Creative Conflict
The Politics of Welsh Devolution

By the same author
The Centralist Enemy

CREATIVE CONFLICT

The Politics of Welsh Devolution

John Osmond

Published jointly by
Gomer Press, Wales
and
Routledge & Kegan Paul, London, Henley and Boston

First published in 1977
by Gomer Press,
Llandysul,
Dyfed and
Routledge & Kegan Paul Ltd,
39 Store Street,
London WC1E 7DD,
Broadway House,
Newtown Road,
Henley-on-Thames,
Oxon RG9 1EN and
9 Park Street,
Boston, Mass. 02108, USA

Set in 'ACM' 10 pt English 49 T
and printed in Great Britain by
J. D. Lewis & Sons Ltd, Gomer Press, Llandysul, Dyfed

Osmond, John
　　Creative Conflict.
　　1. Decentralization in government—Great Britain
　　2. Wales—Politics and government
　　I. Title
354' .41 '082　　　　　　　　　JN329.D43　　　　　　　　77—30410

ISBN 0-7100-8741-1

Owing to production delays
this book was published in 1978

To

ELIN ANGHARAD

Contents

		Page
Preface		ix

Introduction	THE COMMUNITY VERSUS THE STATE	1
	The party political dilemma	4
	The Welsh community	10

Part I Why Devolution?

1	THE CORPORATE ATTACK ON DEMOCRACY	23
	The centralised state	26
	The patronage state	35
	The corporate state	39
	The democratic response	46

2	THE FAILURE OF BRITISH REGIONAL POLICY	53
	The centralist versus decentralist view of economic development	57
	The impact of regional policy on Wales	61
	The Welsh Office role	66
	Why British regional policy cannot succeed	67
	The colonial analogy	74

3	THE EMERGENCE OF WELSH POLITICS	81
	The historical basis	90
	The administrative basis	99
	The national basis	107
	The trade union basis	115
	The Labour party: arbiter between Welsh and British politics	122
	Wales in Europe	130

Part II   Making Devolution Work

4   FRAMING A CONSTITUTION   141
    Labour party manoeuvres   142
    An unstable system   149
    The drift to federalism   163
    A confederal approach   170

5   FINANCING AN ASSEMBLY   179
    The Labour party compromise   180
    The block grant   184
    The case for decentralised financial control   194
    Towards Welsh financial responsibility   198

6   FORGING A WELSH ECONOMIC POLICY   209
    Labour holds its ground   210
    An embryo department of state   212
    The challenge   218

Conclusion   THE RECOVERY OF COMMUNITY   229
             Size, alienation and democracy: the pluralist
                 tradition   231
             The Welsh decentralist tradition   245

Appendix 1   DEVOLUTION AND LOCAL
             GOVERNMENT   253

Appendix 2   DEVOLUTION AND THE WELSH
             LANGUAGE   267

Notes   269

Index   297

Preface

This book has a threefold objective: to analyse why and how devolution for Wales has appeared on the agenda of British politics; to examine the Welsh Assembly proposals brought forward by the Labour government and to suggest constructive ways they might be developed in the future; and, finally, to attempt to set devolution in a philosophical context of political ideas. In this last endeavour I have drawn on many sources but I should lay on record the debt I owe to Ioan Bowen Rees, presently secretary to Gwynedd County Council for his book, *Government by Community,* to which I have constantly referred. My thanks go, too, to David Reynolds, of the University College of Wales, Cardiff; J. Barry Jones, of the University of Wales Institute of Science and Technology; and to my colleague, Geraint Talfan Davies. All read the book in draft and made many helpful suggestions. I should also thank my wife for her help and encouragement. Responsibility for the contents is, of course, entirely my own.

John Osmond

August 1977

Introduction: The Community versus the State

'Devolution is the passing of property from a person dying to a person living.'
Halsbury, *Laws of England.*

The politics of devolution are to a large extent obscured, some would say deliberately obscured, by the language that has been devised to embrace the question. As Sir Harold Wilson said in the debate on the Scotland and Wales devolution Bill in the House of Commons, devolution is a cold, inelegant and unharmonious word. What the Commons was debating, he said, was a much warmer concept: 'There is a need to bring the essential processes of government nearer to the people and to secure identification with them in both Scotland and Wales and to do it without weakening the vital unity of the United Kingdom.'[1]

Though this might be taken as a general definition of what devolution is about, as intended by the Labour government, there is no unanimity. Enoch Powell, for instance, has insisted: 'Devolution is not the same as the transfer of power; it is the opposite; power devolved is power retained, and that retention is the very reason which makes devolution acceptable and possible.'[2]

Powell's definition was supported during the devolution Bill's Second Reading debate by the Prime Minister, James Callaghan, in his opening remarks: 'Devolution as expressed in this Bill is the delegation of a part of Parliament's powers and not a surrender of them.'[3] But on the other hand devolution, as it is understood by most people, is interpreted in a more full-blooded way. As Michael Foot, in a speech to the Labour Party in Wales's conference in 1976, put it: 'Devolution means a real measure of Home Rule for Wales and for Scotland combined with the determination to keep the United Kingdom united.'[4]

Ambivalence in interpreting the meaning of devolution has also been reflected in the way the government has projected the policy. Directed at the people of England, the Labour government described its policy as only a modest change:

> The Government see devolution to Scotland and Wales as a means of enabling the domestic affairs of these two parts of the United Kingdom . . . to be administered in close accord with the people living there . . . Devolution will not, however, affect the supreme authority of Parliament and its ability to make laws on any subject for the whole of the United Kingdom or any part of it.[5]

This was in the December 1976 consultative document *'Devolution: the English Dimension.'* But when the government was addressing the people of Wales and Scotland, as opposed to the people of England, the matter was put differently. For instance, the November 1975 devolution White Paper, addressed to Wales and Scotland, described devolution as 'a massive handover to the new elected Assemblies of responsibility for the domestic affairs of Scotland and Wales'.[6]

There is uncertainty and lack of confidence in discussions about devolution in Britain because of the nature of the British constitution. The constitutional foundation of British politics has never been clearly defined, simply because as soon as it is attempted the idea of a British consensus rapidly becomes undermined. Traditionally the reaction to this state of affairs has been to make a virtue of necessity and praise the imprecision that exists. For example, Britain has no written constitution, a fact which is often taken as a source of flexibility and strength. But there is a great ambivalence over whether Britain is a nation, a state or both. Indeed, most English, and many Welsh and Scottish politicians, have been brought up to consider that there are no important distinctions to be made in this regard. Prime Ministers, in their political broadcasts, happily refer to the 'nation' and most often when making a moral appeal for sacrifice or further effort. But few British Prime Ministers would seek to deny that England is a nation. And when in Wales or Scotland Prime Ministers of both parties have readily conceded the nationality of these countries. Yet the ideas of nation and state, and whether nations can continue to have meaning when politically absorbed by other nations (or whether the correct designation here should be nations within states) are little explored in British political theory or in everyday discussion.

On the whole it would be true to say that the large majority of people in Britain, certainly politically active people, would prefer not to discuss these matters. The problem with devolution, of course, is that it forces them into the forefront of discussion. The reaction has tended to be of two kinds: either to say that devolution, being simply a question of delegating power, has nothing to do with defining the political identity of Britain and its component parts; or alternatively to say that it has everything to do with the question of political identity and so should be opposed or supported because of that.

There is a deeper level to this argument, however, and that is about where power lies in society. Jo Grimond has summarised the issue well:

Devolution suggests that power is centred at the top, that is, in Westminster, and some of it has to be handed down. But in the view of myself
and many other people, power inheres in the people themselves and their
basic communities.[7]

This view, which is the standpoint of this book, is at odds with a
fundamental principle of British constitutional practice, that sovereignty lies at the top with Parliament. As Dicey has stated it:

The principle of Parliamentary sovereignty means neither more nor less
than this, namely, that Parliament has, under the English [sic] constitution, the right to make or unmake any law whatever; and, further, that
no person or body is recognised by the law of England as having a right
to override or set aside the legislation of Parliament.[8]

It is highly significant that in an effort to help its devolution
legislation through the House of Commons the Labour government
was forced to undermine this principle of parliamentary sovereignty
by agreeing to a referendum on devolution, albeit a consultative one.
This signified the acceptance by the House of Commons of the
principle that the future of Wales should be determined by the
people of Wales; that is, that sovereignty is popular rather than
parliamentary. Thus, although devolution in itself suggests, as
Grimond says, that power emanates from the top, the politics of
devolution profess the opposite. They are a debate about whether
government should be viewed from the top down or the bottom up.
Ioan Bowen Rees, in his *Government by Community* defined the two
approaches as follows:

Those who look from the top down consider that the whole authority of
the state is concentrated at the centre. To them, the centre is the only
legitimate source of power: it is from the central government that local
authorities receive their powers: indeed, the central government actually
creates the local authorities, dividing up the state into more or less
uniform divisions in the process. The central government does this for
the more efficient and economic provision of its services. It involves the
leading citizens of every locality in the business of government, not so
much in order to hear their views, as in order to embrace them and make
them identify themselves with the system. This school of thought might
be called the classical school of local government. It is more interested in
efficiency than in democracy, in uniform standards than in local responsibility: it regards the citizen more as consumer of services than
participant in government. Even at its best, it is apt to be patronising.
   The opposite is true of the other school, the romantic school, as it
might be called or, in some countries, the historical school. This school
sees the state itself as a conglomeration of localities, each of which has,
it is true, surrendered much of its authority to the centre, but each of

which retains some authority in its own right as well as a basic identity of
its own. The romantic school places the emphasis on local authorities as
nurseries of democratic citizenship, revels in diversity and local initiative, is impatient of central control and wishes to involve the citizen in
government, not so much to bring him into contact with the state as to
foster his self reliance.[9]

The politics of devolution are about conflict between the classical
and romantic views of government as defined here. The conflict
consists in a reaction of the romantic view against the classical view
which, in the rigidly centralised British state as presently constituted, holds the dominating position. The contention of this book is
that the conflict inherent in the politics of devolution is creative,
since it can only lead to a moderating of the position where local
communities are increasingly subjugated to the uniformity, author-
itarianism and centralism of the British state.

The party political dilemma

Devolution divides all the political parties. It is an issue that cuts
across the more conventional Left/Right divide in politics to
embrace questions of democracy, economic development, nationality, the constitution, and party expediency as well.

In Wales, the most important devolution division is to be found
within the Labour party. As the devolution debate has increased in
tempo the party has found itself in an invidious position of
arbitrating between conflicting ideas of Welsh and British politics.
Consequently the concept of devolution, as defined in the Scotland
and Wales Bill presented to Parliament in December 1976, is inevitably blurred. For it is an attempt to reconcile Welsh and Scottish
aspirations for greater recognition of their political identity, with the
Labour party's own overwhelming desire to maintain an integrated
British political identity.

To illustrate this dilemma it is necessary to trace the history of
Labour's attachment to, rejection of, and finally, re-attachment to
devolution. In the early part of the twentieth century, when Labour
was a growing party, it saw great virtue in radical decentralisation of
government. In part, no doubt, this was a necessary nineteenth-
century Liberal inheritance, but Labour argued the policy on its own
merits as well. Keir Hardie, who became the Labour party's first MP
in 1900, representing Merthyr Tydfil and Aberdare, was a dedicated
Home Ruler (he included it in every election address from 1888 to
1910). The clearest commitment, however, was made in 1918 by the
Labour party's General Secretary at the time, Arthur Henderson.

The party, he said, was pledged to the 'widest and most generous measure of Home Rule' for Wales that could be devised. After stating that the claims of Wales were analogous to those of Ireland, Henderson outlined the following reasons for Labour's commitment to Home Rule for Wales which, in the 1970s, strike a remarkably contemporary note:

> The House of Commons under existing conditions is incapable of dealing with the urgent public business it is required to handle.
> Local legislatures on the federal plan will help very materially to deepen and strengthen the national spirit in each of these self-governing communities. Nationalism means the vigorous development of the material and moral resources of the whole people. It is hardly possible to conceive an area in which a scheme of parliamentary self-government could be established with better chance of success than Wales. All the problems that embarrass statesmen and challenge the imagination of reformers, are to be seen in Wales reduced to manageable proportions. Given self-government Wales might establish itself as a modern Utopia and develop its own institutions, its own culture, its own ideal of democracy in politics, industry and social life, as an example and an inspiration to the rest of the world.[10]

This commitment remained with the party for another twenty years and was written into Labour's manifesto for Wales as late as the 1945 general election. But effectively Labour abandoned its Home Rule policy in 1931. In the general election of that year the party was almost wiped out in England—in Wales it lost only one seat. It was a lesson Labour took to heart. A Welsh Parliament might entail a smaller number of Welsh Labour MPs at Westminster, thereby reducing Labour's chance of forming a government. This proved to be so: but for Wales, there would have been no Labour government in 1950 (majority seven) or in 1964 (majority five). And if there had not been one in 1964 would there have been one in 1966? Certainly, without Welsh support there would not have been even a minority Labour government after February 1974 and Labour would not have been maintained in office after October 1974.

At the same time, from the mid-1960s onwards, Labour's support in Wales began to falter and this fact alone, as much as any other single element, served to place devolution on the agenda. The 1966 general election saw the Labour party reach what will probably prove to be the zenith of its performance in Wales: winning 32 of the 36 Welsh constituencies and 60·7 per cent of the vote. But by the October 1974 general election this support had slumped to 23 of the Welsh seats and 49·5 per cent of the vote, with every indication that

Labour's base level of Welsh support had still to be reached. During this period it became evident that Labour might have as much to lose by not having a policy on devolution as by the establishment of an Assembly.

But there was a positive aspect to Labour's rediscovery of a devolution policy. The Executive Committee of the Labour Party in Wales became committed to an elected Assembly in 1965, long before fortunes at the polls began to indicate this was an electoral necessity. The commitment has been affirmed and re-affirmed at annual conferences of the party in Wales since 1966, the latest being by a large majority at the 1977 Llandudno conference. Indeed, the Labour Party in Wales has been far more positive and consistent on devolution than the Labour Party in Scotland which has gone through a number of about turns in response to the advance of the Scottish National party.

There are broadly two explanations for the positive approach of the Labour Party in Wales. To begin with, it is particularly sensitive to the undemocratic appointments to the nominated boards and committees that administer so many areas of Welsh life. An elected Assembly is seen as the essential means of injecting democratic accountability into the government of Wales. Secondly, the mainstream Labour Party in Wales has, since the mid-1960s, viewed an elected Assembly very much as the top tier of a reshaped local government system. This largely accounts for the more consistent attitude of Labour in Wales than in Scotland. To be credible any all-Scottish elected body is bound to take significant powers from Westminster. On the other hand, an all-Wales elected body can be conceived simply in terms of local government. A precedent can be found in the local government reorganisation that came into force in Scotland in April 1975. Scotland is now split up into eleven regions and the largest, Strathclyde, is virtually the size of Wales. It has a population of some 2,600,000 and embraces an area covered by 35 parliamentary constituencies. Wales sends 36 members to Parliament and only has about 150,000 more people. The parallel is clear. The kind of government system Labour envisages for Wales would have at its head an elected Assembly. Beneath it would be a single tier of 25 most-purpose authorities. Under such a system the 37 Welsh district councils and 8 county councils that came into being in April 1974 would disappear.

Labour believes that a government structure of this kind in Wales would achieve a more equitable spread of resources and services across the country. As a Labour pamphlet put it in 1976:

Reports from a number of Local Government commissions showed that many important services in rural Wales were well below requirements. There was a need therefore, for services within Wales to be co-ordinated, to enable the stronger, more heavily populated areas to help the weaker areas, and thus maintain adequate standards throughout Wales.[11]

It is this emphasis on local government reform that has allowed a consensus, within the postwar Labour Party in Wales's annual conference, to develop in favour of an elected Assembly. The dilemma has been that any all-Wales elected body would inevitably have wider implications: for economics, for politics at Westminster, and for the kind of political entity Wales would become. These implications have been fully reflected by a number of Welsh Labour MPs who have rebelled against the line of their government and of their party in Wales on devolution.

The antipathy of the anti-devolution Welsh Labour MPs has largely coincided with that of the Conservative Party in Wales. Instinctively sceptical of change of any kind, Conservatives have approached the devolution issue from the point of view of their attachment to Unionism. Hence they have dubbed the Labour government's policy a response to nationalism and the starting point of something much more profound. Quite simply many Conservatives have described an elected Assembly as an institution standing at the top of 'a slippery slope to separatism'. This is a powerful source of antipathy, particularly when combined with fears that devolution is also a threat to British identity however that is defined. These attitudes were perceived and articulated by Enoch Powell very early on in the modern debate. In a speech at Prestatyn in 1968 he stated:

If ever it were felt right and necessary for Wales or Scotland to be represented in a separate and exclusive parliamentary institution, to deliberate on matters affecting the kingdom as a whole, because their inhabitants did not consider themselves duly represented by the United Kingdom Parliament at Westminster, then the great question would already have been answered. It would not matter whether the Assembly at first were merely advisory or also legislative or authorised to grant supply—though the same reasons as argued for its establishment would speedily be seen to require that it should be all three. The very decision to establish such an institution would be a declaration that one nation no longer existed.

A Parliament for Wales or an elected Scottish Assembly would not be an extension of that local or even regional democracy whereby elected representatives of the ratepayers administer the expenditure of the rates upon defined purposes, however substantial may be the additions that are made to their resources from national taxation. It would be the watershed, the parting of the ways, the sign that a separate nation had been consciously, deliberately and once-for-all admitted to be there.[12]

8   Creative Conflict

Yet, as with so much of Powell's analysis, the clarity of his expression does not correspond to the complexity of the issue. The
Conservative dilemma is that they recognise devolution to be a
reaction against over-centralised big state government. Lord Hailsham, for instance, observed in a lecture in October 1976 that as a
result of the sovereignty of Parliament becoming, in practice, the
sovereignty of the Cabinet, there is in Britain an elective dictatorship rather than a real democracy. He continued:

> If it were not for the fact that they aim at the destruction of the United
> Kingdom—and that, so far as I am concerned, means my country—I
> might have had most sympathy with the nationalists. They alone wish to
> get rid of the whole incubus of absolute central authority, and manage
> their own affairs themselves on a more modest scale. So far, if they only
> wished to achieve their purpose within the ambit of a new federal const-
> itution, I cannot see anything unreasonable about their aim. After all,
> nations as diverse and as free as the Swiss, the Americans, the
> Canadians, the Australians, and the Germans have all managed to
> achieve stability, efficiency and prosperity on these very lines.[13]

Hailsham's answer was in fact a full-blooded federal solution with
devolved English regional Assemblies as well as Assemblies in
Scotland, Wales and Northern Ireland. A written constitution would
define their powers in relation to Parliament and there would be
added a Bill of Rights: 'Thus Scotland, Wales, and Northern
Ireland would all obtain self-government in certain fields, within the
framework of a federal constitution.'[14]

Although they have been amongst the most rigorous opponents of
Labour's devolution policy, many Conservatives would therefore
favour a radical measure of decentralised elected government for
Wales and Scotland, as long as it could be contained within a new
federal constitution for the United Kingdom as a whole, to protect
their overriding consideration for the integrity of the British identity.
In Wales, Conservative leaders who would support this approach
include Sir Raymond Gower (MP for Barry) and the Shadow Welsh
Secretary Mr Nicholas Edwards (Pembroke). It is intriguing that the
Welsh Communist party at its 1976 biennial conference developed
a very similar line. Although the Communists have long been in
favour of a Parliament for Wales for very different reasons from
those that Conservatives would support, they share the same concern
to maintain the integrity of Britain. The federal solution offered to
them a similar means of achieving the twin objective of devolution
and British unity.[15]

Federalism, of course, has long been Liberal policy since the
nineteenth-century days of Gladstone and 'Home Rule All Round.'

But even the Liberals are split on their attitude towards devolution. The Welsh Liberals are divided on how far they should accept devolution to Wales and Scotland alone, compromising on federalism for the whole of Britain. Emlyn Hooson (Montgomery) is the most reluctant of the two Welsh Liberal MPs on Labour's devolution policy, with Geraint Howells (Ceredigion) staunchly in favour of a Welsh Assembly. Following the defeat of the timetable motion to ensure the passage of the Scotland and Wales devolution Bill in February 1977 Hooson suggested a reconstituted Welsh Grand Committee as the way forward, while Howells insisted the government should press ahead with its proposals for a directly elected Assembly.[16]

The 1976 British Liberal Party conference at Llandudno revealed the party as a whole to be in some disarray over defining their federal policy for England. They ended up with the least practical of the possibilities—a federal Assembly for England, instead of Assemblies for the English regions that would balance more closely the Welsh and Scottish Assemblies. The Liberals' difficulty reveals the inherent difficulty of applying a federal solution to the problem of a constitution for Britain as a whole. In short, the problem is the sheer size of England's population in relation to those of both Wales and Scotland and the consequent imbalance of any federal constitutional settlement based on the three units.

Plaid Cymru's dilemma is that devolution is a British policy. Although it has been formulated to some extent in response to Plaid Cymru pressure, it by no means fulfils the party's objective of full national status for Wales within the European Economic Community. In fact, some leaders in the party believe devolution would ultimately frustrate their objective by integrating Wales into a more decentralised British system. Though decentralised, such a system would still be British with the ultimate focus of power still at the British level. They fear that James Callaghan was right when he told the Labour party's 1976 annual conference at Blackpool:

> My political instincts tell me that the successful implementation of devolution offers us, as a party, the best way of keeping the United Kingdom united, while at the same time enhancing the vigour of national diversity within these islands.[17]

Thus it was with a sense of relief that many Welsh nationalists greeted the failure of the Scotland and Wales devolution Bill to win its crucial guillotine vote to timetable debate in the House of Commons in February 1977. As Saunders Lewis, one of the founders of Plaid Cymru, wrote shortly afterwards:

I hope that serious Welsh nationalists are as cheered as I am by the treatment of the Devolution Bill in the House of Commons. It confirms my forecast of many years ago, and I think it an axiom worth repeating: as long as there is a Welsh Nationalist parliamentary party in the English House of Commons there will be no responsible self-government for Wales.

While Plaid Cymru holds only a minority of Welsh parliamentary seats it is right that it should remain in the House of Commons to declare and defend as well as it can Welsh interests. But if ever, or when ever, Plaid Cymru becomes the majority party in Wales, or in the greater part of Wales, it must forthwith abandon Westminster and set up its own legislative assembly in its own territory.

Then, and only then, after frantic police activity, will the English Parliament pass a measure to recognise and legally establish a Welsh government.[18]

This brief survey of the dilemmas of the political parties over devolution explains why any measure of devolution is so difficult to push through Parliament. Devolution was essentially what the Irish Home Rule debates in the House of Commons were about towards the end of the nineteenth century. The arguments deployed at that time are paralleled remarkably closely in the contemporary debate over devolution for Scotland and Wales. Gladstone's Home Rule for Ireland Bills of 1886 and 1893 were both killed in Parliament. In this failure lay the seeds of Irish partition and the collapse of the Liberal party. Whether devolution or Home Rule for Wales succeeds in this century, whether events follow a similar course to the Irish constitutional experience; or, indeed, whether the issue quietly fades away —the least likely possibility—it is the politics of devolution, rather than devolution itself, that will determine the outcome.

The Welsh community

Much use will be made in this book of the idea of community, a term that in the British context is vague and ambiguous. At the British level it is difficult to insist on community rights, not only because the idea of community is not entrenched, but also because it is customary to think first of individual rights such as freedom of speech, association, and the franchise. The politics of devolution have arisen because of the belief that it is necessary to establish community rights as an indispensable framework for individual freedom.

The idea of community has many levels and in the final analysis can only be defined through assertion. Matters of history, geography and economics apply, but ultimately people identify with communities because they say they do. The basic community, beyond the family, is to be found in locality which is infinitely variable in terms of size, though it tends to be small. If there is one thing that unifies the people of Wales who, considering their relatively small number are amazingly diverse, it is their preoccupation with locality and community. They are an abiding theme in the work of Welsh writers, both in Welsh and in English. Point of origin is practically the first information exchanged when any Welsh people meet. Wales boasts hundreds of celebrated communities and though, of course, there is no unanimity on their order of rank, nothing could be calculated to unite Welsh people more than to threaten any one of them. The most infamous modern instance was the drowning of Tryweryn in Meirionnydd.[19] Nearby is another famous community, Llanuwchllyn. 'The people of Llanuwchllyn, the land of Llanuwchllyn, the history of Llanuwchllyn'—to Owen Edwards, who had such an influence upon Welsh medium education, this was Wales; and if Llanuwchllyn was essentially 'a collection of homes' so was Wales, her history 'not the history of kings . . . but the history of the counsellors and leaders of the people'.[20] The border village of Pandy in Gwent is as different from Llanuwchllyn as any other Welsh rural village could be, yet it has produced another influential figure, Raymond Williams, who is preoccupied with the development of a 'common culture' and communities which govern themselves, and are not governed by Them.[21] And as Williams has stated:

> Community can be the warmly persuasive word to describe an existing set of relationships, or the warmly persuasive word to describe an alternative set of relationships. What is most important, perhaps, is that unlike all other terms of social organisation (state, nation, society, etc.) it seems never to be used unfavourably, and never to be given any positive opposing or distinguishing term.[22]

The difficulty in expressing unambiguously the concept of community and then relating it to a specific situation is reflected in the controversy that surrounds any attempt at defining 'nation'. Possibly the most famous attempt was made by Stalin: 'A nation is an historically evolved, stable community of language, territory, economic life, and psychological make-up manifested in a community of culture.'[23]

However, this definition rests on the imprecise idea of 'psychological make-up'. Without it a community like Anglesey could qualify for national status according to the remainder of the definition. More helpful is Herman Dooyeweerd's phrase: 'A nation is a people . . . which has become conscious of its internal political solidarity.'[24]

It is the quality of political solidarity, therefore, that most distinguishes the idea of nation from the idea of community. And it is this quality which makes 'nation' a controversial, some would argue a pejorative, term. However, even at this point, where the distinction between the two is most marked, there are great connections between the ideas of nation and community. As Nisbet has expressed it:

> By community I refer to much more than what is denoted by mere local community. I use the word . . . in its oldest and lasting sense, of relationships among individuals that are characterised by a high degree of personal intimacy, of social cohesion or moral commitment, and of continuity in time . . . All that is essential is that the basis be of sufficient appeal and of sufficient durability to enlist numbers of human beings, to arouse loyalties, and to stimulate an overriding sense of distinctive identity.[25]

Thus political solidarity is very much bound up with the idea of community. Where the two are found together it is justifiable to conclude that therein consists a national identity. Certainly, this is the closest to a definition that can be found in the Welsh context. As Saunders Lewis, one of the founders of Plaid Cymru, has put it:

> cymdeithas o gymdeithasau yw cenedl rydd, a dyma'r awr i gymdeithasau bychain ymuno mewn cyfundrefn gydweithredol ac amrywiol er maentumio rhyddid. Canys peth lleol yw rhyddid . . .
> *free nation is a community of communities, and the hour has come for small communities to join together in a co-operative and diversified system in order to maintain freedom. For freedom is a local thing.*[26]

For the purpose of this book, the political definition of a community will be taken as a level of human affairs where both power and responsibility can be brought together. The politics of devolution are about giving the community of Wales a political expression in this sense. At the British level there is power—centralised in the Cabinet and civil service and interest groups like investment funds, trade unions, and large companies rather than the elected House of Commons. At the Welsh level there are deep feelings of responsibility for the community but very little power. The politics of devolution are a response to the ideal of bringing power and responsibility together and resting them on a community base.

This is verified in that pressure for devolution has arisen in reaction to chronic erosion of the economic foundations of the Welsh community, an erosion that has continued for generations. Cultural decline, often described in terms of the rapid reduction in numbers of Welsh speakers this century, is a consequence of economic decline. Wales has consistently high unemployment rates relative to Britain as a whole,[27] but these are only half the story. Depopulation, emigration and low economic activity rates have been consistent features of the Welsh economy this century as well. For instance, in 1973-4 in Wales the average number of persons per household at work was 1·2, only 88 per cent of the United Kingdom average.[28]

On almost every indicator of social need Wales compares unfavourably with England and the regions within it. It has a population that experience more illness and more avoidable premature deaths than England. The male death rate for all causes for Wales in 1974 was 13·76 per 1,000 population; in England it was 12·2. The figure for the worst English region, the North, was 13·3.[29] The death rates for heart disease in Wales are 35 per cent above the United Kingdom average; for many parts of Wales bronchitis death rates are 50 per cent above average.[30]

Men in Wales have 32·2 days of certified incapacity for work each year; men in England only 15·5.[31]

Not surprisingly, in view of the above figures, Wales has a far higher proportion of its population in 'need' of personal social services than the rest of Britain. With 5 per cent of the United Kingdom population, Wales has 9 per cent of those receiving invalidity pensions, 12·5 per cent of those receiving industrial disablement pensions, 6·1 per cent of those receiving family income supplements.[32]

Poverty and ill-health are caused or compounded by poor housing and education standards in Wales relative to the rest of Britain.

Welsh housing is older than than of the rest of Britain: 25 per cent of Welsh houses dating before 1891, compared with only 18 per cent in England and Scotland. It is also of much poorer condition: 147,500 houses out of a total stock of 985,000 were reckoned to be 'unfit' in the Welsh Housing Condition Survey of 1973, a proportion of 15 per cent compared to the figure of 10 per cent 'unfit' in the worst English regions of the North and North-West. At the time of writing more than 60,000 people are on local authority housing waiting lists in Wales. Yet between 1969 and 1974 Welsh local authorities were building only 75 per cent of the number of houses being built by English local authorities and only 40 per cent of those in Scotland and Northern Ireland.[33]

Although Welsh schools provide a high proportion of children who go on to further education, they also provide a high proportion of educational failures. In England only 20 per cent of all school-leavers leave school without GCE or CSE passes at grade 5 or better. But in Wales 31·6 per cent of children do so.[34] According to a Department of Education and Science survey, in England, on one day in January 1974, 9·6 per cent of all pupils were absent from school. But the equivalent figure for Wales was 13·9 per cent.[35]

All these figures add up to the inescapable conclusion that if you happen to be brought up in Wales rather than, say, the South-East of England, you have a far higher chance of becoming unemployed, being sick or injured, being forced to move to another part of the country by economic circumstances, and dying sooner. At the same time, if you are brought up in Wales, you are more likely to leave school without any qualifications and more likely to be homeless, on a council house waiting list, or living in a home without an inside toilet, where the roof leaks, where there is overcrowding and rising damp.

These are the harsh realities that lie behind the pressure for devolution. They are given political focus because of the sense of community identity, and with it, community responsibility that exists in Wales. Indignation is added to resentment when the record of the central British state in tackling these problems is examined. In view of the high relative need in Wales one might expect an equivalent response in terms of government social and welfare expenditure. But the latest figures, at time of writing, show that overall spending in Wales on these services is only 4·5 per cent above that of England, with much of the difference being simply the result of high levels of unemployment benefit and supplementary benefit.

Table 1   Public expenditure per head 1975/6 (£)

	(1) England	(2) Wales	*Difference between* (1) *and* (2)
Housing	81	72	-11%
Education, science, arts	128	134	+4·0%
Health and personal social services	111	116	+4·5%
Social Security	173	193	+11·5%
	493	515	+4·5%

(Source: *The Times,* 6 December 1976)

In his *Poverty: The Facts in Wales,* Paul Wilding, a senior
lecturer in social administration at the University College of Wales,
Cardiff, commented on these figures: 'Given the massive evidence
on the greater social needs of Wales, this very modest extra public
expenditure cannot be regarded as in any way matching what the
situation requires.' Neither were recent public spending trends
reassuring: 'In the early years of the 1970s when public expenditure
was increasing rapidly there was no obvious attempt to allocate a
proportionately greater share of extra resources to Wales.' Wilding
concludes that the devolution debate has raised hopes and
quickened aspirations in Wales: 'A sense of inequality, of unmet
needs and missed opportunities, of ignorance and neglect has quickened the call for a greater degree of internal self-government.'[36]
But the standard response to such descriptions of social need and inadequate government action is simply to say that Wales is, after all,
a poor country and cannot expect the standard of living achieved
elsewhere. Such a response is usually accompanied by the assertion
that anyway, Wales is, in economic terms, merely the projection of
adjacent regions in England: northern Wales being an appendage of
Merseyside centred on Liverpool; mid-Wales the lung of the
Midlands centred on Birmingham; and southern Wales the
appendage of a Severnside region focused on Bristol.
Of course, such a view entirely subjugates politics to economics
and takes no account of history or the importance of community.
Even the areas most adjacent to England have a distinctive cultural and
community life.[37] But even in economic terms it is a superficial
analysis. While there are strong links between these regions of Wales
and England, both in terms of communications and as far as ownership and control of many manufacturing firms are concerned, this is
only part of the economic picture. Wales's main economic strength
is as a producer of commodities—food, anthracite and other
minerals, water, and primary industrial products like steel, tinplate
and electricity. Table 2 shows what Wales produces with 5 per cent
of the United Kingdom's population.
For the first time since the start of the industrial revolution, all
these commodities are in a state of world shortage that can only
sharpen as world population continues to multiply. Awareness of the
value of primary products, their increasing scarcity, and therefore
the need to conserve them, is a major underlying economic theme of
the politics of devolution. Alongside it is a growing appreciation of
the injustice of the relative under-development of one area of the
country compared with another. In Wales, as in Scotland, this
perspective has concentrated on the efficacy of British regional

Table 2

Product	Proportion of UK production (%)
Tinplate	100·0
Hay	11·4
Milk	9·5
Wool	17·1
Poultry meat	7·0
Salmon and trout	8·0
Oats	5·0
Coal	9·0
Coke	34·2
Pig Iron	28·4
Steel	31·0
Electricity	9·3
Oil refining	29.0

(Sources: *Hansard; EEC Quarterly Iron and Steel Statistical Bulletin; EEC Agricultural Statistics*).

policy to create a balanced infrastructure to provide more and better quality employment. As will be argued in chapter 2, traditional regional policy, relying on inducements to firms to develop in Wales combined with restrictions on their development elsewhere, has been inadequate in answering Wales's needs. Moreover, as Britain as a whole lurches into deeper and more prolonged economic recessions that begin to look like a long slow decline, the fabric of the regional policy that has been executed is breaking up. Economic circumstances are forcing areas like Wales to rely more on their own resources and initiative for promoting a more balanced and stable economy.

Thus, as with so many other great political questions, an underlying theme of the politics of devolution is an economic one. Along with the pressing need to find new defences for the protection of the democratic freedom of the local community, the need for more self-reliant economic development is a central theme of this book.

Too much emphasis should not be placed on the economics rather than the politics of devolution, however. This is the main deficiency in an otherwise enlightened Marxist analysis of devolution in its British and European context that has recently appeared: *The Break-Up of Britain—Crisis and Neo-Nationalism* by Tom Nairn, a founder-member of the breakaway Scottish Labour Party.[38] Nairn provides a penetrating analysis of the development of the British State and the pivotal position now occupied by Wales, referred to in the final section of Chapter 3. Nairn's thesis, over-simplified, is that the politics of devolution have their source in the 'structural condition' of capitalism. From the classical 'state-nation' of European countries like Britain and France the uneven development of capitalism breeds nationalism (or neo-nationalism) as an offensive-defensive reaction. In the case of Britain the fact that the creation of the state-nation occurred before any other, together with the peculiarity of its formation around the revolution of 1688, first delayed the reaction and then ensured it was given a unique expression in terms of the rise of Welsh and Scottish nationalism and the devolution response. Nevertheless, the British case has strong links with similar experiences in the rest of Europe and the world, particularly in popular mobilisation being effected first around an intelligentsia and then in wider ranges of the middle class.

Nairn quotes Ernest Gellner's verdict that nationalism is 'a phenomenon connected not so much with industrialisation or modernisation as such, but with its uneven diffusion'.[39] This theme is developed in Chapter 2 in a discussion of the centralist versus decentralist view of economic development. The centralist view, still commonly held by British imperialists, is that economic development and higher standards in the core regions of states tend to spread by a process of diffusion to the periphery. The decentralist position, on the other hand, is that experience shows that the rich get rich and the poor poorer. Important peripheral areas such as Scotland and the Basque Country in northern Spain have reached a reverse situation: they are relatively over-developed compared with the core areas of their states which are now holding them back. Wales, Nairn correctly places in an intermediate position which accounts for so many of the dilemmas of Welsh politics. Whatever the position, the areas affected, as Nairn puts it:

> demand progress not as it is thrust upon them initially by the metro-
> politan centre but 'on their own terms'. These 'terms' are, of course,
> ones which reject the imperialist trappings: exploitation or control from
> abroad, discrimination, military or political domination, and so on.
>   'Nationalism' is in one sense only the label for the general unfolding of
> this vast struggle, since the end of the 18th century. Obviously no one
> would deny that nationalities, ethnic disputes and hatreds, or some
> nation-states, existed long before this. But this is not the point. The
> point is how such relatively timeless features of the human scene were
> transformed into the general condition of nationalism after the
> bourgeois revolution exploded fully into the world. Naturally, the new
> state of affairs made use of the 'raw materials' provided by Europe's
> particularly rich variety of ethnic, cultural and linguistic contrasts. But

—precisely—it also altered their meaning, and gave them a qualitatively distinct function, an altogether new dynamism for both good and evil.

In terms of broad political geography, the contours of the process are familiar. The 'tidal wave' invaded one zone after another, in concentric circles. First Germany and Italy, the areas of relatively advanced and unified culture adjacent to the Anglo-French centre. It was in them that the main body of typically nationalist politics and culture was formulated. Almost at the same time, or shortly after, Central and Eastern, and the more peripheral regions of Iberia, Ireland, and Scandinavia. Then Japan and, with the fully development of imperialism, much of the rest of the globe.[40]

Nairn's analysis brings a vital perspective to bear on both the rise of nationalist parties in Wales and Scotland and the central government response which together make up the politics of devolution. But, at most, it is only half the explanation. For the rise of capitalism and its subsequent uneven diffusion via the agency of the state brought with it an attack on the concept of community, that vital element which gives man his humanity. The politics of devolution are as much a reaction to this attack on community as they are to the uneven spread of economic development. The lack of appreciation of this fundamental point, evident in so much of British political theory, is the result of concentrating on just two reference points of politics, the individual and the state, to the exclusion of the third, the community.

For the politics of devolution are as much a reaction against the erosion of community values by the increasingly omnipresent and intrusive state, as it is to the uneven economic development that has taken place under the capitalist system. Indeed, a condition of the spread of capitalism was the establishment of the modern state framework in the first place. The effect of the state is to promote straight relationships between itself and the individual, cutting out the community as in any way an interface or intermediary. The consequences of this for democracy are explored in the following chapter while the final chapter explores the impact on the individual in terms of anomie and rootlessness.

Because the idea of community and community values has been consistently so strong in Wales this point of view has been articulated in each generation with great force and clarity, albeit most often by a minority. One of the finest, indeed saintly, exponents of the view this century was the Pembrokeshire poet Waldo Williams (1904-71). It is no surprise that today he has emerged as a major influence on Wales's most politically active younger generation. A recent biography of Williams by James

Nicholas judges that his life 'was a protest against the alluring temptation of the powerful state'.[41] In 1956 Williams, a Quaker, delivered an address 'Brenhiniaeth a Brawdoliaeth' (Sovereignty and Brotherhood) at the Baptist Union Assembly, held that year at Fishguard. This work bears the stamp of the Russian existentialist philosopher, Nicolas Berdyaev, who was a major influence on Williams. This comes through in the lecture where he analyses the nature of 'Brenhiniaeth' (Sovereignty). For Williams it denoted the compulsory element found in all forms of states, an element essential to the idea of the State:

> Because it is this element of compulsion that says Do, Go, Come, Pay and sometimes Be Quiet, the State is different from society in its interpretation of the word Belonging.

Williams argues that the real tragedy of man's slavery to the State is that he does not realise the slavery; he becomes so lost in Sovereignty that he feels exalted when in fact he is being humiliated. Brotherhood, in Williams' terms, is another expression for Community and he concludes: 'In the presence of brotherhood sovereignty is judged'. Sovereignty tries to steal the gift of Brotherhood from us by making us servants of its needs, and it does so by claiming that it is the custodian of our happiness. But according to Williams:

> Brotherhood is the keeper of human independence.

Indeed, in Brotherhood lies the foundation of our freedom:

> It is the foundation of our freedom as we were born dependent on one another and it is in that relationship that we discover our rights.[42]

Williams' thoughts in this direction were stimulated by his refusal in the early 1950s to pay taxes as a protest against conscription in Wales and the war in Korea, for which he was imprisoned for a number of short periods. In a moving article published in *Y Faner* in 1956 he explained his position on the issue.[43] He saw a terrible dichotomy existing within the modern State—the order within and the disorder in its relations with other States. Citizens live in a condition of duality, having to agree with the absurdity of the situation in order to accept the advantages which the State provides. But above all Williams stressed that freedom depended upon the right to criticise the state:

> This right is the essential anarchy that lies at the heart of democracy— that there are for everyone, certain things they will not do at the dictate

of the Government. This independence is the necessary free space within
the system, the hole at the centre of the wheel. When a citizen's will is
constrained in respect of some crucial matter, then he is totally enslaved,
however many other advantages are offered him.[44]

In the 1959 general election Waldo Williams stood as the
candidate for Plaid Cymru in Pembrokeshire, the first time the party
had fought the seat. He saw from the start the potential conflict
between his stand against state power and the aspirations of Plaid
Cymru to form a Welsh government. In an election address at the
time he addressed himself to this issue in the following terms:

> We want to see a Welsh state but it is essential to keep this instrument
> in its place. Its powers must be decentralised and responsibility must be
> distributed widely. The power of local authorities can be increased and
> the workers given a voice in the control of their industries. Wales is at an
> advantage here in being a small nation without the temptation of power
> politics and the vast expense they involve.[45]

The philosophy of Waldo Williams is only the most modern
expression of a traditional Welsh concern for community combined
with distrust of state power. As the 1970s draw to a close this
becomes an ever increasing cause for concern. It will be argued in
the following chapter that a corporatist economic system with
political overtones is growing up within the British state, a system
that is inimical to the ideals of democracy and community.

At heart, the politics of devolution are a mobilisation of the
community against the onslaught of a powerful corporatist state
system. They are a drama of the community in conflict with the
state. The title of this book is 'Creative Conflict' because it is written
in the belief that the community will win.

Part I   Why Devolution?

Chapter 1

The Corporate Attack on Democracy

'We don't want intervention to lead to a Corporate State.'
Tony Benn, Labour Party Conference, 1976.

During the inaugural Welsh Day debate in the House of Commons in October 1944 Aneurin Bevan denounced the innovation as a 'farce'. He said: 'My colleagues, all of them members of the Miners' Federation of Great Britain, have no special solution for the Welsh coal industry which is not a solution for the whole of the mining industry of Great Britain. There is no Welsh problem.'

The politics of devolution insist there is a Welsh problem but one related to a wider British problem: the concentration of power but not responsibility at the British state level. This is the conflict that the politics of devolution seek to resolve.

British constitutional theory places responsibility in a Parliament in which the Queen is sovereign. But political reality is that power lies elsewhere, notably in the great interest groups like the City, the trade unions, and also in the government and its civil servants in between whom, R. H. S. Crossman once remarked, Ministers wander like pale shadows. The Welsh experience testifies that feelings of responsibility for the Welsh community do not rate highly in these centres of power. Over the last few generations the Welsh social fabric has been constantly damaged by population loss, unbalanced economic development, high unemployment, and deprivation in social provision relative to average levels in Britain—all of which underpin the gradual displacement of Welsh community and cultural values by a uniformity whose source lies somewhere between London and New York.

The politics of devolution cut across the politics of Aneurin Bevan's generation—politics that subjugated the balanced development of the Welsh community beneath the working-class interest in Britain as a whole; politics that gave precedence to a British class-conflict analysis. Though the politics of devolution would give priority to the concept of community over the concept of class they are not a denial of class as a touchstone of political conflict. Neither are they, in themselves, an affirmation that this is so. Rather, they are an attempt to persuade that if politics are to be carried on in a democratic manner they must take place at a level where both power and responsibility can be brought together. The politics of devolution are an assertion that this conjunction can be achieved if a significant proportion of British state power is decentralised to Wales, Scotland, and eventually to the English regions.

Pressure for devolution within Wales has grown as a reaction to the massive development of state power at the British level, power which has influenced every area of Welsh life. A measure of the development of state power can be seen in contrasting expenditure figures for the hundred years from 1870. British public spending in 1870 was £100m: 9 per cent of Gross Domestic Product and equivalent to £3 per head of population. By 1970 these figures had risen to £20,000m: 43 per cent of Gross Domestic Product and equivalent to £400 per head.[1] Simultaneously there was a massive increase in civil servants. In 1900 they numbered just 50,000, but by 1970 they had increased tenfold to more than 500,000. Another reflection of the growth of government is the increase in legislation. In the decade 1901 to 1910, 458 major public Acts were passed by Parliament, involving 2,696 pages of statute. By the decade 1961 to 1970, the equivalent figures had increased to 708 Acts with 16,882 pages of statute.

These developments were promoted by the two World Wars. Writing of the increase of state power as a result of World War I, the historian, A. J. P. Taylor, recorded:

> Until August 1914 a sensible law abiding Englishman could pass through life and hardly notice the existence of the state beyond the post office and policemen . . . The Englishman paid his taxes on a modest scale. All this was changed by the impact of the Great War. The mass of the people became for the first time active citizens. Their lives were shaped by orders from above; they were required to serve the state instead of exclusively pursuing their own affairs . . . The Englishman's food was limited . . . his freedom of movement was restricted . . . the history of the English state and of the English people merged for the first time.[2]

And, of course, among the people who merged with the English state were the Welsh. The Second World War turned Britain into a planned state with the government as the main source of initiative and power in economic affairs. The best single measure of the extent to which the War affected the economy is provided by the estimates of expenditure before the War and at the peak of the War Effort. In 1938 the expenditure of public authorities on goods and services was equivalent to 17 per cent of British income. During the war the figure rose to nearly 63 per cent.[3] In this period Britain was, in strictly economic terms at least, a corporate state. The state set the

country's economic goals, allocated resources, co-ordinated production and consumption, and controlled the distribution of
rewards. In short, the state moved from a supportive to a directive
role in a privately owned economy, the essence of corporatism. But
war is not the only circumstance in which a corporatist economy can
be introduced. It will be argued later in this chapter that as the
1970s draw to a close Britain is accelerating on the path towards a
peacetime corporatist system. The main indicator is that, although
public spending as a ratio of total British income dropped after the
Second World War, it has since risen steadily, until by the mid-
1970s it was well past 50 per cent and growing.[4]

When the role of the state expands to these proportions, freedom
and democracy are in peril, because under the auspices of the state
the hierarchical systems of business, industry, trade unions, financial institutions, education and other establishments begin to merge
into one. Then the whole life of a person is processed and packaged,
outside as well as inside the workplace. The inconveniences and un-
predictability of individual choice and foibles are gradually elimin-
ated. People serve the system instead of the other way around.

This is allowed to happen because the more the role of the state
expands the less individuals become used to involving themselves, on
their own responsibility, in co-operative community effort. People
who live long under a strong centralised government and its bureaucracy come to rely on it.[5] They find it easier to use the state for the
settlement of their disputes and for the provision of public services,
even where the disputes, and the public for which the services are to
be provided are quite local. In the presence of a strong state the
individual tends to stop thinking about those in his community who
need help. He tends to cease having any desire to make a direct contribution to the resolution of local problems, whether or not he is
affected by them. He tends to feel that his responsibility to 'society'
(a more neutral term than community) is discharged as soon as he
has paid his taxes. For these will be used by the state to care for the
old, sick and unemployed, to keep his streets clean, to maintain
'order', to provide and maintain schools, libraries, parks and so on.
The state releases the individual from the responsibility or need to
co-operate with others directly. The state cuts across community: it
provides the individual with an apparently secure environment in
which he may safely pursue his goals, unhampered by collective
community concerns.

There is, of course, a supreme irony here. For the rise of state
power is based partially on an ideology of collectively imposed solutions—for instance, the Labour party aim of the

1940s to gain control of the commanding heights of the economy and impose equality from above. But the result is to weaken feelings of collective responsibility in people.

Where in this discussion of the rise of state power and its harmful effects on community do the politics of devolution fit in? The answer is that they are central. For the politics of devolution are simultaneously about attacking the power and enhancing the place of community as the vital context in which individuals can be free. The politics of devolution are about the role and power of the state. Devolutionists argue that in Britain the state is too big, has grown too powerful, is undermining community and, as a result, is threatening to extinguish individual democratic freedoms. Reference has been made to the size of public expenditure as a measure of the expanding role of the state. The figures given related to Britain as a whole. But in Wales—and in Scotland—the proportion is much higher. It is hard to find comparable figures. The only readily available parallel measurement is the percentage of people employed in the public sector—in Britain in October 1976 the figure was $29 \cdot 6$ per cent, but in Wales it was much higher, $40 \cdot 5$ per cent.[6] Thus it is no coincidence that a strong reaction against the power and influence of the state is to be found within Wales.

The positive response must be to reduce the role of the state and enhance the role of the community. This can be done by finding a smaller scale within which government can operate—a scale where the power of government can be brought into a relationship with the responsibility that springs from the community. The politics of devolution are an assertion that power and responsibility can be successfully joined at the Welsh level and expressed through a devolved Welsh Assembly. This involves cutting the state down to size. The rest of this chapter will examine in more detail current developments of the British state—its chronic predisposition to centralisation, its foundation on patronage, and its increasingly corporate character. Devolution is seen as a means for engaging in conflict with these tendencies on behalf of community and democracy.

The centralised state

The growth of state power in Britain has rested, for its moral justification, on the apparent democratic involvement of the mass of the people through universal suffrage. The involvement has only been apparent since the real reins of power, in industry, the financial institutions, and the social services as well as in government itself, have been centralised away from democratic control. Control of those matters that really affect the everyday lives of people—industry, supply of power, the health service, education and so on—have been steadily concentrated in fewer and fewer hands.

Before the First World War, only 3 per cent of insurance companies' assets was invested in ordinary shares and by 1939 the proportion had risen to only 10 per cent. But in the 1950s and 1960s, largely because equities were able to beat the low inflation rates of the period, the proportion was pushed up beyond 40 per cent. Recent figures are not available but it is probable that financial institutions account for around 55 per cent of all shares quoted on the Stock Exchange. In 1972, when the market hit its peak, the institutions' resources totalled £44 billion. Some twenty men in the City of London control the bulk of these vast funds. Few know who they are and to whom they are responsible.

The Labour party's 1961 manifesto, *Signpost for the Sixties,* commenting on the growth of big firms, said: 'The greatest single problem of modern democracy is how to ensure that the handful of men who control these concentrations of power can be responsive and responsible to the nation.' In the 1950s the hundred largest British firms controlled about a quarter of the country's net output. Since then their share has at least doubled. The prospect is that by the mid-1980s the insurance companies, pension funds and unit trusts will own around two-thirds of British industry and the same proportion of its output will be concentrated in the hundred largest firms.[7] Herein lies the basis for the trend towards a corporate state in Britain. The implications for democracy are alarming.

But centralisation in industry is not just a question of ownership and control. The amalgamation of firms, both public and private, has resulted in a stampede of top management away from Wales and the other economically imbalanced areas of Britain to London and the South-East. A 1973 survey revealed that of 49 private sector firms employing more than 1,000 people in Wales, only 7 also had their head office in the country. Of the 94 private sector firms employing between 500 and 1,000 people only 16 had their head office in Wales.[8]

When an amalgamation takes place, whether in private or public industry, the decision as to operating arrangements is usually left to those running the business—a fact which invariably leads to a London headquarters being established. In private industry the headquarters of the large oil companies, the chemical companies,

and many engineering companies—all with big interests in Wales—
are in London. Here, too, are the headquarters of most of the
publicly owned industries, such as the Coal Board, the British Steel
Corporation, British Rail and British Airways. By the mid-
1970s this headquarters centralisation in London had become so
visibly embarrassing that the Bill establishing the new British Shipbuilding Corporation instructed that it should be based outside
London—much to the chagrin of its management.[9]

It is the centralisation of decision-making centres of large organisations, as much as the concentration of ownership of industry, that
is critical for peripheral areas like Wales. Decision-makers in highly
centralised organisations do not attach great importance to the
regional and social implications of their operation. As Mervyn
Jones, Chairman of the Wales Gas Board until 1969 (after which it
became submerged in the British Gas Corporation) said in his
written submission to the Commission on the Constitution: 'A
London taken view of any nationalised, particularly service, industry
must today incline to a contraction of its activities in Wales and the
outer parts of the United Kingdom and a concentration on the prosperous over-active Midlands, London and South of England.'[10] Here
a number of interlocking factors ensure that the interests of Wales
and other peripheral areas rarely enjoy priority:

(a) The capacity of the *section* of an industry operating in Wales
    to take a long view, to take an initiative based on a measure of
    financial independence, diminishes just because it is a
    section.

(b) When the management headquarters is in London there will
    be little internal pressure for locating new advances in areas
    like Wales, for the decision-makers will predominantly be
    people with knowledge of the South-East and its interests.

(c) To the extent that plans are made locally in Wales they cannot
    be publicly discussed or advocated in Wales since loyalty
    demands that proposals remain private within the London-
    based organisation.

(d) When for any reason an industry is concentrating its resources
    there is a strong tendency for a London headquarters to allow
    contractions to take place first at places furthest from
    London.

This analysis supports Leopold Kohr's 'Law of Peripheral Neglect'
which states that concern for remote districts diminishes with the
square of the distance from the seat of power. In other words, in

large states the regions close to the capital progress, while the distant ones regress for the same physical reason that is behind the melancholy saying: 'Out of sight, out of mind'.[11]

There are two sides to this coin. The most obvious is the tendency to create a branch-factory-oriented economy in the periphery—a tendency that is promoted by regional economic policies, as will be seen in the following chapter. At the same time, the decision-making centres of such economic development must, by definition, be located at the core and not the periphery. This is the other side of the coin. For where decisions are taken—in the case of Wales, the metropolitan South-East of England—economic rewards are highest and people with drive and energy concentrate. For example, in an electronics company the tendency will be for the best scientific and engineering brains to be drawn near the centre so they may participate in the policy-making process. In turn laboratories and therefore employment prospects for graduates also gravitate towards the centre. This was graphically illustrated in a study commissioned in 1973 by Y Gymdeithas Wyddonol Genedlaethol (National Scientific Society) which found grave shortcomings in scientific employment in Wales.

The study discussed the two categories of scientific employment: one dependent on specific communities and their day-to-day requirements; the other without direct links to a particular community and therefore untied to a particular location. The second category of appointments are attractive to science graduates and provide research facilities not normally available to those in the first category. The study showed that the proportion of British graduates in the physical and biological sciences produced from Wales in 1972 was slightly greater, at 5·15 per cent, than the Welsh proportion of the population of the United Kingdom. However, of some 99 government research establishments in the United Kingdom employing a total estimated graduate staff of 13,825, only 2 small ones were located in Wales employing an estimated 50 graduates. Following a similar pattern, not one of 38 industrial research associations was located in Wales and of 26 research establishments attached to nationalised industries and other public bodies, two (a British Steel Corporation laboratory employing 13 graduates at Swansea, and a small Post Office laboratory at Cardiff) were located in Wales. Another indication of the lack of scientific opportunity in Wales was afforded by the 458 United Kingdom graduate posts advertised during 1972 in the scientific journals *Nature* and *New Scientist,* of which only 3 were located in Wales. Total government spending on research and development in 1970/71 was £645 million (Cmnd

4814). Complete figures for separate Welsh spending are not available but the National Scientific Society's study (Scientific Employment in Wales, 1973) claimed conservatively that it would be surprising if it exceeded £8 million. The study, which contains much evidence of this kind, concludes: 'The chance that a science graduate will obtain a satisfactory research post in Wales outside the University are poor; in the case of the biological sciences they are almost non-existent.'

Now all this has grave consequences for the vitality of peripheral communities like Wales. Any community's activities depend upon the qualities of the men and women who have achieved positions of leadership in industrial, commercial and research and development organisations. Centralisation of such people away from a community reduces the calibre of leadership in its social institutions. The politics of devolution are very much a reaction to the adverse consequences of centralisation. Nevertheless, if it could be shown that centralisation led to increased productivity or efficiency the reaction to it would no doubt be more muted. But this has not been the Welsh experience. Most attention has focused on the public sector since it forms the foundation of the Welsh economy. What has been experienced is not only centralisation in the organisation of major state concerns—a centralisation that in the mid-1970s was still very much under way—but a series of centralised decisions resulting in large-scale redundancies, reduced services, and massive misjudgments of market prospects. Wales can testify to the bitter consequences of centralisation in the coal, steel, gas and electricity industries, and in services ranging from local government and the railways to the water and health services.

Under the nationalised Coal Board the coal industry in Wales collapsed in the 1960s. On average one pit was closed every seven weeks—150 all told—and the number of miners fell from 91,000 in 1960 to less than half that by the early 1970s.[12] Hindsight and the 1970s oil crisis soon revealed how short-sighted these centralised State decisions were.

At the time, in the 1960s, the government pointed to high stockpiles of coal, claiming there was no market for it. But that was a state decision, since the biggest customers (taking 72 per cent of Welsh coal in 1967) were British Railways, the Central Electricity Generating Board, the British Steel Corporation, the Gas Board and the National Coal Board itself.[13] Including the steel industry (which was renationalised in 1967) between 1963 and 1967 the sale of coal to the nationalised industries fell by about 2·1 million tons a year, or 64 per cent of the total fall. Over the same period coal sales in the private sector rose by about 3 per cent.[14] Thus the precipitate decline of the Welsh coal industry was a purely state decision.

Steel followed on coal. Figures published by the British Steel Corporation revealed that in September 1975 the Welsh steel industry employed 60,860 people—a drop of 10,800 on the number employed at nationalisation in 1967 and proportionately more than any other steel-making area in Britain.[15] Following nationalisation the new Corporation came up with a long-term strategy involving the closure of steel-making at many small (and often profitable) works, including Shotton, Ebbw Vale and East Moors (Cardiff) in Wales, and the concentration of steel-making in just six very large centres. As I have argued elsewhere[16] this strategy was the outcome of a series of internal reorganisations of BSC's management which concentrated decision-making completely in the Corporation's London headquarters. The motivating factor was simply that a small number of large works could be more easily controlled and governed from the centre than a large number of smaller ones. This analysis was subsequently upheld by a number of key personalities inside the BSC's management, including Stephen Gray, managing director of BSC's Strip Mills division until 1972, and Dr John Kay who, before retiring in 1976, was in charge of planning at the BSC's London headquarters (until 1969) and then director of engineering and planning with the Strip Mills division. In a letter to the *Financial Times* in July 1976 Dr Kay argued, contrary to the BSC, that development at the Port Talbot steelworks could go ahead without prejudice to Shotton in North Wales, which he said should be modernised and not closed. He concluded his letter: 'If anyone is holding up the modernisation of the British steel industry . . . it is the present top management of the Corporation who appear to be clinging to a dogmatic belief in size and concentration for its own sake.'[17]

The centralisation of the Welsh gas industry took place between 1968 and 1972, when Parliament blandly enacted legislation establishing the monolithic British Gas Corporation.[18] Prior to this the gas industry was run by a federal system of Welsh and Scottish gas boards together with ten English regional boards. For practically the whole of its existence (from 1949 to 1969) the Wales Gas Board made a profit. Losses began as soon as the new centralised system came into operation, though after the formal takeover of the Corporation in 1972 no 'regional' accounts were published. These losses occurred despite the closure of 50 Welsh showrooms in the remoter areas of mid and northern Wales after the new centralised regime took over.

The pretext for the reorganisation of the gas industry was the discovery and exploitation of natural gas in the North Sea. In the House
of Commons debate on the change in 1971, the Minister for Industry
responsible, Sir John Eden, declared, 'This transformation needs to
be reflected in a new organisational structure for the industry involving increased central direction with the maximum possible management flexibility.'[19] But the fact that suddenly there was one source of
supply for gas—beneath the North Sea—did not necessitate there
should only be one sales organisation. Most of the world's oil is to be
found in the Middle East but there are many oil companies. In the
United States virtually the whole gas supply is from natural sources.
Yet the industry there is made up of a large number of comparatively
small local utility companies, many covering a smaller area than
the old Wales Gas Board.

Moreover, the crude exploitation of North Sea gas under the new
regime is one of the most compelling indictments of those who claim
efficiency to be characteristic of centralised control. The sales of
natural gas, a highly specialised fuel, were raised by 365 per cent in
a matter of three years from 1970 by pouring it into heavy industry—
a criminal waste of resources in a decade filled with forebodings of a
coming energy crisis.[20] By the mid-1970s industrial demand was
outstripping supply, the Corporation was buying gas from the
Norwegian fields, and gas was more expensive than coal. As early as
May 1973 the chairman of the Gas Corporation announced that it
would not be taking on any 'sizeable new industrial sales contracts'.

And in Wales in 1973 the Corporation's decision (reversed after
two bitter years) to build two enormous gas tanks 500 yards away
from the village of Hirwaun involved the whole upper Aberdare
Valley community in prolonged direct action. A few years earlier this
decision would have been taken by the Wales Gas Board which,
because of its responsibility at the local level, would have been more
sensitive to local reaction. As it was, vital gas installations were
delayed for more than four years, causing industries in South Wales
to close and discouraging new development.[21]

At the time of writing further centralisation of the electricity
industry is under consideration—already seven of the eight offices
that organise electricity generation and distribution are located
outside Wales. In January 1976 the Plowden Committee report
advocated setting up one centralised Electricity Corporation to
replace the, at least semi-autonomous, generating and supply
boards in England and Wales (Scotland has its own separate electricity industry and was not considered in the Plowden review).[22]
The Committee rejected a Welsh Electricity Board largely because

Wales generates a large surplus of electricity (more than twice as much as it consumes) and might have difficulty in persuading England to consume it under a decentralised management structure. It is, to say the least, strange to argue against a unit's viability because it produces a surplus. On the other hand, the Committee's main argument in favour of a centralised corporation was the current system's alleged 'slow and cumbersome central policy-making, caused by divided responsibilities and rigid statutory framework'. But while it wanted strong leadership from the top, the Committee said that not all decisions should be taken at the centre: 'The operating units must retain a substantial degree of authority, but there can be no fully effective safeguard against over-centralisation which would not frustrate the whole purpose of unifying the industry.'[23] The contentious nature of this report was recognised by the Energy Minister, Tony Benn, who, shortly after its publication, called for a wide public debate on its proposals. He said, 'The question of centralisation versus decentralisation needs to be explored fully and local and consumer opinion needs to be taken into account against a background of growing pressure for devolution and a suspicion of centralised power.'[24]

Centralisation of the water industry is also being actively promoted. A consultative document brought out by the Department of the Environment with the Welsh Office, in March 1976, advocated a 'National [sic] Water Authority for England and Wales'.[25] The intellectual deficiencies in the argument put forward by the government departments in favour of this new centralised body must themselves stand as a comment on the competence of centralised management. The document noted that the current structure of the water industry in England and Wales—nine English regional authorities plus the Welsh National Water Development Authority—had been formed out of 1,400 mainly local authority bodies at the 1974 reorganisation. The argument for further centralisation was limited to just four sentences in the 33-page document:

> The new [i.e. 1974] system was designed to enable water resources to be managed comprehensively at river basin level. It did little, however, to ensure that the combined policies and operations of the authorities provide the most effective or economical answer to needs seen in national terms. Nor did it provide an adequate framework for the national planning necessary to meet such an objective. Given that the water industry is one of Britain's largest, with water authorities' annual capital investment running at about £500m and their income (for 1975/76) at £900m, the lack of adequate central guidance and monitoring to ensure that it operates in the national interest must be regarded as a major deficiency.[26]

Must it? The co-ordination of the water authorities by the England and Wales Water Council, together with their individual responsibility to the government, is surely a perfectly adequate system for ensuring control and accountability. The principle at work here is simply that if a public organisation spends a lot of money it should be completely controlled from the centre. It is stated as though it is self-evident.

The Welsh National Water Development Authority, under the Conservative peer, the late Lord Brecon, supported the formation of the centralised authority, though it did add: 'Water authorities' freedom of local action and decision in matters not of inter-authority significance should in no way be allowed to be eroded by the establishment of the National Water Authority.'[27] The naiveté of this position was highlighted by the Water Council's view: 'The proposals to strengthen the centre stop a long way short of full centralisation [since the existing Welsh and English regional administrative structure would remain]. However, the strategic planning function would give the National Water Council a powerful new influence . . .'[28]

The centralisation that has been highlighted here with reference to the coal, steel, gas, electricity and water industries has affected practically every area of Welsh life in similar ways. Centralisation within British Rail facilitated the Beeching 1960s closure policy when, in Wales alone, 200 miles of track were lifted and 80 railway stations closed. The telephone service for Mid and North Wales is run from Shrewsbury and Chester. In the early 1970s the Welsh-based airline, Cambrian Airways, was assimilated, after protest, into British Airways. The result was to transform the Cardiff airport at Rhoose into a peripheral operation. The pilot base at the airport was closed, administrative staff transferred, and the future of the airport itself threatened.

Bus services throughout Wales have been taken over by the nationalised bus company and run down, particularly in rural areas. The 1974 health service reorganisation abolished the Welsh Hospital Board and centralised administration inside the Welsh Office.[29] The reorganisation of local government in 1974 was itself a massive operation in centralisation. It reduced the number of elected authorities in Wales from 181 to 45[30] and halved the number of councillors. Speaking of the reorganisation throughout Britain, Lord Crowther-Hunt said in March 1976: 'We now have fewer elected representatives per head than any other country in Western Europe.'[31] Apart from this, the new structure (8 counties and 37 districts in Wales) does not correspond to established community patterns, and is remote from the people served, especially in rural areas—classic characteristics of any centralised structure.

The politics of devolution are in part a reaction to the state centralisation that is afflicting the services and industry most essential to everyday life in Wales. Experience of centralisation has proved that it is inefficient, a disincentive to balanced development, erodes democratic involvement, saps initiative, denudes the community of leadership, and is harmful to community identification.

In the short term devolution—the setting up of an all-Wales directly elected institution—will do little to combat these evils, since the proposed Welsh Assembly will initially have no power over large-scale industry (though it will have control of education, local government generally and the health service). Nevertheless devolution will be an essential element in mobilising political will in Wales to reverse centralisation and return power to the level of community where responsibility can be exercised over it. As one resolution, condemning the effect of the British Steel Corporation's policies on Wales and passed by the Labour Party in Wales annual conference as early as May 1975, expressed it:

> . . . a new structure for the Steel Corporation is required. Policy making is at present over-centralised and there is a clear need for management and workers in the regions to have a much bigger say in major policy decisions. To achieve this, a regional structure is needed, with the regions able to play a full part in the decisions on management and future policy of the industry. One further advantage of such a structure is that this could be closely linked with the proposed Assembly, so that the people of Wales, through the Assembly, could be in close touch with plans for the future and could exercise greater influence over the future strategy and employment prospects of the Industry.

Devolution does not just apply to superficial political and constitutional superstructures. It is part of a philosophy that envisages decentralisation in every aspect of the economy and the life of the community. However inadequate the constitutional beginning, devolution is a means of creating a determination in the Community to decentralise and so control the decision-making carried out on its behalf.

The patronage state

The attack on democracy inherent in the centralisation of government, services, and industry has been accompanied by the appointment of placemen to manipulate the centralised levers of power.

Directly elected personnel might reflect the demands of the mass of
the people too faithfully.

It can be argued that centralisation and the consequent denial of
power to directly elected representatives are inevitable in any state as
highly populated as Britain. In the mass people do not behave as
rationally or responsibly as when they are in the context of their
immediate community. They do not relate benefits to costs in the
same way and are more inclined to make contradictory demands,
such as wanting taxes reduced at the same time as wanting welfare
provision extended. And, all too often, directly elected representatives, engaged in a competitive struggle for votes, respond. Thus in
the economic and political crisis year of 1974, when inflation was
spiralling, the Labour government froze the rents of council tenants,
from whom it expected to draw a large vote, and the Conservatives
promised '$9\frac{1}{2}$ per cent mortgages', appealing to their own constituency.

The British state system has protected itself against these tendencies simply by limiting the extent of democracy. At the top a political
consensus has developed conceding that in practice most issues
are too complex to be decided by a competitive vote-seeking process.
Thus, although Ministers may introduce legislation and Parliament
may vote, their actions are purely formal, as the real decisions are
made elsewhere. This applies particularly to major economic
matters which, it is declared, are determined by the foreign
exchange market, commodity prices and world inflation and recession. Together with Cabinet control, via the Whip system, over
the House of Commons, appeals to such outside forces ensure that
the field of political decision-making is restricted to a limited few.

But while British state decision-making is carefully controlled in
this way there is a much looser arrangement in dispensing authority
for state executive action. The area for this can be widely extended
by delegation to authorities, boards, corporations and agencies
whose members are nominated by the state and so do not have to
please the electorate on pain of removal from office. This is the
source of the 'patronage state' whose development has been hastened
since the Second World War by the need for administration at a
regional level in Britain where no form of democratic accountability
has been at hand.

Apart from the civil service (three-quarters of whom operate from
regional outposts) there are many special agencies whose 'non-
political' nature is constantly stressed both by themselves and by the
government of the day. Agencies like the BBC, the University
Grants Committee and the boards of the nationalised industries are,

at least theoretically, only influenced by the organisations they are supposed to regulate, rather than responding to political pressure as such. Consequently Members of Parliament are unable to ask questions about the day-to-day running of the nationalised industries. And it is no coincidence that bodies such as the Prices and Incomes Board, the Pay and Prices Board and 'ad hoc' committees presided over by judges, have been used to extend state control into the most sensitive areas of economic life.

Taking just the major nominated authorities affecting Britain as a whole, there are 304 public bodies to which Ministers make appointments, employing about two million people at a cost of £2,500 million a year (at 1976 prices).[32] Seven Cabinet Ministers alone have between them the patronage of 4,223 jobs worth £4,200,000.[33] In his two periods as Prime Minister between 1964 and 1976 Sir Harold Wilson appointed 100 Cabinet Ministers, 403 junior Ministers, 243 peers, 24 chairmen of nationalised industries, and 21 chairmen of royal commissions.[34]

The Secretary of State for Wales, Mr John Morris, confessed in December 1975, that he personally made 628 appointments to 73 nominated bodies operating in Wales.[35] Since then he has become responsible for appointments to two more major authorities, the Welsh Development Agency and the Land Authority for Wales. Between them these 75 bodies administer nearly £1,000 million of public funds. The Welsh Development Agency, for instance, has a budget of £150 million. The eight Welsh Health authorities spend more than £200 million a year. The Welsh National Water Development Authority spends more than £150 million a year.

In themselves these nominated bodies, operating on an all-Wales basis constitute a major part of the case for devolution: a Welsh Assembly is necessary to democratise a wide area of administration that already exists. Many of the functions administered by nominated bodies—health, gas, electricity, water, sewerage, and trunk roads —were once the responsibility of local authorities in any event. The development of their administration at the Welsh level indicates that with the allocation of resources stemming from Whitehall (the top) downwards, and demand emanating from the local community (the bottom) upwards, this is simply the most convenient meeting point for the two processes.

Moreover, Wales is administered as a unit by the Whitehall outpost, the Welsh Office. In theory this is accountable to Parliament. In practice it is not, certainly far less than other parts of the civil service machine. Between 1964, when it was established, and 1974, Welsh Office spending rose from £48,000 to £1,170,000 per annum. Its civil servants run the equivalent of half-a-dozen English ministries with a brief covering health, education, housing, roads, local government, economic planning, industry and its promotion, town and country planning, and much of agriculture.

These wide-ranging responsibilities are the subject of just eight question-days a year in the House of Commons (each of some thirty minutes), one Welsh-day debate a year and no more than four sittings of the Welsh Grand Committee. Moreover, in England the House of Commons offers scope for specialisation, as each of these responsibilities has a separate ministry whose affairs are scrutinised at a separate full period of questions and are the subject of several debates each session. So one group of English MPs concentrates on health, another on education and so on and these members can watch closely over the work of the relevant ministry. For Welsh affairs, one question-time every four weeks or so has to suffice for all the activities of the Welsh Office. As a result, it is not worthwhile for Welsh MPs to specialise in Welsh policy areas, the effect being to give civil servants in Wales greater freedom of action than is permitted to those administering the same functions in England. No major investigation into any aspect of the Welsh Office's responsibility has ever been mounted by the House of Commons.

When the Commission on the Constitution was taking evidence in Wales, Sir Goronwy Daniel, then Permanent Under-Secretary at the Welsh Office, was asked if there was any danger of an elite civil service controlling the affairs of Wales. He replied:

> I think dangers of that kind might arise for two reasons. One is that if accountability is only to Westminster, then the amount of time which can be made available is limited, and the amount of interest shown by members generally is also limited. The other factor is that, as the functions of the Secretary of State grow, it becomes necessary for him to delegate more and more work to officials. If the Secretary of State had full responsibility for education, for agriculture, for child care, and for various other things one can think of, the volume of work would be pretty considerable.[36]

Since this evidence was given in 1969 the Secretary of State has been given responsibility for primary and secondary education in Wales, child care, and complete control of the health service with the abolition of the Welsh Hospital Board in April 1974. And, in July 1975 the Welsh Office gained discretionary powers for aiding industrial development under Section 7 of the 1972 Industry Act together with factory building powers under the 1972 Local Employment Act. These last economic powers were the most significant extension of the Secretary of State's role since the post was established in 1964. Despite Conservative opposition to a directly elected Welsh Assembly the Shadow Secretary of State for Wales, Nicholas Edwards, pledged in May 1976 that the next Conservative administration would transfer full responsibility for agriculture to the Secretary of State.[37]

And in July 1977 the Labour Government announced that the Welsh Office would be taking over full responsibility for the Ministry of Agriculture in Wales, adding 683 civil servants to its complement of 1,500.

Because of the expansion of the Welsh Office and the spread of a rash of nominated boards, authorities and agencies, Wales, more than most parts of Britain, is administered by a non-accountable bureaucracy held together by state patronage. Pressure for devolution is therefore understandably strong in Wales where the patronage state runs strongly contrary to democratic instinct. The patronage state is the outcome of democracy conceived on too large a scale. Devolution, as has been argued, is about bringing government into a more meaningful relationship with the governed; about placing the state in the context of community so that power and responsibility can be brought together. When government is operating on a reduced scale it is reasonable to expect greater understanding and co-operation from the electorate. For then they have an appreciation of the problems being tackled based on their own knowledge and, as a result, are less likely to make inconsistent and excessive demands. In these conditions it is possible to dispense with the patronage state and make government truly democratic.

The corporate state

Thus far this chapter has described the growth of state power in Britain and analysed its attack on democracy in terms of centralisation and patronage. The politics of devolution have been seen as a reaction to these trends—as a means of defending democracy by mobilising the community against the state. To those who would say that the politics of devolution are merely about replacing a big state with a number of smaller states it has been countered that only at the smaller-scale level can power and responsibility be brought together. It is this that makes the politics of devolution justifiable. The politics of devolution are an assertion that state power is only acceptable when it can be subjected to community responsibility. The Welsh experience, as will be further demonstrated in the next chapter, testifies that in this part of Britain at least, community interest has been sacrificed on the altar of British state power. The politics of devolution are a claim that if at least some British state power is decentralised to the Welsh level there will be greater hope of the community exercising control over it.

But there are those who defend the growth of British state power and advocate its continued extension as a mechanism to bring about greater equality and social justice. Prominent amongst these in Wales is Neil Kinnock, MP for Bedwellty, and one of Labour's most articulate backbenchers. In a House of Commons devolution debate in 1975 he summarised his point of view:

> If I had to use a label of any kind, I should have to call myself a 'unionist'. However, I am a unionist entirely for reasons of expediency. I believe that the emancipation of the class which I have come to this House to represent, unapologetically, can best be achieved in a single nation and in a single economic unit, by which I mean a unit where we can have a brotherhood of all nations and have the combined strength of working-class people throughout the whole of the United Kingdom brought to bear against any bully, any Executive, any foreign power, any bureau-cratic arrangement, be it in Brussels or in Washington, and any would be coloniser, either an industrial coloniser or a political coloniser.
>
> I believe that the organised strength of working-class people has brought the only benefits to have been secured by those whom I came here to represent. Their misfortunes are not the result of being British, Welsh or Scottish. They have come about because their fate has been, in the system of economic organisation or disorganisation that we have had hitherto, to be workers—people who have no source of wealth or economic independence other that their work from day to day.[38]

Kinnock's theme is that only through centralised working-class unity on a British basis can further progress be made towards social justice and equality. Only within this framework can his working classes have the strength to confront those that would exploit them. Kinnock would further argue that democracy can only be assured at the British level so long as the main levers of economic power are progressively taken into public ownership and subjected to Parlia-mentary control.

This is a strong argument since it rests on the creation of the wel-fare state by a Labour government in the 1940s. But the belief that Parliament has provided democratic control over the state institut-ions created and can guarantee democracy in the future is weaker. Parliamentary surveillance has not prevented the state centralisation and patronage described in earlier sections. Nevertheless, it might be argued that people in Britain have greater control over, say, the British Steel Corporation because it is owned by the state than if it were in the hands of multi-national capital—though it is unlikely that in private ownership the industry would have become so highly centralised.[39]

But in the context of the last quarter of the twentieth century a stand in favour of British democratic centralism contains two fundamental contradictions: it is neither democratic, nor even centralist in the sense that ownership is being concentrated in *public* hands. It is neither of these things because the British State system is rapidly becoming Corporatist in character.

The argument of Labour's Left wing in favour of more public ownership, developed in Opposition between 1970 and 1974, rested on fear of the ownership of industry centralising into fewer and fewer private hands. As the Labour party's research group on the subject put it: 'The "mixed economy" of the years since 1950 has, indeed, been a mix which assists the capitalist system by undertaking the unprofitable infrastructure of the economy and providing a base for successful private profit-making.' The proposal was for the next Labour government to set up a large and powerful National Enterprise Board to introduce public ownership 'into the strongholds of industry'. About a third of the turnover of the top 100 manufacturers (which accounted for a half of Britain's net output) should be vested in the NEB:

> Dependent on their size the take-over of some twenty to twenty-five companies would yield control of an area of the economy of this degree, which we believe is essential if the public sector is to exercise an effective role in economic planning . . . Before 1980, the top hundred manufacturers will control two-thirds of the key sector in the economy, unless we intervene directly to change the public-private balance.[40]

This last sentence makes clear a deep-seated fear of control of the economy falling into fewer and fewer hands—fear, in short, of centralism. But the panacea offered, public ownership, is merely the substitution of one kind of centralism for another. All experience of British state enterprises, certainly from the Welsh point of view, is that they have ended up in the hands of a centralised managerial bureaucracy just as removed as the private corporations both from dictation by the government and solidarity with the workers.

But even if state ownership at the British level was the answer, the reality of politics since the 1950s is that this is just not happening. Instead, under both Labour and Conservative governments, there has gradually developed a system of state corporatism in Britain. The National Enterprise Board that was actually implemented by Labour when in office was the clearest indication so far that Britain is developing into a corporate state.[41]

The essence of corporatism as an economic system is *private* ownership and *state* control. It contrasts with Soviet socialism's state ownership and state control, and pure capitalism's private ownership and private control. Going beyond Keynsian aggregate-demand management and counter-cyclical intervention ('fine-tuning'), corporatism attempts detailed control of economic activity and conscious direction of resources. In contrast to the 'mixed economy' —partly nationalised and state regulated; partly unregulated private enterprise—a corporatist system attempts total control across the whole spectrum of economic life, at least over larger companies. Unlike the 'technocracy' of Galbraith's *New Industrial Estate*,[42] where experts rule in the name of science and efficiency, corporatism openly acknowledges political control directed towards ends determined by the state.

The corporatist solution was advocated in Britain during the interwar years by many who saw it as a compromise between capitalism and Bolshevism, for instance, Harold Macmillan.[43] The beginnings of its actual implementation in Britain began with the acceptance by the Conservative government in the late 1950s/early 1960s of the need for some form of economic planning. This led to the establishment in 1962 of the National Economic Development Organisation, which subsequently made four attempts at 'consensus' planning— the Four Per cent Plan (1961-2), the National Plan (1964-5), The Task Ahead (1968-9) and the Industrial Review 1977 (1971-2). From that beginning there developed a progressive trend by successive governments to exert control over increasing areas of the economy.

The principal steps in this development have been the 1964-70 Labour government's establishment of the Industrial Reorganisation Corporation to restructure (that is, concentrate) manufacturing industry; the imposition of statutory controls over prices and wages; and the first, unsuccessful attempt at legal regulation of industrial relations (In Place of Strife—1969), followed by the enactment of the Industrial Relations Act under the subsequent Conservative government. During its 'Selsdon phase' the Heath government attempted to suspend Labour's controls, but the event that most strongly confirmed the trend towards corporatism was the acceptance by a Conservative government in 1972 of the need for peacetime controls on prices and incomes. Indeed, it supplemented these with others on dividends, profit margins, and capital movements, and its own interventionist Industry Act 1972.

By the time of the 1974 elections all three British parties were committed (the Liberals most strongly of all) to various sets of statutory controls on economic activity, in an atmosphere of general

criticism against the 'anarchy' of the market which could simultaneously force the collapse of major companies (for example, Rolls
Royce), generate 'unacceptable' capitalist profits for property
speculators, put more than a million out of work, yet allow strong
unions (like the miners) 'to hold the country to ransom'.

The post-1972 Conservative interventionism was recognised at the
time by Tony Benn for what it was—not the latest strategy for the
strengthening of capitalism, but the 'most comprehensive armoury
of government control that has ever been assembled for use over
private industry . . . exceeding all the powers thought to be necessary
by the last Labour government'. Indeed, he went so far as to con-
gratulate the Conservative Prime Minister: 'Heath has performed a
very important historical role *in preparing for* the fundamental and
irreversible transfer in the balance of power'.[44]

Benn was inferring that the transfer would be from capitalism to
socialism. But, in the closing stages of the 1970-74 Conservative
government, its Trade and Industry Secretary, Peter Walker, stated
that, in fact, the transfer was to corporatism. He propounded what
amounted to a tentative theory of corporatism: the Government
was developing a 'new form of interventionism', in which the role of
the state was to harness capitalism to the interests of all and the role
of business was to 'make a profit for Britain'.[45]

Peter Walker's interpretation was confirmed by Labour's 1975
Industry Act which set out in detail how the harnessing was to take
place—through two new institutions, the National Enterprise Board
and the Planning Agreements system. Together they embody three
essential ingredients of corporatism:

(i) A limited commitment to *public* ownership. Nationalisation of
whole industries was restricted to aircraft and shipbuilding which
were already effectively controlled by the state through a combination of subsidies, government orders and research grants
(for example, the aircraft industry's biggest postwar commitments, the Multi-Role Combat Aircraft, Bluestreak and
Concorde, were wholly the state's responsibility). The National
Enterprise Board will work by taking over or participating in
only one leading company in each of the principal economic
sectors and, through control of its activity, use it as a lever to
influence and control other companies in that sector.

(ii) Detailed control over the internal decision-making of privately
owned business through the Planning Agreement system.

(iii) The extent of State control not being explicit in law. No list of items to be covered by Planning Agreements is contained in the Act, which merely says they should serve 'national needs and objectives'. However, departmental discussion documents on the agreements system, prior to the Act, indicated that the areas covered would be comprehensive: prices, investment, productivity (including both technology and employment levels), exports, import saving, industrial relations, product development, consumer protection (that is, product quality) and environmental protection.

Thus the Industry Act expresses the basic character of corporatism outlined above—an economic system which combines *private ownership with state control*. It enabled J. T. Winkler to observe:

> Of course, the emasculated piece of legislation that finally emerged does not establish corporatism in Britain but it should not be underestimated. It served to bring out into the open the principles of the economic system toward which Britain has been evolving over the past 15 years. It created two corporatist institutions which may become more powerful in the future. It indicated the likely course of Britain's medium-term economic development, unless there is a significant shift in political power. That is its historical significance.[46]

Winkler has defined corporatism as a comprehensive economic system in which the state directs and controls predominantly privately owned business according to four principles: unity, order, statism, and success.[47] The first operating principle is *unity,* the idea that economic goals are best achieved through co-operative effort rather than competitive processes. Whether it be through 'joint consultation', 'co-determination', a 'social contract' or 'tripartism', working together as 'one nation' was by the mid-1970s seen by Conservative and Labour alike as the way forward. The pursuit of individual or group interests was labelled 'sectionalism' (when it involved workers) or 'unacceptable capitalism' (when businessmen). On the basis of three years' research into the behaviour of British business firms, Pahl and Winkler maintain that businessmen, as well as politicians, see little merit in price competition or competing sources of supply. Instead, they increasingly favour a system of price control and state-organised cartels with, perhaps some industrial reorganisation. They conclude:

> A corporatist government will attempt to create order by the final overt killing-off of the various still-existing markets (land, labour, money, shares, raw materials, for example), which some neo-classical and socialist economists alike have been prematurely assuring us were long

since dead. It will be done by imposing intensive state control in all major areas of private economic activity.[48]

The second corporatist principle is *order*. Market economies are seen as inherently liable to unintended fluctuations and instrumental disruptions. In order to guard against latent 'anarchy', submission of the particular interest to the general will is a corporatist principle. Discipline, compulsively enforced if required, is regarded as a state necessity 'for the good of all'.

Corporatism is *statist* in a dual sense. First, it is a collectivist system, not an individualistic one. The economic performance of the state has moral primacy over personal affluence or mobility. Second, it is economically aggressive towards the rest of the world, involving protectionist trade policies. The statist characteristic of corporatism was illustrated in the 1974 elections by the Conservative slogan, borrowed from the National Front (they used it in 1970)—'Putting Britain First'.

The final corporatist principle, according to Pahl and Winkler, is *success*. This means giving conscious direction to the economy by establishing priorities and targets and by restricting work done towards other objectives. It means controlling and concentrating investment and the allocation of resources. The goals of mid-1970s Britain were 'beating inflation' followed by moving Britain up a notch or two in the international growth league table. Corporatism is an ends-oriented system, rather than a means-oriented one. It seeks results, not efficiency: it puts greater value on achieving targets than, say, on the maintenance of legal rights.

After listing these four principles of a corporatist system, principles which progressively underlie the British state system, Pahl and Winkler deliver their judgment:

> Let us not mince words. Corporatism is fascism with a human face. What all the major parties have done is take over the core elements of the economic strategy which the Italian fascists, Salazar in Portugal, the Falange in Spain, and the Nazis adopted to deal with the inter-war crisis. . . . What the parties are putting forward now is an acceptable face of fascism; indeed, a masked version of it, because so far the more repugnant political and social aspects of the German and Italian regimes are absent or only present in diluted form.[49]

Since these words were written (in October 1974) the diluted political and social aspects of corporatism in Britain have become more visible. Democratic control over the economy via Parliament has become even less meaningful, with attention firmly focused on closed doors behind which the TUC, Cabinet, and CBI wheel and deal. Racialism is very much on the agenda with the Conservative party taking up many of Enoch Powell's themes, including advocacy of some form of repatriation. Prominent politicians, for example William Whitelaw, make repeated calls for the police force to be strengthened. Meanwhile, there is growing advocacy of a suspension of such party politics that exist in favour of a 'national' or coalition government.

The democratic response

What should be the democratic response to the developing British corporate state? The Left wing of the Labour Party, led in Wales on this issue by Neil Kinnock, call for more intervention at the British state level. But, as the National Enterprise Board has demonstrated, the state intervention they advocate leads directly towards a corporatist system. A Right-wing representative of the Labour party, David Marquand, former MP for Ashfield and now with the European Commission, has suggested that nothing can be done about the trend towards corporatism in Britain:

> . . . corporate power is now a fact whether we like it or not. Governments can propose as much as they like but in the end it is the great producer groups that dispose . . . Governments that try to force their policies down the throats of the producer groups will fail, and deserve to fail. And the only alternative to force is negotiation . . . To try to dismantle the Corporate State and return to the imaginary golden age of parliamentary supremacy, in the way that some Liberals and Conservatives want to do, would be a foolish and destructive waste of energy.[50]

Marquand is right in pointing to the futility of any attempt to dismantle corporatism within the framework of the established British state. This is the answer to those who would believe that the interests of working people in Britain can be best served by attempting to manipulate the British state system. The only way the corporate state can be dismantled is by approaching the task from the bottom, not from the top, and decentralising the state to a level where the community can control it.

Devolution is the means through which reaction to corporatism is being most effectively channelled, the immediate agents being the national movements in Wales and Scotland. But throughout Britain reaction to corporatism can be seen in many disparate groups. On the Right wing there is growing protest from middle-class organisations like the self-employed, while on the Left there are growing demands for workers' control—as opposed to 'workers' participation' which is a classical corporatist co-option technique. At grassroots level there are local action groups; consumer groups;

residents' and conservationists' associations; and 'non-political' pressure groups in fields like housing and poverty. All these various groupings and pressures have in common a reaction to the rise of big business, big industry, big financial institutions, big trade unions, and big government: reaction, in short, to developing corporatism.

The reaction is also bringing a curious intellectual alignment of thinkers who, in conventional political terms, would never be thought of together. Thus the apostle of government non-involvement, F. A. Hayek, would draw a sympathetic response from many radical thinkers today with this comment he made in the 1940s: 'Planning leads to dictatorship because dictatorship is the most effective instrument of coercion and the enforcement of ideals, and as such essential if central planning on a large scale is to be possible.'[51] Since the 1940s writers like Leopold Kohr, E. F. Schumacher and Ivan Illich have been building the conceptual foundations for the anti-corporatist alternative: decentralised communities with a commitment to slow down material consumption, move towards greater self-sufficiency, and place the community over and above the state. For Illich the choice is between two types of institutions: manipulative or convivial. In the manipulative breed of institution scientific discoveries have been used to achieve the 'specialisation of functions, institutionalisation of values and centralisation of power [which] turn people into the accessories of bureaucratic machines'.[52] These are 'treatment institutions'; they induce individuals to use them to consume their outputs, and they become addictive: they produce the demands for their own services and are run by self-certifying elites. Illich's two celebrated case studies on this theme are his *Deschooling Society* and *Medical Nemesis* which attack the manipulative institutionalisation and hierarchy of education and medicine.[53] Instead, Illich advocates what he terms 'Convivial' institutions in which scientific discoveries have been used 'to enlarge the range of each person's competencies'.[54] Whereas manipulative institutions are activated by professionals, their convivial counterparts are client-oriented, and used spontaneously without artificial promotion. Examples include postal systems, telephones and public parks. They are institutions people use without having to be institutionally convinced that it is to their advantage to do so. They exist to be *used* rather than to produce. Whereas manipulative institutions identify satisfaction with the mere act of consumption convivial networks serve a purpose beyond their own repeated use: a telephone, for instance, is used in order to convey a message. According to Illich society is overloaded with manipulative institutions and as a result is hell-bent on productivity, faster economic growth, and the destruction of democracy.

The relevance of Illich's ideas to the politics of devolution in the Welsh context has been drawn by Paul Luke, who has pointed out that Illich relegates the issue of 'ownership' to a position of comparative insignificance.[55] The important thing about manipulative institutions is that they are congenitally destructive. Thus it is irrelevant whether enterprises such as hospitals and schools are state owned or privately owned. Luke adds:

> Equally, and this would mortify traditional devolutionists, it matters little whether they are centrally or peripherally owned. . . . The corollary of conviviality is community, and only devolution-all-round can check the rise of economic growth as the supreme target of all modern society. Indeed, Illich's ideas seem to be to be nothing more than devolution massively applied, devolution freed from its over-concern with the geographic locus of decision-making. The sooner that Welsh devolutionists are able to recognise, with Illich, the real obstacles to the realisation of a decentralised society, the better.[56]

The endpoint of such a perspective on the politics of devolution appears to be a rediscovery of the philosophy of anarchism. And, indeed, it is here that is to be found the source of the required democratic response to the rise of the corporate state. A leading contemporary exponent of anarchism, Paul Goodman, has given it a highly significant definition from this point of view. Referring to the student demonstrators of 1968 (the black flag of anarchism flew side-by-side over the Sorbonne with the red Marxist flag), he has written:

> They believe in local power, community development, rural reconstruction, decentralist organisation. . . . They prefer a simpler standard of living . . . they do not trust the due process of administrators and are quick to resort to direct action and civil disobedience. All this adds up to the community Anarchism of Kropotkin, the resistance Anarchism of Malatesta, the agitational Anarchism of Bakunin.[57]

In Wales the contemporaries of the Sorbonne students are to be found within the ranks of Cymdeithas yr Iaith Gymraeg, the Welsh Language Society. The inspiration also spreads into the wider, more mainstream, national movement. The thinking, as a recipe for practical political application, has been laid down at length by Plaid Cymru's MP for Meirionnydd, Dafydd Elis Thomas, as follows:

> Our task is not to liberate Wales, but to liberate the Welsh people. It is not self-government for Wales we should be seeking but self-government for every individual and community in Wales. That does not mean

anarchy, for I have stressed that there must be a system to determine our extra-personal relationships with one another in society; but that system must be biased *towards* self-determination throughout that society and full participation in it. This means workers' control at plant level; it means tenants' control of housing estates; it means increasing consumer control of demand and a reassertion of direct responsibility for a community's future.

It means building up a system of direct democracy and direct control over economic and social relationships, as far as that is physically and psychologically possible. That is the real meaning of decentralisation and devolution, except that it is not really devolution but a revolutionary demand which communities will have to make on the existing system. This is why nationalists in Wales must see the logic of the fundamental basis of our position: we must not fear the radical, liberating vision implied by real self-government. Self-reliance; ecological self-sufficiency; self-management in industry; self-government in the widest and deepest meaning of that word;—these must be our objectives, and in that view we find that we share not only the vision of some Marxist humanists, but also what can be seen as a modern development from the core of the Welsh radical tradition. In a sense we are moving beyond both blind collectivism and blind individualism to stress the values of human community and of community control of its historic destiny. This means nothing less than the destruction of British welfare capitalism, in order to replace it with an economic structure totally different from that of bureaucratic state socialism.

Of course, there are qualifications which must be made: there must be a framework of central economic planning, as there must be a framework of intercommunity and international relationships. The ideology here is radically different from that of Labourism or Conservatism, individualism or collectivism. Our starting point in Plaid Cymru as nationalists has been the historic distinctiveness of the people of Wales as a cultural group. But we must now move to stress the functional importance of Wales in organising a radically different system of social relationships. And in going along this road in Wales we will not be isolated. In Latin America and in Africa, in Eastern Europe and in Western Europe, there are individuals, organisations, and a few political parties, who are groping toward similar aims.[58]

Of course, the realignment of politics away from the conventional Left/Right conflict to a perception that the real choice is now between corporatism and centralisation on the one hand, and devolution and decentralisation on the other, is not confined to political ideology. The consensus road to corporatism between Labour and Conservative administrations since the 1960s has made the traditional Left/Right electoral debate increasingly unreal. More and more people are contracting out of the Labour versus Conservative setpiece battle, by opting for third parties—the Liberals, who won

6,063,470 votes at the polarising February 1974 election, and also the Scottish National Party and Plaid Cymru. The extent to which the two-party fight has lost activist support was measured by the Houghton Committee recommendation that the parties be financed out of public funds.[59] This, of course, was another lurch towards corporatism. The moment governments are able to control the purse-strings of their political opponents is also the moment at which dissent in any society makes an unconditional surrender to conformity. As the Minority Report of the Houghton Committee report put it:

> We are sceptical about the concept of public money as in some way laundered, and therefore 'neutral'. On the contrary, we find it as dubious as the concept of a free lunch. It is only a short step from the injection of state funds to direct demands on the party organisations for a quid pro quo in the form of radical changes in their rules and practices.[60]

In this chapter some attention has been paid to the question of working-class unity on a British basis as advocated by leaders like Neil Kinnock since, quite apart from the national issue, it is a powerful argument deployed against devolution. In the first place, of course, it is an argument that relies on expediency, as Kinnock has conceded. The level of Britain as the one where working-class forces should unite is a matter of convenience. For instance, most of those who press this case also campaigned against Britain's entry into the European Economic Community. They judged that working-class interests would be more difficult to mobilise at that level though, in terms of unity there would be more to gain. Of course, the idea that the Labour party—even its Left wing—puts the interest of class to the fore is to misconceive the basis of the movement. For as Tom Nairn has pointed out:

> Labourism stands not for class and nation—this is the ideological halo—but for class-in-nation; or more exactly, for nation-over-class. Labour is (to employ one of its own historic programme-words in a different sense) the *Nationalisation* of class. What it represents is not the class, in a sociological sense—the raw or material social reality of class—but the class as seduced by the nation. . . . The Labour Party's real basis may be a popular and proletarian mass; but a *political* movement, surely, is what it does—and what Labourism does is to translate that real mass into terms of the nation, to spiritualize it into the 'national interest'. By enshrining the real in the unreal, it allows the unreal to govern the real—and hence, allows the real power behind that unreality, the profane secret of capital, to maintain its grip.[61]

Even if it were accepted that the Labour party is a class party in the sense that its *raison d'être* was to further the interests of the 'working class' there is still the question of whether the British level is the most expedient context in which to achieve this. A major conclusion of this chapter is that those in the Labour party who cling to the maintenance of the British state apparatus as presently constituted as a prerequisite for furthering the interests of the community or the working class are undermining their own cause. For the direction of the British state is towards centralisation, patronage, and, ultimately, corporatism—all of which comprise a concerted attack on democracy.

It may be argued, finally, that devolution is a classical co-option technique of a corporatist system. In a way analogous to worker participation, rather than worker control, it is a means whereby a corporatist state seeks to create a structure in which dissident groups —in this case the Welsh and the Scots—are given the maximum amount of responsibility for co-operating with the system but the minimum amount of power for interfering with centrally determined policies. As Christopher Smallwood, a financial adviser to the government who worked in the Cabinet Office during the preparation of the devolution policy put it: '. . . devolution is supposed to . . . calm people down and convince them they've got a reasonably good deal'.[62]

This might be true if devolution was confined to the spirit and intention of the scheme devised by the Labour government in 1975.[63] But this would be to ignore the pressures that persuaded the government to draw up its scheme in the first place, to assume that such proposals would remain static, and to underestimate the resilience and power of national communities. As Leopold Kohr has put it, the British state has retained centralised control only by destroying the political identity of its component nations and replacing them with small, easily controllable units of approximately equal size, the counties:

Politically, there is today neither an England, nor a Scotland, nor a Wales. What little chance a union of British nations rather than of British counties would have had can be seen from the fact that the moment one of them, the Irish, succeeded in reorganising itself as a national unit, it burst the frame of the United Kingdom and broke away. There are similar attempts at national reorganisation in Scotland and Wales. Should they succeed also, it would mean the end of the United Kingdom altogether. It would break the small-county organisation which now enables London to rule effectively in all corners of the British

Isles. Once this gives way to national organisation, London would confront accumulations of political power which could be kept under control only by military pressures of such magnitude that, as the case of Ireland has proved, not even a great power can impose them indefinitely.[64]

Such would be the nature of the conflict if the British state sought to use devolution, once implemented, as a means for enrolling the periphery more effectively in the further development of a corporatist system.

But the politics of devolution are about a more creative kind of conflict. Devolution to Wales and Scotland is only setting the pace for decentralisation within England itself. On this basis the peoples of Britain can move forward to a progressive dismantling of the British corporate state. It would be naïve to suggest that this can be achieved without conflict. That would be to underestimate the forces of centralisation. In any event, without conflict there would be consensus which, in this context, is the objective of the corporatist system. Thus the conflict implicit in devolution is creative since the alternative is acceleration to an authoritarian system of government in Britain and the death of democracy.

Chapter 2

The Failure of British Regional Policy

'We are seeking a Wales where we can have growth from within. We are not carrying a begging bowl into the next century.'
George Wright, General Secretary Wales TUC,
Address to Llandudno Conference 1976.

Between 1965 and 1975 the number of men at work in Wales fell by 97,000, a drop of well over 10 per cent. More than any other statistic this provides the economic background to the pressure for devolution. In June 1965 there were 708,000 men in employment in Wales; by June 1975 this figure had fallen to 611,000.[1] This steeply declining economic activity in Wales is more fundamental than the country's persistently high unemployment rates in comparison with the United Kingdom as a whole, set out with other figures in the accompanying tables. Put in the simplest terms, a smaller proportion of the population of Wales is at work than of the population of Britain or of most of the English regions. Paul Wilding, in his *Poverty: The Facts in Wales* (Child Poverty Action Group, 1977), identified this as the underlying cause of poverty and relative deprivation in Wales:

> Low rates of economic activity mean two things—a sluggish economy and low levels of per capita income. If a smaller proportion of the population is at work, then a larger proportion of the population is dependent upon them. In our society, where it is only income from work which provides a satisfactory standard of living, the result of low rates of economic activity is deprivation . . .
>
> It is the low economic activity rates which underlie the low per capita gross domestic product in Wales. In 1974 GDP per capita was £1,030 in Wales, £1,176 in Scotland and £1,321 in England. In 1973 the figure for Wales was lower than any English region. It was 5 per cent below the average for the 'assisted regions' and nearly 25 per cent below the average for the unassisted regions. On the other hand gross domestic product *per person employed* shows the Welsh in a much more favourable light, producing more than the British average. The problem is not that Welsh industry is unproductive. It is simply that there is not enough of it.

The people of Wales today have to cope with a legacy of exploitation of their economy, particularly of raw materials, which lasted for generations without any significant investment being ploughed back. This has gone hand-in-hand with the creation of an economic

Table 2.1 Comparative economic statistics for the countries and regions of the United Kingdom

	1 population 1974 mid-yr estimate (millions)	2 gross domestic product at factor cost 1973 £ million	3 £ per capita	4 identifiable public expenditure 1974-75 (provisional) £ million	5 £ per head	6 unemployment Nov. '75 %	7 increase in % age points Nov. 73-Nov. 75	8 average gross weekly earnings of full time employees April 1975 men £	9 women £
Country									
England	46.4	53,368	1,150	27,011	582	4.7	+2.7		37.7
Northern Ireland	1.5	1,220	788	1,169	756	9.4	+4.1	n.a.	n.a.
Scotland	5.2	5,345	1,026	3,611	691	5.9	+2.1	60.3	35.9
Wales	2.8	2,624	954	1,657	601	6.9	+3.8	59.0	35.8
English regions									
East Anglia	1.8	1,786	1,027	n.a.	n.a.	4.2	+2.6	36.2	34.3
East Midlands	3.7	3,732	1,082	n.a.	n.a.	4.2	+2.5	58.6	34.9
North	3.1	3,238	983	n.a.	n.a.	6.7	+2.7	60.5	36.2
North-West	6.6	7,228	1,070	n.a.	n.a.	6.2	+3.3	59.1	35.8
South-East	17.0	22,590	1,305	n.a.	n.a.	3.5	+2.2	65.3	41.0
South-West	4.2	4,027	1,039	n.a.	n.a.	3.9	+3.6	56.2	35.7
West Midlands	5.2	5,836	1,130	n.a.	n.a.	5.2	+2.5	58.4	35.1
Yorkshire and Humberside	4.9	4,931	1,021	n.a.	n.a.	4.8	+2.4	58.4	35.6

Note: Considerable care should be used in the detailed interpretation of this table. The original sources should be consulted for explanations of the methods and definitions used. Also note that these latest figures do not all relate to the same year.

(*Sources*: *Social Trends*, HMSO, 1975; *Hansard*, 15 December 1975, cols. 831 and 850; *Department of Employment Gazette*, December 1973, November 1975 and December 1975.)

structure grossly overdependent on a few basic industries. Thus, today, the key feature of the Welsh economy is that it has an industrial structure with a higher proportion of industries for whose products demand is falling, or growing relatively slowly.

In table 2.1 note the very poor Welsh gross product per head, £954: only Northern Ireland with £788, is worse. Wales also has the highest unemployment percentage figure in the table. The general message, however, is domination of the English South-East region, both in terms of population size and economic prosperity. The inflationary pressure exerted by this region on Wales is examined in chapter 5.

The dominant declining industry in Wales has been coalmining, whose employment has fallen from about 130,000 at the beginning of the 1950s to less than 50,000 at the beginning of the 1970s. Prior to this, and also during the same period, there was a large drop in the number of farmers and agricultural workers—from more than 80,000 in the early 1950s, to less than 50,000 by the mid-1970s. Then it was the turn of the steel industry. In 1970 it employed 65,000 people in Wales. With the axe poised over Shotton, Ebbw Vale and East Moors (Cardiff), this figure had dropped to 59,000 by the mid-1970s, with plans for it to fall to about 50,000 by 1980 and to between 40,000 and 45,000 by the mid-1980s.

Though many of these jobs have been replaced by more diversified employment in manufacturing industry, the drastic fall in Welsh activity rates referred to at the opening of this chapter, combined with continuing high unemployment levels, tell their own story. And all this has occurred when the infrastructural standards in Wales—roads, railways, housing and other amenities—have declined relative to most other areas of Britain. At the same time, the skills of the Welsh workforce have not been developed to keep pace with the demands of modern industry.

This, in short, is the 'Regional Problem' which is about the relative deprivation of whole communities and, to that extent, more fundamental than inequalities between individuals. By the 1970s this was being recognised by mainstream Left-wing British political theorists. It was voiced, for instance, by one of the architects of Labour's 1974 Election platform, Stuart Holland:

> The regional problem is nothing less than the spatial dimension of inequality in the market economy. It is the social and economic problem writ wide. It is an area which socialists have tended to neglect, in favour of concentration on inequalities of class and social structure. Yet economic and social opportunities often are determined as much by the region as the class into which people are born.[2]

Figure 2.1 Gross Domestic Product per Head as a percentage of the UK average.

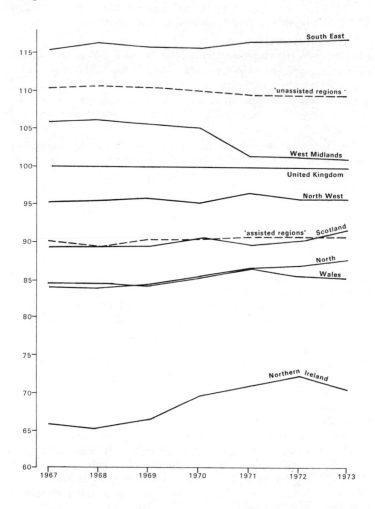

In 1973, Welsh gross domestic product per head was £954 compared with £1,118 in the United Kingdom as a whole. The difference is largely explained by lower activity rates in Wales—approximately 84 per cent of the United Kingdom average in 1971 (see table 2.2).

(*Source: Welsh Economic Trends* (No. 3, 1976), Welsh Office).

Table 2.2 Numbers economically active as a percentage of the population aged 15 and over.

| | 1961 | | 1971 | |
	Males	Females	Males	Females
Wales	85·1	28·1	78·5	35·7
Great Britain	86·3	37·5	81·4	42·7

Table 2.2 shows male activity rates declining in the 1960s in both Wales and Britain as a whole, though more sharply in Wales. On the other hand, female activity rates increased more rapidly in Wales though still remaining substantially lower than the general rate for Britain in 1971. No Welsh county—not even South Glamorgan which embraces Cardiff—has a rate of female activity which even approaches the average for Britain. In latter years the relative decline of Welsh activity rates has been worsening. Thus between mid-1973 and mid-1974, for example, the number of male employees in Wales fell by 2·3 per cent as against a fall of 0·9 per cent in the United Kingdom as a whole.

(*Source: Welsh Economic Trends* (No. 3 1976), Welsh Office).

The centralist versus decentralist view of economic development

The centralist response to the 'regional problem' has been 'regional policy'. This promotes a redistribution of growth, usually manufacturing industry, from the more prosperous English South-East and the Midlands to Scotland, Wales, Northern Ireland and the North of England which are officially classed as Development Areas. The declared object is to achieve more balanced development and social equality in the interests of the United Kingdom as a whole.

This is regional policy viewed from the centre. The decentralist perspective, from the periphery, is different. Here the overwhelming perception is the inadequacy of regional policy to fulfil its promise. Why, it is asked, is the regional problem still with us after forty years of policies to counteract it? And, though the government has conceded the existence of a regional problem, why has it never specified what would constitute a solution? Is the aim to reduce unemployment in the regions to the British average? Is it to create equivalent living standards in the depressed regions to those in the prosperous regions? Or is it merely to keep disparities within politically acceptable limits rather than to make a serious attempt to remove them?

Figure 2.2   Unemployment Rates

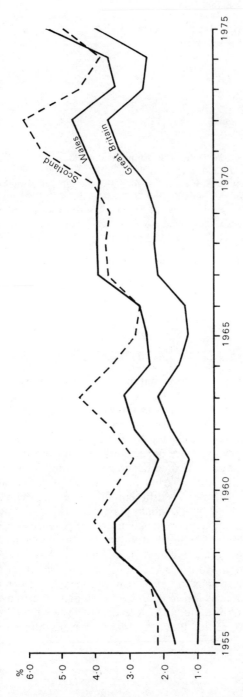

During the postwar period the unemployment rates in Wales have been higher than the rate in Great Britain as a whole. In the past decade the position has deteriorated. In 1975 the monthly average number unemployed reached a peak of over 55,000 compared with 37,000 in 1974—an increase of 49 per cent. The figure rose steeply to nearly 80,000 by mid-1977 with every prospect of it worsening (8 per cent compared with 5·9 per cent for Great Britain as a whole). Unemployment loomed as the major economic issue in Welsh politics for the forseeable future.

(*Source: Welsh Economic Trends* (No. 3, 1976), Welsh Office.)

Questions like these underpin the devolution debate. In economic terms the devolution argument is about whether regional policy, as traditionally practised, can work. The devolutionist, who at this point is beginning to use nationalist arguments, says that regional policy has not worked and by its very nature cannot work. He might even point to Franz Fanon's assessment of European colonialism in Africa:

> In the first phase of the national struggle colonialism tries to disarm national demands by putting forward economic doctrines. As soon as the first demands are set out, colonialism pretends to consider them, recognising with ostentatious humility that the territory is suffering from serious underdevelopment, which necessitates a great economic and social effort. And, in fact, it so happens that certain spectacular measures (centres of work for unemployed which are opened here and there for example) delay the crystallisation of national consciousness for a few years.[3]

The devolutionist/nationalist contends that this analysis of regional policy is confirmed by the government's response of setting up Development Agencies for Wales and Scotland (in early 1976). This initiative, it is asserted, signalled the beginning of the end of the old British regional policy, and was an essential component both of why devolution was happening and what it would be about when it did. For the implication of the new policy was that traditional regional policy with its 'carrot' of incentives and 'stick' of limiting expansion in the richer regions, had failed. The further implication, it is insisted, was that the only hope of greater regional equality was a new departure, involving more economic self-management and more self-generated growth from within.

This is the political argument about regional policy. Underlying it is a related academic argument about the nature of economic development within an area like Britain. Here, the centralist view holds that economic development will tend to occur fairly evenly over the whole area. This will happen because the relative overdevelopment of any one region will cause costs to rise there, as factors such as land and labour become scarce, and therefore the operation of the market mechanism will cause industry to move to other regions, where costs are relatively low. Occasionally some regions will leap ahead, others will become depressed; but such distortions will be temporary and the system will tend always to return to a state of equilibrium. Enoch Powell was presumably subscribing to this centralist interpretation in a television interview with Vincent Kane on BBC Wales in May 1974:

Kane: Is it not a significant feature of a United Britain, of a Great
            Britain, that you tend to find the area around the central
            government in London economically prosperous and the
            areas which do not have the seat of government at hand...

Powell: No. No!

Kane: . . . like Wales and Scotland and Northern Ireland are
            economically depressed?

Powell: No, this is not true. Because if you look at the history of the
            United Kingdom since the Union with Scotland, you will
            find that for the majority of that period it was the South-
            East which was relatively poor and depressed and that the
            great centres of wealth were remote from the political
            centres.

Kane: But if you look at the per capita income now, you will find
            that in Wales and Scotland and the North-East and North-
            ern Ireland it is a lot lower than it is in the South-East.

Powell: But you were asking me to say that this was the inevitable
            consequence of a central government. I have disproved
            that by pointing out that during most of the period that the
            central government of the United Kingdom has been in
            London, the centres of economic growth and power were
            elsewhere.[4]

   Against the centralist view of economic development the decentralist view maintains that development does not spread evenly
throughout the regions of a country. One of the principal exponents
of this approach is Gunnar Myrdal[5] who argues that it is the nature
of the process of economic development to produce rich and poor
regions, and moreover, the rich tend to get richer and the poor,
poorer.
   Myrdal proposes a theory of 'cumulative causation', arguing that,
when initial economic development takes place in one region of a
country, this leads to further development in the same region, not to
balancing development in other regions. The market mechanism, in
fact, increases rather than decreases the advantage of the developing
region over the others. This happens because in the process of
economic interaction between the developing region and the other
stagnating regions, the stagnating regions suffer what Myrdal calls
'backwash effects'. That is, their local resources of labour capital
and so on are sucked away to the growth region. Moreover, goods

and services from the growth region flood into their markets, putting local firms out of business.

As the stagnating regions become relatively poorer, their authorities will find it difficult to provide equivalent services to the growth region, and differentials will appear in the standards of services like health care, education and also of the infrastructure generally.

Myrdal does suggest that this basic pattern of increasing inequality between the growth and stagnating regions may, at some point, be modified by factors such as congestion in the growth region, leading to some dispersal of growth. Thus 'spread effects' may develop, by which growth is transmitted to other regions, but these will generally be in proximity to the original growth region.

Myrdal's theories have not been systematically applied to the British situation. They have been more developed in relation to the underdeveloped countries of South-East Asia. But, applying his ideas to Britain, it can be suggested that the South-East is the main growth region, while the peripheral regions of the North and West suffer backwash effects. Spread effects can, perhaps, be discerned in the Midlands, East Anglia and the Bristol area.

Thus the centralist view of economic development holds that the process will naturally tend towards stability and equality, while the decentralist view suggests that the process embodies fundamental inequalities. The decentralist view was conceded by the retiring EEC Commissioner for Regional Affairs, George Thomson, in November 1976. Commenting on the Regional Commission's performance, he said: 'Whether you look at the division of expenditure between countries, between regions within countries, or between districts within regions, the story is the same. The rich get richer, the poor, poorer.'[6]

The rest of this chapter will examine economic development as it has affected Wales, to see how far the experience confirms the centralist or decentralist view of regional development. The outcome has political consequences since the economic pressure for devolution rests upon a decentralist analysis of economic development. Devolution, or in economic terms 'growth from within', is claimed as the correct decentralist response to this analysis.

The impact of regional policy on Wales

British regional economic policy, which emerged out of the experience of the 1930s unemployment trauma, began to be more rigorously applied in the 1960s and 1970s. Central government claimed it was an attempt to restrain growth in the South-East and the Midlands and to redistribute economic advance to the under-developed English regions, Northern Ireland, Wales and Scotland. Nationalist opponents of the government claimed the policy was a response to their pressure.

Labour administrations have tended to favour grants towards the capital costs of new plant, machinery and industrial buildings in these areas whilst the Conservatives, until the volte-face of their 1972 Industry Act, when they were forced to return to grants, have tended to favour allowances against tax. These capital grants (or allowances) have often been accompanied by accelerated depreci-ation, training grants and a direct labour subsidy in the form of the Regional Employment Premium. This last has been, in effect, a devaluation in favour of Wales and the other underdeveloped areas, to give their products a competitive advantage over those of the Midlands and the South-East.

These 'carrots' have been accompanied by a 'stick' in the form of constraints on expansion in the South-East and Midlands, where Industrial Development Certificates have to be obtained before expansion of premises can take place. The policy was to limit the size of expansion in terms of square footage in the developed areas, with no limit in the development areas. Labour administrations have tended to be more stringent in the application of IDC policy than Conservatives. (One study[7] of the period 1960-9 shows that the attraction of industry to the development areas was more successful in the latter half of the period when a Labour government applied the restrictions more rigidly.)

Within Wales, the general strategy was to use the wide range of incentives to stimulate widespread industrial development at a large number of small industrial estates. A detailed analysis of the activity of regional policy in Wales and its effects during the 1960s and early 1970s was commissioned by the Welsh Office and published in July 1975. Carried out by the Cambridge economists Barry Moore and John Rhodes, it included a detailed breakdown of expenditure.[8] This showed that well over £100m was spent on regional policy in Wales during the 1960s. At the time they published their report, mid-way through 1975, Moore and Rhodes indicated that annual expenditure had risen to around £36 million.

The main conclusion of their analysis was that the strengthening of regional policy generated some 70,000 to 80,000 new jobs in Wales between 1960 and 1972, that is, about 6,000 jobs per year. Just over half these jobs were created by an acceleration in the establishment of new plants after 1960, while just under half were created by the induced expansion of firms which had already been operating in Wales prior to 1960.

Despite this, at the end of the day, the impact of regional policy did not come anywhere near what was officially predicted for it. The *Digest of Welsh Statistics* and the Welsh Office annual report came out regularly with the number of Industrial Development Certificates approved for Wales, together with estimated additional jobs they would bring. But when put against the actual number of IDCs completed, and the estimated job increase at that stage, the contrast is striking:

Table 2.3   Industrial Development Certificates (Wales) 1964-75[9] (Schemes of 15,000 sq. ft and above)

Year		IDCs approved Number	Estimated additional employment	Certificated schemes completed Number	Estimated additional employment
1964	...	61	5,230	28	2,640
1965	...	57	5,790	31	1,810
1966	...	110	21,390	40	4,300
1967	...	81	9,520	49	5,260
1968	...	119	14,930	48	4,470
1969	...	131	14,560	97	10,110
1970	...	103	13,690	65	10,510
1971	...	56	4,440	67	8,630
1972	...	46	3,050	28	3,650
1973	...	40	3,660	30	2,790
1974	...	25	2,300	19	3,440
1975 (January—November) ...		9	870	17	750

Notes:

1. Since July 1972, IDCs have not been required in special development areas and development areas. These include most of Wales.

2. The figures are in respect of schemes, not firms. Some firms may have had more than one IDC during the period.

3. Schemes approved in a period are not normally completed in that period.

4. Approvals details cover all IDCs issued. Completions details cover schemes involving new building, including extensions, but do not cover changes of use.

Allowing a generous time scale of up to two years between granting an IDC and the completion of the scheme, of the 498 schemes approved between 1965 and 1970, promising a total of 66,000 jobs, just over 300 were completed, promising a total of 39,000 jobs.

Nevertheless, in 1970, the Labour Party in Wales had no doubt that the policy had proved a success. In giving evidence to the Commission on the Constitution, a list was provided of 153 firms that had been granted IDCs for new projects, or expansion, in the Welsh Development Area between 1965 and 1970.[10] In 1976 Plaid Cymru undertook an analysis of what had become of the firms listed.[11]

The party discovered that of the 153 firms, 24 never arrived in Wales; and a further 22 had closed down or were on the point of closing down at March 1976: 'We should also subtract the firms who were not attracted to Wales for the first time or planning a genuine new project, but who took advantage of the Development Area grants by moving their factory a few miles to cross the Development Area boundary', stated Plaid Cymru's memorandum:

> It is a little difficult to know where to draw the line between those firms which moved lock, stock and barrel—even to the point of encouraging the whole labour force to move with them—and those firms already committed to a genuine expansion who prudently located the development inside the Development Area.
> The first category have made a move that seems totally pointless; the second category may at least bring new employment prospects to the areas hardest hit by unemployment. In neither case are any extra jobs created in Wales as a whole, and wherever we draw the line the number of genuinely new projects that actually come to Wales, and are still operating successfully, falls below 100.[12]

Of the firms that actually came to Wales, Plaid Cymru found that many were employing far fewer people than they had promised:

> The pattern varies considerably. In one case a firm which originally promised to provide 40 jobs rising to 100 is now employing 330. But only six miles away another firm promised 50 jobs, rising to 200. At its peak it actually employed 15; as far as we can tell it now employs two. Generally speaking it is the smaller firms that inevitably give the least accurate forecasts, and on the whole the bigger firms have developed according to plan. One well-known firm, however, made a firm promise of 2,500 jobs by 1974. It is now employing under 400.
> We have not been able to obtain the number of jobs promised or even the number actually employed for every firm on our list. However, we have complete figures for three counties, which together cover over half

of the projects examined. These suggest that the number of jobs provided—even before the present wave of redundancies—ranged between 70 and 75 per cent of the 'estimated additional employment' in each county. This proportion agrees well with the number of jobs actually provided in Government-owned advance factories, where the full figures are available.

We understand that in the 1960s total employment in advance factories was predicted on the basis of 40 jobs per 10,000 sq. ft. Later this figure was abandoned for the more realistic 30 jobs per 10,000 sq. ft. In fact, the 2.5 million sq. ft. available in advance factories in Wales provides a total of 5,500 jobs—corresponding to a figure of 22 jobs per 10,000 sq. ft., or 72 per cent of the 'norm' . . .

In summary we therefore conclude that the number of jobs actually created in the period 1965 to 1970 was not 66,000 or even 39,000, but more like 28,000.[13]

There are serious deficiencies in this analysis, however. The most important is that it ignores completely the creation of additional jobs in existing factories—a factor emphasised by the Moore and Rhodes study. As stated earlier, this showed that just under half of their estimated 70,000 to 80,000 new jobs generated in Wales between 1960 and 1972 came from the indigenous sector. Moore and Rhodes noted that the indigenous expansion coincided, in the early 1960s, with the introduction of incentives that existing Welsh industry could tap. Their report commented:

It may be that there is a limit to the number of potentially mobile firms which can be induced to relocate in Development Areas in order to 'solve' the problem within an 'acceptable' period of time. In which case more active measures designed to increase the growth of employment and output in the indigenous sector may be appropriate.[14]

There is also the added advantage that indigenous expansion tends to be more secure against the 'branch factory closure syndrome' that threatens immigrant firms during recessions.

Apart from the question of indigenous expansion, neither the Moore and Rhodes study nor the Plaid Cymru critique of regional policy estimate the number of existing jobs that might have been lost, but for the impact of regional policy measures. Nevertheless, whatever the argument about the number of jobs actually created by British regional policy in Wales there is unanimity on their being insufficient. In the conclusion to their report Moore and Rhodes state: 'Whilst regional policy contributed at most 80,000 new jobs between 1960 and 1972, a full solution to the imbalance in the Welsh labour market would have required between 200,000 and 250,000 new jobs'.[15] Thus, for regional policy to have solved the problem by 1972 it would have had to have been about three times more effective than it actually was.

The Welsh Office role

It cannot be said in defence of the government, that the Moore and Rhodes analysis of the Welsh unemployment problem, or indeed their figures, had the benefit of hindsight. For, as early as 1965-6 the Welsh Office economic planners were presented with an astonishingly accurate diagnosis of the problem—which they, together with their political masters, chose to ignore.

In April 1965 the Welsh Office and the nominated Welsh Economic Council were charged by the Secretary of State for Economic Affairs, George Brown, to produce an Economic Plan for Wales which he could slot into the British 'National Plan' he was then trying to get off the ground. The response of the Welsh Office was its ill-fated White Paper *Wales: the Way Ahead,* eventually published in July 1967.[16] The key ingredient in this document was a prediction of employment prospects into the early 1970s. With the drastic coal rundown under way, a steel shake-out on the horizon, and Welsh unemployment figures already twice the United Kingdom average, this was the major problem confronting the Welsh Office planners. The critical area of analysis centred on estimating how many jobs would be available in Wales by 1971.

It so happened that one of the members of the Welsh Economic Council, Professor Edward Nevin, then Professor of Economics at University College, Aberystwyth, was involved in a theoretical study of this very problem. Sir Goronwy Daniel, then the Welsh Office Permanent Under-Secretary, asked him to speed up his work with the aim of providing the Welsh Office with a figure. The method of his team at Aberystwyth was to devise an input/output table for the Welsh economy. Taking the year 1965 as a starting point and assuming the economy would grow at the average rate of the previous five years, the table looked at the input of labour and raw materials and the output of finished products for each industry. After complex computer processing of the figures, a global production level was forecast for 1971 and from this was deducted the level of employment.

The Aberystwyth economists concluded that taking all available data into account the number of male jobs available in 1971 would be 59,000 fewer than in 1966.[17]

This was a figure totally unacceptable to the Welsh Office. Existing government policies—industrial incentives and so on—would be unable to cope with the scale of redundancies implied by the figure. Inside the Welsh Office the reckoning was that by 1971 there would be 25,000 fewer male jobs available than in 1966. By April 1967 the Welsh Office planners managed to persuade themselves that, due to the Government's newly introduced Regional Employment Premium, the figure of 25,000 fewer jobs available in 1971 could be reduced to 15,000—happily coinciding with the number of jobs they estimated could be attracted to Wales. The 'impossible' Aberystwyth figure of 59,000 fewer jobs was rejected. Professor Nevin resigned from the Welsh Council. And five years later the statistics revealed that there were 57,000 fewer jobs available in 1971 than in 1966. Nevin had over-estimated by a marginal 2,000 jobs.[18] Despite the fanfare of publicity given throughout this period to the government's regional policies as a response to growing unemployment, the underlying reality of Wales's steeply declining activity rates was ignored.

Why British regional policy cannot succeed

Despite the considerable resources pumped into British regional policy, the discussion of its impact on Wales concluded that for the policy to have been effective at least three times as much should have been spent on it than actually was in the 1960s—£300 million rather than £100 million. This is a conservative estimate based on a government-sponsored analysis of its own policy. The reality probably is that even more would have been required. In attracting new industry into an area, a law of diminishing returns must apply, as the process is a competitive one with other regions in the market and only so much new industry to go round.

In so far as central government has a policy for coping with the persistent 'regional problem' it consists in applications of more of the same medicine. In their report on *Regional Policy and the Economy of Wales,* for instance, Moore and Rhodes advocate strengthening the 'carrot' and 'stick' traditional approach: 'The present policies should lead to some continued improvement. But unless regional policies are strengthened further this improvement will be very gradual and it could take two or three decades for a full "solution" to Wales's unemployment problems to materialise.'[19]

Moore and Rhodes based their analysis of the operation of regional policy in Wales on the centralist view of economic development discussed in the opening to this chapter—that it is only a matter of adjustment and time before the Welsh economy can be brought into line with the more prosperous and industrially balanced areas of Britain. The argument of this chapter is that this is a sanguine assessment of the position in view of the inadequacy of regional policy so far. Moreover, the position rests on confidence that Regional Policy can be made to operate more effectively in the future. But, on the contrary, there are three powerful factors which suggest that continued reliance on the traditional regional policy approach will not succeed.

(i) The problem has worsened

Since Moore and Rhodes completed their study the problem facing traditional regional economic policy has increased. As the report of the Wales TUC's Economic and Industrial Committee to the 1976 annual conference commented:

> It is worthwhile noting on the Moore and Rhodes study that their data only permitted analysis up to 1971/2. Consequently, recent events such as the actual and potential cutbacks in the steel industry in Wales, have not been taken into account. Given the key role played by steel in the Welsh Labour Market, as a generator of both direct and indirect employment, it would seem reasonable to assume that the number of jobs needed to correct the regional imbalance, as defined by Moore and Rhodes, is currently in excess of the 178,000 figure estimated for 1971. Indeed, the effect of public expenditure cutbacks in Wales on employment make this a certainty.[20]

A few months later the Wales TUC were claiming that the government's July deflationary package of expenditure estimate cutbacks, involving £1,000 million more on employers' National Insurance Contributions for 1977/8, would push Welsh unemployment beyond 10 per cent.[21]

Not only is the Welsh regional problem worsening, it has been demonstrated in the preceding section that under the Welsh Office political framework there is not in Wales the 'will' to strengthen the regional policy approach that Moore and Rhodes advocate. When their report was published, in July 1975, the Secretary of State for Wales, Mr John Morris, commented:

> This is a valuable analysis which clearly shows that the policies adopted for the development of the Principality have had a substantial measure of success . . . nevertheless, the government, fully recognising that much

remains to be done, is taking steps to improve the position. Last year we doubled the Regional Employment Premium, we brought Cardiff into the Development Area, and we upgraded a large part of North-West Wales to special development area status.[22]

In this statement there is no reference to the 'stick' element of regional policy—the all-important Industrial Development Certificate control which is the mechanism for steering industry from prosperous areas into the under-developed regions. John Morris was right in pointing to the fact that the year before, Regional Employment Premium had been doubled to £3 a week for men and £1.50 for women employed in manufacturing industries in the development area. But a year later, in July 1976, the government announced that REP was being reduced to £2 a week for both men and women, and in December 1976 REP was abolished altogether. This cost Wales about £30 million a year at a stroke. In July 1977 Moore and Rhodes estimated that the abolition of REP would result in the loss of between 30,000 and 50,000 jobs in the Development Areas by 1980 (Centre for Environmental Studies Review, No. 1).[23] The announcement, part of a spending cut-back to satisfy the conditions for another loan from the International Monetary Fund, was the beginning of the collapse of British regional policy.

(ii) England's position is worsening

At the same time as the economic situation in Wales has worsened, so has that in the English South-East, the Midlands, and the Northern England intermediate industrial development zones. The unemployment differentials and other social indicators of disparity between Wales and these areas have been maintained, and in some cases, for example health provision, have worsened. But, at the same time, the position of the English regions relative to many European countries has worsened, too. For instance, in early 1976, a study made by the team revising the *Strategic Plan for the South East* (1970) indicated that the region stood seventeenth in the table of incomes among the 49 EEC regions.[24] English people, particularly those in middle-range income groups, are increasingly comparing their living standards, both with past experience and with levels in other Common Market countries, and finding them wanting.

This has great implications for traditional regional policy. Since it was forged—in the twilight of Empire when expansion was still assumed and by a country outside the Common Market—conditions for the United Kingdom as a whole have altered drastically, making the 'carrot' and the 'stick' approach if not irrelevant, certainly far less relevant.

By the mid-1970s the South-East was fundamentally revising its expansionist expectations. In 1970 the *Strategic Plan for the South East* expected a population growth of around 2·8 million between 1971 and 1991. By 1976 the team updating the plan expected that the increase would be a mere 367,000. By the mid-1970s, too, there were nearly as many unemployed in Greater London as in the whole of Scotland, and almost twice as many in London as in the whole of Wales.

Unemployment is only one aspect of a rapidly growing crisis for the inner-city centres of urban England. Net outward migration combined with deteriorating buildings and services is being compounded by a worsening race problem. At the time of writing the latest official mid-year estimate, in 1973-4, by the Office of Population, Censuses and Surveys, gave Britain's total non-white population as 1,744,000. If similar calculations are made for 1974/5 they suggest that the equivalent figure for then would be 1,815,000. Thus, if the non-white population continues to increase at a similar rate the figure of two million will be passed well before 1980. These people are concentrated in English inner-cities like London, Birmingham, Leicester, Wolverhampton, Manchester and Bradford, places already below standard in service provision. In July 1976 Birmingham's council appealed to the government for more help to deal with the problem, as did Smethwick's council in 1964 and Wolverhampton's in 1968. Birmingham's resolution spoke of 'a likelihood of deterioration in race relations arising from the increased housing, educational, environmental and social problems' associated with 'the settlement of a large number of immigrants in the inner crowded areas of cities like Birmingham'.

The worsening of the economic position of the more prosperous English regions in comparison with neighbouring regions on the Continent—brought harshly into focus by Britain's entry into the EEC—has thus been compounded by increased social problems. Taken together the effect has been to weaken the political resolve necessary to enforce the 'stick' element in traditional regional policy. The 'stick' in the form of Industrial Development Certificates, began to be flailed far less vigorously.

In a report prepared for the Centre for Environmental Studies in July 1977, Moore, Rhodes and Tyler revealed that in the 1970s the strength of IDC policy had declined by 50 per cent compared with the average in the 1960s.[25] Their research showed that in the 1950s

5 per cent of applications for IDCs in the Midlands and the South-East were refused each year. In the 1960s, when regional policy became more active, the percentage of applications refused increased over fourfold and varied between 20 and 30 per cent. But in the 1970s the percentage of IDC applications in the Midlands and the South-East fell and averaged 10 per cent in each year.

This downward trend was picked up by the *Western Mail* in April 1976. It reported that IDCs in the non-assisted areas[26] were being more easily obtained following pressure from local authorities:

> The recession means that areas like the Midlands and the South-East are worried by rising unemployment and this has resulted in increased efforts to get greater Government assistance to counter their problems. Areas like Avon, across the Severn Estuary from Wales, are concerned about their heavy reliance on the threatened aircraft industry and feel that restrictions in issuing IDCs is a major barrier in getting replacement jobs.[27]

Thus, not only is the problem facing traditional regional policy in Wales getting worse, but its major weapon—pressure on firms to expand in Wales rather than the more prosperous areas of England —is being weakened by the declining economic position and social problems of urban England itself.

This leads to the third and final strand in the argument against placing reliance on traditional regional policy as an answer to Wales's economic problems. This is that the basis on which traditional regional policy has been constructed—compensation of industry for the disadvantages of operating in the peripheral Development Areas, rather than attempting to remove those disadvantages—has been wrong from the start.

(iii) The inherent deficiency in regional policy

The most convincing reason why the 'carrot' and 'stick' regional policy has not done more to reduce Wales's unemployment levels relative to even the British average is because it has not tackled the root economic problem in Wales—that the conditions industrialists so often find here are not amenable to development. Wales's poverty-stricken infrastructure can be best illustrated by the standard of her roads. By the mid-1970s the two major Welsh cities, Cardiff and Swansea, were still linked by what was in many places a rural road, not even dual carriageway let alone a motorway. Throughout Wales roads are a major problem. The Welsh valleys are regarded as difficult places for attracting new industry. Yet nowhere in Britain could compare with, for example, the Rhondda, in having provided the outside world with so much wealth but having had so little in return to sustain it, after its natural resources have been largely exploited. The road through Rhondda is terrible.

On top of this the strategy of road investment that has been carried out has not been tailored to Welsh needs. More priority has been given to east-west links with England rather than a Wales-oriented system that would have led to a more balanced development of the Welsh economy. Seen from the Welsh point of view a clear priority is a north-south link between Cardiff and Merthyr, a route that would serve a quarter of the Welsh population. By the mid-1970s this route was still only constructed as far north as Abercynon. By now this road should have been taken through Merthyr Tydfil as a spine road of dual carriageway construction to Caernarfon with a branch to the Wrexham area. Together with an improved north—south trunk road on the western side, Wales would then have a road system geared to a balanced development of industry. But the government has refused to consider such a Wales-oriented road system on the grounds that there was no industry in most of Wales to justify its construction. Defenders of the needs of the Welsh economy, on the other hand, point with some justification to the attitude of the Italian government which constructed the Autostrada del Sol linking the prosperous north with the impoverished south. 'There is no industry', the Italians argued. 'Therefore we must have a major highway.'[28]

Roads are only one aspect of infrastructural needs. They are a prime requirement but other essential services are housing (in 1975/6 more than 60,000 Welsh people were on council house waiting lists), sewerage and water facilities (in 1976 much of southeast Wales was cut off from its water supplies because under-investment meant the local reservoirs could not cope with drought), gas and electricity supply, adequate telephone and telex systems and, not least, attractive recreational facilities. In these and other basic amenity areas (railways and airport provision, for example) Welsh provision need only be stated for their inadequacy to be demonstrated.

But all these essential provisions are not within the capacity of traditional regional policy. Though in many instances the policy has helped persuade industrialists to ignore Wales's infrastructural inadequacy, it has not touched the heart of the problem. Bribery, in whatever form, is never a long-term option.

This was the major lesson drawn by Plaid Cymru in its paper 'The Failure of Regional Grants' referred to earlier:

> Only in those areas served by reasonably good roads and railways and where there exist large industrial estates and a wide range of industrial services, has the Development Area policy been a partial success.
> Wrexham, for example, is a centre reasonably near to the M6 motorway, served by a railway, where a large industrial estate has developed. We notice that of the 10 firms that actually came to the Wrexham area (between 1965 and 1970), nine are still operating successfully and providing over 2,000 jobs.
> Similarly Llantrisant is a well-endowed site, reasonably close to the M4 and within 20 minutes of the service facilities available to Cardiff. The four projects on the list (of 153 firms presented by the Labour Party in Wales to the Kilbrandon Commission in 1970) that moved to the Llantrisant area are still operating successfully and also provide over 2,000 jobs.
> On the other hand, the region between Aberdare and Brynmawr has suffered badly from the interminable delays in completing the 'Heads-of-the-Valleys' road and the Cardiff-Merthyr dual carriageway. Of the 12 firms that came to the Special Development Area at the north of the South Wales Valleys, six have already been closed and one is being phased out—a bad omen for the men who will soon be redundant in Ebbw Vale. Similarly, of the 10 firms that were attracted to what is now the Special Development Area in Gwynedd, one has closed and two are on the point of closing.
> Overall, we find that of the 21—23 firms known to have closed or are on the point of closing, 14—15 were in a Special Development Area, and this small sample suggests that the probability of a factory closing is two to three times as great in a Special Development Area as in a Development Area, despite the large grants.
> We conclude that while there may be room for debate as to the best 'mix' of cash incentives and improved infrastructure, there is no doubt that if the infrastructure is totally inadequate even very high cash incentives are insufficient to guarantee continued employment in a new project.[29]

In this section three compelling arguments have been marshalled to persuade that British Regional Policy cannot succeed in the future: (1) the 'regional problem' in Wales is worsening and experience of existing Welsh institutions does not inspire confidence that they are capable of generating the political will to tackle them, rather the reverse; (2) the problems of the English regions, both economic and social, are increasing relative to Continental countries, though not to Wales, resulting in a less rigorous application of regional policy measures; (3) finally, and most importantly, the measures themselves have been shown to be

fundamentally misconceived in that they do not tackle the root
problem.

The final section of this chapter will explore how these underlying
economic realites have been channelled into the political debate in
Wales; how they have been focused on the devolution argument. In
economic terms, devolution is a reaction to the failure of British
regional policy. It is seen as a means of generating the political
muscle necessary to tackle the 'regional problem' in a more fundamental way: from within rather than from without.

The colonial analogy

Regardless of the arguments about the long-term efficacy of British
regional policy, it has until now proved far from adequate in meeting
actual job losses. The Welsh Office-sponsored Moore and Rhodes
study, examined earlier, estimated that in Wales regional policy
would have had to have been three times as effective as it actually
was in the 1960s, to have fully compensated for the jobs being lost in
older industries. And, in terms of the quality of jobs brought, the
inadequacy is as great. Branch factories dependent on headquarters
in prosperous areas outside Wales predominate. A Welsh Council-
commissioned report, published in 1973, revealed the figures for
Welsh firms run from outside the country (Table 2.4)

Table 2.4

Location of Head Office			Number of Employees		
	25—99	100—249	250—499	500—999	over 1,000
Wales	907	142	40	16	7
Outside Wales	1062	372	139	78	42

Sources: C. Tomkins and J. Lovering, *Location, Size, Ownership and
Control Tables for Welsh Industry,* 1973.

This preponderance of outside control has a number of conse-
quencies. First, top management opportunities tend to be concentrated outside Wales with all that means for the drainage of talent,
drive and energy. Second, in any recession, it is always the branches

of firms that are most vulnerable to closure. But, more importantly, where grants are a significant factor in attracting industry, for example, in the Special Development Areas, they can be counter-productive. They can attract firms that are not viable except with the help of grants. Such ventures are, therefore, at best marginal and often fail. Most major companies, when taking investment decisions regarding the location of new plants, ignore the grants and only consider them when seeking to choose between two or more equally attractive sites. The figures for the number of firms that have closed in Welsh Special Development Areas given at the end of the last section, support the argument that here grants have tended to attract firms with only a marginal potential for success.[30]

When the issue is placed in the Common Market context which, since Britain's entry in 1973, grows ever more relevant, the outlook for regional policy as traditionally practised is even less reassuring. The first annual report of the European Regional Development Fund in July 1976 made this abundantly clear. The report stated that the wealth gap between Britain, Italy and Ireland on the one hand and their richer EEC partners on the other, was wider than ever before. Whereas in 1970, for example, the richest areas of the EEC, like Paris and Hamburg, were four and five times richer than the poorest regions of southern Italy, in 1976 they were five and six times better off respectively. And with the probability that poorer countries will join the EEC—Greece certainly, and possibly Turkey, Spain and Portugal—the potential of the EEC Regional Fund for reducing disparities is likely to decrease.

The feebleness of regional policy at the European level in providing a solution only highlights the reality of its operation at the British level. The object of the discussion in this chapter of the impact of British regional policy upon Wales has been to put into focus the conflicting centralist versus decentralist analyses of economic development described at the opening.

The contention here is that the record of British regional policy's operation in Wales supports the decentralist thesis which maintains that the 'regional problem' is part of an inherent conflict between the *centre* and the *periphery*. It is one result of the general tendency towards centralisation and increase in scale of twentieth-century Western industrialised society. The periphery (Wales), suffers as life increasingly revolves around the centre (London and the South-East) where power, wealth and decision-making are concentrated. (The decentralist theory of economic development as expounded by Myrdal explains how this happens.)

If this decentralist thesis of conflict between the centre and the periphery is correct why has the conflict not been more visible? To some extent, of course, the answer is that the conflict becomes steadily more visible, with the growth of the Welsh national movement from one more pressure group, in the 1960s, into a formidable political force in the 1970s. Nevertheless, to the mass of people in the periphery the idea of an inbuilt conflict between themselves and the centre, the South-East, would not register. The reason for this is central government policies intended to defuse protest.

The policies, which have grown steadily more sophisticated, are all interlinked, but for convenience they can be separated into three: regional policy, the establishment of the Welsh Office and devolution itself.

The role of regional policy has not been to eliminate disparities between the periphery and the centre—it has been shown that it is impossible for it to achieve this. Rather, the role has been to reduce the disparities to manageable proportions.

The role of the Welsh Office has already been illustrated, in the section of this chapter that described how it rejected 'unacceptable' but accurate estimates of future Welsh job requirements. The Welsh Office, of course, is not a Welsh institution as such but an outpost of Whitehall in Wales, merely impressing a Welsh imprint on hundreds of circulars that are directed from central government ministries, like the Department of the Environment, to Welsh local authorities each year.

As has been described, the Welsh Office's major contribution to Welsh economic planning, its 1967 White Paper, *Wales: the Way Ahead,* only succeeded in frustrating development by adopting a complacent assessment of future Welsh employment needs. Even after 1971, when time had proved the assessment grossly inaccurate, *Wales: the Way Ahead* continued to be commended to local authorities. One circular, advising Gwent and the three counties of Glamorgan on drawing up their structure plans, commented in 1975: 'On the whole the original ("Wales: the Way Ahead") strategy for Industrial South Wales has needed little change and although constrained somewhat by the overall problems and uncertainties of the national economy, the rate of progress has been satisfactory.'[31] Of course, by the time this sentence was written much of *Wales: the Way Ahead*'s strategy—growth in the context of an expanding economy, development concentrated at the mouths of the valleys and priority for the M4—was disintegrating. Wales was in deep recession and population forecasts were being drastically revised downwards. The main valley-mouth development proposal, Llantrisant New Town, had been axed and emphasis was shifting to

the rescue of older heads-of-the-valleys communities like Ebbw
Vale.

In fact, all that was really left of *Wales: the Way Ahead* in terms
of a coherent strategy, was priority for the M4. An indication of the
frustration of Welsh local-authority planners, with the lack of
proper planning framework, was given in a *Western Mail* report in
January 1976. One planning officer was quoted as describing the
Welsh Office structure-plan circular as 'An insult to a professional's
intelligence'.[32]. Later in the year even the British Town and Country
Planning Association was roused to comment on the fact that,
unlike English regions like the South-East and the North-West,
Wales had no economic plan: 'The data base of the 1967 White
Paper *(Wales: the Way Ahead)* is now over ten years old', said a
statement issued by the Association. 'There is no coherent over-view
or regional strategy to which decision-makers can relate their
policies.'[33]

The third central-government-policy mechanism aimed at
defusing Welsh protest against economic underdevelopment has
been devolution itself. The establishment of the Commission on the
Constitution was in the first place a delaying tactic, an interpretation confirmed by John Mackintosh, the Labour MP for Berwick
and East Lothian:

In 1966 and 1967 Welsh and Scottish Nationalists won by-elections and
by 1968 these parties appeared to mount a serious challenge to the
Labour Party in its Celtic strongholds. Within the Labour Cabinet there
was a division over the policy that should be pursued. The Welsh
Council of Labour favoured an elected Council for Wales but the
Scottish Council of Labour, led on this issue by the Secretary of State
Mr. William Ross, was strongly opposed to anything of the kind. Among
the English members of the Cabinet Mr. Crossman spoke favourably of
devolution, while Mr. Callaghan (sitting for a Welsh constituency) led
the opposition. The outcome was a victory for those who wanted to do
nothing but resist the pressure, arguing that by the next General
Election, the Nationalist threat would have dwindled. Naturally, other
more fundamental arguments were advanced, the chief ones being that
elected all-Scottish and all-Welsh authorities would only serve to
encourage and provide a platform for the Nationalists and that the
correct policy for Labour was to capture control at the centre and then
push through policies dealing with the entire United Kingdom.

But, having won this battle, the opponents of any measure of devolution felt they had to have some answer to those who pointed to the rise
of the Nationalist arguments and then asked Labour leaders: 'What are
you doing about it?' To meet this, it was decided to appoint a Royal

Commission with whom the whole subject could be safely left until after the next General Election . . .[34]

And when the Commission finally reported in 1973 it proved a fascinating attempt to offer Wales enough seeming self-determination to take the wind out of the Nationalist argument, while not disturbing the hold of central government on the fundamentals of economic power (an attempt emulated by the government in its devolution proposals and analysed in Part II). The report also had the effect of fogging and confusing the whole issue with its half-million words, complex alternative schemes, and plethora of recommendations.

Thus regional policy, the Welsh Office, and the devolution proposals, combine to present a rising scale of effort to frustrate and defuse peripheral protest against exploitation by the centre. This is the ultimate statement of the decentralist view of economic development within the single state system. The periphery provides labour, raw materials, food and the products of the heavy end of industry for the centre, and simultaneously a market for more sophisticated centre-produced goods. The colonial analogy cannot be avoided and has been explored by Michael Hechter in his book *Internal Colonialism: The Celtic Fringe in British National Development, 1536—1966,*[35] which is discussed in the following chapter.

But, while devolution is an attempt to confuse and defuse the decentralists' protest at the nature of economic development it is simultaneously a concession to the decentralists' argument. Thus, the case against British regional policy, as set out in this chapter, was implicitly conceded by the Labour party at the October 1974 general election. In its manifesto it committed the next Labour government to the setting up of Development Agencies for Wales and Scotland. When the Development Agency Bills were introduced in Parliament in February 1975 the county of South Glamorgan's Industrial Development Officer, Rhodri Morgan, felt able to write:

Simultaneously in London, Glasgow and Cardiff the Government announced the death of 30 years of British regional policy. The traditional 'stick and carrot' method of attracting industry to development areas is being put away and regional and industrial policy will from now on go on to the offensive. Instead of waiting for firms to come to the Government, the new agencies, the National Enterprise Board and the Welsh and Scottish Development Agencies, will spot the industrial opportunities and will go out to exploit them.[36]

Morgan was over-stating his case. The government was only implicitly announcing the 'death' of British regional policy and the

Welsh Development Agency was far from being a fully fledged body capable of aggression or even great initiative. The government still clung to the notion that British regional policy was the answer. For instance, in August 1976, the new Prime Minister, James Callaghan, visited Scotland to inspect the site of the proposed Scottish Assembly and took the opportunity to say that too much was made of the economic differences between Scotland, Wales and South-East England. He said:

> The plain truth is that our regional policies have been much more successful than we have admitted in the past. They have brought about a greater equality between different parts of this country than exists in any other major country in Europe, and this is something we have to drive home much more than in the past.[37]

Of course, when politicians declare they are about to pronounce a 'plain truth' it is wise to be wary. How can regional inequalities in Britain be smaller than any other large European state when comparable countries in the EEC received far lower proportions of the EEC's Regional Fund during the first three years of its operation from December 1974? While Britain received 27 per cent of the fund, West Germany was given only 6·4 per cent and France 15 per cent. In fact, Britain, Ireland (6 per cent share) and Italy (40 per cent) were the only net beneficiaries from the fund. The other six member states—the Netherlands (1·7 per cent share); Belgium (1·5 per cent); Denmark (1·3 per cent, mainly in Greenland); and Luxembourg (0·1 per cent)—were all net contributors.[38]

When the Welsh Development Agency finally got under way in January 1976, its powers, and above all its meagre finance, meant that it was still very much at an embryonic stage. Nevertheless, its existence combined with a government commitment that it would be made accountable to the Welsh Assembly,[39] meant that the case against British regional policy had been privately, if not publicly, conceded.

The decentralist case against British regional policy as set out in this chapter, is twofold: first, instead of attempting to right the poor conditions and inadequate services that make so many parts of Wales unattractive for new industry, it merely aims at partial grant compensation; and second, its aim is to defuse the protest that might provide the energy to tackle Wales's economic problems in a more fundamental way.

It has been argued that devolution, viewed from the centre, is a response in the same mould as regional policy—aimed at defusing

protest against regional economic injustice, which has taken an irrit-
ating political form, namely the rise of the national parties. But,
viewed from the periphery, devolution provides an opportunity to
mobilise sufficient energy in Wales to tackle its economic problems
from within. This is the economics of devolution and the context of
the statement by Wales TUC General Secretary, George Wright,
quoted at the opening of this chapter: 'We are seeking a Wales
where we can have growth from within. We are not carrying a
begging bowl into the next century.'

Chapter 3

The Emergence of Welsh Politics

> We were a people and are so yet.
> When we have finished quarrelling for crumbs
> Under the table, or gnawing the bones
> Of a dead culture, we will arise,
> Armed, but not in the old way.
>
> *R. S. Thomas*

During 1975 the Executive Committee of the Labour Party in Wales held a series of meetings to work out its attitude to a range of devolution issues. One of the most important was convened in March when the Secretary of State for Wales, John Morris; his Parliamentary Under-Secretary, Ted Rowlands, and other Ministers concerned with the policy were also present. The Executive's main spokesman was its Secretary, Emrys Jones. The minutes of the meeting recorded his opening remarks in the following terms:

> He emphasised that the setting up of a Welsh Assembly should be part of a radical reform of the whole machinery of Government throughout the United Kingdom, involving the decentralisation from Central Government of some of the massive responsibilities it had taken on in recent years, and the democratisation of many of the ad-hoc nominated bodies which had been set up. The establishment of assemblies in the regions of England was an essential part of this reform, and no part of the United Kingdom should be given powers which, after allowing for historical differences, were incompatible with the powers given to the rest of the U.K. Unless these principles were followed, there could develop a real danger of the break-up of the United Kingdom into separate states.[1]

This is a classic British expression in favour of devolution and one which the Labour Party in Wales, from its first formal, post-Second World War commitment to the policy in 1965, has consistently sought to maintain. Devolution is seen as necessary for the whole of Britain, to democratise a growing regional tier of largely nominated *ad hoc* government and to facilitate decentralisation of decision-making in industry as well as government. The minute, quoted above, added:

> The Secretary outlined the Executive's view that there was need for a new look at the structure of nationalised industries, with the aim of introduc-

ing measures of decentralisation. In this process, there should be
Assembly participation in the decisions of nationalised industries as they
affect Wales.[2]

In itself, this position (also the one adopted by Lord Crowther
Hunt's Memorandum of Dissent to the Commission on the constitution) is perfectly tenable: there are sound factual arguments to
back it up—some of them have been argued in chapter 1—and in its
own terms the position is logically consistent. The major difficulty in
the approach, however, is simply that devolution has been almost
exclusively debated in Wales and Scotland and that proposals have
been brought forward in respect of these countries rather than the
English regions. To this British devolutionists counter that, though
it is true that the policy will be first applied in Wales and Scotland,
this is only the first stage. Once devolution is accomplished there it
will soon spread to the English regions.

This reply both raises and avoids the question: why is devolution
happening first in Wales and Scotland? The answer is that there has
developed in these countries a politics different from British politics.
Wales and Scotland have histories, cultures (or interaction of
cultures), economic interests, problems and priorities different from
other parts of Britain. Welsh and Scottish politics have arisen
because these issues have come to be regarded in their own right and
not purely in the British context. It is arguable that devolution
would never have reached the agenda in Britain were it not for
Welsh and Scottish politics, despite the compelling democratic and
decentralist case that can be marshalled independently for, say, a
devolved Yorkshire Assembly. The Liberal Party is the only British
party that has advocated English devolution with any conviction, yet
even this has largely been a consequence of pressure from its Welsh
and Scottish membership.

Quite apart from the democratic and economic case that can be
made out for a Welsh Assembly, as has been attempted in the first
two chapters of this book, the only reason why devolution is on the
agenda for Wales is because of the emergence of distinctively Welsh
politics. There are a wide variety of interlocking factors which have
contributed to this development. First and foremost is Welsh
political, economic and cultural history which has given the people of
Wales a distinctive sense of a separate identity, often manifesting
itself in a crisis of identity. It is the underlying groundswell of so
many people in Wales working out their own personal roots and
loyalties that gives the politics of devolution their edge, tension,
fascination and conflict.

The main question that prompted Hechter's study *Internal*

Colonialism[3] was why distinctive ethnic identities have persisted in Wales, Scotland and Ireland despite centuries of English/British incorporation. The fact that they have is illustrated by exhaustive computer analysis of voting patterns and religious affiliation. Wales's overwhelming allegiance to the Liberals in the last century and to the Labour party in this, for example, is shown to run contrary to what would be expected from conventional sociological data such as class, income and occupation.

The rise of twentieth century Welsh nationalism is viewed as surprising in that most political sociologists have theorised that the social base for such a movement would tend to disappear in industrial society. It has been believed that the urbanisation, increasing mobility and mass communications that accompany industrialisation should lead to homogenisation and a lessening of conflict between a country's core and its peripheral regions. The fact that this has not happened in Britain leads Hechter, in his book, to advance 'internal colonialism' to explain the relationship between the core (defined as England) and the periphery: Wales, Scotland and Ireland.[4] The main characteristic of this has been what he describes as a cultural division of labour between the peoples of the core and the periphery—with the peripheral population undertaking less-skilled, less-varied and consequently less-rewarded occupations than the core.

Thus the increasing contact between the core and the periphery through industrialisation has heightened conflict rather than lessened it. People have been able to compare differing standards and draw conclusions accordingly. Hechter notes that in the period of his study, 1536 to 1966, the English economy became highly diversified while the peripheral Welsh economy became extremely specialised in lower-grade activities in terms of reward (farming, mining and metal extraction). Apart from straightforward inequality, the specialisation in the Welsh economy made it highly vulnerable to trade fluctuations and price changes:

> The persistence of such systematic disadvantages may partially result from the institutionalisation of policies which have the effect of discriminating against the Celtic periphery in a manner similar to that which has been described as institutionalised racism . . .[5] No one would argue that there is much discrimination against Welshmen as individuals in the United Kingdom today. Nevertheless, the fact that Wales as a region is disadvantaged in terms of income, employment, housing and education has decisive consequences for the individuals living there. To the extent that the region is materially deprived, the average Welshman competes with the average Englishman at a disadvantage in many free

market situations. When such long-term differences in aggregate rates of development are the result of ethnic stereotypes, it is appropriate to speak of institutional racism.[6]

It is the perception of disparity that accounts in great measure for Welsh politics. Of course, the disparities between Wales and England are articulated to great effect by Nationalist politicians. But what has been promoted by them goes deeper than envy or even a sense of moral outrage at the injustice. Underlying the debates on the issue is the emergence of a political philosophy that cuts across the basis of British politics. It is a philosophy that gives precedence to the idea of the Welsh community over and above individual Welsh people and, more easily, over and above the state, since there is no Welsh state—only a British one.

This approach has been nurtured just because it is the Welsh community as a whole, rather than individuals within it, that is perceived as suffering injustice. The philosophy rests on historical circumstances as much as any inherently theoretical justification, though this has been provided[7] and forms part of the distinctive background to the emergence of Welsh as opposed to British politics.

Another vital element in the development of Welsh politics has been the visible decline, since the Second World War, of the British dimension, both in terms of its world imperial role and in its effectiveness in producing economic advancement. The two are to some extent interlinked since the desire of some British politicians to behave as though they were still directing an imperial world force, for instance, by maintaining a high defence budget, leads to distortions (usually cut-backs in social spending) in other areas of the economy. And this in turn leads to disenchantment. When he was head of the Central Policy Review Staff (created inside the Cabinet Office by Edward Heath) in 1973 Lord Rothschild warned that Britain would be one of the poorest states in Europe by 1985, if it continued with its imperial pretensions:

> Unless we take a very strong pull at ourselves and give up the idea that we are one of the wealthiest, most influential and important countries in the world, in other words, that Queen Victoria is still reigning, we are likely to find ourselves in increasingly serious trouble. . . . We have to realise that we have neither the money nor the resources to do all those things we should like to do and so often feel we have the right to do.[8]

The position of Wales inside a state whose imperialism now only consists in expensive pretensions is an important element in the devolution debate. Lord Chalfont was referring to it when he remarked in a radio talk on Welsh politics in September 1973:

> One of the principal arguments for keeping Wales locked into the present constitutional and political framework of the United Kingdom is that on its own it would not be economically viable. This is, in fact, a proposition which cannot be conclusively either proved or refuted by hypothesis or economic theory. Welsh Nationalists claim, with a wealth of comparison and analogy, that Wales could be as prosperous as any Scandinavian minipower; such sturdy centralists as Mr. George Thomas dismiss such fantasies out of hand. The argument, of course, is fundamentally political, not economic. Yet it is possible for those who favour a large measure of independence for Wales to point to contemporary Britain and to suggest that it is not much of an advertisement for the virtues of central government. Apart from its chronically precarious state of economic health, there has been a disastrous deterioration of the general quality of life—a decline which has led the Socialist writer, Paul Johnson, in the course of a violent attack on the trade unions, to describe the British working class as the coolies of the Western World and Britain as a 'stinking, bankrupt industrial slum'. Even making allowances for the natural hyperbole of the betrayed radical, it is difficult to refute the proposition that an independent Wales could hardly be worse off than Paul Johnson's England.[9]

Such sentiments have been enormously reinforced by Britain's entry into the Common Market. As the focus of decision-making moves away from London to Brussels and Strasbourg, the sense of remoteness from the centre of power is correspondingly intensified. Simultaneously the psychological links between Wales and England are undergoing a slow and subtle, but, nevertheless, irreversible change. London is no longer the political centre of the universe—it is just one of nine capitals in a Common Market that is moving progressively, via direct elections for the EEC Assembly in the first instance, towards a European state structure. As devolution to Brussels on the one hand and to Cardiff on the other, gains momentum the case for any direct control over Wales from London will be progressively diminished. It is in this context that Wales's first representative in the indirectly elected EEC Assembly, Tom Ellis (Labour MP for Wrexham) was able to talk of 'a new watershed in our history'—the end of the classic sovereign European nation-state—after which 'the Labour Party can once again become a crusading party applying Socialist measures designed to shape our lives in Britain, and significantly, perhaps for the first time exclusively, in Wales'.[10]

The new European context is an expression of a twentieth-century fluidity of power and power structures, including a breakdown of the idea of sovereignty, that continues to be an important explanation of the emergence of Welsh politics. Tom Ellis has noted that the political structure of the nineteenth and early twentieth centuries was pyramidal, characterised by the location of political power at the top of the pyramid. But in the twentieth century, certainly since World War II, this pyramidal or hierarchical political power structure has been breaking down, and power—and with it sovereignty—has become more diffuse throughout society. The main agent of this change has been the requirement of technology and knowledge at all levels of expansionist industry, particularly electronics, which in turn has required decentralisation of decision-making. As Tom Ellis has put it in his essay 'Why a Federal Britain?', *New Europe* (1976):

> Knowledge has become a fourth factor of production to be added to the classical triumvirate of land, labour and capital. As such it must be spread broadly across the mass of the people rather than be held in a few hands . . . Since knowledge in modern society is both synonymous with power and conducive to its being exerted, the new proletariat is now in the remarkable position of being able not so much to establish a dictatorship of the masses as to insist upon a democracy for the masses. Jack has now become as good as his master. The pyramid of power is in the course of collapse and we are facing the need to change from a vertically structured to a laterally structured society.
>
> Our problems have become those of interdependence because power is no longer localised. The real political issue therefore is not Aneurin Bevan's of where to find power (even in his day the seat of power, as he himself admitted, was becoming something of a mirage) but how to differentiate between various facets of it in their various locations and how best to exercise these facets of power.

The decline of Britain, the rise in significance of the European dimension, and the diffusion of knowledge-based power through society has coincided with another element in the strands that go together to make up the distinctiveness of Welsh, as opposed to British, politics: a recognition of the importance of roots and community and the orientation of politics upon their recovery. As Patricia Elton Mayo has put it:

> Modern industrial society tends to be uniformist and rootless, and the citizen far removed from those who control his destiny. He has lost his personal identity. His day-to-day existence gives him greater wealth than his parents knew, but on the other hand denies him a sense of belonging to the place where he lives or even a knowledge of what he himself really is or what he really wants. The unhappiest people may be those who know that something is the matter with them, but do not know what.

Psychoanalysis has helped the individual to understand his own personality and problems, thereby making some solution more possible, but what of the normally balanced man when society itself deprives him of a sense of purpose? The faceless bureaucrat is an unsatisfactory object of hate. Small wonder then if a Welshman, Basque or Breton, the distinctiveness of whose region or culture may be diminished but far from dead, should grasp at the idea of regional autonomy as the last chance of giving his life individual meaning.[11]

Such feelings are intimately connected with an economic reality that by the 1970s was becoming steadily more appreciated—that, in a world of finite resources, primary products are most important. There is more acceptance that economic policies must tend more towards self-sufficiency and ecological containment rather than relying on ever higher economic growth as the way to quantitative (but, significantly, not qualitative) higher standards of living. In Wales in the first part of the twentieth century coal was exploited by the British state at such a rate that there was no time for balanced community development; no thought given to the long-term implications for devastated valley communities. In 1966 Aberfan spoke eloquently of that experience. A determination that it will *never* happen again is a motivating force among those, mainly young, people who are forcing the pace of Welsh politics today.

These varying pressures, from an acutely felt sense of economic and social deprivation relative to England, to the decline of Imperial Britain, coupled with growing environmental and community concern, form the background to the emergence of Welsh politics.

Welsh political debate has been fostered by the development of a wide range of specifically Welsh institutions which, themselves, have reinforced the pressures that created them. These institutions embrace most facets of Welsh life, including cultural, social, educational, economic and sporting activities. In the political sphere there are four broad institutional areas which between them have channelled most of the thrust of Welsh politics: the creation of Welsh administrative institutions, most importantly the Welsh Office; the founding of Plaid Cymru in 1925 and its subsequent development from a pressure group into a political party; the creation of the Wales TUC in 1972/3 and its affirmation of a specifically Welsh economic interest; and the Labour Party in Wales, particularly in its role since the mid-1960s of attempting to steer a middle way between Welsh and British politics.

After a consideration of the historical background, these four institutional areas will be discussed in greater detail in the rest of this chapter. Together they provide much of the explanation of why

Table 3.1   General elections in Wales 1945-74

General Election	Conservative*	Labour	Liberal	Plaid Cymru	Others	Total Votes Cast	Electorate	Percentage Voting
1945†	316,729 (23·8%)	779,184 (58·5%)	198,553 (14·9%)	14,321 (1·1%)	21,884 (1·7%)	1,330,671	1,798,199	75·7
1950	418,668 (27·4%)	887,984 (58·1%)	193,090 (12·6%)	17,580 (1·2%)	11,232 (0·7%)	1,528,554	1,802,356	84·8
1951	471,269 (30·9%)	925,848 (60·5%)	116,821 (7·6%)	10,920 (0·7%)	4,591 (0·3%)	1,529,449	1,812,664	84·4
1955	428,866 (29·9%)	825,690 (57·6%)	104,095 (7·3%)	45,119 (3·1%)	29,954 (2·1%)	1,433,724	1,801,217	79·6
1959	486,335 (32·6%)	841,450 (56·5%)	78,951 (5·3%)	77,571 (5·2%)	6,950 (0·4%)	1,491,257	1,805,686	82·6
1964	425,022 (29·4%)	837,022 (57·9%)	106,114 (7·3%)	69,507 (4·8%)	9,377 (0·6%)	1,447,042	1,805,454	80·1
1966	396,795 (27·9%)	863,692 (60·6%)	89,108 (6·3%)	61,071 (4·3%)	12,769 (0·9%)	1,423,435	1,800,925	79·0
1970	419,884 (27·7%)	781,941 (51·6%)	103,747 (6·8%)	175,016 (11·5%)	35,966 (2·4%)	1,516,554	1,958,778	77·4
1974 (Feb)	412,535 (25·9%)	745,547 (46·8%)	255,423 (16·0%)	171,374 (10·7%)	8,964 (0·6%)	1,593,843	1,993,931	79·9
1974 (Oct)	367,230 (23·9%)	761,447 (49·5%)	239,057 (15·5%)	166,321 (10·8%)	3,785 (0·3%)	1,537,840	2,008,284	76·6

* Up to, and including, the 1966 general election the total Conservative vote in Wales includes votes cast for Conservative and for the National Liberal candidates, and for candidates of the National Liberal and Conservative Organisation.

† Figures for 1945 adjusted to allow for two-member seats.

(Sources: F. W. S. Craig, 'British Parliamentary Election Statistics 1918-1970', and Political Compound.)

Table 3.2 Division of the vote within the United Kingdom 1970-74

	England			Scotland			Wales			N. Ireland			Total		
	1970 %	Feb. 1974 %	Oct. 1974 %	1970 %	Feb. 1974 %	Oct. 1974 %	1970 %	Feb. 1974 %	Oct. 1974 %	1970 %	Feb. 1974 %	Oct. 1974 %	1970 %	Feb. 1974 %	Oct. 1974 %
Labour	43·2	37·6	40·1	44·5	36·6	36·3	51·6	46·8	49·5	12·6	2·1	1·6	43·0	37·2	39·3
Conservative	48·3	40·2	38·9	38·0	32·9	24·7	27·7	25·9	23·9	54·2	13·1	—	46·4	38·2	35·8
Liberal	7·9	21·3	20·2	5·5	7·9	8·3	6·8	16·0	15·5	1·5	—	—	7·5	19·3	18·3
Nationalist*	—	—	—	11·4	21·9	30·4	11·5	10·7	10·3	24·5	84.7	98·3	2·3	4·5	5·8
Other	0·5	0·8	0·8	0·6	0·5	0·3	2·3	0·8	0·2	7·2	—	—	0·8	0·8	0·8

*Category includes Scottish Nationalist, Plaid Cymru in Wales, and Ulster parties with no ties to parties in Great Britain.

(*Source*: Adapted from *The Times Guide to the House of Commons, 1970*, and *October, 1974*.)

devolution has become a major issue. Their combined effect has been to create a framework for what can be described legitimately as a Welsh political debate. In the broader British context this debate, together with separate debates under way in Scotland and Northern Ireland, has great significance for the British Isles as a whole, as Tables 3.1 and 3.2 illustrate.

It can be argued that since 1968 events in Northern Ireland have put an end to the concept of 'United Kingdom politics' as in any way a unified debate. Since 1970 the remaining concept of 'British politics' has come under attack as events specific to Scotland and Wales have become more important in the scale of priorities of the people of those countries. Thus the emergence of Welsh politics has deep consequences for Britain as a whole. Devolution is providing the arena in which those consequences are being played out.

The historical basis

Wales was forged during the Roman occupation of the country between 47 AD and 383 AD. The Christian culture created in Wales in the fifth and sixth centuries—the Age of the Saints—would have been impossible without the experience of Roman civilisation during the preceding centuries. For the Roman occupation was far more than military. Major communities were established in Carmarthen and Caernarfon as well as Caerleon; a thousand Latin words were absorbed into the Brythonic tongue, being a major part of the evolution of present-day Welsh. The Romans left nearly 1,000 miles of road in Wales. Though their original function was military, the cultural importance of these roads was profound. They enabled the Welsh saints—St David, St Illtud and many others—to travel about Wales easily, allowing Welsh civilisation to flower at a time when England was immersed in her 'Dark Ages'.

At the end of the fourth century AD the people of Wales already had many of the attributes of nationhood, and during the fifth century they shared not only a common land, but also a common history, language, culture and religion. An historical myth is the hitherto widely accepted theory (initiated by the venerable Bede in the eighth century) that Wales evolved as a kind of beleaguered enclave of refugees, driven into the mountains of the west by a succession of English invasions. The truth, now established, is that Wales is, and always has been, the only homeland of the Welsh people.

The year 383 AD marks the end of the Roman period for Wales, though not for England. In that year, at a time when the Roman periphery was under increasing attack, the Emperor Magnus Maximus left Britain from Caernarfon. Before he went (with his Welsh wife, Elen, daughter of Eudwy of Gwynedd) he made the Welsh responsible for their own defence. The legions at Chester and Caerleon moved to eastern England. Thus the Welsh were the first people within the Roman Empire to become self-governing.

And, alone of the colonies of Rome's western Empire, they successfully defended themselves against the barbarians that then proceeded to overrun Europe. Christian civilisation would not have survived in the British Isles during this period if it had not been for Wales. Welsh law was codified in about 900 AD by Hywel Dda whose part in the defence of Wales against the northman was critically important. Like his grandfather Rhodri Fawr, he was one of the half-dozen leaders of this period who succeeded in uniting most of Wales under one prince, despite the fissiparous effects of gavelkind —the Welsh law insisting on equal division of property among sons.

After this period the Welsh continued to defend themselves against the Normans for two hundred years until Llewellyn II—the Last—was killed by Edward I's army in 1283. Edward's policy was to make Welshmen Englishmen as soon as possible, a policy that led to one of the most dramatic periods in Welsh history—the rise of Owain Glyndwr in the fifteenth century. This was, in a very real sense, the political birth of Wales. Owain laid the foundations of a modern nation-state—with a parliament, an effective civil service, a treasury and a central military organisation. The parliament of 1406 proclaimed his policy of establishing a national church and two universities, one in the north and one in the south.

But the century of Owain Glyndwr also saw the accession of Henry Tudor to the throne of England, in 1485; and it was under his son, Henry VIII, that the Act of Union was fashioned in 1536, its declared aim being that Wales should be: 'for ever from henceforth incorporated united or annexed to and with the Realm of England'.

Here then was a break in Welsh politics, so that a more accurate title for this chapter would read: 'The re-emergence of Welsh politics'. A community can only have a political expression when its whole life is engaged, embracing cultural, economic and spiritual dimensions as well as the more straightforward political. A Welsh political era ended with Owain Glyndwr because from then on there was a separation of these things in Welsh life. With the Act of Union in 1536 the Church of England became the established church in Wales; there were no separate Welsh institutions; and, in pursuit of the letter and the spirit of the Act, the Welsh language came under sustained and bitter attack.

Wales survived because there endured a consciousness of cultural identity, focused on the Welsh language—which is why it is so important and still, at the end of the twentieth century, a central and emotive issue at the core of Welsh politics. The language was saved from extinction by the growth of nonconformism in the eighteenth century: the chapels and Sunday schools became bastions of Welsh and defied persistent attempts at linguistic annihilation. At the beginning of the nineteenth century 80 per cent of the people still spoke Welsh, and by 1850, although the population of Wales had doubled to more than a million, 90 per cent were Welsh speaking. It was in 1856 that the Welsh national anthem, 'Hen Wlad fy Nhadau' (Land of My Fathers) was written, with all its passionate expression of the Welshman's love of freedom and his language.

But Welsh politics had died in 1485. When a Welsh prince—who had landed, incidentally, with a few French followers at Fishguard —picked up the English crown at Bosworth Field at the head of a Welsh army, there was a notion that somehow Wales had conquered England. In this mood the leadership in Wales, the land-owning class and native nobility, deserted the Welsh political context for the new English/British one in London. The reality there was made plain in the Act of Union: an individual Welshman might enjoy equality with an Englishman to the extent that he was willing and able to turn himself into an Englishman. Accordingly, the native gentry and nobility were quickly assimilated into English social order, and lost the Welsh language within a few generations. This anglicisation had the important effect that it severed links between them and the ordinary Welsh people—the Gwerin. As a result, the most notable feature of domestic Welsh society became its lack of institutionalised social hierarchy, a quality that provided an essential condition for Welsh nonconformity, for the rise of the Liberal party in Wales in the late nineteenth century and for dominance of the Labour party in the middle years of the twentieth century.

As for the gentry and nobility who, through their decision to become English/British, ended the first era of Welsh politics, their modern heirs are the Welsh Conservative party (or more appropriately, and accurately, the Conservative Party in Wales). This pedigree and its consequences has drawn special scorn from Nationalist leaders like Gwynfor Evans:

> As late as the beginning of this century, Conservatives did not acknowledge Wales to be a nation. Their nation was England though they were more inclined than the English to call it Britain. On the law of averages one would have expected them to have produced a few national leaders for Wales, but in four centuries not one has emerged from people of

their background and class . . . . One looks in vain among the Conservatives for a Welsh conservatism which strives to create the political and economic conditions in which the best Welsh traditions, the highest Welsh values, can be conserved and developed.[12]

By the early 1970s, however, in response to the changing mood in Wales, Welsh Conservatives began to adjust their perspective. In 1972 they held their first Welsh annual conference which has since established for itself an important place in the Welsh political calendar. They also began the painful process of working out Welsh policies to present in a Welsh manifesto at general elections. The landed element in the party began to give way to a younger, more urban-oriented leadership typified by the election in 1977 of Donald Walters, a Cardiff banker, as Welsh Chairman. Such new leaders brought a more flexible approach to Welsh aspirations, though the party as a whole remained firmly Unionist and anti-devolutionist.

In the period of the absence of Welsh politics following Henry VII's accession to the English throne, the chief organised expression of Welshness and Welsh sentiment was religious life and this was the factor most responsible for the continued existence of the language. Welsh isolation from England necessitated the official resurrection of the language in 1563, only thirty years after it had been legally proscribed, in order to enhance the status of the State Protestant religion.[13] The translation of the Bible and prayerbook into Welsh was authorised by Elizabeth I in order to assist in the assimilation of the Welsh into the State church. Undoubtedly, this injection of life prevented the language from becoming little more than a collection of dialects. Though the Welsh did not greet the new religious order with enthusiasm (they were at that time more inclined to the Catholic tradition) they at least became accustomed to hearing good Welsh in church services. The translation of the Bible in 1588 set a literary standard which became familiar throughout Wales. And in this way the foundation was laid for nonconformism which gained majority support in the early nineteenth century.

The flowering of religious nonconformity coincided with the 'take-off' of industrialism in South Wales. In the short term, in the late eighteenth and nineteenth centuries, industrialisation did not promote anglicisation. The new industrial villages were populated predominantly by Welsh-speaking migrants from the rural hinterland. In each village, there was reproduced the pattern of institutions of Welsh life: the chapel, the debating and religious societies, voluntary associations, and the Welsh language press.

With their decentralised structure, lack of hierarchy and reliance

on local co-operation and support, the chapels favoured independence of outlook and the development of a radical perspective. They
expressed and intensified what Hobsbawm has termed 'the
characteristic populism of Welsh society'—a shared sense of deprivation of a relatively homogeneous population with strong links
between urban and rural communities.[14]

This social grouping, though diluted during the century after
1850, is none the less a critical source of Welsh leadership in the
second half of the twentieth century. It is the basis, largely inspirational though to no small extent via direct descent, of a developing
Welsh-oriented middle class which, by the middle-1960s was moving
into positions of leadership in Welsh society. This phenomenon has
been most clearly identified by an American sociologist, Bud Khleif,
who has commented that the key to the resurgence of Welsh politics
and efforts to restore the Welsh language is the emergence after
1945 of a new Welsh middle class:

> The current leaders of Welsh opinion are overwhelmingly sons and
> daughters of coal-miners, steel-workers, shopkeepers and minor civil
> servants, but especially of coal-miners. These leaders are mostly school-
> masters, clergymen, and University lecturers, occupational categories
> highly-prized in a country like Wales with its traditional emphasis on
> education. They come, for the most part, from rural areas both north
> and south, but not typically from Cardiff or Swansea, although they may
> live there now. They are all Welsh-speaking and, in a small country such
> as Wales, know each other well. Their Welshness sets them apart, for to
> have spoken Welsh at home, a generation ago, meant that a person, by
> definition, was working class. They are proud of their Welshness—of
> their ability to speak Welsh and of their ability to live a full Welsh life.
> They consider their knowledge of Welsh a badge of achievement for it
> differentiates them from other middle-class men as well as working-class
> men who are monoglots. This new class, this Welsh-speaking middle-
> class, only a generation removed from working-class, has retained a
> tradition of non-conformity, political awareness, and, in its British
> sense, radicalism.[15]

Their political awareness can be traced to the election of 1868
which saw the return of the first *Welsh* Liberal members: Henry
Richard for Merthyr and George Osborne Morgan for Denbigh.
Their election campaigns marked the re-emergence of Welsh
politics: for the first time since the days of Owain Glyndwr, Welsh
grievances were articulated in a specifically Welsh context. Richard,
in particular, challenged, in the name of Welsh-speaking noncon-
formists, the claim to authority made by the English-speaking
landed gentry who had dominated the social and political life of
Wales for more than three centuries:

The people who speak this language [i.e. Welsh], who read this liter-
ature, who own this history, who inherit these traditions, who venerate
these names, who created and sustain these marvellous religious organisations, the people forming three-fourths of the people of Wales—
have they not a right to say to this small propertied class . . . we are the
Welsh people and not you? This country is ours and not yours, and
therefore we claim to have our principles and sentiments and feelings
represented in the Commons' House of Parliament.[16]

The 1868 election saw the return of twenty-one Liberal members
from Wales as opposed to twelve Tories, but that in itself was not
significant since there had been nominal Liberal majorities in Wales
before; the term 'liberal' still tended to be heterogeneous in
character. But it was Richard, in his attack on the alien ruling class
in Wales, who transformed religious issues like temperance, land
reform, disestablishment and education into national as well as
simply class terms, thereby forging a distinctly Welsh political
debate. Merthyr, of course, has continued to be the scene of new
departures in Welsh politics. In 1900 it returned Keir Hardie as the
first Labour party member in Wales. And a generation later, in May
1976, Plaid Cymru captured overwhelming control of the town's
borough authority, the first in Wales to be controlled officially in the
party's name—immediately claimed as another historic first.

The identification of the Liberals with the nonconformist
conscience combined with an effective, thoroughly Welsh,
leadership brought its reward at the polls. In 1886 Welsh Liberals
were returned from 30 of Wales's 34 parliamentary seats. Among
them was 26-year-old Tom Ellis (Meirionnydd) who, together with
Lloyd George, returned at a by-election for Caernarfon Boroughs in
1890 (aged 27), spearheaded the intrusion of Welsh politics into the
British context in the years 1885-95. This drive was backed at the
local level. In the first elections to the new county councils in 1889 the
Liberals won control of every county except Brecon, most by a wide
margin—in North Wales 175 out of 260 councillors were Liberal,
and in South Wales and Monmouthshire they numbered 215 out of
330. Ellis observed: 'The Monmouthshire victory is of *immense*
importance for it means it will cast its lot with Wales.'[17]

In this period a Welsh party was formed within the ranks of
Parliamentary Liberals. It was based at home on what promised to
become a grassroots national movement, Cymru Fydd (Young
Wales) which was founded in 1896. In the next ten years, with a full-
time organiser, it formed more than a hundred branches closely
linked to the Liberal party. To a large extent the movement rested
on the ideas of Michael D. Jones (1822—98—principal of the

Independent Theological College at Bala) and Emrys ap Iwan
(Robert Ambrose Jones, 1851—1906). Michael D. Jones was one of
the founders of Y Wladfa, the Welsh colony, in Patagonia in 1865
and powerfully influenced Ellis and contemporary Welsh politics
generally with an idealised vision of a future self-governing Welsh
community. Emrys ap Iwan saw the defence of the Welsh language
as a political matter and also demanded the rejection of the idea of
Empire. It was he, in fact, who coined the term 'Ymreolaeth' (Home
Rule). The ideas of these two men were to have far-reaching effects.
They were one of the main sources of inspiration for Saunders Lewis
and the foundation of Plaid Cymru in 1925 and also of the founders
of Cymdeithas yr Iaith Gymraeg (the Welsh Language Society) in
1962. In the nineteenth century, however, they were ahead of their
time, though both Ellis and Lloyd George took up their ideas for a
short period. Lloyd George, for instance, placed self-government at
the head of the list of Cymru Fydd's priorities:

> I am sure that Wales would be an example to the nations of the world if
> it were given self-government—an example of a nation which chased
> oppression out of the hills, and of a nation which gave birth to a glorious
> period of liberty and justice and truth.[18]

In an election address at Bala in September 1890 Tom Ellis spoke
in detail of developing the economy of Wales, of its history and
culture, of a national university, library and museum, and of the use
that should be made of the county councils. He continued:

> for these things we work, but most important of all, we work for a
> Legislative council, elected by the men and women of Wales, and
> responsible to them. It will be a symbol and an emblem of our national
> unity, a weapon with which to work out our social ideals and industrial
> welfare . . .[19]

In the early 1890s self-government was a dominant theme in
Welsh politics. In 1895 the Liberal Prime Minister, Lord Rosebery,
came to address the Welsh Liberal League at Cardiff where he
declared in favour of Welsh self-government. There was to be 'Home
Rule all Round', for Ireland, Scotland and Wales. But this was the
peak of nineteenth century pressure for devolution, or Home Rule as
it was then known. The problem was not without Wales, but within.
There was too much ambiguity of aim; too little conviction and no
bedrock philosophy amongst the wider Cymru Fydd movement to
sustain it. The fatal flaw was revealed as early as 1892 when Tom
Ellis accepted office as a junior whip with the newly returned Liberal
government. As Gwynfor Evans put it, 'He opened the path that

Lloyd George made into a main highway for the Welsh to advance in the English political world . . . this appointment was a victory for the English establishment.'[20]

The collapse of Cymru Fydd was symbolised by a meeting in Newport in January 1896 when an attempt to create one Liberal Federation for the whole of Wales in place of the North and South Federations floundered. Cymru Fydd could not withstand the crude reaction to its pressure articulated at that meeting by a powerful Englishman on Cardiff Corporation, Alderman Robert Bird, who shouted: 'Throughout South Wales there are thousands upon thousands of Englishmen . . . a cosmopolitan population who will not tolerate the predomination of Welsh ideals.'[21]

Why at this point were Welsh ideals so weak that they succumbed so easily to such attacks? The answer to this question provides a vital clue as to why Welsh politics were to survive and develop into the twentieth century. For the Welsh movement of the last quarter of the nineteenth century was not based on a firm enough sense of community. Cymru Fydd was brought together as a collective forum for wide-ranging causes—land reform, educational equality, religious dissent and, to a lesser extent, temperance reform. These diverse issues were essentially individualistic causes and not intimately related to the survival of the Welsh community as a whole. Thus the attempt to base on them a community movement, Cymru Fydd, rested on unsure foundations from the start.

Cymru Fydd was the creature of the Liberal party whose basic philosophy was highly individualistic in any event. The conditions which allowed the rise of Liberalism were nonconformism and the spread of universal suffrage, movements that heightened the role of the individual in relation to the state rather than in relation to the community. Thus Liberalism stressed the freedom of the individual but placed no great accent on the community as such.

This individualistic ethic explains the lack of staying power of the Cymru Fydd movement; its lack of toughness. Its leaders were highly individualistic themselves, symbolised by Ellis's acceptance of a government post as a junior whip. At the outset of his career Lloyd George wrote to Margaret Owen before their marriage: 'My supreme idea is to get on. To this idea I shall sacrifice everything— except, I trust, honesty. I am prepared to thrust even love itself under the wheels of my Juggernaut, if it obstructs the way.'[22]

One of the major twentieth century political arguments is about working out a collectivism that takes into account the prime importance and needs of community at the same time as preserving the integrity of the individual. Cymru Fydd did not recognise or face up to this problem and so withered. In the early twentieth century the Labour Party in Wales did respond to it and won the support of the overwhelming mass of the people. But it was a crude response that struck a path towards the arms of the state. There was in the early Labour movement, particularly in Wales, a syndicalist approach that offered a different direction,[23] but the First World War ensured victory for Labour centralists. After the First World War another political movement began, in the shape of Plaid Cymru, to try to work out a solution. It had some hope because its founders stressed from the start the primacy of community, in the tradition of Michael D. Jones and Emrys ap Iwan.

The Liberals, however, continued to pursue their individualistic path, squeezing the community between the requirement of state and individual, and consigning themselves to the political wilderness in the process. It was a tradition they maintained in Wales into the 1970s. In December 1975, the then Parliamentary candidate for Carmarthen, Terry Thomas, presented the following definition of Liberalism to a Welsh Liberal Party Council meeting at Swansea:

> Liberalism remains the most ambitious creed of our times. What could be more ambitious than to aspire to the best of both worlds? Liberalism is not mere moderation. It strives towards the optimum of social progress and democratic freedom, *the best balance between statism and individualism,* between the quality of life and the quantity of goods produced for mass consumption, between planning and choice, between present and delayed gratification of wants and needs, between social engineering and democratic muddling through.[24]

As Thomas went on to point out, this could equally serve as 'a description of Social Democracy or in other words the philosophy of the right wing of the Labour Party'. The barrenness of the approach is that it is an entirely centralist one. The aim of politics is, via 'social engineering' to achieve a pragmatic balance between the requirements of the individual and of the state. On the other hand, a decentralist perspective asks first: what are the needs of the community? This perspective provides the key to the dynamism of Welsh politics in the last quarter of the twentieth century.

It is a dynamism that has evolved naturally from the history of Wales over nearly two thousand years. A study of Welsh history yields a special appreciation of the importance of community because for much of her history it is all Wales has had—lacking both great leaders and state institutions. Unlike the politics of other, perhaps more fortunate countries, the politics of Wales have been predominantly concerned with the survival of community. From their earliest days a prime concern of the people of Wales has been the defence of their very existence. Hence the feeling and sensitivity many Welsh people have for Jewish people. The Welsh obsession with the Old Testament has deep psychological undercurrents. In the years when it was too dangerous—or, more often, too psycho-logically painful—to think about Welsh politics, the Welsh studied Hebrew politics instead. It was a good substitute.

So in the 1970s, when Welsh politics are very much on the agenda, they are concerned still with survival: with the creation of a context in which Welsh politics can occur.

The administrative basis

Despite the collapse of Cymru Fydd, the significance and achieve-ments of Welsh politics from 1868 to the beginnings of the twentieth century should not be under-estimated. Most importantly, instit-utions were created—the University of Wales, the National Library and the National Museum. Their nature does, however, reveal a great deal about the aspirations of Welsh leaders of that period. The aim was equal participation for the Welsh in the British political system. The new institutions were tangible symbols of achievement in this direction: they conferred status on what was essentially a *petit-bourgeois* regional elite based on Cardiff.

One of the adherents of Cymru Fydd, in an exposition of its aims in 1894, made clear that the movement did not seek Welsh indep-endence:

> It is recognised not only that union with England is inevitable, but that it provides the best opportunity that Wales could have to deliver her mission—if mission she has—to the world. The one condition that is insisted upon is that the connection shall not be made closer at the expense of Welsh nationality.[25]

The establishment of institutions went some way to meet this objective. The pressure of Cymru Fydd bore fruit in the evolution of administrative decentralisation in the twentieth century that provided an embryonic framework for the development of Welsh politics.

Education set the pace, from the Welsh Intermediate Education Act 1889 to the creation of the Welsh Department of the Board of Education in 1907. Welsh interest in education had been stimulated as early as 1846 when the report of a Commission of Inquiry, the so-called 'Brad y Llyfrau Gleision' (The Treason of the Blue Books) exposed the poor educational standards in Wales and blamed them on the Welsh language. Speaking in the House of Commons a century later the Minister for Education, R. A. Butler, said:

> We have also had some courses initiated in the Welsh language. I regard as obscurantist the attitude of the Commission of Inquiry exactly a hundred years ago which went to Wales and took the view that to keep alive a knowledge of this beautiful tongue was tantamount to crippling Welsh initiative and penalising Welsh endeavour. I wish now, a hundred years later, to make amends for that attitude.[26]

At the time the Commission served to sting the Welsh into action to disprove the accusations. The first Welsh teacher training college was opened at Brecon in 1846 and from then on hundreds of new primary schools were established throughout Wales. In 1891 the Welsh Intermediate Education Act authorised the new county councils to levy a half-penny rate (supplemented by a government grant of a pound for a pound) to finance secondary schools—progress in advance of England. In 1896 a Central Welsh Board of Education was established to supervise schools inspection and examinations. There was an attempt to insert a clause into the 1906 Education Bill to set up a Council for Wales to raise money and administer education up to university level. The thorough-going devolution implications of this caused it to fail, but a compromise resulted in the creation of the Welsh Department of the Board of Education in 1907.

Education was followed by agriculture. In 1919 a Welsh Department of the Ministry of Agriculture was established. And the provision, under the Insurance Act 1911, for a separate insurance commission for Wales was followed in 1919 by the formation of the Welsh Board of Health, a major step in administrative decentralisation. The next twenty years of economic depression combined with the philosophy of socialist centralism that became dominant in the emerging Labour party, diverted the Welsh from pressurising for more decentralisation. However, attempts were made in 1921, 1928, 1930 and 1937 in Parliament to secure a Minister with responsibility for Welsh affairs.[27]

It was the exigencies of the Second World War that forced measures of decentralisation. By the end of the war fifteen government departments had established offices in Wales. Modest progress was maintained after the war with efforts to improve departmental liaison and enlargement of the role of advisory bodies. In particular, in 1949, a nominated Council for Wales and Monmouthshire was established, composed of representatives from local authorities, industry and other interests. But, at ministerial level, Wales suffered in comparison with Scotland, whose Secretary of State had been reconstituted in 1895 and given Cabinet rank in 1925 (the Secretaryship of State for Scotland had been abolished in 1746).[28]

The office of Minister for Welsh Affairs was finally created by the Conservatives in 1951, not in its own right but as a curious appendage to the Home Office. In 1957 a full-time Minister of State was appointed, to work in association with the Minister for Housing and Local Government, and in 1964 the Secretaryship of State for Wales was achieved—but not without a good deal of political manoeuvring.

The immediate background was the Parliament for Wales Campaign which lasted from 1950 to 1956. A petition of 250,000 signatures was presented to Parliament in April 1956 by Goronwy Roberts, then Labour MP for Caernarfon. In March 1955 S. O. Davies, Labour MP for Merthyr, had presented a Private Member's Bill to the House, defeated by 64 votes to 16. Only six of the thirty-six Welsh MPs supported the Bill: five were Labour and they were reported to the party's National Executive Committee for opposing party policy.[29] Nevertheless, the campaign succeeded in polarising feelings on the issue, causing a debate, with people and institutions taking sides.

Early in 1957 the Council for Wales and Monmouthshire put forward a detailed and reasoned case for bringing together the various government offices in Wales into a new Welsh Office, comparable with the Scottish Office. Their argument was that there was 'far too little co-ordination of the activities of the Departments operating in Wales' and that this constituted 'the greatest single failure' of government. The existing machinery—a committee of the heads of the Welsh regional arms of central government departments—was, said the Council, incapable of 'decisive action to deal with Welsh problems, being vested with little real independence or power of decision'. Nor had the chairmanship of the committee, by the Minister for Welsh Affairs, 'altered the situation in which Ministers have continued to keep all their executive authority'.[30]

The Government ignored the Council's memorandum. After a nine-month wait, a member of the Council, Sir William Jones, publicly accused the higher civil service of responsibility for stalling and warned that 'there is a breaking-point in the patience of a nation as well as individuals'. The Chairman of the Council, Dr Huw T. Edwards, spoke in similar vein. Stung by these rebukes the Prime Minister himself replied to the Council, but refused to accede to their request on the ground that the Welsh Office would be half the size of the Scottish Office, and its constituent departments would therefore be too small for efficiency. What Wales needed was 'not isolation from the rest of Britain, but concentration of ability and wise understanding on Welsh problems and on the Welsh aspects of general problems'.[31] But he promised some piecemeal devolution, and claimed that the recent transfer of responsibility for Welsh Affairs from the Home Office to the Ministry of Housing and Local Government would mean greater attention to Welsh needs.

The Council complained with some bitterness that none of their well-documented arguments had been dealt with in detail, and contested the validity of the Prime Minister's own arguments in a unanimously agreed memorandum.[32] It is rare indeed that a Council of this character, nominated by the very people to whom it is charged to give advice, should show such accord and spirit. But the government did not give way and the Council resigned *en bloc*. The Chairman, Huw T. Edwards, resigned from the Labour party as well, claiming that only Plaid Cymru could now produce the right solution for Wales.

This episode had the result of forcing the Labour party to take the issue seriously. In the year prior to the 1959 general election a series of meetings of Labour's Home Policy Committee, chaired by Hugh Gaitskell and including Aneurin Bevan (Ebbw Vale), James Griffiths (then deputy Labour leader), Ness Edwards (Caerphilly) and Cliff Prothero (then secretary of the Labour Party in Wales) discussed the problem. The committee was split on whether a Secretary of State for Wales should be included in Labour's pro-gramme, with Bevan leading the case against and Griffiths the case in favour. In his memoirs Griffiths analysed Bevan's opposition:

> Nye's doubts about the wisdom of the creation of a Welsh Office went beyond considerations of administration. He has related how he came to realise that if he was to achieve his objectives, and his burning desire to create a Socialist society, it was imperative to reach out from the valley, and beyond the county, to the centre, where the levers of power were operated. He was impatient of nationalism which divided peoples and enslaved nations within their narrow geographical and spiritual front-iers. He feared that devolution of authority would divorce Welsh political activity from the main stream of British politics, as he felt was already happening in Scotland.[33]

There was deadlock in the committee until its very last meeting when a decision had to be reached. At its outset Bevan dramatically switched sides and ensured Labour's commitment to a Welsh Office. The reason for this change is far from clear. The most likely explanation is that Griffiths persuaded Bevan in private out of the strength of his emotional conviction.[34] In this way the Welsh Office commitment found its way into Labour's Manifesto for 1959 and 1964, after which Jim Griffiths was appointed Charter Secretary of State.

But the Welsh Office was born amidst scepticism, and the rest of the 1960s witnessed a struggle to obtain for it the powers promised— a struggle that well illustrates the innate hostility of Whitehall towards decentralised administration, let alone political devolution. The Welsh Office was extracted out of the Ministry of Housing and Local Government whose new Minister, Richard Crossman, recorded in his diary: 'Another equally idiotic creation is the Department for Wales, a completely artificial new office for Jim Griffiths and his two Parliamentary secretaries, all the result of a silly election pledge'.[35] There was an attempt by Crossman's Permanent Secretary, Dame (later Baroness) Evelyn Sharp, to persuade Griffiths that he should begin without a department, except a secretariat in London attached to her Ministry. This Griffiths resisted, but he was faced with more serious political opposition from a number of Welsh Labour MPs who fought a rearguard action against the Welsh Office. In his private papers that became available after his death, Griffiths records that he sent a memorandum to the Prime Minister suggesting that Welsh functions of the Ministry of Housing and Local Government should be transferred to the Welsh Office in Wales as a beginning. In addition he proposed that he should have oversight over all other government departments operating in Wales:

> I did not have any difficulty at first with the P.M. until some of my Welsh colleagues, led by Ness Edwards [MP for Caerphilly until his death in 1968], sent a memo to the P.M. urging that my duties should be confined to oversight but without any transferred administrative functions. I was angry at this, not because of the views expressed in their memo, but because they had not sent me a copy of it. I learnt of it from No. 10. I did not think this was playing the game and I asked for a special meeting of the Welsh Labour Group to be convened, at which I made this development known to all my Welsh colleagues. I also sent a personal note in my own handwriting to the P.M. to inform him that unless an agreement was reached to set up a department for Wales and a beginning made of the transfer of functions, I would feel compelled to submit my resignation to him.[36]

All this occurred in the weeks immediately following the 1964 general election. The outcome was the announcement by Harold Wilson, in November, that the Welsh Office was to be formed out of the regional branch of the Ministry of Housing in Wales, plus the

Welsh roads division of the Ministry of Transport. Though the
manifesto commitment had also envisaged executive responsibility
for the new Secretary of State embracing health, education, local
government and agriculture, no mention was made of them and they
had to be painfully extracted. As Ted Rowlands, Labour MP for
Merthyr and Parliamentary Under-Secretary of State at the Welsh
Office towards the end of the 1964-70 administration and again after
February 1974, commented:

> Health and education would have seemed obvious candidates for devol-
> ution to the newly created Welsh Office. Both already had honourable
> traditions of administrative devolution to their offices in the Principal-
> ity. A Welsh Department of Education had been set up in 1907; a Board
> of Health in Wales in 1919. Indeed, the latter was a microcosm of a
> Whitehall department, exercising within Wales the full range of admin-
> istrative tasks of the central department. And yet it took nearly five years
> for the Secretary of State to assume full executive responsibility for
> health in Wales. The explanation for the delay lies chiefly in the jealous
> guardianship exercised by Whitehall departments over the principle of
> centralised administration.[37]

But, by the mid-1970s, the Welsh Office had won control over
primary and secondary education, local government, economic
planning, and most significantly, trade and industry powers (July
1975) which established at least the context for an integrated administrative approach to the problems of the Welsh economy.

The establishment and development of the Welsh Office has had
the utmost significance for Welsh politics. Most importantly it has
promoted the idea of Wales as an economic unit. Commenting on
George Brown's 'National' Plan of 1965, James Griffiths recalled
that he had to decide what form its regional machinery should take
in Wales:

> There were then, and still are, some who argue that I should have
> created a number of separate planning regions within Wales, in partic-
> ular that the north and south-east corners should be linked with the
> industrial areas beyond in England. . . . But I was confident that these
> border areas in the north and south would develop under their own
> momentum. It was the economic prospects of west and mid Wales which
> gave cause for concern. I therefore decided that Wales should be treated
> as one unit for economic planning, with its own Planning Board and
> Economic Council.[38]

Much of Welsh political debate after 1964 focused on steadily
mounting criticisms of Welsh Office action, and more commonly,
inaction, in the economic sphere. One logical progression of the

debate was the creation of the Wales TUC in 1973, which put the final seal on the concept of a Welsh economy.

The politics of devolution are intimately interwoven with the developing argument over the Welsh economy which, as described in the preceding chapter, has centred on the efficacy of British regional policy. It has been accepted, even by Welsh Conservatives who initially opposed the Welsh Office,[39] that the position of the Secretary of State for Wales in the Cabinet has given the country a formidable weapon in fighting for scarce resources and protecting Welsh interests, if only from the standpoint of political expediency. The most celebrated example was the saving of the mid-Wales railway line from Llanelli through Llandrindod Wells to Shrewsbury between 1967-69, vividly described by Richard Marsh, who presented the case for closure to the Cabinet:

> I spoke for fifteen minutes at the Cabinet and sat back I confess, with an air of satisfaction—smug satisfaction. The silence was broken by the voice of the Secretary of State for Wales, one George Thomas, who said 'But Prime Minister, it runs through six marginal constituencies'.[40]

But such victories only provided a superficial gloss to the harsh underlying reality that the prospects of the Welsh economy were worsening in relation to the more prosperous neighbouring areas in England. There is no doubt that the Welsh Office has been an important focus of pressure exerted on behalf of Wales in the British government system, but this has merely pointed the way forward. Administrative decentralisation has enabled Welsh needs and grievances to be given a focus. There would have to be political devolution before sufficient political will could be mobilised to tackle Welsh problems at root. But the establishment of the Welsh Office provided another, and more immediately important, arm to the argument for taking the process further: the need for democratic institutions to control the new bureaucratic machine. Concluding his survey of the Welsh Office's performance from the vantage point of 1972, Ted Rowlands commented:

> The major changes of the last seven years, however, may be said to have failed at least in one simple respect. They have apparently not assuaged the demands of Welshmen for a greater say in the government of their own affairs. Indeed, the establishment of the Welsh Office has intensified the demand for democratic institutions to supervise the new growing bureaucracy in Wales.[41]

Four years later, in a speech to a Cardiff Labour party meeting, Rowlands elaborated the argument: 'Let me make a confession,' he

said. 'I have been a sceptic on devolution. In the debates in the
Parliamentary group and outside during the 1960s, I was *not*
convinced. I believed that the Welsh Office and the Secretary of
State could have been made effectively and democratically
accountable through Welsh Members at Westminster.'[42] Rowlands,
in fact, had recommended that a Select Committee of the House of
Commons be established to scrutinise Welsh affairs, which was by then
Conservative party policy as well. But he said that since the 1960s,
two developments had resulted in removing the option of a Select
Committee as 'a viable alternative to a fullblooded Welsh
Assembly':

1. Westminster could not afford the time and energy to scrutinise
    the Welsh Office in the detail required—

    'This trend will become even more noticeable when Westminster really
    starts to come to terms with its EEC role. We have scarcely begun to
    grapple with democratic control and supervision of the whole complex
    of UK/EEC relationships . . . and in an already overwhelmingly
    crowded legislative timetable it is difficult to see Westminster serving
    as the real effective watchdog over Welsh or Scottish affairs.'

2. The second reason was the evolution of Welsh Office powers:
    'There is a danger that one could develop a powerful civil service
    elite accountable less and less to Parliament and to the people
    of Wales'. (Here Rowlands was quoting the evidence of former
    Permanent Head at the Welsh Office, Sir Goronwy Daniel, to
    the Commission on the Constitution.[43])

Apart from providing an impetus to the economic argument about
how best Wales's industrial and infrastructural problems could be
tackled, and apart from adding this democratic justification for
further political devolution, the Welsh Office meant that a home-
based administrative machine was built up. In the first decade
after its inception in 1964, the Welsh Office staff rose in numbers
from a handful to well over a thousand. By 1977/78, with the
addition of full agriculture responsibility, the Welsh Office's
complement was more than 2,000.

Taken together all these elements brought a powerful new
coherence to the perception of Welsh problems by the Welsh people
themselves. The development of the Welsh Office in the mid-
twentieth century has provided an essential prop to the framework
out of which has emerged Welsh politics. Well might anti-
devolutionist and former Secretary of State for Wales, George
Thomas, have judged: 'Our greatest mistake was to have set up the
Welsh Office.'[44]

The national basis

Though there were sound administrative arguments for establishing the Welsh Office, at root it was seen as a means of recognising the separate, national identity of Wales. The Council for Wales, for example, in recommending the creation of a Secretary of State, was motivated by the belief that 'Wales is a separate nation and not just a region, province or appendage of England'.[45]

This fact of community identity, connected with a growing political solidarity, was the source both of the demand for the Secretary of State and its eventual concession. Indeed, Welsh national sentiment was a major causal faction in the provision of Welsh ministerial arrangements from 1951 onwards. The Conservative government regarded the appointment of a Minister for Welsh Affairs (in 1951) as a means of 'recognising the national aspirations and the special position of Wales'.[46] And in the words of James Griffiths, the first Secretary of State for Wales, the post had been created primarily out of a 'recognition of our nationhood' which aimed at providing 'a new status for Wales within the constitution of the United Kingdom'.[47]

The source of Welsh nationhood is to be found in the history of Wales, some of which has been briefly sketched in an earlier section. What is remarkable is that despite the ravaging of the identity of Wales in the hundred years between 1850 and 1950 there was still enough vitality in the community to provide the base for the fight back of the 1960s and 1970s. The attack on the language that gathered pace in the nineteenth century was accompanied by the immense upheavals of industrial change, massive population migration and immigration, two World Wars and the impact of mass media emanating from London: all of which combined to change irrevocably the nature of Welsh society. Nevertheless the idea of Welsh nationhood lived on first to provoke the devolution debate of the 1970s, and then to provide the foundations of the conflicting arguments.

A major cause of the vitality of Welsh nationhood in the twentieth century, in the face of at times overwhelming forces dictating British integration and uniformity, was the creation and development of a Welsh national movement separate from any mainstream British political party. In itself Plaid Cymru—the 'Party of Wales', founded in 1925—has remained only a small element in Welsh politics and has grown slowly, achieving just 10·8 per cent of the Welsh vote in the October 1974 general election. But Plaid Cymru, modelling itself to this extent on the Labour party, is far from being purely a political expression. It is a movement in the broadest sense and its influence has penetrated practically every corner of Welsh life, usually in terms of provoking an adverse reaction but, in doing so, breaking down indifference.

The creation of Plaid Cymru, in the aftermath of the First World War, was a signal that the methods adopted by the old Cymru Fydd movement, working within an essentially British context, had been rejected. One of the founders of the party and a seminal influence on its direction over the next fifty years, was Saunders Lewis. It was he who laid the philosophical foundations of the new party which in 1930 officially adopted Dominion or Commonwealth status for Wales as its constitutional goal. (After Britain's entry into the European Economic Community was confirmed by the 1975 referendum this goal was modified to one of full national status within the EEC.) This constitutional aim was laid down by Saunders Lewis in his pamphlet 'The banned wireless talk on Welsh Nationalism' which was prevented from being broadcast since, according to the BBC, it was 'calculated to inflame Welsh national sympathies'.

The main theme of the pamphlet, published in 1930, is the rejection of a nationalism that is merely cultural. Such a concept, it argues, is based on the premise that a nation 'can divide its life and activities into separate compartments with no communication between them'. This, Saunders Lewis holds, is no more possible for a nation than it is for an individual person:

> If a nation that has lost its political machinery becomes content to express its nationality thenceforward only in the sphere of literature and the arts, then that literature and those arts will very quickly become provincial and unimportant, mere echoes of the ideas and artistic movements of the neighbouring, and dominant, nation. If they (the Welsh people) decide that the literary revival shall not broaden out into political and economic life and the whole of Welsh life, then inevitably Welsh literature in our generation will cease to be living and valuable.[48]

The second part of the pamphlet examined the more immediate Welsh problem of unemployment, particularly in regard to the South Wales mining communities. One of the saddest features of the crisis, noted Lewis, was 'the apathy, the uninventive patience of South Wales itself, the fact that we who live here wait and wait hoping for some god outside the machine to step down and lift us away from our troubles'. It was in this situation that nationalism, a spiritual force, could help men overcome their material difficulties. The past was there to be used as an inspiration for the present:

> There is nothing like the sense of belonging to a noble country and to courageous ancestors for inspiring youth to heroism. Nationalism is

above all a fountainhead of heroism and of brave resolve. It gives a beaten people hope. It gives them resourcefulness and drives away apathy and cynicism and selfishness. It rouses them to co-operation and it kills obstruction and the spirit that says 'No'. In the present economic and social distress of Wales this inspiration is just what we lack.

If Saunders Lewis contributed much to the philosophical foundation of Plaid Cymru he also engineered one of two incidents that have become part of an essential mythology of twentieth-century Welsh politics, and of enormous symbolic importance to the national movement. The first, generally known as the 'Burning of the Bombing School' (or 'The Fire in Lleyn') occurred in 1936. It resulted from Plaid Cymru's despair at the insensitivity of the authorities to Welsh feelings, in the decision to locate a military airfield in the Welsh-speaking heartland. A number of the party's leaders, headed by Saunders Lewis himself, turned to direct action, setting fire to buildings at the construction site. Then they gave themselves up to the police, admitting their technical—but not moral—guilt. There followed a series of celebrated court cases (a Caernarfon jury failed to agree so the trial was moved to the Old Bailey where the three accused were sentenced to nine months' imprisonment). The issue provoked intense condemnation but also generated much sympathy for the Welsh national cause and has been a source of inspiration ever since.[49]

In 1959 a somewhat different issue provoked a similar emotional and moral response. The City of Liverpool proposed to flood the Tryweryn Valley in Meirionnydd and to inundate the community located within it, in order to form a reservoir to service new industrial development on Merseyside. Once again feelings were aroused. A national campaign of opposition was organised, and this met with an extraordinarly broadly based wave of popular support. The outcome of this episode was to have equally long-term implications as the Bombing School incident. It may be said that the myth of 1936 secured a distinctive and separate ideology for Welsh politics. And, in turn, the myth of 1959 resulted in the creation of a political party —as opposed to a cultural and political pressure group—which could put the ideology into practice.

The Burning of the Bombing School was the seminal event. The *Western Mail* noted the historical importance of the subsequent trial: no Welshman had faced 'charges of an insurrectionary character' for a hundred years. Further, 'It is the first time for six centuries—since the days of Owain Glyndwr—that charges of lawbreaking have been brought against the protagonists of Welsh independence.'[50]

Saunders Lewis and the other early Plaid Cymru leaders were demonstrating that nationalism must act as an assault on a psychologically subdued community. The people of Wales under-valued their own life-style and language, and thereby under-valued themselves. They tended to adopt the standards of the metropolitan culture, in place of their own, as a suitable measure of quality. As a result the quality of life in Wales could become nothing but provincial, narrow and parochial. As Saunders Lewis himself put it at the time:

> What is wrong in South Wales, as in all Wales, is fundamental. Economic measures alone . . . will bring no remedy of value. . . . There is no hope for Wales until a generation arises that knows its own past. . . . A people ignorant of its own history, completely ignorant of it, as are the majority of the people of Wales, will inevitably be a community of cowards, of self-regarding, self-seeking opportunists. . . . . Courage in social economic enterprises depends on a true sense of citizenship, of consciously inheriting from the grave and confidently building for the cradle.[51]

Saunders Lewis found his history-conscious generation in the Welsh colleges of the early 1960s. It responded to his 1962 radio lecture 'Tynged yr Iaith' (The Fate of the Language),[52] created Cymdeithas yr Iaith Gymraeg (The Welsh Language Society) and proceeded to emulate the Burning of the Bombing School with direct action on behalf of the language. Throughout the 1960s and in the 1970s the activity of Cymdeithas yr Iaith took on a revolutionary character through which the participants established or affirmed their identity in the way Saunders Lewis had advocated for his generation. As one leader of the Society expressed it: 'We knew the law had to be broken—by breaking the law we would free ourselves from our individually and nationally respectable past . . . one was so subjective, so intense, so preoccupied with one's problems of identity.'[53]

But Cymdeithas yr Iaith Gymraeg parted company from Saunders Lewis in one vital respect, so important that it was the reason why Lewis relinquished the Honorary Presidency of the Society in 1976. The issue was the Society's opposition to a crown being donated to the Cardigan National Eisteddfod by the Royal Aircraft Establishment at Aberporth. In a letter to the Society Saunders Lewis said he was resigning because 'the career of a soldier is noble and honourable and essential in any free country'.[54] The Society's position on violence, laid down in its manifesto,[55] published in 1972, is subtle, distinctive and important:

> Reverence for life is the fundamental value on which all other values are built. Take it away and there are no values left. . . . The core of the

matter has been stated by Waldo Williams elsewhere, where he asserts that the use of violence would 'betray the whole moral strength of the movement, and its true purpose—the development of civilisation, gentleness and love'[56] . . . We are campaigning for the future of the language and this cannot be ensured in the end without the support of all Wales. To use violence, or fail to avoid it, would set us on a slippery slope towards the creation of hostilities and hatreds that are then not easily forgotten. Non-violent methods alone can harmonise the need for heroic and uncompromising action and the need for reconciliation and mutual understanding which is necessary for the revival of the language . . .

Neither have we any doubt that the destruction of property, under special circumstances, is consistent with these principles. In the court at Yr Wyddgrug (Mold)[57] Ffred Ffransis stated what these circumstances are, and they have now become part of the policy of Cymdeithas yr Iaith —that other non-violent means should already have been used, and that it is absolutely certain that no harm or danger will be caused to life. We quote from part of his defence before the assizes at Yr Wyddgrug justifying damage done to the equipment of a television studio:

'Destruction of property may be essential to prevent violence to people, and it is a positive duty to anyone who feels any responsibility to his fellowman to be ready to take this course of action. . . . In Wales, broadcasting equipment is being used as a means of oppression against the language and personality of the Welsh people. It would be quite wrong to use personal violence against broadcasters or controllers in order to stop this oppression, but it is right, and indeed it is the responsibility of every conscientious Welshman to destroy property which is being used to oppress the people.'

This section of Cymdeithas yr Iaith Gymraeg's manifesto is worth quoting at length since it illustrates one critical area where the generation that inherited Saunders Lewis's nationalism modified it, and thereby injected an important new dimension into Welsh politics. But on broader political questions the Society merely translated what Saunders Lewis had been saying into a more modern context. This was particularly noticeable when the society came, in the mid-1970s, to develop a political ideology covering broader issues than those immediately related to the language question. It may be argued that here Cymdeithas yr Iaith Gymraeg was keeping closer to the Welsh political tradition[58] as revived by the founders of Plaid Cymru, than the mainstream party itself which by the 1960s and 1970s was engaged in a more conventional political conflict with the Labour party in the South Wales valleys.

Under the leadership of Ffred Ffransis again—he is, incidentally, the son-in-law of the Plaid Cymru President, Gwynfor Evans— Cymdeithas yr Iaith Gymraeg began to evolve an ideology described as 'Cymdeithasiaeth'. It is difficult to translate this adequately into English but a near approximation might be 'community socialism'. It is an abstract noun based on Cymdeithas (Society) but having Welsh connotations and less of a state orientation then Sosialaeth (Socialism). The term was associated with R. J. Derfel, the late-nineteenth-century poet and philosopher of the early Labour movement in Wales who sought to unite 'the red dragon and the red flag'. The broad principles of the ideology, as worked out by Ffransis, were approved by the annual meeting of Cymdeithas yr Iaith Gymraeg at Talybont, Ceredigion, in November 1975. An extract will give the flavour of what was being proposed. The document approved stated that the development of 'Cymdeithasiaeth' would involve many fundamental changes in the way communities in Wales organise themselves:

The Economic and Governmental System

The nature of the economy: the economy would have to be organised with a social motive rather than a profit motive as its basis. The fate of Welsh communities should not be decided by considerations of vested interest and profit. The economy would serve the Welsh community. It is not feasible to develop an independent Welsh capitalist system due to the inevitable connection between modern capitalism and imperialism. Social control over the economy must be ensured in order to safeguard the freedom of the Welsh communities.

Control: The vast majority of economic and governmental decisions would have to be taken in the local communities if the character and continuance of Welsh communities is to be secured. The remaining functions which would be left to the central level of government would be that of co-ordination, the control and distribution of vital supplies and services, the redistribution of wealth between areas, and international functions, ensuring that the principle of 'cymdeithasiaeth' is widely spread, so that Wales would not exist in a vacuum. This new system would entail the revitalisation of, and new responsibilities for, every local community in Wales.

Production: A fundamental change is needed in the type of goods which is being produced, and the end of policies of exploitation which are rapidly stripping the earth of its resources and leading to a world-wide crisis. Production should depend upon the needs of the area, and widespread use of recycling should be used. One sees, increasingly, a fundamental role for agriculture in the economic and social system.

Finance: Surplus capital, that which is now stashed in banks, insurance companies, building societies, national savings, etc., should be put to use for the benefit of the local community. These changes in control, i.e.

that the major power is in the local community, presupposes a fundamental change in tax and rating systems.

Transport: The enacting of these principles would mean many changes in the needs and priorities of a transport policy. With a situation of increased social stability, the development of a truly effective network of public transport takes precedence over the development of fast connections between areas.

This expression is an example of the national basis of Welsh politics as it developed out of the Burning of the Bombing School episode of 1936. Equally important from the point of view of Welsh politics, was a parallel development that grew out of the other essential mythological event of twentieth-century Welsh nationalism: the evolution of Plaid Cymru into a political party as a result of the Tryweryn experience of 1955-9.

Tryweryn is a large valley in Meirionnydd, in an area known as Penllyn.[59] Like the Lleyn Peninsula, the site for the bombing school of 1936, the area was entirely 'Welsh' in character with important community, historical and literary associations. In 1955 it was learned from a press report that the Liverpool Corporation proposed to inundate 830 acres of the valley, the home of Capel Celyn, a small but thriving rural community, with the intention of forming a reservoir to feed new industrial development on Merseyside. Plaid Cymru, under the leadership of Gwynfor Evans, began a campaign on the issue which in a very short time, awakened the whole of Wales. In September 1956 a rally at Bala was attended by 4,000 people. A defence committee was formed and 125 local authorities, with trade union branches and religious and cultural organisations gave their support, passing resolutions condemning the scheme.

A majority of the Welsh MPs came out against the Bill sponsored by Liverpool Corporation to authorise the scheme—27 of the 36 members voted against and none voted for it. But the majority of English MPs in the House of Commons ensured that the Bill was passed in July 1957. It only took a few minutes, since its promoters and opponents came to an arrangement not to debate it. 'There can be no question that emotions in Wales have been aroused,' said Mr Geoffrey Lawrence, who put Liverpool's case in the House of Lords. 'But Liverpool Corporation have to take the constitution as they find it. There is no separate Welsh government. There is no separate demarcation of Wales from England from the point of view of water supplies.'[60]

The Tryweryn issue caused great strains inside Plaid Cymru. There were calls for direct action when it became clear that the immediate cause would be lost. This was resisted by Gwynfor Evans and his close associate, the late J. E. Jones, then General Secretary of the party. They insisted on a constitutional role for Plaid Cymru. Moreover, the party had doubled its vote in Meirionnydd in the 1955 general election : there were great hopes for the 1959 election. In the event these did not materialise, though throughout Wales Plaid's membership rose significantly and in the election its overall Welsh vote increased substantially (from 0·7 per cent to 3·1 per cent).

Nevertheless, there was no breakthrough and the next three to four years signalled a time of great internal disputes and tension between newcomers and older members, on what the aims of the party should be: should it remain essentially a pressure group on behalf of certain cultural values and 'the Welsh way of life', or should it develop into a modern political party with a professional organisation and economic policies for the whole of Wales; should it retain its commitment to the constitutional path? The key figures in this argument that lasted throughout the 1960s were to move into central leadership positions in the 1970s: Emrys Roberts, spokesman for the party's first group of councillors to control a local authority, Merthyr; Dafydd Wigley, MP for Caernarfon; Dr Phil Williams, Vice-President; Dafydd Elis Thomas, MP for Meirionnydd; Dafydd Williams, General Secretary; Eurfyl ap Gwilym, Chairman. These and others symbolised the transformation of Plaid Cymru during the 1960s, and their domination of the party in the mid-1970s indicated the completeness of the change. But the man who ensured unity throughout the period and indeed, gave the change its greatest boost with his Carmarthen by-election victory of 1966, was Gwynfor Evans, Plaid Cymru's President for more than thirty years.

Writing in the aftermath of the 1970 general election, Emrys Roberts summarised the conflict inherent in Plaid Cymru's approach to the politics of devolution:

> We must face up to the questions: Revolution or Evolution? We should all like the best of both worlds: a revolutionary result achieved by evolutionary means. But it's not on. Now is the time to stop kidding ourselves: to make a choice.
>
> Revolution does not necessarily mean guns and violence. But it does mean at least responsible, direct action outside the ambit of normal, respectable British party politics. It means blocking and stopping any future Tryweryn. It means backing Cymdeithas yr Iaith Gymraeg and their methods. It will alienate some people, inevitably. Its success depends on a polarisation of public opinion—really counting those who are for and those who are against. There is no question of persuasion. It

is a gamble that basically, deep down more people will be for than against.

It could succeed. But it is a gamble. Are we prepared to take that gamble? Are we prepared to make the sacrifices that such a choice would entail? Is Plaid Cymru a red-blooded nationalist movement?

Or is it a political party? Are we to decide that evolution is the better way?

I am not suggesting that such a choice would be a dishonourable one. It may be the only realistic one. But if so, we must be realistic enough to accept, and indeed to work for, an evolutionary development towards the ultimate goal. It is unrealistic for an evolutionary political party to campaign for full self-government. It can and certainly should say that that is the ultimate goal. But it should campaign for the next step in the right direction, in order to take as many people as far along the road with us as possible.

If we adopt this approach, it will be seen that we are not proposing something new and way-out. We are merely pushing an existing development a little further. We already have a Secretary of State and a Welsh Office and a nominated council. Why not an elected council next?— possibly advisory at first, then assuming responsibility for supervising some of the work of the Welsh Office. This could lead to a domestic parliament and then, perhaps, to a pan-Brittanic Confederation.[61]

It is this evolutionary approach that has become the mainstream national basis of Welsh politics. As such it is the foundation on which Welsh politics rests, for it permeates many other institutions and organisations in Wales quite apart from Plaid Cymru. But it is Plaid Cymru, ever one step ahead on the evolutionary road, with a growing, increasingly professional organisation, and with a unifying all-Wales approach to the Welsh economy that has given the momentum to Welsh politics.

The trade union basis

The question of the Welsh economy as an extension of the concept of Welsh politics occupies a pivotal position in the politics of devolution. In 1973 the fulcrum was provided by the creation of the Wales TUC, unquestionably the most important development on the Welsh political scene since the establishment of the Welsh Office in 1964.

The twenty-year debate preceding the decision finally to set up the Wales TUC, and the nature of the arguments involved, parallel the debate and the arguments over the Welsh Assembly itself. Indeed, it could be argued that once the debate over the creation of the Wales TUC had been resolved so, too, had the devolution debate. What is not in doubt is that Wales took a long step down the devolution road with the winning of the Wales TUC. Welsh politics, more than most, are tidal. During the late 1960s the devolution tide was running strong in Wales with a series of Plaid-Cymru-dominated by-elections reflecting an almost tangibly changing mood.[62] But after the 1970 general election the tide and the mood began to recede. So much so that devolutionists inside the Labour Party in Wales began to find it more difficult to hold their ground. Despite the two general elections of 1974 in which Plaid Cymru made its vital breakthrough, first gaining Meirionnydd and Caernarfon and then restoring Carmarthen to the ranks, there was no overall change in the tide for constitutional change in Wales which, if anything, continued on the ebb.

Into this context was injected the Wales TUC, a new dimension that came at a vital moment for the politics of devolution. For the first time in history, Welsh aspirations were to be institutionalised on the broad base of the productive capacity of the people of Wales, giving a previously unknown durability to those aspirations.

The effect was immediate. Devolutionists inside the Labour party, and particularly the Labour government after February 1974, were enormously fortified. It was the Wales TUC that enabled them to weather the intense internal Labour party reaction against devolution, between 1974 and 1976, and ensure that Welsh proposals were alongside those for Scotland when the full-scale parliamentary debate on the devolution Bill opened.

The Wales TUC was born in conflict, between grassroots Welsh trade unionists and the establishment organisation of unionism in Wales. When this establishment had been won, or by-passed, there was a fresh conflict between the new Welsh trade union establishment and the union establishment at the British level. These conflicts again parallel the broader conflict inherent in the creation of a Welsh Assembly. The theme of this book is that this is necessary, indeed creative, conflict since the outcome is institutions with a greater sensitivity to the needs and aspirations of the people of Wales. Certainly this has proved to be so with the Wales TUC.

The idea of a Wales TUC was canvassed many times between 1945 and 1970. The National Executive of the Electrical Trades Union considered, on the initiative of their branch in Pontarddulais, whether to make a move inside the British TUC in 1954 for a Wales TUC.[63] Union leaders in Wales were seriously considering the idea late in 1960, but the problems of financing it were deemed too great.[64] The Amalgamated Union of Foundry Workers came out in favour in 1961, and again in 1964.[65] But the main pressure was building up during this period inside the trades councils and their county federations in Wales. In fact, the first significant step in the creation of the Wales TUC was in 1960 when a South Wales liaison committee of trades councils was created. This proved the focal point for pressure for the Wales TUC.

At this time the establishment union organisation in Wales consisted of a South Wales and a North Wales Regional Advisory Committee to the British TUC, made up of the full-time officers of the individual unions. The trades councils made continued complaints to the British TUC that there was no communication between them and the Regional Advisory Committees. There is no doubt that the Committees were hostile to the idea of a Wales TUC and the fact that pressure for one was mainly originating from the trades councils did not make the Committees over-anxious for a close liaison.

However, the conflict between the trades councils and the Regional Advisory Committees became so marked that in 1966 the British TUC initiated an inquiry. By this time, too, the formation of the Welsh Office and the institution of a Secretary of State for Wales had given strength to the proponents of a Wales TUC. In May 1966 the South Wales miners, in conference, unanimously approved proposals for a Wales TUC, the proposer complaining that the Welsh Regional Advisory Committees of the TUC were unable to make policy decisions.[66]

This pressure spurred the two Welsh Advisory Committees to institute an inquiry into the idea but in December 1966 they announced that the inquiry had been shelved. The main opposition appeared to come from the North Wales Committee. The *Western Mail* quoted its secretary, Tom Jones, Shotton-based leader of the area's Transport and General Workers' Union, as saying: 'Our main objection was that it was impractical to organise as Wales is just not an economic unit. Trade unions and industries in North and South Wales are totally different and have completely different problems.'[67]

In 1967, however, the British TUC directed that the Trades Councils in Wales should be represented on the Regional Advisory Committees. This gave them a new vantage point to press the claim of a Wales TUC. In 1968 the annual conference of the South Wales Federation of Trades Councils gave unanimous approval to the idea. It was suggested that the pit and rail closures, then under way in Wales, might be delayed or avoided if Wales had a TUC to press for more industry to come to Wales and for better planning of the Welsh economy.[68]

The debate had now reached a point to arouse strong opposition to the idea of a Wales TUC from the centre. In June 1968 George Woodcock, then General Secretary to the British TUC was quoted as saying: 'A Welsh TUC would only arise if there was a Welsh government and a Welsh Confederation of Employers.'[69]

Nevertheless, the two Advisory Committees in Wales decided to reinvestigate the issue. A meeting between the Chairman and Secretary of each Committee was held early in August 1968 at Newtown. But the effort again foundered, on a calculation that North and South Wales lacked an identity of economic interest. It was pointed out that most unions administered their Welsh membership in three regions—from the North-West of England, the Midlands, and from South Wales, and that most of the nationalised industries in North Wales were linked with Merseyside.[70]

Underlying this rationalisation was opposition to the idea on the part of the establishment trade union leadership, who felt their record, and to some extent their authority, threatened by the grassroots pressure for a Wales TUC. Their feelings were expressed publicly, later in 1968, at the annual meeting of the South Wales Regional Advisory Committee. Its secretary, Graham Saunders, of the Clerical and Administrative Workers' Union, said, 'In my opinion it is extremely doubtful if we could provide the kind of services that would make a Welsh TUC worthwhile'. At the same meeting Ken Griffin, of the Electrical Trades Union said, 'I don't want this movement to be drawn into any form of nationalism because we have no future in nationalism. The body symbolised in a TUC for Wales is dead and let's bury it.'[71]

But this attitude was rapidly becoming out of touch with the sentiment and the organisation of the trade union movement in Wales. In 1968/9 a highly significant organisational change was undertaken by the Transport and General Workers Union. It replaced its separate North and South Wales structures with a single Wales area organisation. The immediate reason was economic need. The all-Wales structure gave the union in the country a membership of 110,000, a stronger base in terms of financial contributions on which to rest the full-time secretariat.

The effect of this change was to remove at one stroke the foundation of the separate North and South Wales Regional Advisory Committees of the TUC. Along with the change in structure came a change in the Union's leadership in Wales. Tom Jones, of Shotton, became the first all-Wales secretary of the TGWU but he was close to retiring. His deputy and destined successor was George Wright, a young aggressive English union leader brought up on disputes in the car industry of the Midlands. Unlike some of the older Welsh union leaders he had no fears of South Wales dominating North Wales, or vice versa, was uninhibited by expressions of nationalism, and perceived more clearly the opportunities and advantages of harnessing the moral pressure of Wales on behalf of the workforce.

At the same time there was a growing appreciation of the development of Welsh politics amongst rank and file trade union membership. D. Ivor Davies, Chairman of the Glamorgan Trades Council Federation, and also Chairman of the Wales TUC in 1976/7 explained,

> It became clear that the leaders of the old Regional Advisory Committees were not really grappling with the problems of Wales. They wanted to concentrate on the problems of their own unions. But the establishment of the Secretary of State for Wales and the Welsh Office symbolised a developing awareness of nationhood amongst the people. In this situation the trade union movement was at a disadvantage.[72]

But the critical factor that precipitated the creation of the Wales TUC, in 1972/3, was unification of the Transport and General Workers' Union organisation on an all-Wales basis, plus the leadership of the union passing to younger, less inhibited and more dynamic hands. The TGWU in Wales formed an axis with the Welsh Miners' Union, which had long supported a Wales TUC, and early in 1972 they jointly decided to establish a Wales TUC.

This was a unilateral decision made in the face of opposition from the London-based British TUC. During 1972 an organising committee was formed, embracing representatives from a dozen unions in Wales and the Trades Councils, a constitution was drawn up, and an inaugural conference held at Llandrindod in February 1973.

This conference, attended by 250 delegates from throughout Wales, was held in defiance of an instruction issued by leaders of the British TUC, who said that Welsh unionists should wait until the regional structure of the TUC in England and Wales could be considered as a whole. The North Wales Advisory Committee of the TUC supported the conference. But the South Wales Advisory Committee did not and many delegates attended the conference in defiance of the ruling of their own union leadership.

The draft constitution of the new Wales TUC was moved by the Transport Union's Welsh regional Secretary-designate, George Wright: 'I recognise, as an Englishman, that Wales is geographically separated,' he said. 'It has a separate culture, a separate people, and a separate language, and it has special problems. We intend to defend Wales against the economic and social neglect of the last 50 years.'[73] He was supported by Dai Francis, Welsh Secretary of the NUM who became the first Chairman of the Wales TUC and its most inspirational leader in the early years, and Tal Loyd, South Wales regional officer of the Amalgamated Union of Engineering Workers, who chaired the inaugural conference.

There were two especially distinctive features about the constitution of the Wales TUC approved at this conference. One is related to the structure and politics of the Welsh community and the other is worthy of note in relation to the wider trade union environment outside Wales.

The first concerns the relationship between the trade unions and the Labour party: the two wings of the Labour movement which have developed more closely in Wales than perhaps anywhere else in the British Isles. On the platform at the inaugural conference was Jack Brooks, of Cardiff, representing the Executive Committee of the Labour Party in Wales. Written into the draft constitution being considered was provision for the Labour executive to be represented on the Wales TUC's General Council. But objection to the intimacy of this relationship was raised from the floor and the conference voted against the Wales TUC having any formal links with the Labour Party in Wales or any other party. Of course, no such relationship exists at the British TUC level. But this decision, made in the Welsh context, was significant in that it measured the extent to which Welsh politics have altered from their monolithic character of the 1930s to the fluidity of the 1970s.

The other distinctive feature of the Wales TUC's constitution is the position in it of the Trades Councils, a position fundamental to an understanding of the role and influence of the Wales TUC. The Trades Councils make up a third of the Wales TUC's annual conference membership with forty-five delegations from most sizeable towns in Wales, together with the eight County Associations of Trades Councils. But more than this, the Trades Councils have fifteen members on the 45-man Wales TUC General Council—the governing body—and written into the constitution is that the Chairman of the Wales TUC should be elected from one of these fifteen every third year.[74]

This is in sharp contrast to the power structure of the British TUC which is confined solely to mainstream trade union organisations. The Wales TUC's constitution reflects the deep tradition in Welsh politics for community and the importance of democracy. The Trades Council delegations provide a political and social perspective to the Wales TUC's deliberations which, if con-

fined to the union delegations—as with the British TUC—would be
more concerned with purely industrial and economic matters. The
result is to make the Wales TUC more representative of the Welsh
community as a whole.

The influence of the Trades Councils has been most powerful and
effective on devolution. At its second conference in May 1973 the
Wales TUC overwhelmingly passed a resolution calling for the
establishment of a Welsh Assembly with legislative powers. This was
a more radical position than the Labour party's policy which was for
an Assembly with only Executive powers. In terms of practical
politics, over the next few years, the Wales TUC's position served to
make Labour's proposals appear modest. As the *Western Mail*
commented after the Wales TUC's 1976 conference at Llandudno:

> Without the creation of the Wales TUC three years ago it is doubtful
> whether the Government's Welsh Assembly proposals would have got off
> the ground. And without the Wales TUC's persistent and unfaltering
> pressure, it is doubtful whether the Assembly would reach fruition. The
> Wales TUC's stand against a referendum as being an anti-devolution
> tactic, for instance, has put the Secretary of State for Wales, Mr. John
> Morris, in a strong position when he goes to meet his critics at the Welsh
> Labour Party's conference at Swansea in two weeks' time.[75]

But quite apart from its specific support for a strong Welsh
Assembly, the creation of the Wales TUC, as stressed at the opening
of this section, has had a far deeper impact on the politics of devolution. The Wales TUC ensured that Welsh politics also embraced
the Welsh economy and consequently made the devolution
argument more broadly based.

The British TUC, faced with the *fait accompli* of the Wales TUC's
inaugural conference in February 1973, rapidly, if reluctantly,
adjusted to the new situation. A document drawn up in April 1973,
on the British TUC's organisation in Wales, noted that repeated
attempts in the 1950s and 1960s to establish a Wales TUC had
foundered on disunity of economic interest between North and
South Wales. But the document concluded that this disunity had
been overcome in the 1970s because of a growing sense of Welsh
national cohesion. It was because of this that the British TUC
should respond positively to the creation of the Wales TUC:

> It was argued that South Wales was linked economically with the south
> west of England and that North Wales had a closer affinity with West
> Lancashire, Cheshire and Merseyside than with the rest of Wales.
> However, recent events imply that this view has to be modified. The
> resurgence of interest in Welsh nationhood and in Welsh culture which

is reflected in the actions of the Government in treating Wales as a separate entity—particularly by the establishment of a Welsh Office and a Secretary of State for Wales—mean that the case for establishing an all-Wales trade union body is considerably strengthened.[76]

The acceptance of the economic unity of Wales and the idea of a Welsh economy, confirmed by the establishment of the Wales TUC, was a stage-marker in the emergence of Welsh politics. It was also a prerequisite for the politics of devolution.

The Labour party: arbiter between Welsh and British politics[77]

Historically, Wales has exhibited all the characteristics of a one-party state, giving its political loyalty exclusively to one or other of the major political parties. Until 1867 and the electoral revolt of tenant farmers, Wales returned an overwhelming number of Conservative MPs to Westminster. During the last quarter of the nineteenth century a similar Liberal hegemony was established and the political history of Wales in the twentieth century has been concerned with the growing political dominance of the Labour party, culminating in the 1966 general election, in which 32 of the 36 Welsh constituencies returned Labour MPs. But by October 1974 the number of Labour seats had been reduced to 23 and the Labour vote, which had been 60·7 per cent in 1966, was only 49·5 per cent. It was during this period and against this threat to its political domination that the Labour Party in Wales initiated and developed its devolution policy.

Apart from the crude electoral threat which provided the impetus —most notably the series of by-elections in Carmarthen, Rhondda and Caerphilly between 1966 and 1968—a variety of more subtle factors conditioned the Labour Party in Wales's approach during this period. These largely consisted of internal changes within the Labour movement. The most important, the pressures leading up to and the creation of the Wales TUC, have already been discussed. A parallel development was the growing influence of the Welsh Council of Labour, the formal organisational structure of the Labour Party in Wales; and the changing character of the Welsh Parliamentary Labour Party.

Any party which can win up to 60 per cent of the vote must enjoy a wide range of support. Labour has always had a substantial following in areas outside the industrial south-east and north-east of Wales. In the eyes of some Welshmen it inherited the mantle of radicalism from the Liberal party; for others it was regarded as the anti-English party if only because its electoral enemy, the Conservatives, were so obviously the 'English' party. For such reasons[78] Labour has won many constituencies which in England (and even Scotland) would have been expected to return Conservatives. Anglesey, Conwy, Caernarfon (despite its slate-quarrying tradition), Meirionnydd, Ceredigion, Carmarthen, Brecon and Radnor, Monmouth and Pembroke are all constituencies which, in a context other than Wales, the Labour party should never expect to win.

Taken together they represent the most agricultural and Welsh-speaking parts of Wales. Sometimes the Labour breakthrough was caused by the anti-Labour vote being split (as when Cledwyn Hughes won Anglesey in 1950) or by Labour presenting itself in a Liberal guise (as in Carmarthen in 1957 when the magic of her name enabled Megan Lloyd George to attract many non-socialists to the Labour fold).

Because of this advance into erstwhile Liberal strongholds during the 1940s and 1950s, the Labour Party in Wales was able by the early 1960s to present itself as the national party of Wales, sympathetic not only to the steel workers of Ebbw Vale and the miners of Caerphilly, but also to the hill farmers of Meirionnydd and the dairymen of Anglesey. The grievances of Welsh speakers were of concern to the Labour party as well as the decline of the coal and steel industry.

This capacity to represent all sectors of the Welsh community was reflected by the 1966 intake of Welsh Labour MPs, eleven of whom were Welsh speakers. Labour MPs from the western seaboard (representing 'Welsh Wales') were responsible for continually reminding the Labour Party in Wales of its responsibilities to its non-industrial supporters and for pressing the claims of Welsh nationhood. Thus, in the 1950s, Cledwyn Hughes (Anglesey), Goronwy Roberts (Caernarfon), Tudor Watkins (Brecon and Radnor), T. W. Jones (Meirionnydd) and S. O. Davies (Merthyr Tydfil) were the only Welsh Labour MPs to support the Parliament for Wales campaign—James Griffiths (Llanelli) and James Callaghan (Cardiff South) for instance, opposed the Parliament for Wales Bill presented to the House of Commons by S. O. Davies (Merthyr) in March 1955. But it was the pressure sustained by the Welsh-oriented Labour MPs that prepared the ground for the acceptance by the Labour party of the establishment of a Welsh Office and a Secretary of State for Wales.

But after the establishment of the Welsh Office, Labour pressure on behalf of Welsh national aspirations, inside Parliament, fell away dramatically. The explanation is that during the decade 1964 to

1974 the number and character of the Welsh Parliamentary Labour Party underwent a fundamental change. After the 1966 general election Labour held all the nine Welsh seats referred to above as representing the most agricultural and Welsh-speaking part of Wales—seats that elsewhere in Britain would have been more likely the territory of the Conservative party. By 1974 Labour had lost control of all but two of these seats, Anglesey, and Brecon and Radnor, and these had become marginal, in a four-party situation.

Moreover, in Labour's southern Wales stronghold the character of its representation altered radically. Between 1964 and 1974 the Welsh Parliamentary Labour group's remaining eight miners' MPs all retired and were replaced by young, second-generation socialists whose background was more likely to be university, and the Bar than the local Miners' Lodge. They were more middle-class. Lecturers and lawyers outnumbered miners and metal-workers and they were more likely to base their families in prosperous parts of London than their constituencies.

In successive elections the loss of crucial seats thwarted attempts to achieve a consensus on devolution inside the Welsh Parliamentary Labour Party. In 1970 the loss of pro-devolutionist Ednyfed Hudson Davies in Conwy was balanced by Gwynoro Jones winning back Carmarthen from Plaid Cymru. But during the next four years the ranks of the supporters of devolution were drastically thinned: S. O. Davies (Merthyr), Elystan Morgan (Ceredigion), Wil Edwards (Meirionnydd), Goronwy Roberts (Caernarfon) and Gwynoro Jones (Carmarthen) all lost their seats and Jim Griffiths (Llanelli), the elder statesman of the party, who might have held a consensus by force of personality alone, retired from the political scene. In short, the Parliamentary Labour Party ceased to be a national party of the whole of Wales. Consequently, by the summer of 1974, when Labour finally began to grasp the devolution nettle, the Welsh Parliamentary party was suddenly divided. In late 1973 a series of group meetings had resulted in it achieving a united consensus on a directly elected executive Assembly for Wales and it was on this platform that it fought the February 1974 general election. But by the summer of 1974 a small group of Welsh Labour MPs (led by Neil Kinnock, a young graduate from University College of Wales, Cardiff, who was first elected to Bedwellty in 1970), began to campaign actively against devolution. Their tactics did not include outright opposition at this stage. Instead they demanded a referendum.

But if the character of the Welsh Parliamentary Labour group altered in the decade 1964 to 1974, becoming less sympathetic to

Welsh national aspirations, the character of the Labour party organisation in Wales changed in the reverse direction. Between 1966 and 1976 the Welsh Council of Labour emerged as an influential and authoritative force.[79] Together with the Wales TUC it provided the foundation on which the Labour government constructed its devolution policy in the mid-1970s.

Originally established as the South Wales Council of Labour in 1937, to counteract communist influence in the mining valleys, its responsibilities were extended shortly before the Second World War to include the whole of Wales. Like other regional councils of the Labour party, its concern was (and to a large extent still is) organisation, the checking of candidate credentials, ensuring proper procedures are followed, co-ordinating and communicating with constituency parties, women's sections and so on. But in 1965 the Council's Secretary, Cliff Prothero, retired and was replaced by Emrys Jones, a party organisation man who had served his apprenticeship in the English regions. Jones brought a new emphasis to the Welsh Council, which reflected his belief that the Labour Party in Wales should be concerned with policy as well as organisation.

Many of his Executive needed no prompting in this direction, having recently been involved in the campaign for a Secretary of State for Wales. In May 1966 the annual conference of the Labour Party in Wales endorsed a demand, voiced the previous year by the Executive, for a directly elected Welsh Council as being the top tier of a reformed local government system. This was two months before Plaid Cymru's by-election victory at Carmarthen, indicating that the shift in Welsh opinion, signified by Plaid's success, was also reflected within the Labour Party in Wales.

But there is no doubt that the nationalist upsurge provided an edge for those inside the Labour organisation in Wales who were pressing for new policy initiatives. The new Secretary, Emrys Jones, established a series of study groups to investigate different aspects of Welsh life: bilingualism, broadcasting in Wales, the decline of traditional industries, and rural depopulation. In February 1969 the most important study group was established to prepare evidence for the Commission on the Constitution (the conflicts aroused by this group's activities will be probed in the following two chapters). The study-group members were drawn from all sections of the party— academics, local councillors, trade unionists, and people with professional expertise, for example, solicitors and local government officers. Although the terms of reference of the groups were laid down by the Executive, the nomination of individual members was the responsibility of Emrys Jones and it was he who chaired the first meeting of each group, as well as exercising a guiding influence. In the late 1960s and early 1970s a wide range of policy discussion documents were produced by the Labour Party in Wales central office, whose establishment at Cardiff was increased by a secretary/ typist and a publicity and research officer. Finance for the additional staff came from Transport House in London, concerned to win back Carmarthen (the new publicity officer was Gwynoro Jones, the constituency's prospective Parliamentary candidate) and to sort out the political mess in Desmond Donelly's Pembroke constituency. However, the new resources gave the Cardiff office more room to manoeuvre, room which it used to great effect when it came to preparing evidence for the Commission on the Constitution.

Further evidence of the party's growing self-confidence was the initiative, in the summer of 1970, to run a bilingual monthly news-paper—*Wales Radical Cymru*—and to grant it editorial independence. Furthermore, the party stood by the paper when it provoked the anger of several Welsh Labour MPs for being too radical on devolution and insufficiently respectful of George Thomas, then Shadow Secretary of State.[80]

Whereas the Cardiff office had previously only prepared Welsh language translations of the central Labour party manifestos, in 1974 the office published its own programme in both English and Welsh, highlighting concerns particularly relevant to Wales. Prominent amongst these was a commitment, in the February 1974 Welsh manifesto, to establish a directly elected Welsh Assembly—a pledge that went unmentioned in the British manifesto.

Final confirmation of the increased status and authority of the Labour Party in Wales, as distinct from the British Labour party, is provided by its annual conference. In the decade from 1966 to 1976 attendance at the conference steadily increased, accompanied by a marked improvement in the quality of debates. This development was assisted by the emergence of specifically Welsh political issues, by the recognition by the trade union movement that the conference provided a valuable additional forum, and by improved and extended coverage from increasingly Welsh-oriented newspapers and television.

A culmination of this last development was the annual conference at Swansea in May 1976, when all the Welsh Labour MPs were present, an unprecedented occurrence. For some, mainly the anti-devolutionist MPs, it was their first conference, and others had not attended for more than fifteen years—a point that was frequently and vehemently raised. The critical debate of this conference was devolution and the issue of a devolution referendum. In the face of strident opposition to the government's policy by a number of MPs, notably Leo Abse (Pontypool), Neil Kinnock (Bedwellty) and Donald Anderson (Swansea East), the conference overwhelmingly backed the government's proposed Assembly and rejected a referendum.[81]

The position of the anti-devolution MPs at the conference was that the proposed Assembly should be opposed since, they alleged, it was merely appeasement to nationalist pressure, confined to Welsh-speaking Wales. But this illusion had been shattered just a week before by the Welsh district council results. The Labour party was decimated, losing eleven of the nineteen districts they had previously controlled, including such strongholds as Swansea, Cardiff, Newport, Afan, Merthyr, Wrexham, Islwyn, and Rhymney. There were a variety of factors influencing the results: charges of corruption and nepotism in Swansea and Afan, for example, as well as natural public reaction against the governing party during a period of rapid inflation and rising rates, which led to victories by Conservative ratepayers and tenants' associations. But the most ominous results for Labour were the losses of Merthyr, where Plaid Cymru won control, and Rhymney, where Plaid Cymru emerged as the largest single party.

The delegates at Labour's conference a week later sensed that survival lay in adjusting to the new situation by reaffirming their devolution commitment, rather than following the lead of some of the MPs and reacting by reneging on the policy.

The county council elections the following year, in May 1977, supported this judgment. Superficially the results were not as dramatic as those in 1976. But in key areas the election demonstrated a significant shift in voting patterns that was not revealed in the simple statistics of gains and losses. The Conservatives captured control of South Glamorgan, moving from 36 to 64 seats, but elsewhere Labour held on to power. It lost an overall majority in Gwent but formed an administration with the support of two new Plaid Cymru councillors against the Conservatives. In Mid and West Glamorgan its majority was significantly reduced, but it still retained control by a comfortable margin. Clwyd in north-eastern Wales shifted towards the Conservatives, though the county remained in no overall control. Independents held sway in Dyfed, Gwynedd and Powys. The line-up of councillors in Wales as a whole is given in table 3.3.

Table 3.3 Nominations and results for the 1977 county council
elections in Wales (1973 figures in brackets)

	Labour	Conserv-ative	Plaid Cymru	Liberal	Independ-ent	Com-munist	Rate-payer
Nominated	363 (418)	250 (150)	233 (99)	60 (59)	301 (349)	17 (24)	96 (23)
Elected	194 (274)	142 (71)	37 (21)	12 (20)	128 (185)	2 (2)	20 (4)

(*Source: Western Mail.*)

The immediate impression from these figures is of a slump in
Labour's fortunes, impressive gains by the Conservatives, and a
small gain by Plaid Cymru. But a closer analysis of the voting
indicates support for Plaid Cymru that must be deeply worrying for
Labour (the Conservative gains were overwhelmingly in their
traditional areas on the periphery of Wales—South Glamorgan and
the coastal belts of Gwent and Clwyd). In Dyfed and Gwynedd, for
instance, Plaid Cymru won the majority of votes given to political
parties (see table 3.4).

Table 3.4   Total votes cast for the political parties in Gwynedd and Dyfed
in the 1977 county council elections in Wales. (Note: Independents not
included.)

Gwynedd		Dyfed	
Plaid Cymru	13,088	Plaid Cymru	21,037
Tory	8,897	Labour	18,076
Labour	6,593	Liberal	6,198
Liberal	1,341		

But more worrying for Labour was evidence of an expanding Plaid
Cymru presence in a wide valley belt stretching from Llanelli east-
wards into Gwent. Plaid won three seats from Labour in the Llanelli
constituency and two in the Neath constituency. But Plaid's
strongest showing was in Mid Glamorgan and neighbouring areas of
Gwent. Here the party's average vote for each ward fought was 1,000
compared with Labour's average of 1,300. The Plaid Cymru threat
to Labour in this area, the heartland of Welsh politics, can be
illustrated by totalling the votes cast on a constituency basis as in
table 3.5.

Table 3.5 Votes cast for the political parties in key Valley constituencies in the 1977 county council elections in Wales.

Parties	Votes	%
Merthyr Tydfil		
Labour	10,900	48.5
Plaid Cymru	9,300	40.5
Conservative	900	4.0
Liberal	700	3.3
Communist	600	2.5
Aberdare		
Labour	11,300	48.6
Plaid Cymru	10,100	43.3
Independents } Protectionists	3,000	8.0
Rhondda		
Labour	16,200	46.2
Plaid Cymru	8,300	23.8
Independent	4,800	14.4
Conservative	3,400	9.4
Communist	2,200	6.2

Parties	Votes	%
Pontypridd		
Labour	8,800	31.5
Plaid Cymru	5,100	18.3
Conservative	5,100	18.3
Independent	4,700	17.6
Liberal	2,900	10.2
Caerphilly		
Labour	13,600	41.4
Plaid Cymru	11,300	34.4
Conservative	4,300	13.0
Independent } Ratepayer	3,600	11.2
Bedwellty (Gwent)		
Labour	12,582	46.7
Plaid Cymru	5,583	20.7
Liberal	2,088	7.8
Conservative	492	1.8
Others	6,169	22.9

Thus, as the 1970s draw to a close Labour faces a major threat in its most traditionally loyal Welsh heartlands. Plaid Cymru leaders are able to claim that by the 1980s it is their party that will have taken over the role of combating the Tories in Wales.

·In the emergence of Welsh politics since 1945 the role of the Labour party has been to reconcile Welsh aspirations to the reality of the British context within which they are pressed. The essential argument in this process has been how far to lean in which direction. The Welsh Parliamentary Labour Party has leaned towards the British position while the grassroots party in Wales has leaned towards the Welsh position. The politics of devolution, from the Labour point of view, are an attempt to reconcile this conflict. The stakes are high. If Labour misjudges the point of reconciliation it is in danger of being by-passed in the argument. It was significant that at the Labour Party in Wales's 1977 annual conference at Llandudno there was an atmosphere of drift. Conference again over-whelmingly backed the government's devolution policy and also rejected a referendum despite, by now, a government declaration in favour. But the failure of the Scotland and Wales devolution Bill in the House of Commons had rendered the pro-devolution majority of delegates frustrated, angry and impotent.

Wales in Europe

At the end of the last chapter reference was made to the analogy of a colonial relationship between Wales and England. This followed an examination of economic development in the two countries. Wales was seen as a producer of labour, raw materials and the products of the heavy end of industry, while at the same time providing a market for generally more sophisticated English goods. As discussed at the opening of this chapter, Hechter has advanced the theory of 'internal colonialism' to describe the relationship.[82] Hechter's exhaustive study of the Celtic fringe of Britain and its relationship with the English 'core' provided some valuable insights. But, as Tom Nairn has pointed out, it suffers from defining the relationship of Scotland and Wales with England in the same terms.[83]

Nairn's critique is particularly valuable in that it highlights the European dimension of the problem and the pivotal position that Wales occupies in the future development of European politics. Nairn identifies two types of nationalist dilemma in contemporary Western Europe, exemplified in Britain by Wales on the one hand, and Scotland on the other:

The two types of nationalist dilemma in Western Europe are, respectively: under-developed or pillaged regions that have finally begun to
react against this treatment; and quite highly-developed epicentres of
industrialisation, middle-class cultures who are for one reason or
another out of phase with the ruling nation-state, and want separate
development to get ahead faster.[84]

Hechter's thesis concentrates on the former perspective and
attempts to force Scotland as well as Wales into its mould. The
reality is that Scotland is an example of an economically over-
developed area while Wales is a curious amalgam of over- and
under-development, thereby occupying a pivotal position in
European politics.

Nairn lists Corsica, Occitania, Brittany, Galicia, Friesland and
the Highland Region of Scotland as typically 'under-developed'
areas. They tend to be peasant communities that were exploited as
sources of manpower, food and raw materials during the first
hundred and fifty years of the industrial revolution. Today they have
often become tourist centres, subject to summer-holiday development: 'In all these cases uneven development has simply thrust back
regions and peoples. It has induced depopulation, cultural impover-
ishment, a psychology of powerlessness and dependency, and fostered
particularly fragmented or distorted kinds of economic growth.'[35]

There are fewer areas which are distinctive because of their
relative 'over-development'. Nairn lists four such zones in Western
Europe: Catalonia and the Basque Country (Euzkadi) in southern
Europe, and Protestant Ulster and Scotland in northern Europe. In
Spain the industrial revolution took place in the periphery of the
state, and in countries with strongly marked identities. As a consequence strong bourgeois societies developed around Bilbao and
Barcelona and these have constituted a permanent threat to the
relatively backward and parasitic state centred on Madrid. In
Ireland the industrial revolution also occurred mainly in an ethnic
periphery, creating the large Protestant 'city-state' of Belfast. Here,
too, uneven development worked to separate the successful middle-
class enclave from the more backward land-mass around it.
Scotland is another example of such uneven development, but, as
Nairn observes, it has only recently entered the category:

Although an old industrial society like Catalonia, with its own cities and
native capitalist class, it previously developed at approximately the same
rate and with the same cadences as the larger society it was linked to,
industrial England. Only with the dramatic decline of the latter, and the
sudden differential impetus given to the Scottish middle class by North
Sea oil production, has a crisis of uneven development arisen. Although

recent, this fissure is growing extremely rapidly, and creating a political situation basically similar to the others. Even more clearly, the outlook of the previously rather quiescent Scottish bourgeoisie is one of restive impatience with English 'backwardness', London muddle, economic incompetence, state parasitism, and so forth.[86]

Wales, as Nairn notes, does not fit neatly into either of these categories of under-development or over-development. Instead, it shares features of both. It has experienced depopulation, cultural oppression, fragmentary and distorted economic development—features shared by many other areas in Western Europe like Brittany, Corsica and Galicia listed above. But unlike these areas Wales has also experienced massive industrialisation, albeit directed overwhelmingly from outside. In contrast to Scotland Wales does not have a comparatively recent history of statehood and surviving institutions, like, for instance, Scotland's separate legal system. But unlike other under-developed areas in Western Europe Wales does have, as described earlier in this chapter, a whole range of administrative institutions built up on the foundation of the nineteenth century Cymru Fydd movement and extended in response to twentieth century nationalism, most notably, the Welsh Office.

Because Wales is suspended between what Nairn terms 'the standard alternatives of European neo-nationalism', Welsh politics are unusually divided, particularly between Welsh speakers and the Anglo-Welsh, between North and South industrial and rural communities, and, within the national movement, between Adfer—who insist on linguistic purity—and those who advocate bilingualism. But because of this middle position and the resulting conflicts, Nairn, a Scotsman, observes that what happens in Wales will be of central importance to the development of European politics, of more importance even than what happens in Scotland:

> All Western Europe's deprived and re-awakened peoples want and need stronger economic development, for example. Given the condition they start from, such development is bound to be in large measure from outside, whether by multinationals or by investment and aid from other countries. Wales has already gone through this, in the most violent and chaotic fashion: such de-centred, invasive industrialisation created the whole problem of modern nationalism in Wales. . . . If Welsh nationalism can arrive at a viable political integration of its contending elements, then many others can hope to. If the ideal, 'cultural' nation can be reconciled with the industrial one here, then the formula may be eventually copiable elsewhere.[87]

Thus the emergence of Welsh politics is not only relevant in terms of its impact upon British economic and constitutional development; it has a wider European reference as well. As has already been stated, Welsh politics have always been primarily concerned with obtaining a distinctive and secure context in which the peculiar conflicts and aspirations of Welsh life can be resolved. To this extent Welsh politics are the politics of devolution. In the 1970s a specific agenda for devolution has been provided. It is to this that we now turn.

Part II Making Devolution Work

Thus far the book has been concerned with the democratic, economic, and political pressures that have pushed devolution into the forefront of British politics. The next three chapters will be concerned with arguments about putting devolution into practice: the constitutional, financial and economic problems involved in establishing an Assembly for Wales.

The practical issues of making devolution work were thrown back into the melting pot at the end of February 1977 when the Labour government's attempt to pass a guillotine motion to timetable debate of its devolution Bill in the House of Commons failed. This failure was to a great extent the result of opposition of English MPs to the whole principle of devolution. Although the devolution Bill won its Second Reading vote by a comfortable margin in December 1976—a vote usually taken to be a vote for the principle of a measure —the guillotine motion provided an easier opportunity for Labour MPs to rebel against their government's policy. The guillotine motion was lost, by 29 votes, because 22 Labour MPs voted against the guillotine and 18 others abstained. That this was an English veto was demonstrated in that two-thirds of Welsh and Scottish MPs supported the timetable motion that would have ensured passage of the Bill.[1]

The crucial opposition which stalled the devolution Bill thus came from English Labour MPs who saw the advantages over their own areas elected Assemblies would give Scotland and Wales. This suggests that it was not any inherent defect in the proposals themselves that provoked their opposition: it would have occurred whatever the proposals that were brought before Parliament. Nevertheless, the obvious points of conflict, inconsistencies and complexity of the devolution Bill that was offered allowed opponents to declare themselves in favour of the *principle* of devolution but to say at the same time that this particular Bill was a bad one and so should be opposed. When pressed on what would be a good Bill the response was usually to argue for a measure federal in character, which ensured a clear and symmetrical division of functions and responsibilities.

This approach stems from the view that power and sovereignty reside in one place, usually at the top of society, and consequently are capable of being neatly parcelled out and delegated. But, as was argued in the Introduction, the politics of devolution are an assertion that this is not the case. Instead, they insist that sovereignty is a diffuse quality, a question of balance that shifts, and that if it is to be found anywhere it resides morally at the bottom of society with the community.

The devolution Bill presented to Parliament by the Labour government in December 1976 was more in line with this latter view than with the former. It had the advantage of responding in a complex but flexible way to a situation that was both of these things. Inherent in the Bill was conflict, as will be demonstrated in the following three chapters. But politics are about conflict. Devolution is about bringing conflicts that already exist—for example, arguments about resource allocation and distribution—into the open, into the forum of an Assembly chamber, where they would have greater prospect of democratic and creative resolution than behind the closed doors of secretive central Government.

The politics of devolution are tidal. But experience has shown that each wave reaches further up the shore.

It will be suggested in the following chapter that devolution will tend to drift toward federalism and, eventually, in a confederal direction. But the problem of finance is the decisive devolution issue. As the first Chairman of the Commission on the Constitution, the late Lord Crowther, remarked to a Labour party representative during an evidence session in Wales: 'Does not the whole history of administration show that he who pays the piper calls the tune?'[2] It will be argued, in chapter 5, that the failure of the Labour government's Scotland and Wales devolution Bill to grant taxation powers to the Assemblies, and to rely instead on central-government block-grant funding, was its greatest weakness.

The renewed proposals for separate Welsh and Scottish Bills brought forward in July 1977 following the collapse of the Scotland and Wales Bill the previous February merely repeated the error. The separation of tax raising from tax spending means that the Assemblies would face no financial discipline from their electorates. In these circumstances the Assemblies' main economic policy would be simply to increase the size of their block grants, which would always be regarded as inadequate. Moreover, the absence of significant taxation powers would deprive them of an important mechanism for influencing the development of the. Welsh and Scottish economies and, consequently, one of the major potential gains to be had from devolution would be lost.

These are examples of some of the arguments involved in making devolution work that will be explored in the following three chapters. But ultimately the politics of devolution are not about such arguments, as the debates in the House of Commons on the Labour government's Scotland and Wales Bill amply demonstrated. The future of devolution depends on the will of the Welsh and Scottish people. Though the arguments about the mechanics of devolution are important they are predicated by the will of the people. This perhaps is the main message of the politics of devolution. Sovereignty lies not with Parliament, but with the people, and in this matter with the communities in Wales and Scotland.

Chapter 4

Framing a Constitution

'The good or bad fortune of a nation depends on three factors: its Constitution, the way the Constitution is made to work, and the respect it inspires.'
George Bidault.

In drawing up its devolution proposals after the October 1974 general election the Labour government adopted two widely differing approaches to Wales and Scotland. This was made clear in a paper produced by the Cabinet Office Constitution Unit at an early stage of interdepartmental discussions on the preparation of the November 1975 devolution White Paper. The following quotations are taken from a short introduction to a series of longer papers discussing problems of devolving industry and employment powers, the implications of Common Market membership and most of the key devolution issues.[1] The introductory paper, written towards the end of 1974 or early in 1975 described the proposals for Scotland in the following terms:

> For Scotland, the picture emerging is of a system which, despite formal subordination to Westminster, would in practice, over a wide range of subjects, have characteristics and powers much like those of a full government. In general, the 'subject' powers devolved would cover not merely freedom to operate existing institutions and methods but also to recast or abolish them. . . . There would be a fully fledged legislative and executive capacity, modelled in general fairly closely on the Westminster pattern and possessing most of the customary attributes of a Government.

This description of the Scottish Assembly's status contrasted sharply with the anticipated powers for Wales:

> For Wales, the picture is of a system devolving wide executive powers but within a constitutional framework much more akin to a major regional authority, and in much more evident and practical subordination to Westminster. The combination of powers and structure proposed is untried and in some ways complex. . . . Wales would have an administration analogous to that of a local authority in that the Assembly would itself be the Executive and would work via Committees; but the scale and scope of powers, including subordinate legislation, would go far beyond the local authority pattern. (This combination of method and powers is novel).

Legislative power made the Scottish Assembly proposals akin to Westminster parliamentary government, while executive power meant the proposed Welsh Assembly was nearer regional government along the local authority pattern. Note the language used in describing the Welsh system: the structure proposed is said to be 'untried and in some ways complex' and also 'novel'. It is evident that devising the Executive proposals for Wales proved more difficult than the Scottish legislative proposals. For Scotland the division of powers between Westminster and Edinburgh was more straightforward.

The following section will reveal that the initial decision to devolve only executive powers to the Welsh Assembly was the result of internal Labour party manoeuvres during 1974. They left the Labour government with an awkward legacy in Wales; both politically, because of the unfavourable contrast with Scotland, and practically, because of the difficulty of devising a hybrid constitutional scheme.

Labour party manoeuvres

The issue of whether an elected Welsh Council or Assembly[2] should have legislative powers was first brought to a head inside the Labour Party in Wales during the preparation of its evidence for the Commission on the Constitution. In 1969 a party research group pressed for legislative powers in the following fields: housing, roads, health, education, local government, regional planning, police and fire services, environmental services, tourism, cultural and countryside amenities, and forestry. These were described as 'powers which presently reside in the Welsh Office and the Welsh departments of certain other ministries'. The main argument for allowing the Assembly legislative power was as follows:

> Wherever possible responsibility for the function of government should be seen clearly to reside at a specific level. This would appear to be intrinsic to the democratic principle of accountability. Ambiguity and confusion might well arise if responsibility were to be divided between Parliament and the Assembly. Indeed, confusion of this sort already exists as regards public knowledge of local authority services.[3]

The paper qualified this by advocating that in some areas powers should be shared by Westminster and the Assembly 'in the general interests of good government and the maintenance of common standards throughout the United Kingdom'. Thus for economic planning, industrial development, agriculture and fisheries, it anticipated that a Joint Committee would establish criteria for Assembly Policy. The paper concluded:

> The logic of these proposals indicates that the Welsh Office would become the nucleus of a Welsh Civil Service which would be accountable to the Assembly. It is further anticipated that a structural re-organisation of the Welsh Office would be necessary so that the various powers and functions of the Assembly might be properly administered.
>
> Differences between Parliament and the Assembly might arise as regards policy or as the result of a disputed interpretation of the proposed Government of Wales Act. In the former instance, the appropriate arbitrative machinery would lie in the proposed Joint Committee or in the informal negotiation at department or ministerial levels. Where differences were related to interpretations of the Act it is proposed that the Judicial Committee of the Privy Council be designated as the appropriate body to determine such differences.[4]

These proposals provoked a storm of controversy between the Labour Party in Wales and the Labour party centrally which was keeping a watchful eye on the preparation of evidence for the Commission on the Constitution. The proposals for giving the Welsh Assembly legislative power were only one aspect of the package that was questioned in its entirety by London—the other key element was taxation powers for the Assembly, explored in the following chapter. Amid a flurry of train journeys between the two capitals the main issue became one of whether the Labour party in London, which included the then Secretary of State for Wales, George Thomas, would accept the principle of a *directly* elected Assembly. The possibility of Labour pressing for an *indirectly* elected Assembly, with its membership drawn from local government councillors, was canvassed by London.

This was unacceptable to the Labour Party in Wales, and eventually its Secretary, Emrys Jones, struck a compromise. In return for Labour committing itself to a *directly* elected Assembly his people would drop all notions of legislative powers for the Assembly (and, indeed, tax-raising powers).

The then Assistant General Secretary of the British Labour party, Gwyn Morgan, was called in to draft a compromise paper which would satisfy both the Cardiff and London ends of the party. It was Morgan's draft that finally emerged as the Labour Party in Wales's evidence to the Commission on the Constitution. On the legislative issue it stated: 'We anticipate that the Assembly would work within the legislative decisions of the House of Commons. Thus it would in no way be akin to a legislature.'[5]

At this point in 1970, the debate over legislative powers for the

Assembly would probably have been resolved inside the Labour
Party in Wales, had it not been for the creation of the Wales TUC.
At its May 1973 conference and again in April 1974 the Wales TUC
. called unanimously for a Welsh Assembly with legislative powers capable
of dealing effectively with industrial, economic and social problems.
At the 1974 conference a Mid Glamorgan Trades Council delegate,
Les Rees, said unless a Welsh Assembly had power to legislate 'we
shall be castrated from the start'.[6]

This initiative had an immediate impact on the Labour Party in
Wales Executive Committee. Later in the same month the Executive
put out a statement declaring that the Assembly should have a legislative role sufficient to enable it to influence the drafting of Parliamentary bills: 'A Welsh Assembly must, as part of a new procedure,
have the opportunity to consider proposed legislation and have the
means to influence the drafting of bills to take into account matters
of importance to Wales.'[7] The statement continued that the
Assembly should have a structure designed to enable it to undertake increasing powers. Central government should legislate
broadly, leaving the maximum possible area of discretion for
decision-making to the Assembly:

> This is felt to be necessary in the interests of democracy, of participation
> in government, and of efficiency. . . . Not to give an elected Welsh
> Assembly these powers of discretion and decision-making . . . would
> destroy its very purpose.[8]

The role of the Wales TUC in maintaining pressure for devolution
during this period was crucial. It lent an edge to the debate inside
the Labour movement and ensured that the question at issue was
always whether more should be devolved rather than less. After its
conference in April 1974 and the Labour party response outlined
above, the issue was taken to the Labour Party in Wales's annual
conference at Swansea in May. Here there was a clash between trade
union delegates and mainstream Labour politicians. One motion
from the South Wales Union of Mineworkers called for an Assembly
with full legislative powers to be set up without delay. But another,
from the Swansea Labour Association, supported an Assembly with
executive powers only.[9]

Though the conference was divided, had the question been put to
the test, the big union delegations would have demanded a card vote
—an unprecedented move—and on that basis won the day for a
legislative Welsh Assembly.[10] But instead the Conference platform
used the excuse of an imminent government consultative paper on
devolution[11] to avoid a confrontation on the legislative versus execut-

ive issue. It was a ruse, since it was known that the consultative paper would not aid debate on the matter but merely summarise the possible devolution schemes laid down by the Commission on the Constitution, and ask for comments.

But the ruse worked. Its object, to gain time for a compromise to be reached on the issue, between the Labour Party in Wales and the Wales TUC, was successful. The Labour party persuaded the TUC that if the devolution sights were set too high there was a danger of nothing being won. A compromise was achieved on the basis of extending the economic horizons of devolution: a crucial phase of the development of Labour's devolution policy, since it laid down the foundation on which the Welsh Development Agency could be erected the following year. Nevertheless, at the time the main object was a reconciliation between the political and industrial wings of the Welsh Labour movement. An agreed paper was drawn up avoiding the legislative powers issue but advocating broader economic powers, particularly power for the Assembly to control the operation of the nationalised industries in Wales. The Labour party also accepted the Wales TUC line that the Assembly should have a hundred members (instead of between seventy and eighty) and that it should be served by its own independent civil service. A compromise paper *Devolution and Democracy*[12] was approved overwhelmingly by the special Labour Party in Wales conference called to consider it in July 1974.

But, on the same day, the Executive Committee of the Labour Party in Scotland came out strongly against the creation of a Scottish Assembly. 'Constitutional tinkering does not make a meaningful contribution towards achieving our Socialist objectives,' declared the Scottish Executive. This was the very development that the Labour Executive in Wales feared. They had favoured devolution consistently since 1965 but were aware of the hostility of the Labour Party in Scotland to the policy. Indeed, the Welsh Executive had resisted pressing for full legislative powers not only because of the deal struck with Transport House in London but also to make it easier for the Scottish Executive to fall in line with devolution.

There followed a series of events which completely out-manoeuvred the Labour Party in Wales. The context was that this period— July, August and September 1974—was mid-way between two general elections and the Labour party centrally knew that the next one was only weeks away. When Labour's leaders in London heard of the Scottish Executive's decision on devolution they were appalled. They believed it exposed their flank in Scotland to the Scottish National Party which had already captured seven seats in

the February 1974 general election. A confidential report which was
later 'leaked' to the press had told them that party organisers felt
thirteen 'safe' Labour seats in Scotland were vulnerable to the
Scottish National Party.[13] With the Labour government already in a
minority, such losses could prove fatal in the forthcoming election.

Swift instructions were sent out from London to the Labour Party
in Scotland to shore up the gap and regain a defensible position on
devolution. Labour's Scottish leaders called a special conference for
August. And here came the rub for the Labour Party in Wales. The
special Scottish Labour conference which ensued did not just back
the previously established Labour line. It went further and called for
full legislative powers for the Scottish Assembly.

This series of events was the source of the Government's policy of a
legislative Assembly for Scotland but only an executive Assembly for
Wales: the Scots had asked for legislative powers while the Welsh,
apparently, only wanted executive powers. The reaction of the
Welsh executive after it first heard of this discrepancy has been
chronicled by Ann Clwyd, the *Guardian*'s correspondent in Wales
but also a Labour parliamentary candidate in 1974. Referring to a
meeting of Welsh, Scottish and English Labour party devolution
policy-makers in mid-August 1974 when the separate policy for
Wales and Scotland was revealed, she wrote:

> At the meeting representatives of the Welsh Labour Party were horrified
> when they heard the draft proposals. One recalls nearly falling off his
> chair since up to that time the Scots on the working party had appeared
> to be totally opposed to any sort of devolution. But this time there were
> new and younger Scots present and they were clearly anxious to pocket
> as much as they could get.
> When the Welsh protested that it would be politically impossible to
> sell unless Scotland and Wales were treated the same there was some
> surprise at their ingratitude. Surely they had got exactly what they had
> asked for, pointed out Ted Short (then Leader of the House and respons-
> ible for devolution). The working party was merely following the resol-
> utions of the two conferences in Wales and Scotland.[14]

Early in September 1974 this position was rationalised in a pre-
general election statement put out by Transport House in London.
The statement stressed the similarity between the needs of Wales
and Scotland but said that because of legal and historical differences
Scotland alone should be given a legislative Assembly:

> In matters of fundamental constitutional practice, reasonable men do
> not lightly break with the traditions of the past. They are, after all, part
> of our heritage. Scotland, for example, has always had a distinct legal
> structure and legislative process, firmly bedded in hundreds of years of

history. And many Scottish laws today are significantly different from those of England and Wales—and are indeed separately enacted for Scotland.[15]

The issue of parity with Scotland revealed the split within the Labour Party in Wales's ranks on devolution. The *Western Mail* reported that Cledwyn Hughes (Labour MP for Anglesey) was 'very disturbed' that Wales was being given a different deal from Scotland on devolution.

> I would not want the difference between the Welsh and Scottish Assemblies to be anything other than in relation to the different system of law. Legislative proposals for Scotland could cover housing in so far as Scottish property law is concerned because that is quite different from England or Wales. But I would not have thought this should also extend to the broad fields of education and health if Wales were not similarly involved. After all, it is quite clear that we in Wales have united more on the question of devolution than in Scotland where a far bigger element are satisfied with the status quo.[16]

On the other hand, Alec Jones (Labour MP for Rhondda) said that to insist on legislative powers for a Welsh Assembly could merely involve duplication. 'The test of the proposals should be whether they meet our needs in Wales and not whether they entail parity with Scotland,' he said.[17]

In terms of presentation of the government's devolution policy in Wales the resort to legal and historical differences between Wales and Scotland to explain the disparity between their two proposed Assemblies was, on the whole, successful. An additional argument was made, for instance, by Gerald Fowler, Minister of State in the Privy Council Office and one of the Ministers responsible for devolution between 1974 and early 1976, that the highly populated border between Wales and England made legislative powers for the Welsh Assembly inapposite. Thus in a speech in Cardiff in January 1976 he stated, 'The English/Welsh boundary in both the North and South cuts through densely populated areas, and quite separate legal systems for the two countries would seem to be undesirable even in principle.'[18]

Explanation of this kind only served to emphasise the artificiality of the rationale given. But after Labour survived the October 1974 general election reasonably intact in Wales, devolutionists inside the party lost the initiative. Freed from any electoral imperative, Labour opponents of devolution then sought to undermine the policy. Hence the main issue in 1975 and early 1976 became a referendum on devolution, sought by a group of Welsh Labour MPs all hostile to an

Assembly, though for different reasons: Leo Abse (Pontypool); Don
Anderson (Swansea East); Neil Kinnock (Bedwellty); and Fred
Evans (Caerphilly).

The object of the referendum campaign was to stop devolution
completely. The campaign was lost inside the Welsh Labour movement (though a referendum was ultimately conceded by the government), largely due to the solid pressure in favour of devolution
exerted by the Wales TUC, who took their stand to successive
Labour Party in Wales conferences in 1975 and 1976.

Nevertheless, the effect of the referendum campaign was to take
the steam out of the debate on legislative powers for the Welsh
Assembly. In this period the Labour Party in Wales Executive
Committee adopted a strategy of playing down the legislative powers
issue. In this they followed a lead set by John Morris (MP for Aberavon) shortly before he became Secretary of State for Wales, after
the February 1974 general election. In January he told a meeting of
his Aberavon Constituency Committee at Skewen that the debate
over whether the Assembly should have legislative or executive
power was 'phoney'. He said, 'It is not beyond our wit to fit the
Welsh Assembly into the legislative process. I cannot conceive of a
worthwhile body being set up without it having the opportunity of
expressing its views and influencing the actions of central government on its proposals for Wales.'[19]

A paper prepared for a special meeting[20] of the Labour Party in
Wales Executive on devolution in January 1975 summarised their
position on the legislative powers issue:

> The procedure through which an Assembly would exercise its powers has
> been bedevilled up to now by sterile arguments as to whether an
> Assembly would have 'Legislative' powers, 'Executive' powers,
> 'Administrative' powers, powers to make 'regulations' or 'ordinances'.
> These words have become emotive, and MPs, some Ministers and others
> have used these phrases loosely without appreciating how these various
> methods of Government vary in degree and overlap in use. We have tried
> to avoid the pitfall of misuse of these words, by trying to indicate in a
> broad general way the relationship, as we see it, and the decision-
> making responsibility of Central and Regional Government. Our central
> theme has been expressed in a number of ways:
>
> 1. Central Government must be the supreme legislative body.
>
> 2. Nothing must be done in the allocation of powers to Regions to
>   reduce the right of Regions to participate in decisions taken at
>   Westminster.
>
> 3. Wales must continue to have the right to exercise a full influence at
>   Westminster.

We decided that:

1. The Assembly would 'not be akin to a Legislature'.

2. Parliament should legislate broadly, leaving a wide area of discretion for decisions at a more local level.

3. That if a decision can better be taken at a lower geographical level then it should be taken at that level.

This paper put a brave face on the Labour Party in Wales's commitment to an Executive Assembly. The events outlined in this section indicate that Labour's decision to grant legislative powers to its proposed Scottish Assembly but only executive powers to a Welsh Assembly, had as much to do with political compromise and accident as with any rational argument.

Plaid Cymru seized upon the absence of legislative powers for Labour's proposed Welsh Assembly from the outset. The grounds for the distinction made between Wales and Scotland—Scotland's separate legal system and her comparatively long possession of a Secretary of State—were rejected as spurious. Neither the Swiss cantons nor the Länder of West Germany had a distinct legal system yet they both had legislative powers. Moreover, Scotland was being given law-making powers in areas which had no connection with her separate legal system—social work, the environment, transport planning, roads and aviation. Plaid Cymru concluded: 'The Government's dilemma has been to avoid yielding real power to the Welsh Assembly whilst appearing to bestow upon it important decision-making and policy forming functions.'[21]

There is no doubt that this kind of appeal found a ready response. While some people, perhaps a majority, were apathetic about the devolution proposals as such, the thought that Scotland might be stealing a march rankled. An opinion poll conducted at twenty-five interviewing points throughout Wales in March 1976 (by Research and Marketing, Wales and the West on behalf of the Welsh-language weekly, *Y Cymro*) found that 75 per cent of the respondents said 'Yes' to the question 'Should a Welsh Assembly have equal status and power with a Scottish Assembly?' (14 per cent said 'No' and 11 per cent didn't know).

An unstable system

The question of an Assembly having legislative as well as executive powers is important, not only because of the amount of freedom it means, but also because once this decision is made a whole series of constitutional implications follow. For instance, under the government's devolution policy, powers are not devolved to a Welsh executive, but vested in the Assembly as a whole, blurring the parliamentary distinction between an Executive sponsoring policies and an Assembly discussing and questioning them. As the November 1975 devolution White Paper commented: 'This system, *which is well suited to a body which will not have to deal with primary legislation,* will allow wide democratic participation in making decisions, since all Members will have a positive role' (my emphasis).[22]

This proposal resembled what the Bains Committee thought a modernised and streamlined local authority should be like.[23] Another logical consequence of an Executive Assembly was a committee structure, as opposed to the legislative Scottish Assembly's cabinet structure of administration. The Welsh Assembly was required, under the devolution Bill, to set up Standing Subject Committees to cover all its main devolved functions. These would do most of the detailed work, and their composition would reflect the political balance of the Assembly. Each Subject Committee would have a Chairman to conduct the business impartially and a leader known as the Executive Member who would take the main policy and administrative initiatives. The Chairmen and Executive Members would be appointed by the Assembly. A central co-ordinating committee (known as the Executive Committee and surely the equivalent of Bains's Policy and Resources Committee) would oversee general policy and the allocation of resources. This would consist of Executive Members from Subject Committees plus any other Members (but not exceeding one quarter of the total) appointed by the Assembly.

Following on from the Welsh Assembly's executive power and committee structure is a further, more directly political, implication, surrounding its proposed fixed four-year term between elections. In the Scotland and Wales Bill this proposal applied to both Assemblies. But, following the collapse of the Bill in the February 1977 guillotine vote, the proposal was modified for Scotland. In his statement on the new separate devolution Bills for Wales and Scotland the Lord President, Mr Michael Foot, proposed 'a power of premature dissolution for the Scottish Assembly dependent on a vote of at least two-thirds of its members' (*Hansard*, 26 July 1977). This decision was in response to criticism that the Scottish Assembly could break down in the chaos if the ruling executive lost its majority in the Assembly and had no recourse to a dissolution. But because executive authority in the Welsh Assembly proposals was vested in the Assembly members themselves, the government decided there was no parallel argument for a power of dissolution for Wales. But, as will be discussed below, a Welsh Assembly would be likely to operate more like central rather than local government. Although in theory its executive authority would be vested in all 80 members, in practice authority would be concentrated in its Executive Committee. In this event it is easy to imagine a situation arising in which the Assembly could be frustrated by its inability to dissolve itself.

Figure 4.1   Constitution of the Welsh Assembly

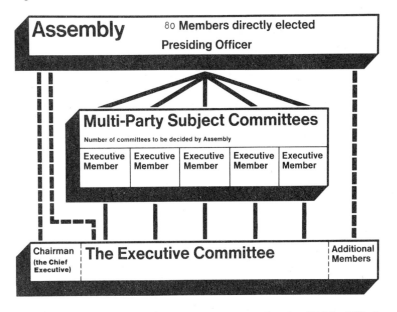

The structure of the Welsh Assembly as seen by the Welsh Office's Information Division the day the November 1975 devolution White Paper was published. The Executive Member apportioned to each subject committee is drawn from the Assembly's majority party and is also a member of the Assembly's Executive Committee, in effect the Welsh Cabinet. The subject committees have 'non-partisan' chairmen. The total membership of the Assembly, 80, is that revised by the August 1976 Supplementary devolution statement.

A broader consequence of limiting the Assembly to Executive powers was that the constitutional system became very complex with the Assembly having to mesh into the Westminster Parliamentary process at many more points than if there were a clear-cut separation of legislative authority. The result was to build into the proposed constitutional structure for Wales stress-points that could have been avoided. There were at least six constitutional areas likely to lead to instability and probable conflict between the Assembly and Westminster: (i) the division of responsibility for primary legislation, the province of Westminster, and for execution, the province of the Assembly; (ii) the division of responsibility for primary legislation, the province of Westminster and secondary legislation,[24] the province of the Assembly; (iii) the likely ambition of the Assembly for its committee structure to develop into something more akin to a cabinet system with a Welsh Premier; (iv) the role and possible redundancy of the Secretary of State for Wales; (v) whether the Assembly's civil service remained part of the United Kingdom unified structure, as the White Paper proposed, or whether it forms a separate Welsh body; and (vi) the incipient conflict contained in the 'over-ride' powers reserved for Westminster: the White Paper speaks of the ability of Parliament to intervene in the Assembly's affairs 'on grounds of policy' (para. 210).

The first three of these stress-points are a direct result of the Assembly having only executive powers. The last three were problems shared with the proposed Scottish Assembly which had additional constitutional strains associated with the separate Scottish legal system. The six stress-areas identified as applying to Wales will be discussed in order:

(i) Primary legislation

The November 1975 devolution White Paper conceded that, in the case of Wales, the division of responsibility for primary legislation (Parliament) and for execution of policy (the Assembly) 'presents some problems'.[25] The essential problem for the government policy-makers was that though, formally, the Welsh Assembly may be denied legislative power it might, nevertheless, in practice come to wield it through influence. A confidential paper prepared by the Welsh Office Devolution Unit, written early in 1975,[26] on 'The Role of the Welsh Assembly in Primary Legislation' clearly stated this position. After arguing that no formal procedure needed to be laid down in the Devolution Act to allow the Welsh Assembly to participate in the primary legislative process, the paper stated:

It may be objected that this would give no greater legislative role to the Assembly than is possessed by any other body or individual, since these too can make their views known to Parliament and attempt to influence legislation through MPs. This, of course, is strictly true but the objection ignores the fact that the Assembly's views will carry more weight than those of most other bodies. First, the Assembly will represent the people of Wales and will speak with a virtually unique political authority on matters affecting the Principality. Second, the Assembly will be responsible for implementation of legislation on devolved matters in Wales; it will know the situation 'on the ground' and will speak with knowledge on proposals relating to that situation. In reality, therefore, the Assembly's *influence* on legislation could be substantial.

And, of course, once Assembly Members saw themselves having influence—but only influence—the power to legislate would be an obvious focus for their ambition. This was recognised by the formulators of the government's policy and in an effort to anticipate the ambition they sought ways of formally integrating Parliament's legislative authority more closely with the Assembly's executive role —but failed. One such attempt was chronicled by Ted Short himself some six months before the appearance of the November 1975 devolution White Paper. He was then Lord President of the Council and responsible for devolution policy. The difficulty that Wales was presenting in drawing up a policy was reflected in his paper for the Cabinet Office Devolution Unit on 'The legislative roles of the Welsh Assembly—Note by the Lord President of the Council'. On the issue of primary legislation he observed:

The Assembly will reasonably wish to be able to convey views to the United Kingdom Government on the effect upon Wales of proposed Westminster primary legislation on the devolved subjects; it may even wish sometimes to request such legislation. This can be expected to work in the main through ordinary processes of administrative contact. . . . The question arises, however, whether there should be more formal recognition of a public voice for the Assembly in this field. Draft Bills are confidential, and there could be no question of giving the Assembly any official opportunity to see and comment on them before they have been revealed to Parliament on formal introduction. Once introduced, however, they will be available to the Assembly as to any member of the public; and there will be no means (even if we so desired) of preventing the Assembly from giving views, whether by holding a debate or otherwise. The question of express provision in the Bill is therefore presentational rather than substantive. I would judge that such provision would be liked in Wales. On the other hand, it might lend force to complaints

that we had ignored Welsh views, if we had not managed to accom-
modate them; and when action was urgent or our legislative programme
was tight we might not welcome the enhanced risk of criticism for not
giving the Assembly long enough to comment, whether before second
reading or later. On balance, I should prefer not to make express
provision.[27]

In this paragraph Ted Short described the very frustrations that
would be likely to feed the ambition of Welsh Assembly members to
be able to legislate for themselves and not depend on the whim of a
Parliament that would probably have different priorities.

(ii) Secondary legislation

The Welsh Assembly's role in secondary legislation (also known as
subordinate or delegated) was to exercise powers conferred by
Westminster statutes. These powers would, at least initially, be of
uneven scope and depth since different arrangements have evolved
in each area of legislation. The November 1975 devolution White
Paper envisaged that, over time, broadly consistent fields of responsibility between Westminster and the Assembly in the various
devolved functions might develop: 'In time Parliament might wish
to give the Assembly greater discretion by passing legislation which
would lay down only broad guidelines, leaving the Assembly to fill in
the rest' (paragraph 198).

The problem with this is that primary and secondary legislation
are essentially two parts of the same process. To separate their
enactment between two bodies with different electorates is bound to
provoke instability. Secondary legislation, with its Statutory Instruments and Orders, has evolved as a convenience for governments,
Ministers, and the drafters of Parliamentary Bills to fill in gaps and
modify primary legislation in the light of experience. It is not a
separate class of legislation that can be formulated by a body apart
from the central government or central Parliament: it is not a
rational base for the division of legislative powers.

In his paper on 'The legislative roles of the Welsh Assembly'
(referred to in the preceding discussion of the primary legislation
issue) Ted Short listed five 'unavoidable limitations' in any progress
towards a convention where Parliament laid down the broad framework of policy leaving the Assembly to fill in the detail:

1. It will not be easy to devise exact guiding principles.

2. Parliament could not in any event bind itself to abide by them.

3. Framing statutes differently for Wales and for England would be an unwelcome addition to Parliament's legislative burden. It might also be objectionable to some that Parliament should tie Wales less closely than it tied England (or, put another way, that the Assembly should be free to move into areas which in England were judged matters for primary legislation).

4. If, conversely, the loosening of the statutory framework were made common to both England and Wales, this would imply giving 'English' Ministers wider delegated powers than Parliament would otherwise have chosen; this too might be criticised.

5. The line between primary and secondary legislation has often in the past been a matter of convenience (related, for example, to considerations of Parliamentary time). In the 'devolved' situation it would have much greater importance. This might sometimes be an additional complication in the management of the Westminster legislative programme. It is possible also that Parliament might choose actually to draw primary legislation more tightly, rather than more loosely, in order to constrain the options of the Welsh Assembly (which might have a different political majority).

After listing these 'limitations' Short offered a very revealing comment. He wrote, 'I have no proposals for countering these limitations, nor do I suggest that they should deflect us from our course —but we should be aware of them.' There is every likelihood that a Welsh Assembly, too, would be aware of them—and want to remove them.

(iii) The committee versus Cabinet structure

The government's committee system for its Welsh Assembly, outlined at the beginning of this section, was a novel blend of the present local government committee operation and central government Cabinet operation, with the emphasis towards the former. Separating the Chairman from each Committee's Leader (the White Paper referred to him as the Executive Member) was the way in which the blend was achieved. The 'impartial' Chairman together with the multi-party complexion of the Committees (to reflect the party balance in the Assembly) was the local government committee element. The Executive Member, also a member of the single (majority) party Executive Committee of the Assembly, comprised the central government Cabinet element.

This blend had been advocated by the Executive Committee of the Labour Party in Wales. A paper it considered in March 1975 set out the argument:[28]

The Labour Party in Wales has firmly rejected the notion that the new Assemblies in Scotland or in Wales should set themselves up as shadow 'Parliaments' with 'Cabinets', 'Ministers', and 'Prime Ministers'. We have expressed a preference for a Committee system similar to Local Authorities.

We accept that both systems have advantages and disadvantages. A Cabinet system—in which the powers to be devolved from Central Government would be vested not in the Assembly itself but in Ministers who would be responsible to the Assembly—would have advantages of clear individual and collective responsibility for decisions and action taken. But it would involve many of Westminster's disadvantages: the inadequacy of Parliamentary control over the Government, the ineffectiveness of backbench members, the exclusion of the opposition—and back-bench government supporters—from access to Civil Servants.

A Committee system, in contrast, would give better opportunity for minority parties and back-bench members of the majority party to participate in decision-making. But opponents of this system point out the lack of co-ordination, of executive effectiveness, and of clear personal responsibility which such a system would involve.

We would therefore seek a system which would be a hybrid between the Westminster and the Local Government patterns, and which in our view would combine the strong points of the two.

As indicated at the opening of this section, this hybrid committee structure was only possible because the proposed Assembly did not have primary legislative power. But the instability created by the absence of primary legislative power, together with the instability inherent in the separation of primary and secondary legislation for Wales, both described above, would in themselves produce instability in the committee structure, ingenious though it is.

The likelihood of the scheme was that there would be an inbuilt movement towards either a cabinet structure or a more pure committee system. The nature of a Welsh Assembly, focusing as it would the aspirations of a nation, would be such that it would probably tend towards the status of a cabinet system. As the devolution policy statement of the Wales TUC declared: 'If the Assembly is to have any kind of credibility a Cabinet System of Government must operate. To introduce a Committee System of Government would give the Assembly the image of a County Council rather than a forum of Welsh Affairs.'[29]

(iv) The Secretary of State

One of the difficulties that faced the Government's devolution policy-makers when they drew up the November 1975 White Paper package was to find a role for the Secretary of State for Wales when so many of his functions were being handed over to the proposed Assembly. The answer was to build up the Secretary of State's responsibilities as an economic Minister to compensate for the health, education, housing, roads, local government and other functions he was losing.[30] This process was begun in July 1975 when the Secretary of State took over much of the responsibility of the Department of Trade and Industry in Wales, particularly powers of selective regional industrial assistance under section 7 of the 1972 Industry Act.

The November 1975 White Paper proposed that, in addition, the Secretary of State for Wales should take over complete responsibility for agriculture and also for the activities in Wales of the Manpower Services Commission, the Training Services Agency and the Employment Service Agency. When added to the Secretary of State's existing responsibility for planning and promotion of the Welsh economy this decentralisation would give him, in the words of the White Paper 'an enhanced and very substantial economic role.'[31]

The problem here was that these transferred economic powers were the very ones an Assembly would covet most. It was argued in chapter 2 that problems of the Welsh economy, particularly the failure of British regional policy to have an adequate impact on Welsh unemployment, is a major driving force in the pressure for devolution. By its very nature an Assembly would not rest until it had within its control the power—that is, the Secretary of State's economic responsibilities—to tackle the problem for itself. Indeed, there were concessions in this direction long before an Assembly was in prospect. The November 1975 White Paper envisaged that responsibility for the Welsh Development Agency would be split between the Secretary of State and the Assembly. By the following May the government had already conceded full control of the Agency to the proposed Assembly.

Thus the economic aspirations of the Assembly would ensure from the start a built-in tension between it and the government, represented here by the Secretary of State. This tension would be focused by the annual negotiations for the Assembly's block grant. Though there is no explicit statement in the White Paper of the Secretary of State's role in the negotiations there is little doubt he would be involved in them on behalf of the United Kingdom government.[32] If the government attempted to use the Secretary of State in this way, if only for presentational purposes, he would be seen as the granter (or, more likely, denier) of funds to the Assembly. His role would then become an ambiguous one especially in light of his traditional function of lobbying himself on behalf of Wales—a function that would, in part, remain.

The Secretary of State would hardly be the most popular man in Wales in these circumstances. But from the point of view of Whitehall such an arrangement would have two attractions. First, the Assembly would be seen, at least in public, to argue about its grant with a Welshman. And, secondly, the Treasury would continue to exert its influence behind the scenes rather than face public scrutiny which, wherever possible, it scrupulously avoids.

A further general point should be stressed. By definition the Secretary of State's position is a highly political one, and given the likelihood of different political control at Cardiff and London for much of the time, this would accentuate any differences between them. The political nature of the problem is compounded by the fact that the Assembly had a fixed four-year term in the government's proposals. Thus an Executive which lost its majority because of by-election losses or defections could not try and restore its majority immediately by calling an election. Under these circumstances it is probable that there would be much more instability in the Assembly than at Westminster and that the Welsh Executive's policies would also be defeated more frequently. The White Paper did not speculate on the Secretary of State's role in such eventualities but the potential intricacies and dangers of his position can be imagined.

The tenor of the above argument opens the question whether it would be desirable, in the long run, to keep the Secretary of State as a United Kingdom Minister. In the debate on whether there should be an Assembly or not this question has been largely avoided, since everybody, whether for or against devolution, has united in agreeing that the office of Secretary of State has benefited Wales.[33] Indeed, some of those against an Assembly have argued that an Assembly would weaken the Secretary of State's influence and should therefore be opposed on that ground.

But once an Assembly was established it would be sure to quarrel with the argument that, while it makes sense to devolve economic functions administratively to a Secretary of State, such functions are not suitable for political devolution. The Assembly would be likely to take the view that if something can be run separately for Wales as an administrative package, then it makes sense for this to be transferred to the Assembly.

The government's line on this was that certain things, particularly economic policy-making, need to be done centrally because of the desirability of uniformity throughout the United Kingdom. But in these matters pressure for uniformity is a real pressure—pressure from consumers—and does not have to be protected by constitutional arrangements. An Assembly would be likely to take the view that central government fear of too much diversity was misplaced. And, of course, the more this view prevailed, as it surely would once an Assembly was established, the more the Secretary of State's functions as a United Kingdom Cabinet Minister would be undermined. The proposed role of the Secretary of State in Labour's devolution proposals was therefore likely to be a continuing source of instability until that role was removed.

(v) The civil service

The first step in the erosion of the position of the Secretary of State would be the establishment by an Assembly of its own civil service. Though the November 1975 devolution White Paper insisted that there should be a unified United Kingdom civil service for both Assembly and Westminster Parliament, it conceded there was an argument the other way:

> The Kilbrandon Commission [on the Constitution] thought that there would have to be a separate civil service, on the grounds that a devolved administration would wish to choose its own senior officials, might not be content for general personnel matters to be handled by a Government Department, and would want to be able to rely on the undivided loyalty of their officials dealing with the Government, for example on the block grant. There are however strong arguments for maintaining a unified service. It would help the consultation and co-operation on which the success of devolution will heavily depend. Present experience does not suggest that with a single service there need be divided loyalty; civil servants by tradition give wholehearted service to whichever Ministers are in charge of their Departments.[34]

This last argument is not very strong. It is one thing for a civil servant to transfer his loyalty from a Labour Minister to a Conservative Minister when there is a change of government in Britain, but this is a quite different situation from that in which officials might be expected to work to *two* sets of political masters *at the same time*. If civil servants did find themselves being pulled in different directions by Welsh administration and the British government, which would likely to be the stronger? The suspicion among members of the Welsh Executive would be that, in any conflict episode, officials who were members of a United Kingdom civil service would tend to protect their good standing and their career prospects in the larger entity centred upon Whitehall, even if this should mean less than total support for their 'political masters' on the Welsh Executive.

Such fears were voiced by the Wales TUC early in 1976 when it declared that if the civil service in Wales was not answerable to the Assembly, 'the Whitehall Civil Service Machine would begin to exert unnecessary and unwanted influences on the working of the Assembly'.[35] And a document approved by the Labour Party in Wales Executive Committee in March 1975 said it was 'crucial' for the Assembly to have control of its own civil service:

> One of the weaknesses of the Regional Economic Planning Councils in England has been that, because their permanent officials are responsible to Whitehall, it is very difficult for the Councils to express a distinctive regional point of view. Such an arrangement for a Welsh Assembly would be a recipe for intolerable tensions. It is essential that the officials who administer services which are the responsibility of the Assembly should themselves be responsible to the Assembly.[36]

A radical solution to the problem of servicing an Assembly would be to adopt the principle of a Welsh public service. This could be created by hiving off civil servants working in Wales from the British civil service and integrating them with Welsh local government, health, water, university and nationalised industry staff. Such a system, which is supported by the National and Local Government Officers Association,[37] would allow officials to gain experience with local government, an Assembly, and the other public services that together would provide a wide and varied career structure within Wales. Under the Labour government's proposed Welsh Assembly only about 2,000 permanent staff would be involved in servicing it, a limited number on which to build a self-contained service. But in Wales there are some 100,000 full-time local government officers, 45,000 people working in the health authorities, and 5,500 with the Welsh National Water Development Authority—without taking into account the thousands of administrative personnel in the national-ised industries and the University of Wales. Taken together they would provide a firm basis on which to build an efficient, widely experienced, and integrated public service for Wales: an essential condition for making devolution work.

(vi) Westminster 'Over-ride'

The area of clearest potential confrontation between Labour's Assembly and central government was the 'United Kingdom Reserve Powers' outlined in the November 1975 devolution White Paper.[38]

These were so draconian that they were substantially modified in the supplementary statement that appeared seven months later in August 1976. In November 1975 the government proposed that if the Welsh Assembly took or failed to take action which it judged to have harmful consequences for the United Kingdom as a whole, three courses of action would be possible:

(a) The UK government could issue a directive prohibiting a certain prospective course of action if it had anticipated the action in time.

(b) It could issue an annulment order revoking an action already taken by the Assembly.

(c) It could resume responsibility for a devolved subject if the Assembly refused to comply with Westminster's request to revoke earlier actions or to put right omissions.

In the Supplementary Statement that appeared in August 1976 the government announced that in the case of the first two possibilities they would be operated 'only if their exercise is considered by the Government necessary to prevent unacceptable repercussions on matters for which they remain responsible'. As to the third possibility it was simply cancelled: 'There will not be a power for the Government to take back devolved functions.'[39]

Nevertheless, Westminster would still, in theory at least, have the right to veto, reverse or annul any act or contemplated action of the Assembly where it judged its own responsibilities were adversely affected. The blunderbuss nature of this provision, even in modified form, was revealing as to the spirit in which the devolution proposals were drawn up. In this they reflected the timidity of the Commission on the Constitution itself. The Commission wanted to devolve legislative powers but remained most uneasy at the possibility of regional assemblies adopting 'policies so extreme as to be regarded as intolerable in other regions or by Parliament and the central Government'; or 'policies, which, while not unreasonable in themselves would, when taken together, be so incompatible as to undermine political and economic unity'.[40] In other words devolution of power was acceptable provided it did not lead to genuine diversity.

But the most damaging aspect of the 'over-ride' provision, even in modified form, was that it was designed for 'circumstances in which the Government need to intervene on grounds of policy'.[41] Very little political sophistication is needed to appreciate that this was a guaranteed recipe for conflict as virtually any decision emerging from

Cardiff might be regarded as unacceptable on policy grounds, especially in cases of political control in Westminster and Wales resting in opposing hands.

Following the failure of the Scotland and Wales Bill in February 1977, the government remained sensitive to this problem in its consideration of'what fresh devolution proposals to place before the Commons in the following session. In his statement on the form of the new proposals being brought forward in separate Bills for Wales and Scotland, the Lord President, Mr Michael Foot, said:

> We believe that it is possible to dispense with certain of the detailed controls on the actions of the devolved administrations to provide more clear cut arrangements. We will propose that the Government's general reserve powers should be available only in cases where a matter is prejudiced for which there is no devolved responsibility. The powers will remain as an essential safeguard to protect matters which are not devolved, for example defence, trade, the economy and industrial relations. (*Hansard*, 26 July 1977.)

The above detailed examination of the Labour government's proposed devolution settlement has been intended to demonstrate that it was littered with opportunities for either Assembly or Westminster to provoke confrontation. But the essence of politics is conflict. The essential question is how conflict is resolved. One of the justifications for devolution is that it would bring conflict into the open. Grievances and disagreements would be more capable of being debated democratically and in open forum rather than behind closed doors. There is an argument, too, for allowing new institutions to evolve through experience rather than attempting to anticipate every difficulty with elaborate constitutional safeguards. A central theme of this book is that the conflict underlying the devolution debate, and the conflict institutionalised in Labour's proposed devolution settlement itself, was creative, since the experience of working through it would tend to bring power and responsibility together in government. The final sections of this chapter will examine two constitutional directions towards which such creative conflict would be likely to lead an Assembly: a federal solution, and, more problematically, but more desirably, a confederal approach.

The drift to federalism

When the government was drawing up its constitutional proposals for devolution it had five broad options:

(i) the status quo;

(ii) a 'minimalist' alternative to the status quo based upon an indirectly elected, or possibly even directly elected, advisory
council;

(iii) a devolutionary alternative to the status quo which is neither
minimalist nor maximalist—in other words, broadly the
government's choice;

(iv) a 'maximalist' alternative (short of independence) of a federal
or quasi-federal nature, based upon a Welsh Parliament with
some exclusive, as well as shared powers to legislate;

(v) outright independence for Wales.

It will be argued towards the end of this chapter that there is a
sixth alternative: a confederal solution based upon a decentralist
philosophy of government, a philosophy that holds that sovereignty
lies at the bottom of society (with community) and not at the top
(with the state) and that, further, sovereignty is something that is
conditionally surrendered and not something handed down. But
given that such a philosophy, by its very nature, must be alien to any
British view of government, then the effective choice open to the
Labour government in framing its proposals was the five options
that have been listed. The government argued that the status quo
was not an option—political pressure proved there were Welsh
aspirations for change that had to be met. Independence for Wales
was also ruled out, which left three choices: an advisory council,
federalism, or middle-of-the-road devolution.[42]

An advisory Welsh elected Council would offer little more than a
forum for debate of Welsh problems. But it would at least have the
practical merit of being compatible with such features of the existing
British system as (a) maintenance of 36 Welsh MPs in the House of
Commons; (b) representation of Welsh interests at Cabinet level by
the Secretary of State for Wales; and (c) the responsibility of the
Secretary of State for the work of the Welsh Office, staffed by
members of the British civil service.

A Welsh Parliament within a federal system would not be compatible with most features of the British governmental structure and
would involve problems of its own—such as the need either to divide

England into provinces or to accept permanent domination of the federation by a much more populous England. But it is at least possible to conceive of a system (novel to Britain but not to Canada, say, or West Germany) in which Wales would have a legislature with powers of final decision in designated fields, a Welsh Cabinet answerable in such matters to a Welsh Parliament, and a Welsh civil service quite separate from the United Kingdom civil service.[43]

What the Labour government offered was neither of these 'minimalist' or 'maximalist' solutions, either of which would have, in accepted constitutional theory, held out some prospect for stability. Instead, the government offered 'middle-of-the-road devolution', a compromise which, like all compromises, was vulnerable to attack. It enabled politicians like Enoch Powell to argue that the scheme must lead either to a federal system or to the dissolution of the United Kingdom into two or more independent states. As Powell put it shortly before the publication of the November 1975 White Paper:

> The devolution debate will be based upon a proposition no less objectively false than to assert that two and two make five. It is the proposition that it is possible to establish one or more local parliaments within the unitary parliamentary state known as the United Kingdom. I am using the word 'parliaments' in the perfectly precise sense in which it will be the subject of the debate, namely elected assemblies endowed with legislative power.
>
> The difference between such assemblies and local authorities is clear and unambiguous. Local authorities, large or small, high or low, have no power themselves to make or alter the laws which they apply: they take decisions only at the administrative level within the limits which the law, not made by them, lays down.
>
> In the context of the devolution debate the theorem which corresponds to the equation two and two makes four is this: the establishment of one or more local parliaments must have one of two consequences; either the conversion of the unitary parliamentary state into a federal state, with a written constitution which prescribes the respective spheres and powers of the federal parliament and the local parliaments, or alternatively the dissolution of the unitary state itself into two or more independent states. No third possibility exists.[44]

Given his premises, Powell's logic is impeccable. But, as usual with Powell, it is his premises that are suspect, not his argument. In this case it is his view of sovereignty. The politics of devolution are a challenge to his claim that sovereignty is immutable and to be found at the top of society, in Parliament. Nevertheless, Powell's point bears examination, and particularly the possibility of a federal solution. The government's rejection of federalism derived, in part, from the dismissal of the system by the Commission on the Constitution. But the legislative scheme the Commission recommended and also the direction of the government's own proposals have distinct federal overtones. Moreover, a movement pressing for a Bill of Rights is gathering force in Britain which, if successful as appears increasingly likely, would set Britain well on the way to having a written constitution.

The Commission on the Constitution's rejection of federalism was unequivocal:

> If government in the United Kingdom is to meet the present-day needs of the people it is necessary for the undivided sovereignty of Parliament to be maintained. We believe that only within the general ambit of one supreme elected authority is it likely that there will emerge the degree of unity, co-operation and flexibility which common sense suggests is desirable.[45]

This statement of principle that Parliament symbolises an inviolable unity touches a deep nerve in the English subconscious. Dicey expressed it towards the end of the last century in his case against Irish Home Rule:

> Under all the formality, the antiquarianism, the sham of the British constitution, there lies latent an element of power which has been the true source of its life and growth. This secret source of strength is the absolute omnipotence, the sovereignty, of Parliament.[46]

The institutional place of Parliament combined with absence of a written constitution are rightly regarded as being among the finest expressions of English nationhood, the fruit of centuries' growth. But part of England's problem is that these quintessential characteristics are bound up with her imperialism as well as her nationalism. This was perfectly illustrated by Enoch Powell during 1971 in the course of a series of speeches he made in Europe warning that England/Britain would never in the long-term accept the abandonment of nationhood that, he said, membership of the European Economic Community would mean. The confusion of England and Britain fatally weakened Powell's case, as was to be proved four years later in the referendum. In the course of one of the speeches he stated:

> It is a fact that the British parliament in its paramount authority occupies a position in relation to the *British nation* which no other elective assembly in Europe possesses. Take Parliament out of the

history of England and that history itself becomes meaningless. Whole
lifetimes of study cannot exhaust the reasons why this fact has come to
be; but fact it is, so that the *British nation* could not imagine itself
except with and through its parliament (my emphasis).[47]

It was out of such confusion that the Commission of the Constitution's scheme for legislative devolution for Wales and Scotland
emerged. Despite the Commission's outright rejection of federalism,
their scheme can be fairly described as a plan for 'semi-
federal' or quasi-federal government, or 'federal devolution'.[48] The
Commission was anxious to assert that the transfer of powers under
its scheme of legislative devolution would in no way detract from the
ultimate and complete supremacy of Parliament. At the same time
the Commission, encouraged by the experience in Northern Ireland
up to 1972,[49] forecast that the power of Westminster would be
invoked only in exceptional circumstances and that, for instance, a
convention would arise that Parliament would legislate for Wales on
a transferred matter only with the agreement of the Welsh
government.[50] In a paper on 'Wales and Legislative Devolution'
presented at a Cardiff conference on comparative law in September
1974, D. G. T. Williams, a Fellow of Emmanuel College,
Cambridge, commented on this aspect:

> It is remarkable that such an interaction of law and convention should
> be contemplated in advance for an entirely new system of government,
> and in making its forecast the Commission came perilously close to pro-
> posing federal government without the courage of its convictions.[51]

In fact, one of the objections to legislative devolution was that it
would introduce an element of rigidity into the relationship between
Parliament at Westminster and the Welsh Assembly. Those among
the Commissioners who supported such devolution replied that this
rigidity would be a source of strength in protecting the Assembly
'from what would otherwise be an inevitable whittling away of its
powers through the centralising tendencies of government'.[52] Thus,
although the Commission rejected the federal solution, its scheme
for legislative devolution is effectively a drift towards federalism.

And in Scotland the government's amended proposals for a legislative Assembly were hailed by one of their leading proponents,
John Mackintoch, Labour MP for Berwick and East Lothian as
'Federalism without the faults.'[53] This was in March 1976, immediately after the annual conference of the Labour Party in Scotland
that year had passed a resolution seeking greater economic powers
for the Scottish Assembly and weakening Westminster's veto powers

over it, both confirmed by the government later in the year.
Mackintosh argued that a full federal scheme would be highly
inflexible, particularly for economic co-operation between Scotland
and England, and that there was no strong English demand for it. In
these circumstances, the improved devolution scheme on offer had
most of the advantages of federalism without its defects. First, the
reduction of Westminster's power of veto gave the Scottish executive
virtually untrammelled power in its own area of competence. (This
entrenchment was political rather than legal as in a fully federal
system.) Second, the improved devolution proposals could easily be
altered in the future, unlike federalism with its legally entrenched
arrangements. Mackintosh argued that because the devolution
scheme was now essentially a federal one, the Scottish Assembly
should be called a Parliament, the executive described as a Cabinet,
and its leader a Prime Minister: 'The Scottish Prime Minister will,
in this scheme, be wielding powers quite commensurate with those
of the Prime Minister of Bavaria, Queensland or British
Columbia.'[54]

It may be argued that the solution outlined here would result in
the Scots having it both ways: a full-blown Parliament and complete
integration within the United Kingdom. This is probably right. But
given the political pressures (both of the wishes of the Scottish
people and the question of the disposal of North Sea/Scottish oil) it
is the most likely medium-term outcome for Scotland. And given
that the Scots achieve the best of both worlds in this sense it is probable that the Welsh will want the same.

At this point the drift towards federalism would be well under
way. And by then another current would in all likelihood be flowing
in the same direction—pressure for a Bill of Rights which, if
achieved, would form the basis for a written constitution (a necessary condition for federalism). In the vanguard of this pressure has
been Sir Leslie Scarman, a judge of the Court of Appeal. His views
were first set out in the 1974 Hamlyn Lectures.[55] In a public lecture
at the University College of Wales, Cardiff, in April 1976 he
reiterated them more forcefully, claiming that unless the rule
of law was placed on a firmer footing in four key areas of
policy there was danger of political anarchy developing in
Britain.[56] The four areas where he said the place of the law was
unclear were devolution policy, Britain's new position inside the
European Economic Community, the welfare state, and industrial
relations.

In all these areas there was a growing or potential need for arbitration by the courts, yet in none of them were any procedures laid

down on how this might be achieved. 'One of the most remarkable
omissions from the Devolution White Paper is any discussion of the
legal implications of devolution,' said Sir Leslie. He had spelled
them out himself in his Hamlyn Lectures, arguing that the probable
need for legal arbitration between devolved Welsh and Scottish
administrations and Westminster should be anticipated:

> It is said that very few such problems arose during the 50 years of the
> Stormont Constitution. But there is no parallel here: Stormont, backed
> by a majority of Northern Irish public opinion was desperately anxious,
> up to the very moment of its suppression, to foster links with the United
> Kingdom. It would be surprising, given the current trends of Scottish
> and Welsh national feeling, if an Edinburgh or Cardiff assembly would
> be as enthusiastic for the link with London as was Belfast for 50 years.
> Such assemblies may reasonably be expected to explore the extent of
> their legislative powers and to seek the independent arbitrament of the
> courts if they find themselves at variance with the central Parliament in
> the interpretation of the extent of their powers. Inevitably, therefore,
> legislative devolution will bring with it a role for the courts.[57]

In his Cardiff lecture Sir Leslie said that entry into the EEC
posed an unsolved and largely undiscussed problem of the legislative
role of Parliament faced with laws binding on Britain made by
Community institutions. He foresaw an inevitable clash developing
between the United Kingdom Parliament and Brussels which the
courts would be called upon to resolve: 'If our links with Europe
tighten and we move closer to the Civil Law system of the Common
Market then we might find irresistible a move towards a Bill of
Rights.'[58]

The two other areas where the rule of law was uncertain were the
administration of welfare legislation and the problems of industrial
relations. The courts were not clear on the attitude they should take
in supervising the work of appeal tribunals that decide disputes
between the state, which provides welfare benefits, and the citizen,
who receives them. In industrial relations Sir Leslie quoted the
collapse of the 1971 Industrial Relations Act as a good example of
what happens to major legislation if agreement is not reached before
it is put into practice. The answer still had not been found to the
question of the proper place for the rule of law in industrial
relations. In these areas Sir Leslie said, 'A Bill of Rights and conse-
quential judicial review could reduce the confusion and diminish the
chance of anarchy happening in our society.'[59]

A Bill of Rights would be a United Kingdom statute enacted by
the United Kingdom Parliament, and would be applicable through-

out the whole United Kingdom. It would ensure basic human rights, freedoms and duties in the various nations and regions. It would have to be a principled instrument for ensuring equality of basic welfare state provision throughout the United Kingdom whatever level of devolution had been achieved. It would also have to be an entrenched statute, that is, protected from appeal by a bare majority of Parliament—possibly requiring a two-thirds majority before it could be repealed. Inherent in the proposal would be an element of judicial review, with the courts interpreting the statute in its application to particular circumstances and also enforcing its application. This also implied that the courts might be called upon to invalidate other legislation—whether passed by a devolved Assembly or Parliament—where it infringed the Bill of Rights.

Sir Leslie concluded that the devolution debate and its prospect of constitutional change might well engender the right atmosphere for the introduction of a Bill of Rights, and would certainly provide a need:

> In the new forms of social administration that evolve over the next 15 years we have to ensure that the rule of law has a proper place. If devolution should come to develop a federal character then we would have to consider seriously the introduction of a fully-fledged and entrenched Bill of Rights.[60]

It is unlikely, however, given the very large population of England compared with that of Wales and Scotland, that a federation based on these units would ever in any strictly legal sense be evolved. The question might change if regionalism within England were to develop more distinctly. But from the perspective of the 1970s that seems no more than a long-term possibility.

Yet, given that neither the Welsh nor the Scottish Assembly will be content with the status of a slightly superior but nevertheless *local* government unit subordinate to Westminster, the likelihood must be that the constitutional relationship between Wales, England and Scotland will develop into a federal hybrid. It has been argued that, as well as pressure from the Assemblies themselves, outside developments such as the Common Market and the need to clarify the place of the rule of law in many civil areas, are pressing in the same direction. The first stage in the creation of a Bill of Rights is likely to be an incorporation into the legal system of those parts of the European Convention on Human Rights by which the United Kingdom is already bound.[61]

A semi-federal compromise based on legislative devolution for Wales, would be a likely way for instabilities like those in Labour's devolution proposals to be resolved. In the long term, as the new Welsh institutions evolved and as the European link increased in importance, such a compromise would be likely itself to become unstable, however. The last section of this chapter attempts to outline one way in which such fresh instability might be faced.

A confederal approach

The Commission on the Constitution presented a convincing case why federalism is inapplicable to the United Kingdom.[62] A federation of four units—England, Scotland, Wales and Northern Ireland —would be so unbalanced as to be unworkable. It would be dominated by the overwhelming political importance, wealth and population of England. Any attempt to correct this imbalance by dividing England itself into federal provinces faces a dual problem: first, the concept of the English region remains a nebulous one and, second, even if a solution to this were found the reality of English nationhood would still remain, ensuring that England, by weight of numbers and wealth, would continue to dominate the federation.

On the first point, a major difficulty of dividing England into regions or provinces is the South-East with its disproportionately large share of the population. Using Whitehall's Regional Economic Planning Regions with minor modifications to reflect changed local authority boundaries, the South-East has 17 million of the total English population of 46 million. Using the five English regions proposed in the Commission on the Constitution's Memorandum of Dissent, the South-East has 22 million out of 46 million.

On the second point, England's sense of nationhood can also be demonstrated by referring to the English reluctance to break with tradition and accept the written constitution that an entrenched federal constitution would demand. As Enoch Powell has expressed it, a written constitution

> would replace the Crown in Parliament by a supreme court as the ultimate sovereign authority; for wherever there is a written constitution, the true sovereign in the state is that piece of paper, and its priesthood—the ultimate human sovereign—are the judges who authoritatively interpret it . . . I am extremely doubtful if the people of Britain (sic), when they discovered what was involved, would prefer to be governed by an unelected unrepresentative judiciary, or would be willing to dethrone the Crown in parliament as their sovereign in order to install her Majesty's judges in the vacant space.[63]

Just as a federal system would cut across the generally inarticulated, but nevertheless deeply rooted, sense of English nationhood, so, too, it would be bound to offend the perception of the Welsh and Scots themselves as nations. For in no sense are Wales and Scotland 'provinces' in the way that the English regions might be. They owe their cohesion and also their internal fissures to their separate history, culture and nationality.

Apart from the inapplicability of the federal system to the particular circumstances of the United Kingdom, it is a form of government that evolved during the eighteenth and nineteenth centuries when the role of government was smaller and less complex than in the twentieth century.[64] This meant that separation of powers was more easily defined and consequently that conflict between layers of government more easily avoided. The federal experiences of Canada and the United States demonstrate how force of circumstances have resulted in the modification of original intent of their constitutions.

In the case of Canada, its original constitution, embodied in the British North America Act of 1867, was so centralised that it could hardly be classed as federal at all. But as settlement of the country was extended into new areas of people of different nationalities and languages, the diverse nature of Canadian society became increasingly marked, and the Dominion government found it impossible to exercise effectively from the centre the powers given to it under the constitution. In order to make the constitution work it was necessary to operate it in a quite different way from that originally intended. Over a period of fifty years the Judicial Committee of the Privy Council (until 1949 the final court of appeal in constitutional matters) interpreted the British North America Act in such a way as to reverse its original purpose. Federal powers were restricted and provincial powers were expanded until, in effect, residual power was removed from the federal government to the provinces.[65]

On the other hand, in the case of the United States, its federal constitution, based strongly on 'states' rights', has led to almost unrestricted federal power in the hands of the President. In his research paper for the Commission on the Constitution, Professor M. J. C. Vile suggested that in the United States the concentration of power at the centre has become so great that the country may be moving out of a system of federalism into one of decentralised unitary government.[66]

Thus the experiences of federal government that might be considered most relevant to any British attempt to embark on the system suggest that it would not lead to a stable settlement.

Thus far, much of this chapter has consisted in ruling out a

variety of constitutional options that have been suggested might
ensure stability. 'The status quo is not an option'—to use the government's own words.[67] Moreover, the case has been pressed that the
government's devolution policy, full as it is of points of dispute, is a
recipe for instability rather than stability. It has been argued that
any drift towards a federal alternative is unlikely to be stable either.

If this analysis is correct it creates a dilemma for the centralist
view of government. It means that the only alternative left is
independence. As the Commission on the Constitution expressed it:

> Parliament could transfer powers to a region in one of three ways. It
> could transfer complete sovereignty in all matters, in effect creating a
> separate state; or it could transfer sovereignty in certain matters only,
> retaining sovereignty in other matters such as defence and foreign affairs
> (that is, federalism); or, while retaining sovereignty in all matters, it
> could delegate to the regions the exercise of selected powers (that is,
> devolution).[68]

This centralist view of government which, when examined
logically in the British context, leads inexorably to Independence as
a constitutional requirement for stability, is based upon two fundamental misconceptions about the nature of government and also
about the nature of sovereignty. It will be argued that a decentralist
view of government avoids these misconceptions and therefore holds
out the prospect of a stable and co-operative constitutional settlement in Britain short of independence.

The four centralist alternatives, from the status quo to independence, are all conceived in terms of government being distributed
from the top (the state) downwards. But the decentralist view holds
that power and responsibility (the basis of government and sovereignty) are not something to be handed down but something which
may be surrendered, from the bottom upwards, either willingly or
unwillingly. When they are surrendered willingly it is through a
recognition of benefits, usually economic, gained in return. Such
leasing of power and responsibility upwards to a higher body is
conditional, however. Many rights are retained and the lease itself
can be terminated at any time.

The decentralist view holds that sovereignty is defined in terms of
freedom and is held jointly between individuals and their immediate
community. This is the most difficult point in the decentralist thesis
since the idea of community is very difficult to specify in any general
way. The only answer is that the concept of community varies in size
and quality according to the perceptions of those involved. Never-

theless, the decentralist view holds that it is here that sovereignty ultimately resides.[69]

So, the first point the decentralist makes in answer to the centralist's thesis of the four possible constitutional options for Britain is that they are limited by a narrow, one-way, downwards view. If, instead, the perspective is reversed with the vantage point being decentralised communities and how far they should join together to create higher levels of government, the way is left clear for what can be termed a confederal approach to government.

A crude definition of a confederation is that it is an association of several states which unite for the purpose of mutual co-operation and defence, but which does not have a direct power over the citizens of the associated states, and is not usually entrusted with the conduct of their foreign affairs. As a framework to fit the decentralist's aspirations this definition needs to be tempered by a greater clarity on terms. Such clarity was provided early in the twentieth century by one of the most remarkable and incisive minds Wales has produced, Saunders Lewis. He, of course, was one of the founders of Plaid Cymru, and in 1926 delivered a classic and formative lecture to the party's first Summer School.[70] In it he laid down a basis for future co-operation in Britain:

> We are so familiar today with hearing such sentiments as: every nation, ought to be free; no nation has the right to rule another nation; a nation must be independent; and sentences of like kind—that we but rarely dispute them or inquire as to what they mean. What do we mean by the terms 'free', 'to rule', 'independence'? Assuredly, meanings could be assigned to each of them which would justify each one of the sentences I have quoted. But they could just as easily be understood in such a way that we could in all sincerity say: no nation ought to be free; no nation is entitled to independence or to rule itself. And these are the truths which most need to be stressed today.[71]

The nations of Europe in the middle ages, he continues, were not 'free' in the sense generally assigned to the word at the time of writing. They all recognised a supranational authority in the form of the Church. 'The whole of Europe shared one law and one civilisation: but that law and that civilisation had varied forms and many different hues.' Under such a system, one form of civilisation was not thought of as a danger to any other forms, nor did a variety of languages militate against the unity based on moral law and a common belief.

In the sixteenth century—the age of Luther in Germany, of Macchiavelli in Italy, of the Tudors in Britain—this was undone,

and replaced by another kind of nationalism, the one still current in
Europe, that which set up the state as the supreme arbiter of
morality and the sole object of loyalty. It placed the power of the
state, its rights, its freedom, beyond restraint and conditions. Each
authority came to be thought of as a threat to its neighbour, one
civilisation as the enemy of another. Diversity could not be conceived
of except as divisiveness. One state became the enemy not only of
other states, but also of all differences in tradition, culture and
language within its own domain. As authority came to be based exclusively on material force, uniformity within the state was insisted
upon, under the tyranny of one law and one language. It is in this
context that the relationship of Wales and England within Britain is
to be seen:

> These, grossly simplified, were the principles of the nationalism conceived
> in the sixteenth century. Such were the ideas of the Tudors in Britain.
> These too were the very principles which destroyed the civilisation of
> Wales . . . the two countries were given one government, one civil law,
> one culture, one system of education, one religion—being the state's
> religion, the state's language, the state's education, the state's culture.
> Sixteenth-century nationalism represented nothing less than a victory for
> the material over the spiritual, for paganism over Christianity. It was
> this pagan and materialist victory which destroyed our Wales.[72]

The task of the new political party, Plaid Cymru, was to reverse
this change, to dislodge one kind of nationalism, that is the one most
commonly practised among the nation states of Europe in the
modern world, and substitute it for another, comparable in kind to
that which existed under mediaeval Christendom:

> What then is our nationalism? It is this: to return to the principle
> accepted in the Middle Ages; to repudiate the idea of political uniform-
> ity, and to expose its ill-effects; to plead therefore for the principle of
> unity and diversity. To fight not for Welsh independence, but for the
> civilisation of Wales. To claim for Wales not independence but freedom.
> And to claim for her a place in the League of Nations and in the
> community of Europe, by virtue of her civilisation and its values.

Several times before the end of the pamphlet, the difference
between the idea of 'freedom' and the idea of 'sovereign independence' is clearly reiterated:

> First of all, let us not ask for independence for Wales. Not because it is
> impractical but because it is not worth having. I have already shown that
> it is materialistic and cruel, leading to violence, oppression and ideas.

already proved to be bad. The age of empires is fast passing, and after-wards there will be no meaning or value in independence. Europe will return to its place when the countries recognise they are all subject and dependent. . . . So let us insist on having, not independence, but freedom. And freedom in this affair means responsibility. We who are Welsh claim that we are responsible for civilisation and social ways of life in our part of Europe. . . . We do, therefore, need a government of our own. Not independence. Not even an unconditional freedom. But exactly that degree of freedom which is necessary in order to make civilisation secure in Wales; that freedom will not only benefit Wales but will also contribute to the welfare and security of England and all other neighbouring countries.[73]

But the idea of freedom rather than independence, an essential component of the decentralist confederal approach to government, was rejected by the Commission on the Constitution:

It is said that sovereignty is no longer necessary for full statehood, the implication being that all states are now so interdependent that none has complete freedom of action and that, in effect, although Scotland and Wales could not have absolute sovereignty they could have as much sovereignty as any other state.

We are not satisfied that the question of sovereignty can be dismissed in this way. We are concerned with the realities of constitutional power, and the fact is that even in the modern world a state is either sovereign or it is not. A state which is already sovereign may make agreements with other states limiting its own courses of action, and for a variety of reasons the number of such agreements is increasing. But they rest on the sovereignty of the independent states which make them, and in the last resort an independent state has complete constitutional control over its domestic affairs and can order its relations with other countries in whatever way it thinks fit. Scotland and Wales could not be independent states in the sense understood by the world unless they had this kind of authority, and they would not have it if their independence rested upon the continued co-operation of England on some very important matters.[74]

This interpretation of the meaning of sovereignty is based on the premise that it rests with the state. It has been argued that this is a premise conditioned by a centralist position. If the decentralist view is accepted and sovereignty is seen as not being the property of the state but a natural characteristic of community, radically different forms of co-operation are possible. It then makes sense to regard communities as completely interdependent but at the same time retaining completely separate identities. After all, this is no more than occurs between individuals in a healthy marriage.

Ultimately, no irrefutable argument of logic can be presented to persuade that the centralist or the decentralist view of Sovereignty is the correct one. It is a matter of judgment having regard to what comes most instinctively and most naturally. Does the state or the community take precedence? Where is the source of moral authority in human affairs—with the community, an organic evolution of relationships, or the state, a product of man-made institutions that rest ultimately on violence?

Out of the choice of the decentralist position can develop a confederal response to the problem of organising the relationship between communities. In Europe the best example of this in practice is the Nordic Union. This was created in 1953 by Denmark, Finland, Iceland, Norway and Sweden which collectively have a population of around 21 million people. A Nordic Council was established as a consultative assembly consisting of parliamentarians and Cabinet Ministers of the five countries. In 1971 there was added a Nordic Council of Ministers with competence for the whole area of Nordic co-operation.

In 1954, the Nordic states signed an agreement creating a passport union and a joint Nordic labour market. Economic planning, particularly with regard to employment, regional development of arctic areas, hydro-electric power and road building, is done in conjunction. There is a joint Scandinavian Airline, a postal union, and a convention on social benefits so they are the same in all the five countries. The electric power grids of Denmark, Finland, Norway and Sweden are interconnected and the power producers co-operate in an agency called Nordel. In many areas the laws of the member countries have been harmonised.

This kind of co-operation was envisaged by Plaid Cymru when it drew up its constitutional proposals for the Commission on the Constitution in September 1969.[75] The party envisaged a 'Britannic Common Market' in which each member state—England, Wales, Scotland and, possibly, Ireland,—would co-operate voluntarily. There would be established a permanent Commission consisting of an equal number of representatives from each country to ensure uniform levels of taxation, customs duties and social security benefits. Their prime function would be to advise on budgetary and trade policy and the social security services. Plaid Cymru's memorandum continued:

> We do not envisage major difficulties in arriving at recommendations acceptable to all four governments because it will be in the interest of all four countries to maintain the free flow of people, capital and goods. . . . The net effect of these proposals would be that there would be no

customs barriers, no frontier or frontier formalities between England
and Wales or any of the four countries concerned. .... This solution on
the one hand avoids the situation which occurs in a unitary state like the
U.K. of the more populous of the four countries, England, dominating
the rest, and, on the other hand, the equally unfair situation which
might prevail in a fully federal system (where Scotland and Wales each
had a vote equal to that of England) of the tail wagging the dog.[76]

The memorandum concluded that such a system might be termed
a 'Britannic Confederation'. But because such a title might be
misinterpreted it suggested, instead, 'Britannic Common Market'.

The theme of this chapter has been the instability of the constitutional position in the United Kingdom. The status quo is unstable
because of three main factors: (i) the rise of national parties in
Scotland and Wales and the continuing problem of Ireland
manifested by the strife in Ulster; (ii) entry in the European
Economic Community; and (iii) the problem of England's identity,
signified by her declining imperial world role coupled with overall
long-term decline of the British economy.

It has been argued that the government's devolution response
was, if anything, guaranteed to create even more constitutional
instability. The drift towards federalism implicit in legislative devolution is also unstable, particularly because the balance of
population in the countries of Britain is unsuited to it.

The conclusion of this chapter is that the instability inherent in all
these systems results from a mistaken centralist view of government.
This looks at the problem of framing a constitution from the top
down, a view that places sovereignty with the state rather than the
community. If, instead, the community is given its proper place as
the source of authority, of sovereignty, a decentralist solution can be
found. It has been argued that the decentralist approach which in
constitutional terms, means confederalism, will be inherently more
stable since it will rest on sure community foundations.

What is the place of devolution in this argument? It has been
shown that any purely devolutionary response to the problem of the
constitution will be unstable and will therefore lead to conflict. But
such conflict will be creative because it will force the participants to
re-examine the centralist position from which they have hitherto
approached the problem. Only when a decentralist philosophy,
which puts the needs of the community first, is accepted will there be
a prospect for evolving stable relationships between the peoples of
the British Isles. Devolution is a means for promoting this end.
Thus, although it will involve conflict it will in the end be a creative
experience.

Chapter 5

Financing an Assembly

'All experience shows that the man who pays the bill in the end collects the power.'

Civil Service evidence to the Layfield Committee. [1]

The central issue and dilemma of devolution is finance. It is the central issue because without a reasonable measure of control over the amount and source of its revenue, no institution can act responsibly. He who pays the piper calls the tune. At the same time financing an Assembly poses a dilemma for central government because it has continually in mind the 'vital and fundamental principle to maintain the economic and political unity of the United Kingdom'.[2] Deeply entrenched in British thinking, indeed, in any centralised state thinking, is that control over taxation, its gathering and spending, is a necessary condition for unity.

But depriving an Assembly of control of its finance has grave inadequacies that will be explored in detail in later sections of this chapter: it divorces tax raising from spending and so engenders fiscal irresponsibility; it prevents fine tuning of demand management in the economy which devolved taxing power would allow; it perpetuates inefficient centralised spending control; and it makes devolution be little more than a rationalisation of local government structure rather than a real decentralisation of power and responsibility from the centre.

The December 1976 devolution Bill proposed that Welsh and Scottish Assemblies should be financed by a block grant from the central Exchequer and by borrowing—the same as the main sources of finance of any local council. (The suggestion made in the November 1975 devolution White Paper that the Assemblies could levy a surcharge on local government rates was removed by the supplementary statement on powers the following August.)

Further consideration of the financial issue following the collapse of the Scotland and Wales Bill in February 1977 did not depart from the principle of central control via the block grant system. The July 1977 proposals for separate Welsh and Scottish Bills the following session did put forward a 'formula approach' for settling the block grants in an attempt to minimise conflict between the Assemblies and Westminster over the allocation. It was also allowed that the

Assemblies might come forward with suggestions on raising themselves some marginal revenue out of their own taxes for a special project or purpose. But the key issues of fiscal responsibility and the use of devolved financial powers to help promote the relatively under-developed Welsh economy were avoided.

It is true that the proposed grant was a block grant, rather than a package of grants tied specifically to certain forms of expenditure, but so is the largest share of the financial support that goes to local authorities. In any event, the government's 'illustrative annual calendar'[3] of the process for settling the amount of the block grant shows that there would be plenty of room for Treasury pressure on a Welsh administration to alter its allocation in ways that Whitehall thought best. Take this pressure away and you have a more than usually independent local authority, but a local authority for all that. The only way to move towards something more like genuine Home Rule would be to give an Assembly the power to raise a significant proportion of its own finance.

The Labour party compromise

The sensitivity of the taxation issue was demonstrated by the evolution of Labour Party in Wales policy on financing devolution between the late 1960s, when the party was preparing evidence to submit to the Commission on the Constitution, and 1974, when the Labour government seriously began putting together a devolution policy.

As described in the preceding chapter, a Labour Party in Wales research group, made up of councillors, lecturers and business people, produced in August 1969 a confidential document intended as the basis for their submission to the Commission on the Constitution.[4] Apart from the principles of devolution and the issue of legislative powers, it also discussed finance. Viewed from the perspective of the late 1970s this aspect of the document is the most interesting and was developed as follows:

> The crucial factor in any relationship between the proposed levels of Government is that of finance. It is apparent that those who framed the Local Government Acts of 1888 and 1894 were well aware of the problem, and made strenuous efforts to ensure that the county and county borough councils were given a significant degree of financial independence. This financial independence, marginal though it has increasingly become, distinguishes the British system of local

government from the more centralised French system of local *administration* . . .

The motivating principle (of our proposals) should be that the financial relationship between an elected Welsh Assembly and central Government should be no less than that originally intended in 1888/94 between central government and county and county borough councils. The Assembly should be given a degree of financial independence commensurate with its responsibilities. To settle for less would be a negation of the principles on which British local government is based.[5]

The paper outlined three ways in which its proposed Assembly might be financed. It could receive an annual block grant from the Exchequer calculated to cover 100 per cent of the cost of the services delegated to it. The paper argued that this would tend to tie the Assembly too closely to central government. Many of the weaknesses and inadequacies of the current local government system would be repeated, but on a larger scale. Thus, this option should be avoided.

Alternatively, the Assembly might itself be empowered to levy and collect the monies it required. This would ensure its financial autonomy but, the paper argued, would give rise to other and far-reaching consequences: 'Such an arrangement would seriously undermine the constitutional authority Parliament to determine the broad strategy of Britain's economic and welfare policies.' The paper suggested that an Assembly with too much financial responsibility would not seek regular consultation and co-operation with central government. Such an arrangement would tend, it said, to lead to conflict and so this option should also be avoided.

The paper concluded that a financial relationship must be developed which gave 'an appropriate freedom of action to the Assembly, while at the same time ensuring that Parliament's authority to finance general policy remained undiminished'. To achieve this the paper suggested a scheme along the following lines:

An amount equivalent to not less than 45 per cent of the Assembly's required revenue should be the subject of an entrenched entitlement. Either such a sum should be levied by the Assembly itself, and collected by means of a convenient mechanism, or, the tax or duty, having been levied by Parliament, should then be automatically available to the Assembly to utilise as it determined. The remainder of the Assembly's required revenue, and anyway not less than 40 per cent of its total receipts in any year, should be made available through the Exchequer from central funds. This would retain in very wide measure the proper ultimate authority of Parliament.[6]

The paper went on to urge that the Assembly should have access to a 'dynamic' tax, that is, a buoyant tax like income tax, which would rise automatically with the cost of living and prices, unlike, for example, the rates. Otherwise the balance between the Assembly's revenue sources would tend to change in favour of funds provided centrally, as with local government. The paper, in fact, advocated that the Assembly should have access to personal income tax levied in Wales, and worked out a proposal on the basis of the 1967/8 Welsh budget. (In response to political arguments about Wales's accounts, this had been provided by the Treasury, see table 5.2.) The paper estimated that the Assembly's revenue requirements in that year would have been £306·2 million. It proposed that a variable amount of between £120 million and £165 million should have come from a block exchequer grant. On top of this the yield from personal income tax, amounting to £135 million in 1967-8, should have been added: 'The size of the yield from this single tax would avoid the administrative complexity of diverting a larger number of smaller taxes to the use of the Assembly', the paper stated:

> A small deficiency of about £28·7 million between the mean level of the exchequer grant (estimated at £142·5 million) and the Council's estimated expenditure would still remain. It is proposed that this sum should be raised by delegation to the Assembly of the right to levy and utilise certain minor taxes on capital, as well as stamp duties, motor vehicle duties and Selective Employment tax. A yield of up to £35 million could be anticipated from this source. There would be an added advantage in that flexibility would be introduced in an area where taxation levels can constitute a useful policy instrument.[7]

As with the paper's scheme for giving the Assembly legislative power (discussed in the previous chapter) these taxation proposals became a focus for confrontation between Transport House in London and Transport House in Cardiff. Eventually the Labour Party in Wales, guided by its secretary Emrys Jones, struck a compromise. In return for London's accepting the principle of direct rather than indirect elections to the Assembly, it relinquished its taxation aspirations, together with legislative powers. Again, the British Labour party's then Assistant General Secretary, Gwyn Morgan, was the author of the final compromise draft that in 1970 was presented to the Commission on the Constitution. This reduced the submission on finance to seven paragraphs. The first four were a preamble using identical wording to the opening of the Labour Party in Wales's research group paper quoted above. The final three paragraphs then proceeded to fudge the issue. They repeated the dangers described by the research group of relying entirely on a block grant or relying entirely on a system of locally raised taxes. But then, instead of following the research group's line of advocating a mix of these alternatives, the submission that reached the Commission on the Constitution concluded:

> We suggest a financial relationship should be established that would give an appropriate freedom of action to the Assembly, while at the same time ensuring that Parliament's authority to determine general policy remains undiminished.[8]

It is a political truth that too clear a definition of a problem can be counter-productive. This is the spirit in which the Labour Party in Wales has approached the key question of financing a Welsh Assembly, ever since they gave their evidence to the Commission on the Constitution. As Gwyn Morgan remarked when questioned on the matter by the late Lord Crowther, the Commission's first chairman:

> We have not gone into the details and nuances of these proposals, but we are very conscious that here is a very thin line to be walked between damaging the ultimate legislative authority and answerability of people to the U.K. Government, for money raised by the central exchequer and disbursed by it, and yet giving the Assembly sufficient independence to make it a meaningful force for the advancement of its areas of responsibility in Wales.[9]

The imprecision was maintained even at the critical stage of the Labour Party in Wales's internal debate on devolution in 1974. A document approved by a special conference on the subject, at Llandrindod Wells in June, stated that a financial procedure should be devised which safeguarded Parliament's financial supremacy at the same time as allowing the Welsh Assembly 'sufficient freedom of action to determine priorities peculiar to Wales'. It added, in the second of only two paragraphs on the subject:

> One way to achieve this would be by an Annual Statutory Grant by the central Government thus ensuring minimum standards, and to provide for higher standards where required by central Government, together with a separate source of income which would give the Assembly financial elbow room.[10]

Thus, although the Labour Party in Wales compromised with the Labour party centrally on the issue of taxation powers for the Assembly, at the end of the day it managed to keep its options open. Finance remains the crucial arena for the advance of Welsh responsibility in any devolved institution.

The block grant

The Labour Government's proposals in their November 1975 devolution White Paper[11] (confirmed in the devolution Bill a year later) relied on a system of block funding for the Assembly from the central Exchequer. The argument for this was as follows:

(i) The basic principle is one of equity for Britain as a whole: resources should be distributed 'not according to where they come from but according to where they are needed' (para. 20). The Assembly's expenditure should thus be determined by the 'needs' of the devolved services in Wales, and not on whatever revenues happen to arise there. 'Needs', however, are not absolute but relative, and must therefore be determined in negotiation with the British government, which is the only body in the constitution in a position to weigh the needs of one region against those of another.

(ii) The Welsh administration should therefore negotiate a block grant with the British government each year sufficient to meet the needs of the devolved services. Fixing the size of the grant would not be an arbitrary matter, but would arise out of the Assembly's public expenditure projections, which would roll forward every year and interlock with the British Public Expenditure Survey Committee estimates (see Appendix C of the White Paper). The last word over the size of the grant would lie with the British Government (para. 226).

(iii) When the block grant is determined, the Welsh administration should have

> the fullest possible freedom to decide how the money should be spent—how much, for example, should go on roads, houses, schools and hospitals, and where in Wales it should be spent. This is a major economic as well as social power, and will give the Assembly a powerful new instrument for shaping developments over a wide range of services (para. 223).

(iv) It would be wrong for the Assembly to have substantial independent sources of revenue because this would infringe the principle of 'distributing resources according to need' on which 'the whole system of allocating public expenditure' in Britain is based. So Welsh taxpayers should continue to pay British taxes to the British government at British rates.

The November 1975 devolution White Paper made two qualifications to this last statement. First, the Assembly would have a general power to levy a surcharge on local authority taxation, that is, the rates. Second, the Assembly could reduce the proportion of local authority expenditure it financed by Rate Support Grant and make the local authorities depend more heavily on rates and charges for services.

The supplementary devolution statement, made the following August, withdrew the first qualification: 'Thorough re-examination has confirmed that no better method of developing some revenue-raising power is available within the current framework of national and local taxation, but in the light of the comments received the Government have decided not to pursue this proposal.'[12]

During the debate on the Scotland and Wales Bill in the 1976-7 Parliamentary session these block grant proposals drew much criticism. It was asserted that the size of the block grants would be a source of perpetual conflict between the Assemblies and Westminster. Following the collapse of the Bill in February 1977 the Government proved sensitive to this charge. The renewed proposals for separate Welsh and Scottish legislation the following session set out a 'formula approach' for determining the block grants in an attempt to avoid an annual wrangle between the Treasury and the Assemblies.

The July 1977 White Paper, *Devolution: Financing the Devolved Services* (Cmnd 6890) recognised that there had been concern that annual discussions of the levels of devolved expenditure would lead to detailed scrutiny by government departments of individual devolved spending affecting public spending levels generally. Accordingly, the White Paper proposed an approach that would relate the total of devolved public spending in Wales and Scotland to comparable expenditure elsewhere in the country on the basis of relative needs. Then it would be expressed as a percentage of comparable expenditure in the country as a whole. The percentage would be maintained over a given period, after which it would be determined afresh on the same basis of relative needs:

> The period might be four years, corresponding to the term of the devolved Assemblies. During that period, it would not normally be open to a devolved administration to propose an increase, or to the Government to propose a reduction in the percentage; but increases or decreases in the level of comparable expenditure outside Scotland and Wales would automatically lead to corresponding increases or reductions in devolved expenditure (para. 76).

It would not be practicable to incorporate such a formula in statute because it would lead at best to cumbersome provisions of doubtful validity and effectiveness. Therefore, the Government said it intended to propose an approach, a formula approach on these lines to the Assemblies as soon as they were set up. The White Paper concluded:

> The Government see no reason why determining the level of devolved expenditure in Scotland and Wales according to relative needs should be a cause of especial political dispute. Nevertheless, in order to minimise any risks studies are in hand on the collection of objective information on needs and standards of public services. The Government intend to explore with the devolved administrations the scope for an independent advisory body and for a formula under which devolved expenditure would be settled for a period of, say, four years ahead as a percentage of comparable expenditure in the country as a whole (para. 91).

Such were the government's proposals for financing the Assembly and the case made out for them. The November 1975 White Paper described the Assembly's ability to shift resources from, say, education to housing as 'a major economic as well as social power' but political reality dictates otherwise. For example, the Assembly might decide that it should spend more money on schools. But under the White Paper system, this could only be done by cutting expenditure on housing, or hospitals, or roads, or something else. That means that Wales would have to accept lower standards on these items than elsewhere in Britain, in return for their higher standards in education. If the voters refused to take that, then the room for the Assembly to vary spending would be gone.

At the same time the White Paper did not allow Wales to consume less in order to pay for more schools. That would surely be no more illegitimate or subversive a decision than cutting spending on hospitals or housing for the same purpose—indeed, most people, faced with the choice, would probably prefer to see consumption cut. Yet because the amount of tobacco or alcohol or petrol that people buy was held to be part of demand management while the relative totals spent on Welsh schools and hospitals were not, this area of genuine political choice was excluded.

Demand management—that is, control of total consumption—raises a fundamental question of democracy, a question that was ignored in the government's devolution proposals. The question is simply that a centralised financial system, as is exercised in Britain through the Treasury, is incompatible with real local responsibility. This was brought out clearly in May 1976 by the Layfield Committee report on local government finance which judged that a deliberate choice has to be made between a centralised financial system and one which provides for greater local responsibility.

The report declared that placing responsibility firmly with central government or with local authorities meant

> either adopting a financial system which frankly recognises a need for strong central direction or taking positive steps to increase the ability of local authorities to manage local affairs. If that is not done we believe that there is bound to be an increasing shift of power to the centre, but in circumstances in which responsibility for expenditure and local taxation will continue to be confused.[13]

Where centralised control is allowed to continue unimpeded, the tendency will be towards greater centralisation, the Layfield Committee argued:

> We are convinced that, unless increased powers of local decision are matched by a greater control by local authorities over their sources of revenue, the combination of financial and political forces will continue to push in the direction of greater, not less, central control. We conclude that there is no prospect of achieving substantially greater local accountability within the framework of a financial system combining high and increasing grants with rating as the sole local tax.[14]

Here, of course, the Layfield Committee was talking about the relationship between central government and local authorities. But the point applies with equal, if not more, force to the relationship between central government and a Welsh Assembly.

But it is just this issue that was ignored in the November 1975 devolution White Paper. However, a chink of light was allowed to penetrate in the Supplementary Statement that Mr Michael Foot, the Minister then responsible for devolution, presented to the House of Commons the following August. After announcing that the government had decided against allowing the Assembly to levy an optional surcharge on the rates to supplement the block grant Foot's Statement continued:

> If future changes are made in the taxation framework, particularly for financing local government, which would make it feasible for the Welsh Assembly to supplement the block fund . . . the Government will be ready to consider incorporating the necessary revenue-raising powers in subsequent legislation.[15]

This suggested that the government wished to avoid becoming immersed in taxation arguments while the devolution Bill was passing through the House of Commons. But the implication was

that a 'green line' was being drawn around the proposals for financing the Assembly—an interpretation confirmed by the government
when it published the Bill in November 1976. Government
spokesmen, including Michael Foot, declared they were not against
taxation powers in principle but that it was extremely difficult to
devise a workable scheme.

Following the collapse of the Scotland and Wales Bill in February
1977, the government's renewed proposals for separate Scottish and
Welsh legislation the following session threw the onus squarely on
the Assemblies themselves. The July 1977 White Paper,
Devolution: Financing the Devolved Services (Cmnd 6890) stated:

> The Government have again reviewed the scope for devolving marginal
> tax powers including a supplementary income tax, a supplementary
> value added tax or sales taxes, a tax on the occupation of property,
> supplementary taxes on companies and a mix of minor possibilities.
>
> The Government's conclusion is that, on balance and taking into
> account the general practicability and likely public acceptability of each
> tax method examined, the disadvantages outweight the advantages. They
> accordingly have no proposals for devolving specific tax powers as a
> means of supplementing the block fund. However, if the devolved
> administrations wish to have available a limited supplementary tax
> power and are ready to meet its administrative cost then the Government
> would certainly be willing to consider sympathetically any such
> proposals, other than in relation to off-shore oil (paras 64-5).

The reality of the position was that in attempting to devise a
finance-raising scheme for its Assembly the government ran up
against total hostility from the Treasury which refused to counten-
ance that any part of its control over taxation be removed. This confrontation, which is central to the politics of devolution, will be
probed in detail in the rest of this chapter. As to the alternative to
some form of tax-raising power, total reliance on central block
funding, one need only quote the Treasury, itself, which has put on
record the major drawback. This is that it is a denial of the fiscal
discipline of joining tax raising with tax spending:

> It can be held as a very general rule of good administration that
> financial and managerial responsibility should go hand in hand. The
> attitude of an authority towards expenditure for which it may be
> responsible could be materially affected by the degree and directness of
> its responsibility, towards an electorate of its own, for raising funds in
> order to defray that expenditure.[16]

Of course, the Labour government's block grant system for financing devolution ignored this 'general rule of good administration'. In doing so it was a recipe for conflict. It placed the proposed Assembly in a position of inevitable confrontation with central government. Social conditions in Wales, as described in the Introduction, compare unfavourably with the rest of Britain, particularly housing, education and health standards. The Welsh economy needs massive resources to place it on a balanced and modernised footing. Yet a major economic concern of central government, at a time of continuing inflation and balance of payments deficits, is curbing expenditure. In these circumstances scope for confrontation between Wales and Whitehall is obvious. Indeed, the 1975 devolution White Paper spoke of the 'political sensitivity' of annual negotiations proposed for settling the block grant and stated that its determination would be 'a matter for political judgement'.[17]

In the circumstances outlined, political judgment would tend to give way to political pressure. The block grant negotiations conceived in the Labour government's devolution policy would become a major arena for conflict between Wales and Westminster. Nevertheless, the conflict would not be new. It would take place in public view instead of behind the closed doors of the Cabinet. Inevitably it would tend to lead to ways being found of placing more financial responsibility at the Welsh level as the essential means of tempering the new-found muscle being exercised on behalf of the Welsh community. It is the central theme of this book that the politics of devolution in action would be creative in this way. The rest of this chapter will explore some of the arguments that need to be deployed in achieving a creative response to this central financial problem of devolution.

The dead hand of the Treasury

The Treasury has consistently brought immense pressure to bear to ensure that it retains complete control over the British economy's taxes and levels of demand. In its evidence to the Commission on the Constitution the Treasury insisted that its control over demand levels was essential because 'on this depends the level of economic activity, our balance of payments on current account, and, to some extent, the stability of the currency'.[18] It made it clear that demand management policy would be easier to carry out 'the more the decisions on the rates and yield of major taxes are concentrated in the hands of central government and the greater the influence of the

Treasury over both the total amount, and the economic composition
of spending of all layers of government'.[19]

The Treasury added that it would be a 'contradiction' to envisage
regions running their own demand-management policies within an
economy in which an overall control had to be exercised by the
central government. It concluded that the central government
should be left with 'sufficient powers to manage the economy
without fear of having its policies thwarted by one or more of
the regions'.[20]

Given that the Treasury must retain responsibility for overall
levels of demand in the British economy the argument centres on the
power and control 'sufficient' to achieve this. The Treasury's
position is, quite simply, that it should have full control, and this
was the position adopted by the Labour government. For example,
the 1975 devolution White Paper stated:

> Economic unity requires a system which considers the expenditure needs
> of the whole United Kingdom, including the claims of regions with
> special problems. This requires a decision each year on public expendit-
> ure for all parts of the United Kingdom by the Government, answerable
> to Parliament.[21]

This is the source of the reliance on the block grant system of
financing devolution, a system that can be easily controlled from the
centre. Early on the government recognised the inherent weakness of
lack of fiscal responsibility in totally relying on a block grant. But
under Treasury pressure it declared that no other practical solution
was to be found. Thus the Prime Minister, Mr Callaghan, when
introducing the devolution Bill to the House of Commons, conceded
that 'in theory' there was a case for taxation powers. He added: 'We
are not against it in principle. We have simply not yet found a
scheme which would be satisfactory'.[22] What he should have said
was that no scheme, however well it might have worked in such economically successful countries as West Germany or the United States,
would be satisfactory to the Treasury.

Any alternative to centralised Treasury control implies some form
of decentralised control over revenue raising. From the Treasury's
point of view the extreme possibility would be that local authorities
or devolved Assemblies would have access to income tax, with a wide
discretion in setting its rate. Income tax is, of course, a key
instrument of government demand management. Decentralising it
could cause problems of overall United Kingdom economic management, since it would reduce the ability of the government to use
income tax changes as a means of stimulating or depressing demand

in the economy. There is a particular danger, from the Treasury's point of view, that action by the government to reduce taxation by means of changes in tax rates or increased allowances would be seen as an opportunity for devolved assemblies to increase their taxes, thereby blunting the effect sought by the government.

But the apparent logical simplicity of this Treasury case can be challenged, first on theoretical grounds, and second, on the basis of the lack of success of the Treasury's centralised system of complete control over income tax:

(i) The limited Treasury control required for demand management

The Treasury is not concerned with the detailed levels of expenditure of particular areas or groups of people within Britain, for instance, with the marginal variations in demand between towns with a heavy rate burden and towns with a light one. Rather, the Treasury is traditionally, and properly, concerned with 'aggregate demand'— that is, with the broad totals of different types of spending in the economy as a whole.

Now the significant factor is that, taken together, the Welsh and Scottish Assemblies could not significantly alter total aggregate demand in Britain. This has been demonstrated by Dr David King in his research paper for the Commission on the Constitution.[23] Taking 1968-9, Dr King showed that the total expenditure in Wales and Scotland by the central government in that year, on services considered potentially suitable for devolution, was £780 million. This was about 2·5 per cent of British gross national product (GNP) and about 4 per cent of total public expenditure. So, with devolution in these areas, Wales and Scotland could raise their spending by a fifth in one year without raising total demand by more than 0·5 per cent of GNP.

If raising total British demand by less than 0·5 per cent in one year, in the case of the Welsh Assembly by itself, was considered serious, then the Assembly could be asked not to change its total spending by more than, say, 5 per cent each year. Such a policy would still allow substantial changes to occur in a matter of a few years.

But this would be leaning over backwards in favour of the Treasury—an assertion confirmed indirectly by no less an authority than the Permanent Secretary of the Treasury himself, Sir Douglas Wass, in 1975. In evidence to the House of Commons Expenditure Committee in that year he stated that, with GNP running at about £100,000 million a year, only sums of £1,000 million or more could have a real effect on demand in Britain.[24]

The 1975 devolution White Paper estimated the Assembly's total devolved expenditure for the financial year 1974-5 to be £910 million. Thus, even if the Assembly had complete control over its own revenue raising this would fall short of Sir Douglas Wass's critical figure. Political reality is, of course, that simply because tax-payers are also voters, it is highly unlikely that the Assembly would ever want to vary revenue in Wales even as much as 10 per cent from the amounts that would be raised by the British government if the Assembly did not exist. It is far more likely, in fact, that variations would be less than 5 per cent (certainly in the first years) and, depending on the type of expenditure undertaken, the effect on demand in Wales would probably be less.

If further support is needed to counter the Treasury's irrationally frigid concern about its ability to control aggregate demand, it was provided by a taxation research paper for the Commission on the Constitution.[25] This gave figures of central government tax receipts for the United States and Canada in 1967 which amounted to 14 per cent of their GNP. At that time the comparable figure for the British government's tax receipts was 26 per cent of GNP.[26] Indeed, in that year, or for that matter in any subsequent year, Britain could have devolved enough taxes to cover all regional current expenditure (including that of the English regions as well as Wales and Scotland) and still have had central government taxes left amounting to 14 per cent or more of GNP—which, as has been shown, was sufficient for a country like the United States to administer aggregate demand.

In view of the foregoing argument, which has demonstrated that the British Treasury could have far less centralised control over the economy and still operate an effective aggregate demand policy, it is not surprising that an increasing number of critics are turning their attention to the institution of the Treasury itself. As the Memorandum of Dissent to the Commission on the Constitution put it: how is it that 'major countries with devolved systems of government manage to be at least as successful (and in some cases more successful) at stabilising their economies?'[27]

The question leads from challenging the theory of the Treasury's adherence to absolute control over any devolved expenditure (via a block grant) to examining the practicality and success of central-ised control. How far, in fact, does the Treasury properly control spending and manage demand?

(ii) The inadequacy of centralised Treasury control of the British economy

In December 1975 the House of Commons Expenditure Committee declared that public expenditure was out of control and concluded: 'the present system of control of public expenditure cannot simply be left as it is'.[28]

The Committee accepted evidence that the Treasury had allowed public spending in 1974/5 to rise by about £5,800 million more than had been planned in its Public Expenditure White Paper of November 1971. The Committee pointed out that on the Treasury's own admission nearly 70 per cent of the excess—£4,000 million—was not the result of announced policy changes. This unplanned expenditure corresponded to 5 per cent of the United Kingdom's gross domestic product, or enough to keep the National Health Service going for a year. The Committee commented, 'The Treasury's methods of controlling public expenditure are inadequate in the sense that money can be spent on a scale which was not contemplated when the relevant policies were decided upon'.[29]

Whatever explanations can be found for this lack of spending control, and there are many including the important problem of forecasting relative price increases, this record is not a good advertisement for centralised control of demand management. The impression of lack of precision was accentuated by evidence the Committee took on the relationship in Britain between taxation and expenditure.

Sir Alec Cairncross, a former economic adviser to the government, told the Committee that Britain is the only country in the world which decides on its public expenditure programme before its tax programme. He said this 'may mean there is a greater readiness to concede an increase in expenditure than there would be if it were necessary on each occasion to impose fresh taxation'.[30]

Beyond performing the valuable function of bringing these and related matters to prominence the Expenditure Committee had few positive suggestions on what changes should be made to improve control of public spending. Its main recommendation was that the Treasury should introduce more 'positive planning' with a tougher scrutiny procedure than operated by its Public Expenditure Survey Committee System. (This produces annual Public Expenditure White Papers projecting spending five years ahead.)

Advocating tougher scrutiny is little more than suggesting merely that the Treasury should improve its existing performance. The Expenditure Committee's lack of any fundamental analysis of its findings at least leaves the way clear for an argument for a more decentralised system of demand management and control of the economy.

The case for decentralised financial control

The argument against the Treasury's insistence on centralised fiscal control of the British economy has so far been directed at:

(i) The excessive degree of centralisation being demanded.

(ii) The inadequacy of centralised fiscal management in operation.

This has been tackling the Treasury's case on its own ground: conceding that there is, in fact, a homogeneous uniform British economy which can be managed by homogeneous uniform solutions. That this should be the underlying assumption of the Treasury's position is in itself a reflection of the distorted view of Britain as seen from Great George Street and the rest of Whitehall. If there be any doubt that this is indeed the Treasury position one need only point to the lack of information and statistics the Treasury has to gauge the regional impact of its policies. The House of Commons Expenditure Committee criticised the Treasury's inadequate information about the impact of its taxation policies on regional economies within Britain.   In particular, the Committee felt there was lack of information on each region's tax yield and its proportion to each region's contribution to gross domestic product:

> The relevance of this to arguments about devolution and local government finance is obvious and once known it could, one hopes, be compared to the regional distribution of public expenditure to produce the net 'effect of government operations upon each region, something highly relevant to all regional policy.[31]

The fact that the Treasury has not sought any complete analysis of the regional impact of its fiscal policies confirms that it has been primarily concerned with aggregate results at the expense of regional variations within the United Kingdom. These variations, so far as unemployment and low activity rates are concerned, have been discussed in chapter 2. Throughout much of the period since the Second World War a major concern of British government has been with the problem of inflation. The causes have grown more complex in the 1970s but an underlying factor has been pressure of demand combined with labour scarcity in the South-East of England and the Midlands. At the same time the Welsh economy (in common with

Scotland, Northern Ireland and the English Development Areas) has been characterised by low demand and a labour surplus partly disguised by emigration of people of working age.

Thus public spending cuts and other deflationary measures have had little relevance to the problems of Wales. Their effect has merely been to worsen the Welsh unemployment situation. This has, of course, been recognised to some extent by the government, and since the late 1960s there has been an attempt to discriminate between the different regions of the United Kingdom in the application of deflationary policies.

This was the prime function of the Regional Employment Premium, a wage subsidy for males in high unemployment areas. It was instituted in the wake of the 1967 deflationary budget which continued running the economy with high unemployment. As a means of attracting *new* industry to Wales and other development areas REP was an ineffective and costly measure. But viewed as a counter-trade-cycle weapon which can cushion the effects of recession in Wales it proved more successful. It was, in effect, a form of regional devaluation. This has been argued by Professor Graham Rees, who has stated that its removal would place Wales in a position of acute disadvantage in the context of the unitary British economic system where there is no other tax adjustment:

> Wales' plight of being so closely integrated with the rest of the UK as to be entirely bereft of separate and independent means of economic adjustment provides the parallel in *extremis* of the ultimate goal now accepted by the British government in relation to the EEC. Clearly, for Wales itself, British entry to the EEC makes the Principality that much more remote from the source of economic decision-making.[32]

The Regional Employment Premium was, of course, abolished in the mini-budget of late December 1976, signalling the end of British regional policy as traditionally conceived in the postwar period. Its removal left a vacuum which the devolutionary movement was poised to fill. But the problem was that the devolved institutions being proposed did not have the facility for inter-regional adjustment inherent in the old Regional Employment Premium. To have that they would have had to have the potential for establishing variations in tax rates.

An approach to presenting the case for a more decentralised financial control of the economy was made by the former Labour Minister, Jeremy Bray, in his book *Decision in Government,* published at the end of Labour's 1960s administration. The central argument of the book was that global economic management at the

all-United Kingdom level was not providing a sufficiently sophisticated degree of control. In its place Bray pressed for what he termed,
disaggregated economic management:

> Its working practice can be stated quite simply: the total productivity of
> resources used should be maximised while the balance of supply and
> demand is maintained not just for the economy as a whole, but within
> the several parts of the economy. Thus demand and supply should
> balance for the overall operations of an industry, for a geographical
> region, for a particular kind of manpower, for a particular resource, or
> for a particular product. . . . By maintaining a higher and smoother
> level of activity in each part, with a rapid rate of internal development,
> the growth of the economy as a whole should be more rapid.[33]

Bray's approach to the problem was modest by the standards of
the debate that was already under way amongst decentralists in
Wales and Scotland. His was a thoroughly British/centralist
analysis. What was required was fine tuning at the disaggregated
level of particular industries and manpower groups as much as at
the regional level which, in any event, is blurred in the book with the
'local level'. The starting point of Bray's argument is the need for
more efficient operation of the British economy taken as a whole
rather than the needs of communities within the country. Indeed,
these are only conceded in so far as they coincide with a
'geographical region'.

Nevertheless, the force of Bray's argument, on grounds of pure
technical efficiency, led him to press the case for stronger *local*
government. He concluded that local government required additional
'responsibility for the management of local aspects of the economy
and for manpower policy, with the power to raise a sufficiently wide
range of local taxes to cover the greater part of their expenditure'.[34]
For as Bray put it:

> It is the age old experience of government, and indeed of administration
> generally, that remote control—disinterested perhaps, but unaware, ill
> informed, and not involved—cannot work satisfactorily. The way the
> chips fall in a particular area from a series of separate national pro-
> grammes in education, housing, transport, employment, industrial
> development, taxation and subsidy does not by any means represent a
> coherent and balanced course of local community development. The
> absurdities, so obvious at a local level, get lost in a national view and
> produce great frustration locally.
>
> This is best seen in particular local situations. The picture that
> emerges is not one of neglect but of a certain ineptitude and clumsiness
> from central government. On Teeside, which I know best, many millions
> of pounds of public funds have been poured into the development of

capital intensive industry without increasing employment. At the same time higher education, lighter industry and service employment were neglected, leaving an unbalanced and unstable local economy. The experiences of Sunderland, West Cumberland, Hull, Cornwall, Oxford, Stevenage, the Swansea Valley, Anglesey, Greenock and Stirling are all different. Simply to list them recalls the diversity of problems they have faced. . . .[35]

No doubt it was Bray's acceptance of the logical consequences of his analysis that required him to resign from the government in order to publish his book—an indication of the insecurity of the Treasury-inspired orthodoxy as much as an indictment. Bray listed the objections to his analysis as follows:

(i) people of sufficient calibre could not be found at the 'local level' to carry out the fine tuning demanded by disaggregated economic control. This he countered with the fact that rising levels of educational attainment point the other way.

(ii) Conflict would arise because policies of a central government of one party could be frustrated by local government in the hands of another political party. Bray countered that if local democracy is to be meaningful this problem should be accepted.

(iii) Economic policies must be uniform across the United Kingdom because the various areas of Britain are so economically interlocked. Bray countered this by demonstrating the wide variation in economic problems facing the different parts of the country. Viewed from outside London blanket central policies can often seem 'perverse in the extreme'.[36]

Bray concluded that these replies were only half the argument:

The full argument is that control should rest in proportion to where need is recognised and people are willing to respond. From the sheer scale of the problem central government cannot recognise and respond to need in all respects. It would be wiser for central government to give way where it can, before the pressures for decentralisation build up to breaking point, and the movement goes too far away from the centre.[37]

Moreover, contrary to Treasury orthodoxy, devolved taxes can build into a financial system a great deal of fiscal discipline. This has certainly proved the case in West Germany which has two main layers of government, the central administration in Bonn and eleven regional legislative governments, the Länder. The constitution allocates different taxes to the two levels of government. Income tax is shared among the central government, the Länder and the local authorities, and VAT between the first two only. The relative share is agreed at a tough round of negotiations which take place about once every two years (at the time of writing Bonn takes 43 per cent of income tax and 69 per cent of VAT). Both levels of government must maintain balanced budgets, a directive that is the more enforceable since each layer of government acts as a check on the other. There is an equally healthy check on taxation levels as a result of the relationship. For instance, in December 1976 the German Federal government proposed to increase VAT from 11 per cent to 13 per cent from January 1978. This was opposed by the Länder governments and they were able to express their opposition through their representation in the Federal State upper house of representatives, the Bundesraat.

Of course, the major gain of the German federal system (more accurately described as co-operative federalism) is the dispersal of economic power centres it encourages. There is no dominating centre like London in West Germany. Bonn, the capital, is a relatively small administrative centre. Länder capitals like Stuttgart, Munich, Dusseldorf and Hamburg are all major power centres which ensure a spread of resources. As a result West Germany has no fundamental problem of regional economic imbalance which so bedevils Britain. The poorest Länder, Lower Saxony on the shores of the Baltic, in mid-1977 had an unemployment rate of only 5.6 per cent (compared with a West German average of 4.3 per cent). In turn this facilitates the achievement of wage agreements since they are not so easily undermined by dissenting groups which are often associated with disadvantaged areas of a country. It is also part of the explanation why West Germany has been able to rationalise its trade union structure down to just 16 unions compared with some 400 in Britain.

The case for decentralised financial control is that devolved fiscal machinery is necessary to enable inroads to be made into the problem of regional unemployment in Britain. Exercising demand management at the regional level—in the case of Wales and Scotland at the national level—is an essential component of tackling the 'regional problem' that was described in chapter 2.

Towards Welsh financial responsibility

Professor A. A. Tait, of the University of Strathclyde, has argued that the economics of devolution are a knife-edge problem where the two extremes are stable but all intermediate positions unstable.[38]

At one extreme, a strong authoritarian central government, which was prepared to use regionally differentiated taxes and subsidies between Scotland, Wales and England, would be a stable position. At the other extreme, total separation which enabled Scotland and Wales actually to devalue and expand their economies, leaving the problem of excess demand in England to the English government, would also be stable. Intermediate positions, such as Welsh and Scottish Assemblies financed by block grants, would be unstable and gradually lead to separation as a result of inevitable constitutional conflict. Tait concluded:

> This is a classic knife-edge position. Either the position is one where a powerful central power is prepared to take politically unpopular decisions to restrain the strong affluent regions, or those regions which are weak and require expansion start to behave as independent countries. The in-between stages are unstable.

Professor Tait insists that the first option requires a regional policy which puts as much emphasis on the 'stick' of restricted growth in the strong areas of the country as on the 'carrot' of industrial incentives to promote development in the economically weak areas. He argues that a powerful central administration with the political will to impose the politically unpopular restrictions in the stronger regions does not exist in Britain. Indeed, he argues that the reverse applies, with the government authorising the London Allowance:

> The Government, as usual, would dearly like to have its cake and eat it by saying that it has to pay the London Allowance to get civil servants to work in London at the same time as saying that it cannot persuade civil servants to disperse to the provinces.

With the Treasury continuing to impose its demand-management restrictions on any devolved institutions, Professor Tait predicts an inevitable slide towards further devolution and independence. The only way this situation could be defused, he suggests, would be to re-think the whole question of the validity of aggregate-demand stabilisation policy in the United Kingdom: 'It might be possible to create a dis-aggregated stabilisation policy under which the regions would have sufficient control to remove the continuous irritation of Treasury dominance.'

Such a solution would have to involve Assemblies receiving a substantial part of their income from taxation for which they were directly responsible and which they could vary. Only then could they make real political choices between expenditure priorities and also directly affect levels of activity and unemployment in their territory.

The remainder of this chapter consists in presenting the outline of a scheme that could bring such financial responsibility to a Welsh Assembly. It owes much to the ideas presented by Professor A. T. Peacock in the Commission on the Constitution's Minority Report.[39] The main difference is that while the Crowther-Hunt scheme was drawn up on the assumption of devolved executive Assemblies in five English regions as well as Wales and Scotland, the pattern suggested here is applicable to Wales (and Scotland) alone. The problem is to devise a scheme which combines flexibility for an Assembly with preservation of sufficient Treasury influence over the British economy as a whole.

However, when Wales and Scotland are considered by themselves the problem is simpler than if Assemblies for the English regions were involved as well. For, as was demonstrated earlier, the devolved budgets for Wales and Scotland put together could only marginally influence total British demand.

The financial scheme outlined in the following pages is considered in three parts. First, methods of assuring a sufficiently independent source of revenue for an Assembly are proposed. Second, a suggested structure to ensure the scheme dovetails with the Treasury's role in managing the whole United Kingdom economy is put forward. Finally, the economic benefits the suggested financial scheme can be expected to bring will be briefly discussed.

(i) Revenue to ensure autonomy

Under the government's proposals (in the November 1975 White Paper) spending on devolved services would have come to more than half of total identifiable public expenditure in Wales in 1974-5. The Welsh Assembly's budget would have been broken down as shown in Table 5.1.

It will be seen that if an Assembly were to have financial responsibility a significant proportion of the £650 million block grant would have to be found from taxes within the control of the Assembly itself. The nature and proportion of taxation raised and spent in Wales can be illustrated by the Welsh budget produced by the Treasury in 1971 for the financial year 1968-9. This is reproduced in simplified form in Table 5.2. The table shows that taken together personal and corporate sector income tax combined with National Insurance contributions (total £289 million) roughly equal taxes raised on

Table 5.1   1974-75 devolved budget for Wales

Income	£ millions	Expenditure	£ millions
Block Grant	650	Education	235
Borrowing	170	Health and personal social services	227
Local Authority taxation	90	Housing	173
		Environmental services	97
		Roads	86
		Other	32
		Local Authority loan charges	60
Total	910	Total	910

(*Source*: Welsh Office [The break-down for expenditure is that decided by the Welsh Office for that year].)

expenditure (£266 million). Thus any scheme to finance an Assembly's budget mainly out of its own accountable taxation would have to draw on both income and expenditure taxation.

A Welsh Assembly's income should consist of three elements:

(a) personal income tax; (b) petrol and vehicle excise duty; (c) a block grant sufficient to ensure equalisation of provision as between Wales and the rest of the United Kingdom.

(a) *Income tax.* It would be impractical to collect income tax from the Welsh corporate sector, that is, any version of corporation tax. This is because corporation tax is assessed on a company at the address of its registered office, usually its head office. Since the majority of industries operating in Wales have their head office outside the country—see last section of the following chapter for the figures—the measurement of tax profits and revenues by Welsh industry would be severely restricted. The most practical approach on the income tax side, therefore, is to limit an Assembly's remit to personal income tax. In 1974-5 this raised some £300 million in Wales.

The basic rate of United Kingdom income tax is now 35 per cent, which is applied to taxable income (gross income minus allowances for family and other commitments). The Welsh Assembly should be allowed to vary this between a range of 25 per cent and 40 per cent. This would allow the Assembly flexibility in managing Welsh demand levels. The tax would be collected on behalf of a Welsh Assembly by the United Kingdom Inland Revenue (due to computerisation Wales was made into an integral tax collection area in 1975/6). Rules about residence would be required. A personal income tax was recommended by the Layfield Committee report for adoption by the eight Welsh county councils. The report stated that it was 'the only serious candidate for a new source of local revenue that could give a substantial yield and at the same time maintain or enhance accountability'.[40]

(b) *Indirect taxation.* The majority report of the Commission on the Constitution described petrol duty as 'one of the stronger candidates for devolution' and vehicle excise duty as 'perhaps the strongest candidate for devolution'.[41] In 1974-5 the total yield in Wales from vehicle excise duty was £24·3 million and since then, due to increases, the yield has become more buoyant (probably reaching about £40 million in 1975/6). The yield from petrol duty in 1974/5 was about £150 million. The Welsh Assembly should be empowered to vary

Table 5.2   Central Government Account for Wales 1968-9*

Receipts	Treasury	Expenditure	Treasury
Taxes on Income:		*Identifiable Current Expenditure:*	
Personal Sector	163	Goods and Services	356
Corporate Sector	31	Local Authority Grants	121
Taxes on Expenditure:	266	*Allocated Current Expenditure*†	
National Insurance, etc., Contributions:	95	Debt Interest	61
Rent, Trading Surpluses, Interest and Dividends:	67	Defence	115
		Central Government Administration and External Relations	14
Total Current Receipts	622	Total Current Expenditure	667
CAPITAL RECEIPTS		CAPITAL EXPENDITURE	
Current Deficit:	45	*Central Government Element of Public Expenditure*	97
Taxes on Capital, etc.:	39	*Grants and Loans to Local Authorities:*	34
Net Borrowing Requirement:	182	*Grants and Loans to Public Corporations:*	47
Total Capital Receipts	176	Total Capital Expenditure	176

*The figures are in £ millions and are Treasury estimates for the financial year 1968-9.

†Allocations of total UK expenditure on 'central' services between Wales and the rest of the UK were based on the ratio of Wales's total population to that of the UK as a whole.

(*Source:* Roy Thomas, 'The Economics of Nationalism' in *The Welsh Dilemma* (Christopher Davies, 1973), p. 76.)

excise and petrol duties by up to 10 per cent above or below the
English rates.

Taken together, personal income tax combined with petrol and
vehicle excise duty would have yielded some £500 million of the £650
million apportioned by the government for the block grant it proposed in the November 1975 devolution White Paper.

(c) *Equalisation grant.* The remaining £150 million should be
derived from an amended block grant system. A leeway of these
proportions would be necessary to provide a measure of equalisation
between Wales and the rest of Britain. The equalisation grant would
be calculated in the following way. First, a sum would be agreed
between the Assembly and the Treasury as to the Assembly's global
expenditure on the assumption that funding was to be entirely on the
basis of a block grant. Then, using standard British rates for the
devolved taxes (for example, a 35 per cent levy on personal income
tax) their yield would be worked out on that basis. The difference
between that sum and the global figure first agreed would be met by
the equalisation grant.

The equalisation grant would vary as the return from the
independently raised revenue varied. Thus if the variable rate of
personal income tax led to an increase in consumption then, via the
multiplier, average income would also rise in Wales. The resulting
increase in return from income tax would enable a decrease in the
equalisation grant.

(ii) Integration with the British economy

The system outlined above would endow an Assembly with considerable flexibility in its finance-raising ability. To begin with it would
be responsible for raising at least three-quarters of its own cash. But
on top of this the system would allow it to vary its basic rate of
income tax between the limits of 25 per cent and 40 per cent. This
flexibility would give it a powerful weapon to protect and promote
the Welsh economy by varying demand rates in it relative to the rest
of Britain.

However, this flexibility, which is discussed below in the third part
of this financial scheme, is also the source of the scheme's main
difficulty. For it would make the Treasury's task of managing
British demand levels more difficult. This is because the demand
effects of tax changes in one particular area cannot be contained
within that area. For instance, if a Welsh Assembly were to lower the
rate of Welsh income tax with the result that the rate of spending by
people in Wales increased, many of the extra goods bought would be

made in England. This would mean that economic activity would be stimulated in England as well as in Wales. This type of effect is known as 'spill-over' effect. Spill-over effects are difficult to trace through economies, making the general management of demand very difficult. The following arrangements would be designed to counteract this difficulty:

(a) The Welsh Assembly would be required to draw up a set of projections of the likely development of the services within its control over the next five years. On the basis of negotiated 'reasonable standards' for each service a total figure for expenditure could be arrived at and its demand effects estimated.

(b) This planning exercise would be repeated every three years, although the projections each time would cover a five-year period: this would ensure that there were always at least three planned years to serve as a background to the Assembly's Public Expenditure Surveys, which would be carried out each year.

(c) Differential rates in the Assembly's taxation would be settled in this planning exercise. Hence the rates decided on in one planning exercise would be fixed and immutable until the next planning exercise, three years later. Thus there would be no question of the Assembly changing its tax rates frequently and at will, making it very difficult for the Treasury to gauge spill-over effect and to control the general level of demand. Indeed, the aim would be to establish a stable differential structure of taxation rates between Wales and England, thereby helping to equalise the pressure of demand on resources between the two countries. If England decided it wanted regional government then there could be even finer tuning in these differentials and hence demand management to meet the particular needs of different areas.[42]

(iii) Economic benefits of the scheme

The major benefit would be that the Welsh Assembly would be empowered to make some inroads into unemployment levels by utilising the techniques of demand management at the Welsh level. It would have broadly three options. It could:

(i) set its rates of taxation below those prevailing in England in order to stimulate demand;

(ii) increase its expenditure in ways most likely to reduce unemployment (for instance, direct spending to relevant areas if unemployment was highly localised);

(iii) do a combination of both these things.

The power to alter the price of petrol within Wales through changing the tax rate would be an added bonus. In co-operation with local
authorities the tax rates for petrol could be varied within Wales in
order to aid areas, particularly in rural Wales, where people are
forced to run cars because of the inadequacy of public transport.

Apart from taxation powers enabling the Assembly to evolve a
counter-cyclical demand-management policy from a Welsh basis, they
would inject a fiscal discipline that is lacking in a financial scheme
heavily reliant on a central block grant. Such a discipline would be
the most efficient check on spending growth and consequently an
essential ingredient of spending control.

The central argument of this chapter has been that the freedom of a
Welsh Assembly would depend very largely on how far it could
control its income. The direct control of its income by the Treasury,
under the block grant system, would impose a rigidity that would
result in the loss of many potential benefits from devolution.
The most valuable benefit to be lost would be the advantages of a
disaggregated demand-management facility.

This is not to deny that a block grant system operated by an
Assembly would be an advance for Wales. Indeed, following the
1977-8 rate-support-grant allocation procedure the Welsh local
authority associations called for a block funding system via the
Welsh Office, for themselves. This was because under the distribution formula for England and Wales the Welsh counties were classed
along with the English shire counties, from which money was being
diverted into the English metropolitan areas. This was despite the
fact that most of the Welsh counties had problems more in common
with the metropolitan areas.[43]

Nevertheless, reliance on any form of block funding for an
Assembly from the centre would be unlikely to prove satisfactory for
long. The simple reason remains that any form of block funding
divorces revenue raising from revenue spending. It is not designed to
ensure efficient control of public expenditure, as the rate-support-
grant system with local authorities has proved. Applied to a Welsh
Assembly it would be likely to result in Wales being permanently
dissatisfied with its grant total. Indeed, the only economic policy
likely to be followed by a Welsh administration financed by a
Treasury block grant, would be to ask for more money from
London. It would be a positive incentive to a begging bowl mental-
ity. On the other hand, if Welsh politicians were faced with the task
of working out economic policy for themselves they would be less

inclined to think that the answer to most problems would be simply more state subsidies.

The Commission on the Constitution stated that a 'general and long term cause of financial frustration among local authorities has been the extent of central influence on their detailed expenditure plans, which springs largely from the central government's general political responsibility for local services'.[44] This is quite correct. But the central political responsibility is overwhelmingly the result of dominant central financial responsibility.

Without a measure of financial autonomy for Wales, devolution would have limited point. Decentralising political responsibility cannot be divorced from decentralising financial responsibility. The two go hand in hand. Devolved taxation powers would also have the advantage of building in fiscal responsibility as well as providing the opportunity for decentralised demand management of the economy. Financial responsibility is the central requirement for any workable devolution scheme. In this sense it is more important than the question of whether legislative as well as executive powers should be devolved to an assembly and how far an assembly should have control over industry and the economy generally. For devolution to work an Assembly must have financial as well as political responsibility for its actions.

Chapter 6

Forging a Welsh Economic Policy

'The key issue is that the economic powers of the Assembly are essential to
its effectiveness and its credibility . . .'

Labour Party in Wales, Executive Committee
memorandum, June 1975.

Like the issue of whether an Assembly should be able to raise its own
taxes, the question of whether it should have the power to promote
and control economic development in Wales is a central dilemma of
devolution. On the one hand underdevelopment of the Welsh
economy has been a major cause of pressure for devolution. But on
the other hand, the granting of industrial powers to the Welsh
Assembly would threaten the British government's ability to control
development from the centre. A related issue is the position of the
Secretary of State for Wales, since the more powers that were
devolved to any Welsh Assembly the less tenable would become his
position as a Cabinet Minister.

The compromise solution, as devised by the Labour government,
was to concentrate power over the Welsh economy in the hands of
the Secretary of State. If not devolution to the Assembly this was at
least administrative decentralisation and had the added advantage
of compensating the Secretary of State for the education, health,
and environmental functions he would be losing.

This strategy began to be put into effect in July 1975 when the
Secretary of State for Industry's powers, under Section 7 of the 1972
Industry Act, and his factory building powers under the 1972 Local
Employment Act, were transferred to the Secretary of State for
Wales. The November 1975 Devolution White Paper indicated that
this would be followed up by making the Secretary of State for Wales
responsible for manpower and industrial training in Wales and
wholly accountable for agriculture.

But the transfer of Section 7 powers marked the most significant
stage in the evolution of the Secretary of State for Wales into an
economic Minister. Under Section 7 the Secretary of State has discretionary powers for aiding industrial development linked with
employment creation in Wales, including medium-term loans at
favourable interests rates, and help with renting and buying government advance factories. In the first year of the Secretary of State's

responsibility for Section 7, after 1st July 1975, £11·4 million was
spent on assisting eighty-seven projects, the total cost of which was
£120 million.[1]

Labour holds its ground

This compromise of denying an Assembly control of the Welsh
economy and concentrating it instead in the hands of the Secretary
of State for Wales was among the least durable of the compromises
in the Scotland and Wales Bill presented to Parliament in December
1976. For it is noteworthy that in the two other main problem areas
where compromise solutions were found—the questions of legislative versus executive powers and taxation powers for the Assembly—
the Labour government managed to persuade the Executive Committee of the Labour Party in Wales to acquiesce. But no such agreement was achieved on the third problem area of control of the Welsh
economy. Debate between the two sides was joined in the summer
months of 1975 when the government was reaching its decisions on
what to include in the forthcoming November devolution White
Paper. A series of papers written by the Labour Party in Wales's research department between May and August 1975, and approved by
the Executive Committee, relate the firm stand taken on the issue.
As the first paper, prepared in May, stated uncompromisingly: 'At
the heart of the devolution policy of the Labour Party in Wales is the
commitment that the Assembly will have real powers in the field of
economic and industrial development.'[2]

The first issue was control of the Welsh Development Agency,
responsibility for which the Government was proposing to divide
between the Assembly and the Secretary of State. The Welsh Labour
Executive argued that the Assembly should have total control over
the Agency and this was eventually conceded by the Government in
May 1976. But at the same time the Welsh Executive pressed the
case for the Section 7 powers of the 1972 Industry Act to be transferred to the Assembly as well. It argued that if this was not done
there would be problems of co-ordination: 'These decisions—to
transfer the Agency together with Section 7 powers to the Assembly
—are implicit in Labour's commitment to a strong economic role
for the Assembly: it is essential that they are carried out if the devolution policy is to have any value.'[3]

Another discussion paper, issued by the research department of
the Labour Party in Wales to its Executive the following month,
dealt with some anticipated objections to this position.[4] The government's approach was that the 1972 Industry Act should be operated

in a uniform way throughout Britain: while it was possible for Cabinet colleagues to operate different parts of the Act in line with overall collective responsibility, there would be problems of discrimination if responsibility for operatir.g any part of the Act were not vested in the government. The Welsh Labour Executive's discussion document countered this as follows:

> The Act already sets out a broad framework of rules. These have been clarified internally within the Civil Service, and when the Assembly took over, a public code of practice would be drawn up based on the present internal code. This would remove some of the secrecy which now exists over the rules for operating the Act (clearly dealings with specific companies must remain confidential). The logic of devolution is that different practices are appropriate to meet different circumstances. Within an agreed framework the code of practice would provide the ground rules, without being so rigid that it removed all room for discretion.
>
> It is most unlikely that powers of this kind vested in the Assembly would jeopardise the wider industrial policy of the Government. Firms who have factories outside Wales as well as within Wales will relate to the National Enterprise Board, not to the Welsh Development Agency. For these large firms the need in Wales is for information and participation in UK decisions: there must be proper arrangements for liaison between the WDA and the NEB, as well as between the Assembly and the UK Government.[5]

The paper then went on to deal with the politically sensitive position of the Secretary of State for Wales. If economic functions, on top of present Welsh Office responsibilities for such activities as health, housing, roads and education were to pass to the Assembly, what role would be left to the Secretary of State? This was politically sensitive since it was believed in the country that Wales gained great benefit from having a Secretary of State to fight for resources inside the Cabinet. But the Welsh Labour Executive's paper insisted that the over-riding need was to retain the benefits of joining together in one authority responsibility for direct contacts with industrialists, together with responsibility for regional planning, roads, water and sewerage services, and the whole range of industry-related infrastructure provision. This conjunction was currently being achieved under the aegis of the Welsh Office. Labour's paper argued that the Welsh Assembly should take over complete responsibility for the two aspects and not be a signal for a splitting of functions.[6] As to the general political problem, the paper concluded:

> The future of the Secretary of State for Wales must be faced. In the medium term there is a clear need for the Secretary of State, who will be

responsible for carrying through the practical details of the devolution policy, who will be able to put the case for Wales at Cabinet level, and who will have a crucial liaison role between the Central Government and the Assembly, particularly in the early years. In the long term, developments within the EEC may well have profound effects on the role of the Secretary of State, and of the Welsh Office, and the Assembly too.[7]

The Welsh Labour Executive's view that integrated economic powers should be given to the Assembly and the implication of this for the future role of the Secretary of State brought it into head-on collision with the government. At this stage, July-August 1975, the government decided that Britain's economic integrity demanded central control of the 1972 Industry Act through the Welsh Office, and also Welsh Office control of the sensitive policy-making capacity of the Welsh Development Agency. But the Welsh Labour Executive held to its ground. In August its secretary, Emrys Jones, produced a further memorandum which emphasised their case:

The Assembly, with WDA powers, and section 7 powers would be able to give more detailed consideration to the needs of every community in Wales, be able to take action to meet the highly individual needs of areas and communities.

There would be greater impetus for experimentation and a more immediate response to difficulties arising in communities and areas if the Assembly had the responsibility for dealing with industrial advancement.

The Secretary of State, in the exercise of Section 7 powers has to conform with criteria laid down at U.K. level—Why cannot these powers with the restrictions which already apply be transferred to an Assembly?[8]

Part of this case was conceded by the government with its announcement in May 1976 that the Assembly would have complete control of the Welsh Development Agency. The argument inside the Labour party over whether the whole case should be conceded, and an Assembly given comprehensive control over the Welsh economy, makes clear the importance of economics in the politics of devolution. The powers that the Welsh Labour Executive insisted should be devolved are the minimum that would be required to forge a Welsh economic policy.

An embryo department of state

In economic terms the politics of devolution are an assertion that British regional policy has failed and that Wales must find within itself the energy and resources to promote its own development. It has been argued (in chapter 2) that the Labour government tacitly conceded this position when, in January 1976, it set up the Welsh Development Agency. The concession was confirmed in May 1976 when it was announced that the Agency would be made wholly accountable to the Welsh Assembly. This was crucial since without an Assembly's political driving force it is unlikely that the Agency will respond adequately to its task.

Indeed, without an Assembly it is unlikely that the Agency will have the means to respond. This is the judgment of the Wales TUC, which, during much of 1975 and the early months of 1976, entered into long negotiations with the Welsh Office about the role and powers of the Welsh Development Agency. The outcome was a disappointment. In March 1976 the Wales TUC's General Secretary, George Wright, declared:

> In the past year we have had a clash between the Establishment and the new thinkers on the way the Agency should operate, and the Establishment have won. The CBI have succeeded in defending their position of no restriction on free enterprise and Wales has lost an opportunity for real change, for at least a decade. What we have is a nominated advisory body with more limited powers than a straightforward commercial bank operating the private market.[9]

Without the stimulus of an Assembly assuming responsibility for the Welsh Development Agency it is likely that George Wright's forecast of a ten-year loss of opportunity will be proved correct. It is possible to identify five critical areas of the Agency's powers where an Assembly would bring crucial political muscle to bear:

(i) Budget

The Welsh Development Agency's £100 million budget for the first five years of its operation (starting 1 January 1976 and capable of being raised to £150 million without further recourse to Parliament) was immediately criticised as inadequate. Indeed, when the Agency submitted its first industrial strategy to the Welsh Office in January 1977 it overstepped its own cash limit, pressing for some £50 million to £100 million more than the £150 million set by Parliament.[10] In March 1976 the Wales TUC, in its comments on Welsh Office guidelines for the operation of the WDA, stated: 'At the very least this limit must be indexed against inflation. However, to provide the basis for an effective Welsh Development Agency there should be provision for £500m, with further substantial sums available if needed.'[11]

(ii) Planning

A consultation paper on the Welsh Development Agency, issued by
the Welsh Office in January 1975, stated that the WDA should
ensure that attractive industrial sites and factory space were available in Wales; develop, maintain and manage government-owned
industrial estates; and build advance factories.[12] This was the extent
to which the government felt the Agency should be involved in
strategic planning of the Welsh economy. But at the first meeting of
the Agency's Board, its Chairman, Sir Dai Davies (Ebbw Vale-born
former General Secretary of the Iron and Steel Trades Confederation), declared that one of the first aims of the Agency would be to
draw up an economic and industrial strategy for Wales as a context
for spending its budget.[13] This brought it into immediate tension
with the Welsh Office which was insisting in circulars to Welsh local
government that the 1967 White Paper, *Wales: The Way Ahead* was
still the valid context for Welsh economic planning decisions.[14] By
the end of its first year of operation the Agency had conceded the
issue of economic planning to the Welsh Office. The Agency's chief
executive, Ian Gray, announced: 'We take the view that even if we
wanted to, it would not be practical for us to produce an economic
plan for Wales. So many elements in such a plan would be totally
outside our control. These include, for example, communications
and the nationalised industries.'[15]

The result was that planning was split three ways between the
Welsh Office, local authorities and the Welsh Development Agency.
The eight Welsh county councils were responsible for producing overall
land-use and transportation strategies for their areas to be co-
ordinated by the Welsh Office. The counties were also responsible for producing industrial strategies which would be co-ordinated
by the Welsh Development Agency. By the end of 1976 this split
responsibility had produced total confusion. The counties were complaining that the Welsh Office had not provided them with an
overall context within which they could slot their ideas for development. The Welsh Office was telling the counties that once they had
submitted their strategies (the deadline was Spring 1977) it would be
at least two years adjudicating them. And at the end of 1976 the
Welsh Development Agency was still waiting for the counties to
produce their industrial strategies so it could proceed with its
priority task of industrial if not overall economic planning.[16]

If a Welsh Assembly had responsibility for the Welsh Development Agency this lack of coherence and direction in planning would
be sure to be a matter for immediate debate. One of the most telling

arguments for devolution to Wales is that it would result in decisive and determined strategic planning of the Welsh economy as a whole.

(iii) Acquisition of share capital

The Welsh Development Agency has the power to invest money for Welsh industry through loans; by taking equity holdings; or by entering into joint holdings. But it cannot compulsorily buy its way into firms it assists. Rather, it was operating by the end of its first year as 'a fairly adventurous merchant bank', to use the words of its chief executive, Ian Gray.[17] However, the early discussions on the Agency's role, between the Welsh Office, Wales TUC and the Wales CBI produced sharply differing views on how aggressive and innovatory the Agency should be in its business practice—a division of opinion that would be bound to be reflected in Assembly debates on the matter. The Wales CBI argued that the Agency should not take equity holdings in any of the companies to which it gave financial assistance:

> Banks do not judge it necessary to take equity in companies to which they make available short or medium-term finance and neither should government. Nationalisation in terms of state ownership is an out-dated method of involvement achieving nothing in itself by way of improved efficiency or the implementation of stable long-term policies.[18]

But the Wales TUC was adamant that the Agency should have powers of compulsory acquisition at the average quoted price of the previous twelve months, or at the current market price, whichever was the lower:

> Any board of directors worth its salt will be able to repulse an Agency bid to buy shares on the open market. At the very least it would be able to fend-off Agency advances for long enough for share prices to rise, thus opening the door to all kinds of speculation.[19]

The Wales TUC added that there would be particular problems in dealing with firms that were run from outside Wales. It suggested that the Agency should have special powers to monitor the activities of such companies, to extract from them guarantees regarding their permanence, their employment requirements, and, where necessary, compulsorily to purchase their establishments in Wales. A suitable way of achieving this, suggested the Wales TUC, would be to empower the Agency to negotiate a planning-agreement type of relationship with the company in question as a precondition of Agency assistance.

There is no doubt that an Assembly would focus pressure for the Welsh Development Agency to pursue adventurous policies along these lines.

(iv) The agency's loan function

When making loans or engaging in joint ventures with companies the Agency is subject to two restrictions. It can only invest more than £1 million in a project with the approval of the Secretary of State for Wales (presumably the Assembly, once it took over responsibility) and it has to charge competitive interest rates. The Welsh Office guidelines specified that the interest rate charged by the Agency should be 'not less than that paid by commercial firms of the highest standing'.[20]

The Wales TUC quarrelled with both these restrictions. It said the £1 million upper limit was unduly restrictive in view of the fact the Agency had a £2 million ceiling on share purchases, and suggested the loan ceiling be raised to the same figure. On the question of competitive interest rates the Wales TUC commented:

> To rule out the use of incentives such as the provision of cheap sources of finance from the means of persuasion open to the Welsh Development Agency, is surely unjustified. At the same time, to charge the current market rate of interest will involve the charging of the highest rates at exactly the time when investment is most needed, during the recession. Finally it would encourage the Welsh Development Agency to become a 'lender of the last resort', in which case, the delay involved could involve serious additional costs.[21]

The Wales TUC suggested that the Agency be given the power to fix interest rates that would maximise the attractiveness of its loans. This would greatly enhance the impact the Agency could have on the investment plans of those industrial sectors it wanted to influence most. Again, it is likely that on this issue a Welsh Assembly would focus pressure for policies along these lines.

(v) The agency's financial returns

A further restriction on the Welsh Development Agency is that where it invests money—whether by buying shares in existing companies, setting up joint ventures or other means—it must ensure an adequate return on its capital. The Welsh Office guidelines state categorically that the Agency must 'always have regard to profitability when making investment decisions'.[33] The Wales TUC's reaction was that nothing could be more restrictive than to interpret this criterion in a simple profit-and-loss sense, or to apply it rigidly in the short term. Instead, the Wales TUC advocated that the Agency should take into account the total economic and social costs and benefits involved in a project, thus inevitably widening the strictly financial cost criterion: 'We would hope to see the widest possible interpretation of "adequate returns on capital employed", rather than the blinkered obsession with profitability.'[23] These kinds of considerations, as they apply to individual cases, would be likely to be raised and hotly debated by an Assembly. The political nature of that debate would inevitably tend towards emphasis being given to the total social costs of investment decisions by the Welsh Development Agency.

These five disputed areas of the Welsh Development Agency—its budget, its planning role, its investment and loan decisions, and its return on capital—would be sure to provide wide opportunities for debate within a Welsh Assembly. The issues would be likely to be so contentious that an Assembly would not be content to allow the Agency to remain a semi-autonomous separate body. All the pressure would be for the Agency to be absorbed into the administrative machinery of the Assembly itself. This possibility was allowed for in the Devolution Bill[24] and was canvassed by the Labour Party in Wales's Executive Committee as early as the summer of 1975:

> It may happen in the future that the Assembly would wish to take over all functions of the Agency itself, with its actions being directly responsible to the Industrial Department and the Executive Committee [of the Welsh Assembly].[25]

One of the strongest arguments for devolution is that it would provide a focus for the political will that is necessary to give the Welsh Development Agency impetus, power and determination to tackle Wales's economic problems. The likelihood is that the Agency would have to be absorbed into the Assembly itself to facilitate the free flow of energy required. The concession of the government in May 1976 that the Agency should be an Assembly responsibility was a recognition of the economic dimension of devolution. At that point the Agency became an embryo department of an evolving Welsh government. The structure necessary to forge a Welsh economic policy was being created. Devolution is about the promotion of the political will to make the structure work.

The challenge

Any approach to forging a policy for the Welsh economy must take account of its inherent weaknesses:

(i) Poor infrastructure and lack of coherent all-Wales economic planning.

(ii) Over-dependence on traditional industries in decline and an inadequately trained workforce to take advantage of alternative more diversified industry.

(iii) Inadequate and inefficient management of investment and a weak private sector combined with a centralised public sector concentrated on the older declining industries.

Many of these aspects have been probed in chapter 2 which analysed the failure of British regional policy, and also in the preceding section of this chapter. It has been argued that devolution is about mobilising the political will, within Wales, to tackle these problems. Once this will has been institutionalised in a Welsh Assembly and these economic problems are viewed in a Welsh context—with the benefit of manageable scale, detailed knowledge and commitment that this perspective would bring—the contention is that solutions are more a matter of common sense than the result of esoteric economic analysis. This is the essence of the devolutionist's case. It will be pursued by examining in more detail the three underlying weaknesses of the Welsh economy that have been listed.

(i) Infrastructure and planning

Wales faces such a formidable challenge in restructuring its economy that it is essential to ensure that basic requirements like efficient communications consequent upon imaginative planning are provided. For instance, Professor Glyn Davies and Dr Ian Thomas, of the University of Wales Institute of Science and Technology, estimated in 1976 that the Welsh economy required an injection of 120,000 new jobs over the next ten years.[26] The areas of greatest need coincide with those having the poorest facilities. Thus the South Wales valleys, according to another 1976 estimate, required 100,000 jobs by themselves by 1991 if they were to maintain their population levels.[27]

The extent to which poor roads have negated financial inducements to industry to establish operations in Wales has never been adequately quantified. But it was established in chapter 2 that only in those areas served by reasonably good roads and railways and where there exist large industrial estates and a wide range of industrial services, has central government's Development Area regional policy been a partial success. Areas where these conditions apply in Wales are far too few. They are limited to eastern Gwent, the South Wales coastal strip and a small area around Wrexham in north-eastern Wales. Of the 112 foreign firms situated in South Wales, for example, 70 per cent are to be found within ten miles of the M4 motorway.[28]

During the ten years to 1976, expenditure per mile on Welsh roads was little above half that spent on roads in England. The motorway position reflects the Welsh road situation as a whole: at the time of writing England has 1,045 miles of motorway, Wales just 27. Wales, which is a larger exporter of electricity, does not have one mile of electrified railway line, compared with 2,150 miles in Britain as a whole.

A large part of the explanation of this under-development is to be found in the fact that Welsh needs are inevitably viewed by central government in an all-Britain context, a perspective that has led to massive distortions both in analysis and in the solutions proposed. A classic illustration was provided in April 1976 with the publication of the Government's consultative document on transport policy in Britain.[29] This does not attempt any analysis of Wales's problems on the grounds that the proposed Welsh Assembly would be responsible for planning and co-ordinating transport in the country. Nevertheless, the document reaches conclusions that embrace Wales on the basis of all-Britain figures, conclusions which are therefore inevitably weighted towards the requirements of the South-East and the Midlands of England. This is amply demonstrated by what the document has to say on railway passengers, freight transport, and car ownership.

Households in the top two income groups (40 per cent of all British households) account for 71 per cent of passenger rail expenditure, notes the report. From this it concludes that 'the predominant users of subsidised rail services are members of better-off households or business travellers' and so proposes a general curbing of subsidies. Yet the document also notes that this pattern of rail travel by the rich is essentially a phenomenon of the London area: members of the top two income groups account for only 54 per cent of rail expenditure *outside* London and the South-East of England. If other prosperous English regions, such as the Midlands, are taken into account, together with the fact that inter-city long-distance travel generally attracts richer passengers, the proportion of rail users in Wales and other outlying areas who are in the richer income groups will be much lower. The fact is that in Wales, and especially the Valleys, rail services are largely used by people from lower-income households. Thus a blanket policy for reducing subsidies which may establish rough justice in the South-East of England, would be bound to penalise the majority of rail users in Wales.

A similar distortion is produced when the document considers freight travel. It estimates that 'bulk goods travelling by road, over 75 miles, now account for only five per cent of road ton mileage'. Further, the document asserts that 'heavy lorries cause relatively few problems when travelling on good roads away from residential areas'. On both these counts the document judges the road-versus-rail argument to be 'a barren one'. But when applied to Wales, rather than Britain as a whole, this generalisation does not correspond to reality. Most of the freight arriving by road in Gwynedd, Dyfed and West Powys has travelled more than seventy-five miles—whether oil, coal, fertiliser or animal foodstuffs—and accounts for considerably more than 5 per cent of road-ton mileage in Wales. And how many towns in Wales can boast of 'good roads away from residential areas'? In the South Wales valleys the distances are shorter, but the road conditions are worse and, indeed, constitute a serious disincentive to industry.

Again, the Consultative Document tentatively proposes the abolition of car licensing duty in favour of higher rates of petrol duty. The object would be to force car owners to meet the costs of urban congestion. The document states that 'car ownership appears to be only moderately sensitive to the price of petrol' and, later, that 'the rate of growth of income seems to be a more important determinant [of car ownership levels]'. But in many low-income parts of rural Wales car ownership is essential in the absence of public transport. Why should low-wage car owners in Gwynedd, Dyfed, Powys and Clwyd be forced to pay higher petrol duties intended to meet the costs of (or reduce) congestion in far-away conurbations?

These are just three key transport areas—rail passengers, freight, and car ownership—where planning viewed in a British context is currently producing serious distortions in Wales, distortions which, if allowed to develop, would prove a serious disincentive to industrial development. When added to the under-development of Welsh infrastructure, particularly road investment, they add up to a powerful case for the management of the economy at the Welsh level and for devolution.[30]

The kind of management that would be possible was illustrated by Plaid Cymru in its Economic Plan for Wales, produced in 1970. This selected ten major growth centres to attract new employment to every region of Wales: at Wrexham, Bangor-Caernarfon, Aberystwyth, Milford Haven, Pontardulais, Cynffig, Llantrisant, Merthyr Tydfil, Ystrad Mynach and Cwmbran-Pontypool. They advocated that a substantial part of the total budget for economic development should be used to establish, at each growth sector, a modern industrial park where a wide range of industrial services could be provided. These included banks, canteens, an accident unit, computer centre, export and design bureaux, shared maintenance and security services and so on. Smaller-scale industrial development would be encouraged at ten secondary growth centres so that employment could eventually be provided for all the people of Wales within about twenty miles of their homes. Each of the growth centres would be linked to an adequate network of roads and railways to provide efficient communication with ports and with the main markets in Wales, England and Europe.

Professor Glyn Davies has pointed to the more general awareness in Scotland than in Wales of the need for growth strategies based on new growth industries in growth areas (as shown, for example, in the Scottish Council's Toothill Report of 1961 and the White Paper *Development and Growth in Scotland 1963-64*). This approach restructured the Scottish economy well in advance of the discovery of oil which 'has simply lubricated the new economic structure and speeded up her rate of advance'.[31] Meanwhile Wales has continued, under Welsh Office guidance, to have excessive concern for the propping up of every community and of every industry and tried to maintain things as they are, in short, to resist the changes which are the essential forerunner of new growth. Growth-point policies were being applied in Scotland by the early 1960s. But in Wales in the mid-1970s the message had still not reached the ears of the Welsh Office and the political establishment. The politics of devolution are in large measure a frustrated reaction against this incompetence. As Professor Davies and Dr Ian Thomas put it in the conclusion to their comprehensive study of investment in Welsh industry:

It is imperative that Wales should produce a comprehensive national economic plan, not simply a series of unco-ordinated plans for particular parts, whether south Wales, or Deeside and so on . . . With the Welsh Assembly soon due to herald a new constitutional advance, the time is ripe for just this sort of co-operative national effort, if a fuller appreciation of the problems and potentialities of Wales is to emerge. Only in this context, can a strategic locational and industrial policy, tailored to the special requirements of Wales, be properly developed.[32]

(ii) Manpower

Industrial re-training would be a major component of a Welsh economic plan. This again presents a formidable challenge to Wales, at a time when large sections of its workforce are being made redundant as a result of the rundown of older industries, particularly steel. Professor Davies and Dr Thomas in their invest-ment study estimated that 30,000 of the 120,000 new jobs required in Wales over the decade to the mid-1980s were the result of the run-down of older industries.[33] An overwhelming need of the Welsh economy is a wider and more diverse industrial base: a need which demands a workforce highly trained in a variety of skills. Yet during 1976, when Welsh unemployment passed the 80,000 mark (8 per cent) only 5,500 people were in government industrial training or re-training establishments.[34] The target for training specifically young people in 1976 was some 1,300 places. But this was less than half the number of 1975 school-leavers registered unemployed in January 1976 (2,921). In July 1975 a total of 29,370 young people under the age of 24 were registered as unemployed in Wales (in the previous year the total had reached 11,586).

In view of these figures it is not surprising that the proportion of young people in Wales who take jobs requiring no training at all outstrips Scotland and all the English regions—in 1974 it was 50 per cent higher than the British average. In that year, too, Wales offered proportionately fewer apprenticeships for boys than any other part of Britain except the South-East of England, where white-collar work predominates (38 per cent of school-leavers compared with the 43 per cent British average and 53 per cent in Scotland). The position with girls was similar: 5·5 per cent for Wales compared with a British average of 6·5 per cent. Secretarial jobs absorbed 31 per cent of girls in Wales compared with 40·5 per cent in Britain.

The Wales TUC pointed out in their report on the problem (January 1976)[35] that this low level of training was bound to lead to critical skill shortages and bottlenecks in particular labour markets. In their survey of 81 overseas firms in Wales Professor Davies and Dr Thomas found that 55 (or 68 per cent of the sample) mentioned the availability of labour in Wales as an influence on their decision to locate in Wales. But 12 of these firms were subsequently dis-appointed with the quality of the workforce. Eight of the remaining 26 firms in the sample cited availability of labour as a problem of operating in Wales.

In their report the Wales TUC emphasised that low skill levels in the workforce tends to attract industrial investment which requires low skills:

> We would argue that the creation of an increasing volume of unskilled and semi-skilled jobs in manufacturing industries would be inappropriate as the major short-term expedient to ease the principality's employment position, and nothing short of a continuing prescription for under-achievement and under-development in the medium and long term context of the economy.

The report called for Welsh training levels to be brought up to the British average by 1980 and for the Manpower Service Commission to carry out a survey of the training needs of key sectors of the Welsh economy. There was no doubt that their analysis was right and the remedy they advocated was little more than the response of common sense. The outstanding question, however, was a political one. Was there sufficient will to push the required programme through, to recognise its priority and to allocate sufficient money accordingly?

In most of the postwar period the philosophy of government in regard to industrial training has been rooted in the belief that responsibility should rest with individual firms. However, the Employment and Training Act 1973 established three new institutions: the Manpower Services Commission (MSC), the Training Services Agency (TSA) and the Employment Service Agency, charged with the task of training workers and finding them jobs in response to industry's needs. These bodies are managed by the two sides of industry and the Secretary of State for Employment provides finance and approves programmes of work. Under the government's devolution strategy of building up the economic role of the Secretary of State for Wales to compensate for the loss of his powers in other spheres, to the Assembly, it was decided that he should take over responsibility for industrial training in Wales.[36]

But on this matter the advice of civil servants to the Ministers drawing up the devolution proposals was more radical. Early in 1975 a team of civil servants in the Cabinet Office Constitution unit considered there was a good case for devolving responsibility in the manpower field to the Welsh Assembly. In its concluding statement to a discussion of the issue the group stated:

> Opinion in the group is divided as to whether to recommend devolution in the manpower field. The Department of Employment opposes the concept but sees decentralisation as giving the Secretaries of State a substantial area of responsibility. In the view of the Constitution Unit, this is an area where Scottish/Welsh aspirations could be met without threatening the basic requirements of a unified economy.[37]

The fact that, despite this view, the government decided to devolve manpower responsibility to the Secretaries of State rather than the respective Assemblies, is good supporting evidence for the interpretation of their devolution strategy, argued in the first section of this chapter—that is, the government wishes to build up the economic role of the Secretaries of State to compensate for their loss of functions to the Assemblies in other spheres such as health, education, housing and the environment.

But as has been made clear, the question of industrial training and re-training is one of the major challenges confronting the Welsh economy. It would be sure to be seen by an Assembly as a major and integral part of any overall economic policy it produced. As such, it is inevitable that an Assembly would insist that it should have control of Welsh manpower policy.

(iii) Investment

The third main challenge to the Welsh economy, listed at the opening to this section, is its unbalanced industrial base. Wales has a weak private sector combined with a top-heavy centralised public sector concentrated on the older declining industries.

The weakness of the private sector has much to do with the small scale of most Welsh private industry. A Welsh Council report in 1973 identified 2,911 private firms in Wales employing 25 people and over. But only 49 of them employed more than 1,000 people. And the large majority, 2,063, employed less than 100. In between there were just 278 Welsh private firms indicating just how weak Wales is in the middle range of industry, the range from which expansion tends to take place.[38]

The Welsh Development Agency should confront this problem by establishing a venture-capital-arm to encourage entrepreneurs to expand or start their own businesses indigenously in Wales. All too often men of vision, and with the ability to establish the companies of the future based on advance products, processes or services, cannot find the capital to produce their prototype, far less get their production line built and moving. They either have to let their ideas wither or emigrate. What the WDA should do in cases like this is to make venture capital available (that is, funds in the region of £50,000 to £100,000 per project, not large sums). In return for the investment of venture capital the WDA would get a minority equity stake in the young or embryo company, and a formula should be prepared whereby the WDA would have a statutory duty to divest itself of its equity share when the company reached a certain level of size and profitability. The WDA would take the capital gain accruing from the sale of the equity and would therefore be able to invest in more venture-capital-situations. As a result the WDA venture-capital-arm would in effect be self-generating.

As well as the small scale of much of Welsh private industry its other major weakness is that most of it is controlled from headquarters outside Wales. The 1973 Welsh Council report revealed that in the 'mainly manufacturing' sector only 113 of 477 establishments in Wales employing more than 100 people had their head offices in Wales. Overall only 205 of 846 private industrial establishments in Wales employing more than 100 people had their head offices in Wales. And of 126 branches and subsidiaries of non-Welsh companies operating in Wales only 64 could vary product mix, 56 fix their own market price and discounts, 16 provide their own finance and 71 make their own capital expenditure decisions.[39]

All this has grave consequences for management opportunity and vitality in Wales. Career structures are centred outside rather than inside Wales. The centralisation of top management away from Wales not only adversely affects the economy but also the community as a whole, which is denuded of leadership potential for other spheres, especially politics. In general the result is that decisions that often directly affect job opportunities are more easily taken with little regard to the condition or requirements of the Welsh economy and are not subject to any Welsh political pressure.

The only long-term answer to this problem is to create the conditions in Wales to encourage the expansion of indigenously based industry. But the present position could be prevented from being eroded further by conferring powers on the Welsh Development Agency to prevent the transfer of control over Welsh-based undertakings, to persons or companies which are not themselves Welsh-based. Such powers would be analogous to those enjoyed by the National Enterprise Board in relation to takeovers by persons or companies not based in Britain. Such powers would of course be employed entirely at the discretion of the Welsh Development Agency. There would be no legal obligation. The probability would be that they would only be used where the Agency itself was interested in taking equity in the firm involved.

As to the provision of sufficient finance to meet Wales's investment needs, the objective of devolution is to establish a Welsh Assembly with the political muscle to ensure that the Welsh Development Agency has the funds and the right investment policies.

The Agency should have a rolling budget for some four or five years ahead so that, for example, the executive of the WDA knows in 1978 what its budget will be in 1982, in 1979 what its budget will be in 1983, and so on. This would have two vital effects: one would be to allow the executive to engage in constructive forward planning; the other would be to take industrial funding out of the political arena in that its confirmed forward money vote would not be subject to erratic change if and when the colour of the ruling party in the Welsh Assembly altered.[40]

The WDA, which has responsibility for funding the Welsh Development Corporation, essentially a public relations body to protect Wales's economic image abroad, should transform this into a more dynamic and aggressive department. It should open offices in the major commercial centres of the world—London, New York, Paris, Frankfurt, Tokyo, San Francisco, and Chicago, and possibly the Middle East, Africa and the Communist bloc. These offices would look two ways: they would look from Wales into the major markets of the world and assist the increase of Wales's exporting effort, and monitor the types of industry of the future that could hopefully be established indigenously in Wales; and they would look from the major markets of the world into Wales, promote the encouragement of licensing and joint venture agreements, and attract industry from these major world centres to Wales.

The extent of the challenge confronting the Welsh economy was made clear in late 1976 by Professor Glyn Davies and Dr Ian Thomas, of the University of Wales Institute of Science and Technology, in their report *Overseas Investment in Wales*:

> Wales needs at least 120,000 jobs within the coming decade; first, in order to reduce the current record of over 80,000 unemployment to about 2%, some 60,000 jobs are required as quickly as possible. In addition, 30,000 jobs will be needed to make up for losses from existing industries like coal and, especially, iron and steel; while another 30,000 jobs need to be created if the very low Welsh activity rates, particularly among women, are to be raised closer to those long established in the more prosperous regions of Britain.
>
> These are realistic if conservative—almost minimum—figures and are in line with other estimates of one million jobs required for the five problem areas of Wales, Scotland, Northern England, Yorkshire and Humberside and the North West.
>
> These jobs should, moreover, be sought chiefly through establishing manufacturing industry, with rather less emphasis on service and administrative employment, with two-thirds or 80,000 coming from manufacturing and one-third or 40,000 from the non-manufacturing sectors . . .
>
> In the absence of a Welsh national plan, and in face of the persistent

official refusal to publish any figure of job requirements, we suggest that the 80,000 manufacturing jobs required will be made up as follows: 30,000 from overseas, 25,000 from the expansion of indigenous manufacturing industry and 25,000 also from manufacturing industries in the rest of the UK.

These figures assume that in future far fewer manufacturing jobs will become available for dispersal to Wales from London and the South-East or from the Midlands, formerly the two major sources. Two reasons are put forward for this most significant change. First, whereas these congested areas were expected to be the main recipients of the officially extra 25 million inhabitants by the end of the century, revision of the population projections has reduced anticipated UK population at the end of the century from 75 million—the 1964 estimate—to less than 60 million today. Secondly, the Midlands, from being the power-house of England, has become virtually a problem region, with far fewer jobs to export—and then probably only to the New Towns within or adjacent to its own region.[41]

The message is clear. As Wales moves towards the end of the present century it can rely less and less on its economy being bolstered by industrial overflow from England. By the mid-1970s the two major sources of future development for Wales were from within and from overseas. The old economic relationships within Britain, which had never provided a full solution to Wales's structural and employment difficulties, were now becoming increasingly less relevant. The initiative must now come from within. The politics of devolution are an assertion that such an economic initiative requires as a necessary condition a political initiative as well: a Welsh Assembly is essential to provide a political focus of pressure which can generate the economic momentum that is required. The first step in this direction was the establishment of the Welsh Office in 1964. But this merely focused administrative pressure, and the record has proved its inadequacy, for example in Welsh economic planning. Full-blooded political pressure to mobilise the collective will of the people of Wales through a Welsh Assembly is vital if we are to meet successfully the formidable challenge of re-shaping our economy.

This chapter has touched on just some of the ideas and approaches that might be involved in forging a truly Welsh economic policy. As has been shown, some of the pattern is already emerging. The evolution is taking place as much by force of circumstances as by conscious pressure and design. For the world of large-scale growth that could contain the disparities between the British nations and regions by generalised overall economic improvement is no longer an even medium-term option. Peripheral Wales can no

longer rely on hand-outs in the form of regional assistance from the
more prosperous parts of Britain, even if that was inherently
desirable anyway. The English South-East and Midlands are relatively less prosperous than they were and will become progressively
more concerned with protecting their own position and progressively
more jealous of greater prosperity within the Common Market
'Golden Triangle' across the English Channel.

Faced with this reality, areas like Wales will have little choice but
to look to themselves for initiative and reliance—qualities that alone
can bring self-generative economic achievement. It demands major
adjustment to new conditions and new relationships—political as
well as economic adjustment. It is an exciting challenge.

Conclusion: The Recovery of Community

'The true problem of our time is not unemployment but the scale of unemployment, not violence but the magnitude of it, not war but big war, not
society but the size of society. Hence, the real conflict confronting us in our
effort to create a better world as the 20th Century draws to a close, is no
longer between black and white, youth and age, poor and rich, labour and
management, colonial liberation and imperialism, socialism and capitalism. They are but the two sexes of the same species of struggle in which
neither has any meaning without the other.

'The true contemporary conflict is between man and mass, between the
citizen and the state, between the small society and the big one, between
David and Goliath'.

Leopold Kohr.

'The problem is to replace the individualism of the bourgeois era not by
totalitarianism or the sheer collectivism of the beehive but by pluralistic
communal civilisation grounded upon human rights and the social
aspirations and needs of man.'

Jacques Maritain. [1]

The politics of devolution are bedevilled by the cross-currents of
nationalism and unionism, socialism and corporatism, ideas of the
community and the state, economic integration and more self-
sustained development, bureaucracy and democracy, cultural crisis
and claims of linguistic racism—to name but a few. The issue is
further complicated in that there is no consensus definition of any of
these terms and no agreement about how, if at all, they relate to the
establishment of Assemblies within a unitary state system.

Since devolution is about the alteration of the context within
which politics are carried on in Britain, the devolution debate is
bound to touch on all these matters and more. In this respect the
politics of devolution are akin to the politics of the European
Economic Community. In fact, the two questions are entirely
complementary because they both form part of the painful process
in which Britain, having lost an Empire, is seeking a new and, hopefully, more rational place in the world.

Though the politics of devolution are complicated by an array of
pressures it is possible to identify two themes which together
describe much of the impetus behind the debate and also point to

future directions. The first is an underlying philosophy of community which has promoted the politics of devolution and which, in turn, is being influenced by them. The second is the relationship of the size of states and their populations to democracy and the evolution of levels of government in the European context. Viewed in these perspectives the politics of devolution are nothing less than a quest for the recovery of community.

As was stressed in the introductory chapter, there is in Wales, as throughout the world, a renewed assertion of the importance of community. In relation to the politics of devolution the concept of community was defined as that level of human affairs where power and responsibility can be brought together. It was argued that there is insufficient responsibility at the British level of government to ensure that the power concentrated there is tempered by community interest. On the other hand, at the Welsh level, great feelings of responsibility for the community are being frustrated by lack of power to respond to Welsh problems. The economic aspect of this was probed fully in chapters 2 and 6 and it was argued that this in itself constitutes in large part the pressure and justification for devolution.

The conjunction of power and responsibility at the Welsh level would not occur in isolation. Below and above any all-Wales level of government new formations are already crystallising. It is widely recognised that devolution entails radical changes in the structure of Welsh local government. The Labour Party in Wales, the Welsh Liberal party, and Plaid Cymru are all committed to the present eight Welsh county councils and thirty-seven district councils being modified, or replaced by a completely different structure.

Following the collapse of the Scotland and Wales devolution Bill in February 1977 the government made an unequivocial commitment to the need for changing the structure of Welsh local government in the context of its renewed proposals for the following session. In a statement to the House of Commons announcing new separate devolution Bills for Wales and Scotland the Lord President, Mr Michael Foot, said, 'Given the expressed concerns about the structure of local government in Wales, we will propose that the Welsh Assembly should have a statutory duty to review the structure of local government'. (*Hansard*, 26 July 1977).

Above the all-Wales level changes are already well under way. The most significant development occurred with the June 1975 referendum when the people of Wales, in common with the people of the rest of Britain, voted overwhelmingly to remain inside the European Economic Community. This was a momentous decision, for it portended fundamental changes. Any new level of government is bound to have an impact on existing levels. For Britain, which in the last 500 years has developed probably the most centralised unitary system of government with pretensions to democracy the world has ever seen,[2] the impact will be profound. Simultaneously, Westminster faces a competing European power centre at Brussels, and embryonic national power centres internally. As Gwyn Morgan, the European Economic Community's representative in Wales since 1975, has put it: 'These are exciting times. With the development of a Welsh Assembly, Westminster's influence will diminish, and the dynamic centres will be Cardiff and Brussels.'[3]

Exciting times inevitably embrace conflict. Great vested interests wish either to preserve existing institutions or to change them. But contemporary politics should not be allowed to obscure the fact that at stake are issues which have preoccupied thinkers since the earliest times of political debate: the problem of what form or forms of government can best enhance the values of civilisation and community; the alienation of the individual from the community; and the question of the relationship between size and democracy.

Size, alienation and democracy: the pluralist tradition

Whether they favoured aristocracy, democracy or a mixed system, influential Greeks from Pericles to Aristotle agreed that the state should be both small in territory and in population. 'If the citizens of the state are to judge and to distribute offices according to merit, then they must know each other's character', said Aristotle, who held that the right population for a state was—'the largest number which suffices for the purpose of life and *can be taken in at a single view*' (my emphasis).[4] Aristotle was, of course, writing in opposition to his teacher, Plato. As Nisbet has put it:

> Where Plato had expressed his craving for and adoration of unity, Aristotle, in less brilliant but no less profound fashion, called for plurality, diversity, and division in the good community and saw in the search for unity carried too far the danger of not only tyranny and suffocation of spirit but even subversion of the political community itself.[5]

Between them Plato and Aristotle began a dialogue, an intellectual conflict, that has remained a persistent theme of Western political thought and one that underpins the contemporary devolution debate. It is the argument of this book that this conflict inherent in the politics of devolution is creative in that it at least holds out the opportunity for an advance towards pluralism and the recovery of community. For the monistic spirit of Plato, demanding always an intensely rational, systematic, and single-view approach to political organisation has been overwhelmingly dominant in Western thinking. It is the spirit that is behind the idea of sovereignty, that constitutional bogy of devolution.

Nevertheless, Aristotle set in train an alternative political tradition of pluralism which is the inheritance of the politics of devolution. This insists that the state is not like a military organisation whose effectiveness depends upon total unity and a blurring of differences. 'In the good state it is important that the dissimilarities among people and their customs be both recognised and protected, so far as is possible,' writes Nisbet summarising Aristotle: 'Failure to do this, and the effort to achieve in the state a form of community as close as that of the family, cannot fail, he emphasises, to result in a monolithic unity: a celebration of the one, rather than the many, and hence a totalitarian type of society.'[6]

The conflict of ideas between Plato and Aristotle has been joined ever since. Possibly the most dramatic episode occurred during the fourteenth, fifteenth and sixteenth centuries when the pluralistic values of mediaevalism clashed with those of the emerging centralised nation-state. This has already been discussed in some detail in the final section of chapter 4 where the basis of Saunders Lewis's confederal approach to the problem of sovereignty was examined. It comes as no surprise that while Lewis walked in the footsteps of Aristotle, the Commission on the Constitution took the line of Plato. As Saunders Lewis pointed out in his *Principles of Nationalism* (1926), the period of the Middle Ages offered a notable example of a society organised along pluralist lines. It started from the idea of the whole and unity, symbolised by the Roman Catholic Church, but to every lesser unit down to and including the individual, it ascribed an inherent life, a purpose of its own and an intrinsic value. It saw society in a European context as a community of communities.

There is, of course, a danger of romanticising the mediaeval system—an accusation often brought against Saunders Lewis—for it contained within it much exploitation, deprivation and cruelty. But as Nisbet points out, it is the

> medieval pattern of social and political life that furnishes the background, the context, and, most important, the actual themes of what we call the plural community in modern Western social thought. Without exception, from Althusius through Burke and to Max Weber, it is the general medieval set of social and political principles that supplies the

substance of pluralist reactions to the modern central-ised, bureaucratised, and collectivist state.[7]

Nisbet sees the Dutch writer Johannes Althusius (1557—1638) as the true founder of the philosophy of the plural community. In his *Politics,* published in 1603, Althusius attacked the ideas of Jean Bodin who in his *Commonweal* twenty-seven years earlier had first defined the unitary theory of political sovereignty. Bodin wrote in the tradition of Plato; Althusius in the tradition of Aristotle. Bodin declared absolute, perpetual and total sovereignty to be the attribute of the political state alone, while Althusius found this conception of sovereignty un-tenable on grounds of natural and moral law. Sovereignty, he declared, belongs with the people—a cry echoed by devolutionists in our own day.

At this point extreme care is required and some subtlety. For the idea of 'the people' is a highly dangerous concept; one capable of easy perversion into becoming merely another name for the state. This was the trap laid by Rousseau with his extremely influential idea of popular sovereignty, an idea that laid the foundation for the French Revolution and the mass state politics of the nineteenth and twentieth centuries. Rousseau's revolutionary doctrine of the 'general will' is one in which the individual achieves freedom through his interests becoming identical with those of the state. In the direct tradition of Plato, Rousseau makes the sovereignty of the people identical with that of the state. His concern is to emancipate the individual from what he sees as the corruption, conflicts and un-certainties of mediating communities between the individual and the state, traditional institutions like the church, guild, extended family, monastery, local community, economic enterprise, and school. In a situation where man is independent from fellow members of the community Rousseau believes it possible to achieve a condition of equality approximating as near as possible the state of nature:

Each citizen would then be completely independent of all his fellow men, and absolutely dependent on the state: which operation is always brought by the same means; *for it is only by the force of the state that the liberty of its members can be secured* (my emphasis).[8]

But for Althusius, as Nisbet notes, the idea of popular sovereignty in no way depended on the state:

For him the people was no abstract or atomized entity, divorced from social and cultural identity bestowed through the various groups, com-munities, and associations which in fact make up a population. On the contrary, for Althusius popular sovereignty lay in the people *considered only in terms of their actual, historically developed traditional communities and groups.* These groups and communities—ranging from family through neighbourhood, parish, guild, or corporate association of any form, to church—would be the true units of the political commonwealth. . . . We thus have what Althusius is most famous for: a principle of federalism, of which the nineteenth-century anarchists as well as political pluralists and guild socialists would avail themselves in their prescriptions for the good society. For Althusius, as for the later pluralists, federalism is a means of governmental decentralisation based upon natural or traditional communities, each of which, along with the formal organs of political government, will participate in the governmental process.[9]

This pluralist, decentralist political philosophy which holds that sovereignty rests with the people in their natural communities is the tradition in which devolution is firmly anchored. As we have seen, its justification is essentially a moral one, Althusius, for instance, holding that it conforms to natural and moral law. But it can also be defended in terms of practicality and efficiency. Possibly the most famous advocate of this aspect of the case was the eighteenth-century philosopher Montesquieu. In his *The Spirit of the Laws* he argued that qualities like self-restraint, obedience to law, dedication to the common good, loyalty, equality, and frugality, are best met in a state of small size:

> It is in the nature of a republic that it should have a small territory; without that, it could scarcely exist. In a large republic, there are large fortunes, and consequently little moderation of spirit; there are trusts too great to be placed in the hands of any single citizen; interests become particularised; a man begins to feel that he can be happy, great and glorious without his country; and then he can become great upon the ruins of his country.
> In a large republic, the common good is sacrificed to a thousand considerations; it is subordinated to various exceptions; it depends on accidents. In a small republic, the public good is more strongly felt, better known, and closer to each citizen; abuses are less extensive.[10]

By this time in history, however, political philosophers had to deal with the existence of large nation-states. Montesquieu saw that the small state could be subjugated by the large state—which in turn could be destroyed by internal weaknesses. 'If a republic is small', wrote Montesquieu, 'it is destroyed by an outside force; if it is large, it is destroyed by an internal vice.'[11] In 1835 de Tocqueville foresaw with uncanny prescience the flaws in the mass societies that were then beginning to develop. In his monumental work *Democracy in*

America, published in that year, he predicted a type of oppression 'different from anything that has ever been in the world before'; for 'that same equality which makes despotism easy, tempers it': the incipient despotism of a democracy would be 'more widespread and milder: it would degrade men rather than torment them'.[12] What Tocqueville foresaw was a mass of men 'alike and equal, constantly circling about in pursuit of the petty and banal pleasures with which to glut their souls'.[13] To each, mankind would consist only of his own family and friends. As for the rest of his citizens, 'he touches them and feels nothing'. A benevolent state regulates everything: 'it gladly works for their happiness but wants to be the sole agent and judge of it'. This state 'does not break man's will but softens, bends and guides it . . . never drives men to despair but continually thwarts them and leads them to give up using their free will'. Little by little the exercise of free choice becomes so restricted as to be pointless. Consoling themselves with the idea that they are sovereign, the people actually become incapable of making a choice. The occasional opportunity of electing the central power is insufficient to develop their political sense: having given up managing affairs which they can comprehend, they are unlikely to make a good job even of that. Disillusioned, Tocqueville predicts they will 'fall back at the feet of a single master' since they have already been slowly falling back 'below the level of humanity': 'It is not easy to fight benevolence.'

Tocqueville's descriptions of the kind of political society that would emerge under these conditions are equally telling. He continued that 'as conditions become more equal among people, individuals seem of less and society of greater importance';[14] that this 'naturally gives men in times of democracy a very high opinion of the prerogative of society and a very humble one of the rights of the individual . . . the interest of the former is everything and that of the latter nothing'; that 'most . . . think that the government is behaving badly but . . . all think that the government ought constantly to act and interfere in everything'; that 'not only are [men] by nature lacking in any taste for public business but they also lack the time for it'; that a man's 'needs and even more his longings continually put him in mind of [the State] and he ends by regarding it as the sole and necessary support of his individual weakness' and that 'every central government worships uniformity; uniformity saves it the trouble of enquiring into infinite details, which would be necessary if the rules were made to suit men instead of subjecting all men indiscriminately to the same rule'.

Tocqueville was firing the opening shots in an intellectual struggle that was to be waged throughout the nineteenth century between those, like him, who rejected the development of large nation-state centralist societies; and others, like Marx, who welcomed the development, believing it was a necessary experience through which men had to pass in order to achieve an ideal society. The contrary view, put by Proudhon and others, was that Marx's road would lead instead to a dead end. They believed that a decentralised order was the only constructive way forward. This decentralist tradition and its relationship to Welsh politics will be discussed in the following section. The politics of devolution, apart from being a contemporary day-to-day political conflict, are also a continuance of this great clash of intellectual ideas. It can be left to the reader to judge which is the most accurate vision of Western European societies today—that of Marx and his class conflict leading to the dictatorship of the proletariat, or that of Tocqueville and his forebodings of the development of a corporate state.

Tocqueville believed in intermediate levels of power as an antidote to uniformity, centralisation and a more powerful state. In the second volume of his *Democracy in America* he does not go into detail about the type of intermediate authority which he believed necessary. But one of the things which lay at the back of his mind was the New England township with, generally, two to three thousand inhabitants. This he described in the first volume and drew from him the much quoted remarks:

> . . . the strength of free people resides in the local community. Local institutions are to liberty what primary schools are to science; they put it within the people's reach; they teach people to appreciate its peaceful enjoyment and accustom them to make use of it. Without local institutions a nation may give itself a free government but it has not got the spirit of liberty.[15]

In the nineteenth century battle of ideas the approach typified here lost ground to the centralised-state followers of Marx. In Britain, for instance, the early Labour movement was decentralist in its political outlook. But the Independent Labour party and the idealist vision of its leaders like Keir Hardie was crushed by the First World War. On the ruins was built the modern Labour party with its commitment to centralised state socialism. The decentralist ideas of thinkers like G. D. H. Cole lost out to the centralism of the Webbs. In Wales the victory was not so immediate or complete but its eventual triumph was symbolised by the emergence of Aneurin Bevan as a key myth figure of Welsh Labour politics.

Centralised state thinking was both a response to and a requirement of the mass industrial society that developed in the nineteenth century. The appearance of an educated urban working class made mass political parties and unions a necessity from the point of view of the traditional ruling elite. And the development of mass communications made mass organisations possible. But even the most efficient communications system is incapable of cementing groups once they grow beyond a certain size. Thus the experience of mass parties and unions is that they tend to splinter into two unequal parts: the leadership and the led. This experience is paralleled in many other spheres of life in modern urbanised mass society. There is separation of home and work. There is an immense range of job opportunities, life-styles, moral values and standards. The values of science and technology have tended to supplant those of religion but only to create uncertainty and confusion as the world wrestles with population, energy, and food crises, continual wars and superpower confrontation amid the threat of nuclear disaster. The mass media tend to be remote and impersonal, education increasingly specialised and bureaucratised.

As has been described, these conditions were foreseen with remarkable prescience by de Tocqueville who emphasised the dangers of the 'tyranny of the masses' and the consequent threat of pressures towards conformity, standardisation and mediocrity. Experience, however, has not been so straightforward. Far from being too powerful the masses have, in fact, been the helpless victims of relentless systems of political and economic oppression. Writers like Herbert Marcuse have argued that modern man, manipulated through the mass media, lacking communal ties, impotent and frustrated before the complexities of life in a technological environment, is left with a sense of powerlessness and alienation. In modern technological societies Marcuse argues that so-called 'free' institutions and 'democratic liberties' are used to repress individuality, disguise exploitation, and limit freedom and the scope of human experience. Society is controlled through the manipulation of false needs created by vested interests; the domination of nineteenth century-style capitalists is screened by their transformation into bureaucrats and corporations. Thus a new totalitarianism is created within which the last reservoir of revolutionary energy lies with 'those who are outside the productive process'—coloured minorities, the permanently unemployed and, above all, students.[16] Marcuse was writing in the context of the United States but the theme is easily transported to the British Isles where a major reservoir of revolutionary potential, in his terms, is to be found in Northern Ireland, Scotland and Wales.

The main agency of Marcuse's new totalitarianism is
bureaucracy, a phenomenon that was analysed by the German
sociologist Max Weber (1864—1920). As he put it:

> The development of the modern form of organisation of corporate
> groups in all fields is nothing less than identical with the development
> and continual spread of bureaucratic administration. This is true of
> church and state, of armies, political parties, economic enterprises,
> organisations to promote all kinds of causes, private associations, clubs,
> and many others. . . . The whole pattern of everyday life is cut to fit this
> framework. For bureaucratic administration is, other things being
> equal, always, from a formal technical point of view, the most rational
> type. For the needs of mass administration today, it is completely indis-
> pensable.[17]

Weber was concerned with the *alienation* that results from
bureaucratic methods of administration. Of course, it was Marx
who first introduced the concept of alienation into political and
sociological theory—for him it arose from the separation of the
worker from his product and from the ownership of the means of
production. But the term has come to have a far wider reference and
one that is central to the politics of devolution. It is not just a
question of alienation from economic processes but from the total
community. A connection was made by Erich Fromm who, in his
The Sane Society (1956) suggested that 'alienation' is that condition
when 'man does not experience himself as the active bearer of his
own powers and richness, but as an impoverished "thing"
dependent on powers outside himself'.[18] It is in this sense that
psychoanalysts use the term: the reluctance of individuals to
advance from the state of childhood dependency to achieve what
Sartre has called truly 'authentic' personalities. The politics of devolution are about the reluctance of whole communities to advance
from states of dependence and realise their freedom and full
potential.

The first step in this process is for the individual to experience a
sense of loss; a sense of estrangement from community. Seeman has
isolated five dimensions of alienation: powerlessness, meaningless,
normlessness, isolation or anomie, and self-estrangement.[19] Each of
these reflects a different kind of 'split' in man's relationship with his
environment. Underlying them all is the sense that man in modern
society has become reduced to an object—a 'thing', isolated and
fragmented. It was the German sociologist, Ferdinand Tonnies
(1855—1936) who pointed out that modern society has ceased to be
an organic community. Instead it is a mass society in which relationships are essentially contractual.[20] Tonnies's work was given an

important extra dimension by a contemporary French sociologist, Emile Durkheim (1858—1917) who introduced the concept of anomie. An anomic society is one in which there are a few strong standards of behaviour, individualism is rife, and the sense of community obligation, group membership, and a purpose greater than one's own is attenuated. Man in such circumstances is in a state of anomie. He is confused, anxious and seeking. Nisbet finds in Durkheim's work an illuminating treatment of 'the consequences of moral and economic individualism in modern life. Individualism has resulted in masses of normless, unattached, insecure individuals who lose even the capacity for independence, creative living.'[21] The importance of community in preventing anomie is the mainspring of Durkheim's political writings. In his *Socialism and St Simon* he sees the whole point of the socialist movement as lying not in a demand for common ownership but as a protest against the suffering of anomie. The restoration of a social order whose norms are meaningful to the individual who participates in it should, in Durkheim's view, be the main arm of modern politics. Thus in his *Professional Ethics and Civic Morals* he advocates a form of guild socialism.

But it was from Conservative, often Catholic thinkers of the late eighteenth and early nineteenth century, like Edmund Burke (1729-97) and Louis de Bonald (1754—1840), that the initial reaction to the anomic society came. Nisbet observed that 'it was to the Middle Ages that most of the nineteenth century conservatives looked for inspiration in their revolt against revolutionary secularism, power, and individualism'.[22] They stressed the positive role of tradition, authority and religion in maintaining a stable community, and insisted that human institutions could only be understood as the product of a long-term organic development. They emphasised the need to maintain the integrity and continuance of existing institutions, hierarchy and tradition. A society lacking continuity with its past heritage will lack a sense of direction and suffer the loss of guidelines for wise action, as well as experience the rise of a mass rootless population.

Thus it is no coincidence that the most influential founder of the Welsh national movement, Saunders Lewis, was a conservative in this sense, became a Catholic, and looked to the Middle Ages as the essential precedent for the recovery of a Welsh community identity.[23] His successor, Gwynfor Evans, can also be considered a conservative in that he is preoccupied with history and tradition[24] but his general political outlook is broader. He would describe himself as a radical, but he would also have much in common with

Durkheim's interpretation of socialism as a protest against anomie
and as a means of restoring a meaningful community context for the
individual.

The idea of alienation, as it has been developed here, was given a
spatial dimension and prescription by Lewis Mumford in the 1930s.
It was at this point that the concept became immediately relevant to
the politics of devolution. It was in the 1930s, too, that
Saunders Lewis was laying the philosophical foundations for the
emergence of Plaid Cymru as a political force in the 1960s.
Mumford's most immediately political work, *The Culture of Cities*,
was published in 1938. Here he expresses the view that our environment is being dehumanised as a result of the mechanised outlook of
the nineteenth century and of the 'psychological complexes that have
been deliberately built up around the idea of national sovereignty
and centralised government'.[25] Human communities should be
based on the region: 'not found as a finished product in nature, not
solely the creation of human will and fantasy'.[26] Though isolation is,
in the modern world, a delusion, it is frontiers which must be cheap-
ened, not local loyalties. No longer must the capital city of a large
state be allowed to 'monopolise advantage or substitute its activities
for those of the whole'.[27] Inter-regional cooperation must take the
place of directives sent down from above—instead of concentrating
in one capital, the elite should travel from region to region.[28]

In delineating the region, the aim must be, not to make men more
powerful, but to make them more human; to emphasise, not the
mechanistic, but the organic; to unify, not by suppression, but by
inclusion:

> one must not confuse the region, which is a highly complex human fact,
> with arbitrary areas carved out to serve some single interest such as
> government or economic exploitation. The country within fifty miles of a
> metropolitan centre is not a region just because it is a convenience for a
> metropolitan advertising agency or newspaper or planning board to call
> it so.[29]

Regionalism is thus a political and cultural movement as well as an
exercise in administration and economics.

Mumford is well aware of the political difficulties of regionalism
within a large state:

> The fact is that real communities and real regions do not fit into the
> frontiers of the ideological pattern of the national state. The state is
> usually too big to define a single region . . . and it is too small to include
> a whole society like that of Western Europe or the North American

continent, which must ultimately become the sphere of a larger system of co-operative administration.[30]

Thus the problem in the last quarter of the twentieth century is how to break out of the nineteenth century nation-state mould into a more creative and fluid system which corresponds more closely with practical requirements and with the over-riding importance of relating government to community, of power with responsibility. As Dahl and Tufte concluded in their book devoted to this problem, *Size and Democracy* (1974):

> Today and in the forseeable future, people will live in a multiplicity of political units. Because democratic theorists, with notable exceptions, have focused on the problem of democratising one sovereign unit—first the city, then the nation-state—they have overlooked the problem of democratising a political system that consists of a collection of interacting units ranging from small primary associations, in which direct democracy is at least theoretically possible, to larger entities in which direct citizen rule is impossible. Rather than conceiving of democracy as located in a particular kind of inclusive, sovereign unit, we must learn to conceive of democracy spreading through a set of interrelated political systems, sometimes, though not always, arranged like Chinese boxes, the smaller nesting in the larger. The central theoretical problem is no longer to find suitable rules, like the majority principle, to apply within a sovereign unit, but to find suitable rules to apply among a variety of units, none of which is sovereign.[31]

Understanding of this reality of power in the modern world has penetrated first to the relationship of Britain as a whole with the outside world. For example, in 1967 Edward Heath wrote:

> The Labour Government of 1945 . . . and Conservative Government after them refused to join the European Community because they were still thinking in terms of Britain's history during the period of the development of the nation state. Whilst the European countries concerned were moving on from the nation state because in their view it was inadequate to meet modern requirements.

From a completely different point on the political spectrum Isaac Deutscher put the same point, but more harshly:

> The nation-state decays and disintegrates whether people are aware of it or not, no matter what their efforts to preserve it. . . . The nation-states of the West have left their golden age far, very far, behind. . . . Like any organism that has outlived its day, the nation-state can prolong its existence only by intensifying all the processes of its own degeneration.[33]

The politics of devolution are in part a reaction to this degenera-
tion. But implicit in the debate over devolution is an argument about
the character of the new level of government that is emerging above
the nation-state level. The debate is also explicit in that the new level,
the European Economic Community, is exerting an increasing
influence over the daily lives of the people of Wales, not least in the
price of food they eat—determined by the EEC's common agricultural policy.

The issue is the quality of the sovereignty that is emerging at the
supra-national EEC level. There are three main supra-national
elements in the Treaty of Rome that established the EEC in 1957-8:
the independence of the EEC Commission, the Brussels-based
executive of the Community; the concept of 'qualified majority'
voting in the Council of Ministers of the member-states; and the
European Assembly. All these elements are important, but the
development of the European Assembly will determine the future
character of the EEC more than any other factor. The Rome Treaty
envisages that the Assembly shall ultimately be elected by direct universal suffrage instead of being nominated by the Parliaments of the
member-states. This immediately raises the fundamental issue that
is behind the politics of devolution: whether power should emanate
from above or below. If the European Assembly is directly elected, it will
signal that power is once more being concentrated at the top. For it
is the experience of Britain, where there are some 55 million people
(there are nearly 200 million in the EEC), that the principle of universal suffrage does not combat the growing distance between
government and governed. As Proudhon expressed the problem
more than a century ago: 'Universal suffrage is a kind of atomism,
by means of which the legislator seeing that he cannot let the people
speak in their essential oneness, invites the citizens to express their
opinions per head.' The result was that the body of the nation was
reduced to: 'a heap of dust animated from without by a subordinat-
ing centralised idea'.[34]

Proudhon's 'heap of dust', which is the experience of British
democracy, would certainly apply at the EEC level of universal
suffrage. But at the level of the older nations and the regions there is
a reasonable chance for universal suffrage to be comparatively free
from the dangers of loss of individual identity, of depersonalisation,
and therefore of dehumanisation in the exercise of government
power. The implication of this view is that the regional level of
government, the level where power and responsibility be best joined
together, should indirectly elect the EEC level. This would weight

decision-making on the regions and older nations of the EEC at the same time as providing for effective co-operation at the EEC level.

Political reality dictates, unfortunately, that this desirable state of affairs has little chance of materialising. The pressure for direct elections to the European Assembly is such that they will probably take place. But those who advocate this development should take into account that it would enormously strengthen the case for full self-government for areas like Wales, within the EEC context. As a Plaid Cymru statement made clear in February 1976:

> If direct elections do take place, this will underline the need for Welsh self-government. A fully self-governing Welsh State would have 13 seats in the European Parliament based on the current proposals, compared to three or four if we are part of the U.K. delegation. For Wales, self-government is the only way of getting a fair voice.[35]

Just as there are important choices to be made about the future development of the European dimension in relation to devolution, the same applies in relation to the future structure of local government within Wales. The present two-tier structure (plus community councils) that came into being at the 1974 reorganisation—the eight counties and thirty-seven districts—is almost universally unpopular. There is overlapping and duplication of functions,[36] and few would argue that the new system has resulted in greater efficiency or reduced administrative costs. This is despite the fact that the reorganisation decimated the number of local authorities in Wales from 184 to 45, a victory for the civil service which has consistently sought fewer local authorities in order to facilitate its central control. Despite this reduction devolution has been used as a pretext for fewer local authority units still. It has been claimed that a Welsh Assembly would constitute 'over-government' and this, combined with the unpopularity of the present system, has been used as an argument to dispense with a tier of local government, usually the counties. Indeed, this prospect has often been presented as part of the case for an Assembly, for instance, by Denzil Davies, Labour MP for Llanelli:

> Those who criticise the plans for the Assembly because—so they allege— the Assembly establishes a fourth tier of government, should recognise that without an Assembly the Labour Party will have insufficient justification for looking again at the present local government set-up which has been so much criticised.[37]

In May 1977 the Labour Party in Wales came forward with a scheme for merging the eight counties and thirty-seven districts into a single tier of twenty-five most-purpose authorities. The new structure, the proposal of a special study group, was based on merging districts in Glamorgan and Gwent, and reverting to the pre-1974 counties in the rest of Wales.[38] A similar policy is advocated by the Welsh Liberal party and it has a strong following in both Plaid Cymru and the Conservative Party in Wales.

The great problem with this apparently straightforward single-tier approach is that it would effectively centralise a great deal of decision-making upon the Welsh Assembly in Cardiff. Basic services, such as health, education and the social services that have been traditionally administered and been accountable at the local community level, would tend to be centralised at the all-Wales level. At one stroke many of the objectives of devolution, particularly decentralising decision-making from Whitehall and bringing government more under the control of the local community, would be undermined.

An alternative approach to the problem of local government in the context of devolution would be to start from the perspective of the 1004 communities (800 of which have councils) that were delineated in Wales by the 1974 reorganisation. These are the traditional units of Welsh administration. It may have been fortuitous, it may have been planned, but the 1972 Local Government Act which preceded the 1974 reorganisation discarded the word 'Parish' as a unit of civil or local government administration in Wales and replaced it with 'community'. This is the English translation of the Welsh *Cymwd*, a unit of administration with its roots in mediaeval and early Wales.[39]

The way forward for Welsh local government should be to reduce in number the Community Councils, making them accountable to reasonably sized communities—perhaps with populations varying between 5,000 and 20,000. These should then operate in the context of the present eight county councils whose boundaries could be altered perhaps to increase their number slightly. The counties do correspond to the historical regions of Wales and to that extent they reflect a community of interest. They are also of sufficient size to be able to raise their own local income tax revenues, as recommended by the Layfield Committee report on local government finance,[40] and to administer on their own account services like education, health and the social services. They would also provide wide scope for policy variations across Wales, particularly in regard to the Welsh language. There are many European precedents for such an approach to local government, with the cantonal system in Switzerland being the most outstanding example and the one most applicable to Wales.[41]

Thus the politics of devolution embrace important debates about the relationship between size and democracy at the European and local level, as well as at the Welsh level. In each case the main consideration should be whether power and responsibility can effectively be fused together in government. The aim of this section has been to highlight this practical problem, the major theme of this book, and place it within a theoretical framework of political ideas. Once this is done the decentralist perspective comes clearly to the fore and makes for a creative response to the conflicts involved.

As has been described, the politics of devolution are not just a twentieth-century phenomenon. They are a continuation of a fundamental conflict that has exercised societies and political writers since the days of Plato and Aristotle: the conflict between 'man and mass, between the citizen and the state, between the small society and the big one' as Kohr was quoted at the opening of this chapter. Nevertheless, the accelerated development of mass society in this century has heightened this conflict and made its resolution in favour of the citizen and the small society an urgent necessity if civilisation is to survive.

In the struggle that is taking place there are three perspectives— that of the individual, the community, and the state. The theme of this book is that if the problem of mass society is to be overcome then the community perspective must take precedence, even over the individual, since without community the individual has no meaning and is quickly subjugated by the state. The politics of devolution are about the projection of community into the debate where formerly its reference points were confined merely to the state and the individual.

Wales is well placed to understand and grasp this challenge. For, although in the British context the perspectives of the individual and the state dominate, Wales, with its decentralist tradition, is sensitive to the needs and place of community. If the recovery of community does not succeed here there is little hope for the rest of the world.

The Welsh decentralist tradition

Viewed from the perspective of the last quarter of the twentieth century, it may seem that socialism has been moving always in the same direction, always towards the centralisation of power and the

increasing authority of the state. This impression indicates the pre-
dominance of Marxist socialist thought: not for nothing were the
early Marxists called Authoritarians.

But, as already touched on in the previous section, there is
another socialist tradition. Known variously as libertarianism,
mutualism, federalism, decentralism, syndicalism, or anarchism,
the tradition has a greater relevance to modern Western European
society than the Marxist. Indeed, its reassertion is a major philosophical undercurrent of the politics of devolution. And it is no
coincidence that the tradition is especially strong in Wales.

The first thinker to give coherent expression to these ideas in a way
immediately relevant to the problems of modern industrial societies
was Henry Saint-Simon (1760—1825). The central element in his
theory of politics was that the industrial society of the future would
be 'administered, as against governed' by a corporate collection of
industrialists, organised labour, scientists, and tech-
nologists.[42] What Saint-Simon envisaged was a transformation of
the nature of politics from an activity concerned essentially with
military and theological matters to one directed towards scientific
and industrial goals; politics would become, as he put it, 'the
science of production'. Saint-Simon, though still generally thought of
as a 'utopian socialist', foresaw more clearly than any other
nineteenth-century thinker four crucial developments which are
visible in contemporary industrial societies. These were the
imposition on society of decisions made by corporate forces, in
particular business enterprises and trade unions; the consequent
necessity for new forms of institutional co-operation between those
forces and government; the growing influence of a new 'technical
intelligentsia'; and powerful integrative pressures at the
international level.

Saint-Simon was a seminal influence on Proudhon (1809-65), a
major prophet of the decentralist tradition. More than any other
Proudhon instilled a moral dimension into socialism which Marx,
who professed a hearty contempt for moral teaching, rejected. It is
Proudhon's moral ethos that imparts such veracity to his writings.
Thus:

> By the word [Anarchy] I wanted to indicate the extreme limit of political
> progress. Anarchy is, if I may be permitted to put it this way, a form of
> government or constitution in which public and private consciousness
> formed through the development of science and law, is alone sufficient to
> maintain order and guarantee all liberties. In it, as a consequence, the
> institutions of the police, preventive and repressive methods,
> officialdom, taxation, etc., are reduced to a minimum. In it, more

especially, the forms of monarchy and intensive centralisation disappear, to be replaced by federal institutions and a pattern of life based on the commune. When politics and home life have become one and the same thing; when economic problems have been solved in such a way that individual and collective interests are identical; then—all constraint having disappeared—it is evident that we will be in a state of total liberty or anarchy.[43]

This is not so much an idealist's vision as an expression of the direction in which society should move. It contrasts vividly with Marxism in that it sees change evolving from below, while Marx saw change being imposed from above. Both thinkers, at least in theory, envisaged the state withering away. But for Marx this would be the result of the 'dictatorship of the proletariat' while for Proudhon it would be the result of a more subtle and democratic process. This argument parallels the key issue in the politics of devolution, identified in the introductory chapter to this book: whether the problem of government should be viewed from the top down, the Classical/Marxist model; or from the bottom up, the Romantic/Proudhon model, which is also the devolutionist's model. Nisbet explains the difference as follows:

In utter contrast to Marx, Proudhon felt it vitally important to deal with the nature of power, the distinction between authority and power, the necessity—for freedom, at any rate—of autonomous associations, of decentralisation of economy, society and state, and of federalism as a constitutive principle in all institutions. Only by the diversification of society, Proudhon declared, can freedom be assured. 'Multiply your associations and be free', Proudhon told workers and all others. Unlike the Marxists, who thought only in terms of a single, centrally led proletariat and, for the distant future, a 'classless society' conceived, so far as we can determine, much in the fashion of Rousseau's democracy of the general will, Proudhon stressed the need for diversification of all society and also the importance of building the good society based on the natural communities that may already be seen forming even under capitalism.[44]

The first time the word 'socialism' appeared in print was probably November 1827, when Robert Owen, writing in his *Co-operative Magazine,* said that, in the argument whether it is more beneficial that capital should be individual or common, there are socialists who held that it should be common. It was Owen, of course, who prepared the ground for both Proudhon and Marx, by insisting that the value of a thing depends on the amount of labour incorporated in it, and that labour rather than money should measure the

different values of commodities.[45] In terms of mainstream nineteenth-century politics such ideas did not occupy the centre of the
stage in Wales, but they did exercise an influence. Tom Ellis,
Liberal MP for Meirionnydd and a leader of the Cymru Fydd movement, in a speech at Bangor in 1892, asked: 'In the . . . great movement for placing upon a stabler and more satisfactory basis the
social relations and duties of man to man, in this movement towards
socialism, what has been the contribution of Wales?' He went on to
answer:

> Though Wales in modern times is largely individualist, we cannot but
> feel that it has been the land of cyfraith, cyfar, cyfnawdd, cymorthau
> and cymanfaoedd,[46] the land of social co-operation, of associative effort.
> It is significant that the initiator in Britain of the movement for
> collective and municipal activity in the common effort for the common
> good was Robert Owen, who embodied in these latter days the spirit of
> the old Welsh social economy.[47]

Decentralisation and the voluntary principle run deep into Welsh
life and 'the old Welsh social economy'. Before the conquest of
Wales in 1282, few Welsh leaders achieved much success in building
up a unitary Welsh state. In England, 'the primary unit was
England. . . . In Wales the primary unit was the "commote", an
area which might on occasion be no larger than a single parish, and
whose name is the basis of the Welsh word for neighbour'.[48] The
tendency to decentralisation in mediaeval Wales was furthered
socially and politically by the Welsh law of property which knew
nothing of primogeniture. Under its system of gavelkind, property
was divided among the sons. This principle of division applied to
kingdoms and principalities as well as to small private estates.

Between 1282 and the Act of Union (or, more accurately, Incorporation) of 1536, the March of Wales remained an area of free lordships. And no sooner had the Tudors accustomed Wales to central
authority than the rise of nonconformity began to fragment Welsh
life once again in the sphere that really mattered. It has been
suggested that, when nonconformity was dominant and government
still remote from ordinary life, Wales virtually had selfgovernment:
by the same token, the localities of Wales were also largely autonomous during the last century. As Ioan Bowen Rees has commented:

> Organised religion carries comparatively little weight in Wales today,
> but the political ethos of non-conformity still colours social attitudes
> over much of the country. People who have seen for themselves that
> ministers of religion subject to little, if any, central supervision and
> control are in no way inferior to those of the hierarchical churches, are

likely to be sceptical about the difference which more administrators and advisers can make to the quality of teaching in schools or to the work of social workers in the field. People who have been used to taking a vote on every question from the selection of visiting preachers to the cost of a new organ—and to discussing abstract questions like 'Are there degrees of sin?' without expert guidance—are not likely to welcome large units in which their votes count for nothing. For better or for worse, democracy is the Welsh way of life. Attitudes rooted in noncon- formity—or in the free principalities and lordships of the Middle Ages—still crop up in the Trade Union, the Flower Show and the Swimming Pool Association.[49]

These attitudes found their way into the early industrial exper- ience of Wales and were dominant, in fact, until the outbreak of the First World War which killed so much more than lives. The out- standing example was *The Miners' Next Step*, first published in Tonypandy in the Rhondda Valley, in early 1912. At once a set of specific proposals and a political pamphlet, it was written by several men including Noah Ablett, Will Mainwaring, Noah Rees, and Will Hay, and was the subject of several delegate conferences and amended accordingly. Democracy was a major theme:

> The men who work in the mine are surely as competent to elect [officials] as shareholders who may never have seen a colliery. To have a vote in determining who shall be your fireman, manager, inspector, etc., is to have a vote in determining the conditions which shall rule your working life. . . . To vote for a man to represent you in Parliament, to make rules for, and assist in appointing officials to rule you, is a different proposition altogether.[50]

The document contains a shrewd analysis of trade union bureau- cracy and lays emphasis upon the power of the rank and file, expressed through the fully democratised machinery of the union. While the document lays emphasis on 'decentralisation for negotiating', with the miners' lodges having 'every stimulus to work out their own local salvation in their own way', it argues for the centralisation of fighting power. Significantly, R. Merfyn Jones's introduction to a reprint of the pamphlet in the 1970s comments: 'It was this industrial unionist emphasis on effective centralisation which caused The Miners' Next Step's programme to be ship- wrecked on the rock-like sense of district autonomy to which the South Wales miners were particularly attached.'[51]

But viewed from the perspective of the 1970s perhaps the most powerful and telling point of the document was its unhesitating rejection of any schemes for nationalisation. These were seen as allowing the industry to fall into the hands of the state and thence, through the backdoor, back to the coal-owners:

> Nationalisation of the mines does not lead [towards the elimination of the employer] but simply makes a National Trust, with all the force of the Government behind it, whose one concern will be, to see that the industry is run in such a way, as to pay the interest on the bonds, with which the coalowners are paid out, and to extract as much more profit as possible, in order to relieve the taxation of other landlords and capitalists.
>
> Our only concern is to see to it, that those who create the value receive it. And if by the force of a more perfect organisation and more militant policy, we reduce profits, we shall at the same time tend to eliminate the shareholders who own the coalfield. As they feel the increasing pressure we shall be bringing on their profits, they will loudly cry for nationalisation. We shall and must strenuously oppose this in our own interests, and in the interests of our objective.[52]

The only quality that separates the politically active youth in Wales in the 1970s from the men who produced *The Miners' Next Step* is experience of brutality. For the rest they reach back, across a generation deracinated by war and ambition, to touch the Welsh decentralist tradition. At once, this combines practical strength with idealism. It takes as its moral starting point the community and community rights. Contrary to the Marxist democratic centralist approach, it views the problem of government from the bottom up rather than from the top down. It does not deny conflict. But instead of a conflict between classes, envisaging a facile dictatorship, it sees conflict in terms of a clash between centralism and decentralism. Centralism is the product of a strong state system. In so far as the Marxist philosophy depends on creating a strong state to effect change it is always vulnerable to perversion into a corporatist system. The conflict inherent in Marxism, because it rests on class, cuts across community and also threatens dictatorship by the corporate state.

On the other hand, the centralist/decentralist conflict—the conflict between the community and the state—offers the possibility of creative reconciliation in a new balance between the two. This is the challenge of the politics of devolution.

The Welsh philosopher, J. R. Jones, originally a Marxist, eventually came to the conclusion that the main threat to humanity was no longer the economic oppression of capitalism, but the spiritual oppression of a strong over-centralised state system, whether operated by socialists or capitalists.[53] As more and more of the things we use are produced in identical units, he argues, the danger is that human beings, too, will be treated as units rather than unique beings. Neither can the uniqueness of individuals be considered apart from the uniqueness of the nations and communities within which they have developed and apart from which they lack integrity and significance. Man needs an anchor in a particular community. It is the source of that moral power which enables him to resist the monolithic State. The nation and the community in which he seeks his roots is not an end in itself: it is man's link with eternity. 'Cadw tŷ mewn cwmwl tystion', as Waldo Williams so movingly expressed it: man's relationship to the community is 'Keeping a home amidst a cloud of witnesses'.[54]

Appendix I: Devolution and Local Government

As was touched upon in the final chapter, the politics of devolution embrace an important debate about the problem of government below the all-Wales level. The outcome of the argument over Welsh local government structure in the context of devolution will determine the character of community and democracy in Wales as much as the establishment of an Assembly itself. A notable contribution to this debate was a discussion paper prepared for a July 1977 meeting of the Welsh Counties Committee by Gwynedd County Council's chief executive, Mr Alun Jones, which is reproduced below:

Discussion Paper on Proposals for Further
Local Government Reorganisation

1. *Preamble:*

1.1   From time to time when its White Paper on devolution was published in 1975, the Government, through its spokesmen in the House of Commons and the House of Lords, was emphatic that its proposals involved only the transfer to regional assemblies of functions hitherto exercised by Central Government and not those which lay within the jurisdiction of local government. The (then) Prime Minister, Sir Harold Wilson, in a letter to the Times in December 1975, said,

> It is not intended that it (the Scottish Assembly) should assume powers from local government—its role is to take over work now carried out at Westminster.

Mr John Morris, Secretary of State for Wales, gave similar, if not stronger, assurances,

> (a) We made it clear in the White Paper that the Welsh Assembly would not be expected to assume existing powers from local government—I repeat that commitment.
>
> (House of Commons—4 February 1975)
>
> (b) I have said repeatedly in the House, that the proposals that we shall put before the House will not materially affect the functions of local government. If it pleases hon. Members, as I am sure it will, I shall say it again.

And Mr Ted Rowlands, M.P., stated,

> The Government's proposals for Welsh devolution do not involve the reorganisation of local government.
>
> (House of Commons—3 March 1975)

1.2   Prior to the publication of the Scotland and Wales Bill, the Welsh Counties Committee had supported the concept of Devolution, and had affirmed its enthusiasm for the establishment of an 'accountable' Assembly for the Principality which would undertake important responsibilities hitherto exercised by the Secretary of State and the Welsh Office, together with the host of activities carried out by numerous (and relatively unaccountable) ad hoc bodies. Such bodies had proliferated greatly in the post-war years, and it is estimated that in 1975 there were about 70 non-elected bodies of importance in Wales, 50 of them spending more than £300m. a year. Whether the Welsh Counties Committee would have adopted this approach in 1974 if Ministers of the Crown and others who have subsequently changed their tune and who now urge further re-organisation as a concomitant to Devolution had not made the statements attributed to them as shown above is open to conjecture.

1.3   Advocacy for further reorganisation of local government in Wales became strident in 1976. The Secretary of State for Wales, Mr John Morris, in a statement quoted in the *Western Mail* on 4 August 1976 said,

> We told the Conservatives at the time of reorganisation that they were putting the cart before the horse. They should have tackled the Kilbrandon report first, and in the light of this, then considered local government. They refused, and they are wholly responsible for the present system, and because of this stubbornness the people of Wales are having to pay for it. Something has to be done, and we believe that the Assembly, with its responsibility for supervising much of the work of local authorities, will clearly have weighty and important views on the structure we need.

1.4   Since 1974, two important lobbies have, almost incessantly, canvassed a further re-organisation of local government. The first is the Welsh Labour Party which, at its 1977 Conference in Llandudno, has called for the establishment of 25 single-tier councils in Wales to replace the present structure of 8 County Councils and 37 District Councils. The Welsh Labour Party, as the Secretary of State implied, had shown great reluctance towards accepting the pattern of local government implemented as the result of the Local Government Act 1972. It had sought postponement of the 1974 reorganisation until the publication of the Kilbrandon Commission proposals.

The other group seeking an early re-organisation of local government is the Council for the Principality.* This body has clamoured persistently for a re-structuring of local government, and some of its constituent member authorities have at some time asserted their desire for a reorganisation on the lines of a straight transfer of some major County functions to the Assembly with the residue passing to the District Councils. It might not be

---

*The body that represents the 37 Welsh district councils.

unfair to suggest that their attitude reflects subjective rather than objective considerations.

As long ago as May 1976, representatives of the Council for the Principality met the Secretary of State for Wales in London to discuss the workings of the Welsh Assembly and the possibility of a further reorganisation of local government in Wales. This may have some relevance to the fact that whilst the White Paper on devolution to Scotland and Wales entitled 'Our Changing Democracy' published in November 1975 stated categorically that the devolution Act would not make any change in the structure of local government in Wales, and that local government administrative areas and boundaries would remain the responsibility of the Secretary of State, a subsequent Supplementary Statement presented to Parliament in August 1976 quoted the Government's intention to ask the Assembly to consider and report, after appropriate consultations, on future local government structure in Wales in the context of the Assembly's own new responsibilities for the whole of Wales. This was reflected subsequently in the Scotland and Wales Bill.

1.5   No detailed arguments in support of a new local government structure have been advanced by the proponents of further change. The predominant argument of political groups is that Wales cannot afford a further tier of government, given the establishment of an Assembly. Some District Council spokesmen repeatedly state that 'people' are disenchanted with the present system, which they regard as inefficient and confusing, and that the present counties are too large and cumbersome for some services; too small and ineffective for others. It is clear, however, that whatever alternative pattern is favoured, a number of county services—the 'strategic' services— are regarded as candidates for transfer to the Assembly. We shall seek to show that such transfers are advocated, not because the existing Counties are unable to administer the relevant services effectively, but because any pattern of unitary or most purpose authorities in Wales with a population more akin to that of existing Districts than to that of the Counties would not give rise to units of local government which would be sufficiently strong and capable in relation to the provision of those services.

1.6   Although it constitutes the primary target of those who propose change, County Government has hitherto remained silent. We welcome the opportunity to present the counter-argument, which will, we hope, enable this controversial matter to be discussed more rationally than hitherto, and with a greater appreciation of the consequences of alternative patterns which have been mooted, often thoughtlessly, and sometimes irresponsibly.

2.

2.1   *Is further re-structuring of local government necessary?*

In recent months, some of those who allege that the creation of multipurpose local authorities in Wales must necessarily follow the establishment of an Assembly have added a new assertion to their argument. It is that local government in the Principality, and County Government in particular has since the 1974 re-organisation, become so ineffective as to give rise to considerable public concern, and that accordingly a fresh look at the local government structure is urgently required. Principally, this assertion comes from spokesmen for the Principality, and is given much prominence in the Welsh press. Certain members of Parliament have appeared ready to adopt this view and to repeat it and the Secretary of State for Wales has clearly been influenced by such assertions (see para. 1.3). The Welsh Labour Party has recently proposed the formation of 25 single-tier most purpose authorities, and wishes this change to take place whether devolution goes ahead or not.

2.2   We think it important that the performance and effectiveness of local government should be examined in the context of this assertion. For this purpose an examination of the criticisms most frequently made of the present system, together with such answers to those criticisms as we can fairly provide, will be useful.

2.3   *Size and Remoteness:*

This is the criticism most frequently levelled at County Councils in Wales. The proposals of the Welsh Labour Party are described in the Western Mail (May 25, 1977) as reflecting the aim 'to create authorities as close as possible to the grass roots at the same time as being compatible with running the major services of education, social services, transport, and housing'. The Association of District Councils are quoted in the same paper as saying that the present County Councils are too large and remote. But of the many who advocate the transfer of 'strategic' functions from local government to an Assembly, there is not one who has considered the size and remoteness of the Assembly in Cardiff as an executive body responsible for some local government functions which, they say, should be transferred to it. Nor would combinations of 'multi-purpose' authorities for services which cannot effectively be administered by relatively small units be regarded as 'remote' in terms of accountability!

We must acknowledge that certain members of one Welsh County Council—Dyfed—have apparently taken the view that that County's effectiveness is hampered by its size, but so far as is known, there has been no genuine concern on the part of members of the other seven County Councils in relation to their size or their remoteness from their electors or, for that matter, from their peripheral areas. Indeed, it would be well to recall that the three Glamorgan counties within whose boundaries live about half the population of Wales, are today much smaller in area than the single pre-1974 County of Glamorgan. Gwent is not significantly larger, whilst the largest Welsh County in terms of acreage is still considerably smaller than the pre-1974 County of Devon.

2.4   In any discussion on the 'remoteness' of a local government unit, it is necessary to analyse the meaning of the expression in relation to the functions and activities of the unit. If 'remoteness' means simply that the headquarters offices of the Council are too far, in a geographical sense, from members of the population who live in the peripheral areas of a County, then the criticism of remoteness becomes ludicrous. County Councils with large geographical areas have almost without exception, established local or area offices geared to particular functions or services which enable the public to seek information or make complaints with relative convenience. In practice, very few members of the public require personal recourse to County Council departments at Headquarters : should a member of the public wish to communicate with 'the Council' his natural practice is to telephone, or write, or contact his local member. In relation to education matters, his immediate point of contact is with the local school headmaster. And, in the context of this criticism, it would hardly be rational to suggest that a ratepayer who resides, say, 30 miles from a County administrative centre, is at a serious disadvantage in comparison with one who lives within 15 miles from County Hall ! Whatever the number of multi-purpose authorities which are proposed, it is highly unlikely that their populations would either be able to enjoy, or wish to have, such a facility.

2.5 'Remoteness', as a perorative expression, may be used to denote a lack of accountability. It is true that since the 1974 re-organisation, the number of elected members in relation to the population has suffered a reduction. To this extent it may be true to say both that electors generally will find greater difficulty in making personal contact with their representative, and that the member, in turn, will be undertaking a greater burden of work in relation to the requests and complaints of his larger electorate. But this, in terms of County Council functions, is not a serious disadvantage. Parents have school governors—all local—for recourse in relation to local problems. Ratepayers and electors in the rural areas are now accustomed to raise local problems, including those which relate to County and District Council matters, with Community Councils or with individual members of those Councils. And, finally, the institution of the Commissioner for Local Government Administration—'the Ombudsman' —has not only provided an aggrieved individual with a channel for a comprehensive examination of his grievance, but has also emphasized to both members and officers of local authorities the need for sensitivity and the importance of accountability in local government activity.

2.6 Most, if not all, County Council services are most effectively organised on a large scale. This has been acknowledged by a number of Commissions and Committees which examined the local government of England and Wales prior to 1974. It was the relative inability of some of the old County Councils to provide services to a requisite standard, because of their inadequate size, that led to the trauma of re-organisation. This fact appears to have been forgotten by those who now seek to create 25 or more multi-purpose authorities which in large measure will perform functions undertaken by County Councils which, prior to 1974, were in most cases considerably larger than those which are now proposed. The pattern of local authorities favoured by the Welsh Labour Party would give rise to no fewer than eight unitary authorities in North Wales alone, six of which would be significantly smaller in terms of both area and population than the pre-1974 Counties in that area. The other two would have populations of 63,000 and 33,000 respectively. It is inconceivable that all these relatively small authorities would, in the period of scarce resources and complex social requirements that will undoubtedly continue well into the next decade, be able to carry out the more important functions currently exercised by County Councils; it is probable that in terms of effectiveness, they would not be able to compete with the pre-1974 Counties, let alone with the 8 present Counties of Wales. In South Wales, the pieces of the jig-saw are even smaller and much more numerous in comparison with the old Counties.

2.7   In justification of the district-based multi-purpose authority, it has been suggested by the Council for the Principality and by certain Members of Parliament that a number of 'strategic' functions should be transferred to the Assembly. The Rt. Hon. Cledwyn Hughes, M.P. is recently reported as having suggested the transfer of the major part of the Education Services to that body. The Welsh Council for Labour suggests merely the transfer to the Assembly of higher education (with some further and special education), together with strategic planning and transportation planning. We will discuss in a subsequent part of this paper the unacceptable nature of proposals to centralize in the hands of a regional body which by its nature is infinitely larger and more 'remote' than any existing County Council, those important functions of local government. What is important to note at this stage is the inappositeness of small-sized units of local government in relation to the administration of major functions such as the Social Services, Highways and Transportation, the Fire Service, and the residue of the Education Service should Higher and Further Education be transferred to an Assembly. All these functions require proficient specialist staffs in relatively large numbers. The expertise and equipment for some of these services has been carefully built up and equally carefully deployed through County areas. It has been possible to provide throughout County areas the flexibility in the use of these resources which efficiency demands, as well as constant standards of provision. Specialist staff resources, like other resources demanded in local government today, are scarce, and it is quite impossible to see how the small multi-purpose units now proposed could operate effectively and to a constant standard in relation to those services presently undertaken by County Councils.

2.8   In defending the County system of government, the Welsh Counties Committee is likely to be accused of being self-protective and subjective in its attitude. Happily, it can quote the views of bodies and individuals whose researches into local government structures and functions in recent years were undoubtedly objective and comprehensive. In its examination of the size of the County Unit in Wales, the Local Government Commission for Wales which reviewed the organization of local government in Wales over a period of three years, found that the costs per head were in general significantly higher in the smaller counties than in the medium and larger ones. They stated (para. 317 of the Report and Proposals, 1962),

> We commenced our task without pre-conceived ideas. By the time that we had completed the first stage of our investigations, . . . it had been borne in upon us that there is a close relationship between the size of a local authority in terms of population and resources and its effectiveness.

The Commission also stressed that the area appropriate to each type of authority must be related to the functions performed.

> County government, as the topmost tier of this three-tier system, must inevitably be carried out over wide areas. It is reasonable, therefore, to take the view that in general at this level effectiveness must set the broad pattern and the factor of convenience should only modify it.
>
> (para. 362)

> If convenience were the only factor to be considered, all local government would be exercised over very small areas.
>
> (para. 360)

The Royal Commission on Local Government in England in 1969 reported as follows in relation to the services specified,

> An efficient highways authority should be large enough in terms of its road mileage and its financial resources to support a team of qualified road engineers and a range of modern roadmaking equipment . . . . they (larger authorities) would have the resources to acquire and keep employed a full range of equipment.
>
> (para. 265)

and, in relation to Education,

> From the return made by Your Majesty's Inspectorate, the Department of Education and Science concluded that the least efficient education authorities tended to have population below the 200,000 mark.

There are many other declarations of similar kind which those who now call for a further re-organisation and the creation of smaller units of local government have not tried to refute; they simply ignored them. The Welsh Counties Committee will no doubt wish to remind the Government, and perhaps the Assembly in due course, of their existence and validity.

2.9   The prime task of a County Council is to provide a wide variety of services to the public in their areas, to do so effectively, and to secure that insofar as is possible, the manner and extent of their provision reflects the needs and the aspirations of the inhabitants of its area. Since 1 April, 1974, there is ample evidence that County Councils in Wales have, in good measure, attained this objective. Despite the complex difficulties and upheavals consequent to the 1974 re-organisation, the ever-worsening economic situation during the past three years, and an inflation rate which gave rise first to a policy of 'no growth' and subsequently to one of negative growth in local authority investment, it is fair to say that the new Council's achievements in terms of significant development of the Social Services, the construction and improvement of new roads, partly under agency to the Welsh Office, and the maintenance of Education, Police and Fire Services to a standard at least as high as that attained by their predecessor authorities, is an indication of their strength and effectiveness rather than of any inherent defect in their size or organisation.

2.10 If tangible evidence of weakness in Welsh local government is sought, it is fair to point to two factors which currently relate to district councils. Very recently, a Parliamentary Debate has disclosed a very substantial failure in Wales on the part of housing authorities to meet the house building target contemplated by the Welsh Office. It seems that there has been underspending to the tune of £25,000,000 during the last financial year, and that a Government Inquiry into the circumstances of the surprising failure to achieve an important Programme objective is to be carried out. The other factor—strangely similar to the first—is that in course of Sewerage work undertaken by district councils as agents for the Welsh National Water Development Authority, only about 25% of the works programmed, has been undertaken in the last financial year. This is despite the fact that the total programme of works sought for the last financial year by the Welsh District Councils was cut by 50% beforehand, presumably on the grounds that their ambitions were not regarded by the Authority as being compatible with their capability. Accordingly, it seems that the district councils succeeded in undertaking only $12\frac{1}{2}$% of the total capital programme which they themselves had proposed. This is yet another indication that much larger and stronger local authorities are required to undertake the planning and design of major works and to ensure even flows of work and expenditure.

On current showing, therefore, small sized authorities (up to, say 200,000 population) do not provide a model of effectiveness so far as building and infrastructure programmes are concerned, and if a pattern of multi-purpose authorities for Wales should ultimately emerge, the virtues of strength and effectiveness could well be in serious jeopardy if the size and nature of the new authorities correspond more closely to the present district authorities than to the County Councils.

3. *The extra-tier argument*

3.1 This has been raised both by those who, in Parliament, have favoured devolution, and by its opponents. Naturally, it has been frequently repeated by those whose prime interest in devolution appears to lie in the opportunity which the Welsh Assembly would provide for a further examination of local government structure, rather than in the undoubted need for an elected and accountable forum which would deal in Wales with Welsh matters currently administered in Westminster and in the Welsh Office. Some commentators assert that the Welsh are already over-governed, and that the imposition of yet another tier of government would be intolerable. We find it difficult to accept this assertion. In the first place, the Government's proposals do not contemplate the creation of a fresh point of contact between government and the governed. The Assembly, given the functions proposed for it in the White Paper, is in no sense to become an 'operational' body, and its primary intent and its undoubted effect would be to remove from Westminster to Cardiff, and from the Secretary of State and his department to an elected forum, an area of Government activity. In other words, the Assembly will not increase, measurably, the amount of Governmental activity in Wales; what it will do is to alter the way in which that activity is exercised. It is for that reason, presumably, that those who have put forward the proposals, i.e. Government Ministers, have patently refused to acknowledge the 'tier-proliferation' argument.

3.2   Obviously, those who would regard the Assembly as an operational and executive body, charged with this direct administration of all or part of the Education service, perhaps of the fire service, transportation, planning, etc. would be happy to see it as the only County Council in Wales. That solution would, of course, go a long way towards meeting the argument of over-government, but it would simultaneously attract the more relevant criticism that *local* government had been immeasurably weakened, accountability reduced, and 'remoteness' considerably increased.

3.3   Most protagonists of a multi-purpose system of local authorities claim that the undoubtedly high costs of establishing and running the Welsh Assembly must be met, in part, by a substantial saving in the local government field, i.e. by dispensing with the allegedly expensive unit of local government—the County Councils. This suggestion is fallacious, and it is of extreme importance, in our view, that the true position be expounded and understood by politicians, members of local authorities, and the public alike. We shall examine it in the paragraphs that follow.

3.4   County Councils are, indeed, the most expensive units of local government in terms of total expenditure. They are responsible for all those services which are strongly labour intensive. They are responsible for the employment—and payment—of teachers (several thousands in most Counties), of staffs of Higher and Further Education establishments, of policemen, of Social Service workers, and of the supporting administrative staffs. Should the provision of the service within which those categories of public employees work be transferred to some other authority, be it to an Assembly or to 'multi-purpose' Councils or to a combination of such Councils, the employees in question would continue to work in their original locations and the financial burden of paying their salaries and wages would remain unaltered. If it is asserted that a streamlined administration based on the Assembly would result in lower administrative costs, our reply is that supervision and administration would still be necessary in each immediate locality, and in addition, extra provision would become necessary for the central administration personnel in Cardiff.

An attempt was made in 1976 to ascertain the cost of administration as a percentage of the total cost of providing Education and Social Services in one of the Welsh Counties. In the case of Education, it was 3.26%, and for Social Services it was 12.18%. It is quite probable that these percentages, small as they are at present, would increase in the event of a splitting of County administrative resources among a number of new multi-purpose authorities covering the same area.

3.5   In Wales, some idea of the relatively higher costs of administering services at district level is provided by the costings of the library service in those Welsh districts which run their own library service. The significant feature of the relevant figures is the higher cost of administration in districts as compared with counties. Small is not always beautiful!

3.6   If the multi-purpose authorities proposed by the Welsh Labour Party and by the Council for the Principality are to undertake responsibility for Social Services, Education (in whole or in part), Road Construction, and other County Council services, a relatively large number of posts will necessarily be created at Chief Officer level and at Senior (qualified or specialist) level. Staffing of those services would undoubtedly become significantly more expensive than it is at present. If, as has been suggested in recent proposals of the Welsh Labour Party, combination of a number of authorities would be effected in order to share specialist skills, the savings thus obtained would be minimal. If Joint Committees of several authorities are established for the purpose of administering those services which cannot easily be administered by relatively small authorities, it is necessary to ask whether such combinations would operate as efficiently in relation to those services as do the present County Councils. Would it not be more rational to vest *all* local government functions in the County Councils? The transfer of the relatively small range of functions undertaken by District Councils to the existing County Councils would without doubt be simpler and more logical than the much more complex and disruptive process of transferring the numerous and more important County functions to 25 or more new authorities.

4.   *Overlapping functions*

4.1   Undeniably, the splitting of planning functions between County Councils and District Councils in 1974 created problems which must be faced and solved. Irrespective of future proposals for re-organisation and indeed, whether a fresh re-organisation ever becomes a reality, there is a clear need for clarification of responsibility in relating to planning functions. Indeed, conflicts between the structure planning authorities (the

County Councils) and the authorities exercising development control (the District Councils) have arisen too frequently in the course of the last three years. The remedies that should be considered include the vesting of *all* planning functions in one type of authority, be it the County Council or the District Council, and alternatively, a complete review of the relevant legislation in order that interface conflicts are avoided.

4.2 In the field of social services, the problem of homelessness has given rise to disagreement between some Social Service authorities (County Councils) and housing authorities. It is astonishing that progress towards legislation designed to remedy these unfortunate 'demarcation' issues has been so tardy, but it is likely that this most prominent source of disaffection between County Councils and District Councils will disappear with the passage of the Housing (Homeless Persons) Bill now before Parliament.

4.3 A criticism of the present system which occurs from time to time, more particularly in large urban areas is the inability of some members of the public who are in urgent need of assistance or advice, and who may often be suffering social deprivation, to contact speedily and conveniently the appropriate social agency. Indeed they may, in many cases, have no knowledge of the existence of the services or of agencies which are available to them. The creation of a unitary or a multi-purpose local authority would go some way towards overcoming this problem, but it is doubtful if this would provide a complete remedy. Those of us who have worked for County Borough authorities will recall, sadly, the inability of agencies and services within the one authority to co-ordinate their policies and activities. And we would be excessively sanguine if we were to claim the ability to proffer a solution which would completely eradicate this important and worrying aspect of the problem. It must, however, be pointed out that *any* agency, be it a housing office, a local social service office, a family doctor, a district nurse or health visitor, or for that matter any elected member of a local authority, should be fully conversant with the responsibilities of all relevant services and of the general nature of the facilities available to those who seek guidance and support. They should, therefore, be in a position to direct the involvement of the relevant service or worker in the cases and inquiries which come to their notice. This is really a question of how information and guidance can better be disseminated and should be examined immediately by local government—outside the context of local government re-organisation.

5. *The process of re-organisation—its costs and traumatic effect*

5.1 Since 1973, local authorities in England and Wales have weathered the storm of upheaval with considerable success. A certain slowing of pace, changes in policies and management processes, and the costs directly attributable to transfers of staff, construction of buildings, and allowances to displaced officers were all contemplated at the time, and were in fact experienced. It is only now that local government is settling down to its routine activity after these burdens of restructuring have progressively lightened. Probably the most debilitating feature of any large-scale re-organisation is the uncertainty and fear which staffs must necessarily experience for a protracted period prior to, and during re-organisations; fear of loss of employment or of career prospects, fear of being uprooted from present domiciles, and the fear and uncertainty of undertaking new roles and relationships. This was a disturbing feature of the 1974 re-organisation, and the prospect of another upheaval so soon after the last one will, we feel sure, create the greatest harm to staff morale. Not only they, but also the public whom they serve, will suffer. For this reason alone, the Welsh Counties Committee will wish to deplore the incessant talk of further re-organisation which has been a feature of the Welsh Scene since the summer of 1974—in fact from within a few months of the date when the present local authorities assumed their functions.

5.2   We would not wish to infer, however, that the present pattern of local government is sacrosant in any way, and that it would be wrong to review it for many years ahead. Changing social patterns, successive economic crises, and serious and justifiable criticisms of any of its aspects all demand a periodic examination of the processes of government—local and central. What we would assert is that such reviews should be based on an objective and 'in depth' study of local government in all its parts, and should never be undertaken as the result of pre-conceived views (often held by political groups or individuals disappointed by rejection of their own theories during the previous re-organisation), however shrilly they are enunciated; the statements of general opinion that have been heard so far on this issue, coupled with a conspicuous failure to examine the elements which make for effectiveness or true economy, are certainly not a ground for a hasty re-drawing of the local government picture.

5.3   Drawing lines on maps of the Principality and attributing to the areas thus defined a neat population figure is a simple exercise. It gives rise to simplistic solutions which, if implemented, could well spell the end of true local government in Wales. For this reason, we would urge an end to exercises of this kind which seek to 'give the answer before the sum has been worked out'. Any further reform of local government must be carefully worked out after detailed examination of the short-falls of the present system, the close examination of numerous issues which have not hitherto been looked at, and the fullest consultations with all sides of local government and the public. Only then would the exercise become an honest one.

5.4   If the pre-emptive action of the Welsh Labour Party to press for multi-purpose local government units is adopted, whether by a Welsh Assembly or by the Government, the possibility of forming multi-purpose units based largely on existing County areas, rather than on district areas or the combination of districts, should be carefully considered for the following reasons:

(a) County areas are coterminous with Area Health Authority Areas. This is highly relevant to the need for co-ordination between the Social Services and the Health agencies. If, in order to retrieve the element of direct accountability now comparatively lacking in Area Health Authorities, these were to return to the local government fold, the County Council area is the smallest area compatible with the Health catchment areas.

(b) Effectiveness, especially in terms of planning and design and performance of Capital Works is clearly difficult to attain in relatively small local government units.

(c) Unit costs of services are generally acknowledged to be lower in large authorities than in small ones. Our previous comment on administrative expenses of library authorities in Wales is an example.

(d) The transfer of a large number of complex and staff-intensive services from eight County Councils to 25 smaller Councils together with transfers from existing District Councils in several areas, would be infinitely more difficult and costly a process than the transfer of the relatively few functions and associated staffs from existing District Councils to the eight County Councils. In this connection, it is necessary to bear in mind such factors as the provision of office accommodation, the splitting of County Council teams between 25 other authorities, hardship and disturbance allowances, and the contentious competition for scarce skills which was experienced during the last re-organisation. The costs of transfers to eight authorities might be bearable: the cost of transfers of functions and staff to twenty-five authorities would be unacceptable in a period of economic restraint.

(e) The disappearance of one tier would follow, given that County Councils would then constitute all-purpose authorities. But the criticism of remoteness, for what it is worth, might be intensified. It is thought that a rational consequence would be the enlargement and strengthening of the Community Councils—the grass-roots authorities, whose function might change but which would gain in purpose and importance through recognition as the most *local* unit of local government at which the whole range of local government problems affecting their immediate areas might be discussed. These authorities would be consulted on local needs and on proposed developments and would, in any case, enjoy a formal relationship with the top-tier authority through statutory measures. They would act as Consultative bodies in relation to all public services.

5.5   A case for local government re-organisation on these lines is not being pressed. Rather, this view is being presented as a better alternative than those which have already been proposed by others. This alternative has the merit of creating a local government multi-purpose unit which is sufficiently large to assimilate some of the many activities and functions now entrusted to a welter of 'nominated' bodies who have no direct responsibility or accountability to the electorate of the Principality as such or to a particular area or locality. Area Health Boards, Regional Arts Associations, Area Tourist Councils, Divisions of the Welsh National Water Authority, are examples of bodies whose administration should be vested, in logic, in multi-purpose authorities which are sufficiently large in size and at the same time directly responsible to the electors.

Appendix 2: Devolution and the Welsh Language

The politics of Welsh devolution are intimately related to the Welsh language, both as a response to its crisis and the conflicts it arouses, and in terms of the impact a Welsh Assembly would have on its future. The attitude of many people in Wales to devolution is conditioned by their prior attitude to the language. The question has been touched upon in the preceding pages, particularly in Chapter 3, but the main preoccupation of the book has been with the political, economic, and constitutional conflicts of Welsh devolution. This is mainly because the Welsh language issue has been exhaustively examined elsewhere, for example, by my colleague, Clive Betts, in his *Culture in Crisis—The Future of Welsh Language* (Ffynnon Press, 1976). See also, Ned Thomas, *The Welsh Extremist* (Gollancz, 1971, and in paperback by Y Lolfa, 1973) and Glyn Jones, *The Dragon Has Two Tongues* (Dent, 1968).

In an address to the American Political Science Association in Washington in September 1977, Peter Madgwick, a senior politics lecturer at the University College of Wales, Aberystwyth, summarised the language conflict well. It was significant that his address, 'Devolution in Wales', concluded that so far as the language was concerned the conflicts arising out of devolution would be creative since a Welsh Assembly would bring the language issue into the open:

> The language is not the most significant issue for the future of Wales, and yet it is at the sentimental heart of 'the Welsh question'. The Welsh language is the strongest centrifugal element in British politics, even compared with Scottish oil. It has profoundly affected the drive towards devolution, and will in its turn be affected by the enactment of devolution (even in a weak form). Two kinds of fear have been expressed. One is that an Assembly dominated by non-Welsh speakers will lack sympathy for the language, and will be more reluctant than a remote and uninvolved London government to take action, especially unpopular action, to protect and promote the language. The other is the reverse, that the Assembly will overrepresent Welsh speakers and the Welshness of Wales, and will establish an official bilingualism, closing many administrative posts to non-Welsh speakers.
>
> The truth lies probably between these two views. There may well be actual overrepresentation, since Welsh speakers are numerous in the political class, and in mixed language areas bilingual candidates are often and naturally enough preferred. But the overrepresentation will not be as substantial as that now operating through the elites, and the clear majority of the Assembly will be monolingual English speakers. The Assembly will certainly operate bilingually, with some consequences for the recruitment of officials, and it will develop and symbolise a Welsh character and style. This after all is one of the objectives of the new institution, to express the distinctiveness of the national area it

serves. Such a development represents a considerable cultural gain, the firm recognition through a prestigious national institution that Wales is bilingual. Beyond this there can be no guarantee of the policies which an Assembly will pursue. Language policy will for the first time be open to discussion and determination in an elected body representative of all of the people of Wales. This is a marked improvement on the present arrangements for the government of the language.

Hitherto the government of the language has been particularly open to the influence of Welsh-speaking elites. This has bought about gains for the language, but not by open procedures which give legitimacy to language policies. Government of the language through an elected assembly would secure political legitimacy for comparatively modest language policies, much less than the linguistic nationalists regard as necessary, but still more than an indifferent public would adopt for themselves without political leadership. The submission of language policy to the judgment of an elected assembly would not diminish, but might civilise, conflict, by diverting it into public and constitutional channels.

Notes

Introduction

1 *Hansard,* 13 December 1976, col. 1008.
2 Enoch Powell, speech at Llwynypia, Rhondda, May 1974.
3 *Hansard,* 13 December 1976, col. 983.
4 Michael Foot, address to Labour Party in Wales annual conference at Swansea, May 1976.
5 *Devolution: The English Dimension* (HMSO, 9 December 1976), paras 11 and 14.
6 *Our Changing Democracy: Devolution to Scotland and Wales*(Cmnd 6348, 27 November 1975), para. 4.
7 Jo Grimond, 'Devolution could do Scotland more harm than good', *The Times,* 9 February 1976.
8 A. V. Dicey, *Law of the Constitution* (1885, quoted from Macmillan 'Papermac' edition, 1962), pp. 39-40.
9 Ioan Bowen Rees, *Government by Community* (Charles Knight, 1971), p. 2.
10 Statement issued by Transport House, London, June 1918. See also a major policy document of that year, *Labour and the New Social Order,* which was approved by the 1918 annual conference. This included the statement:
    Labour believes in self-government. The Labour Party is pledged to a scheme of statutory legislatures for Scotland, Wales and even England, as well as for Ireland, as part of the larger plan of constitutional reform which will transform the British Empire into a Britannic Federation or Commonwealth of British self-governing communities.
11 Labour Party in Wales, *Why Devolution?* (Pamphlet, September 1976).
12 Enoch Powell, speech to the North Wales Conservative Advisory Council, Prestatyn, 27 September 1968.
13 Lord Hailsham, 'Elective Dictatorship' (the Richard Dimbleby Lecture), *Listener,* 21 October 1976.
14 *Ibid.*
15 See *Western Mail* report, 22 November 1976.
16 See *Western Mail* report, 28 February 1976.
17 Reported in *The Times,* 29 September 1976.
18 Saunders Lewis, letter to the *Western Mail,* 11 March 1977.
19 See Part I, chapter 3, pp. 113-14.
20 W. J. Gruffydd, *Cofiant Owen Morgan Edwards* (Aberystwyth, 1937), pp. 1-2.
21 See the last chapter of *Culture and Society* (Chatto & Windus, 1958), and his novel *Border Country* (Penguin, 1964).
22 Raymond Williams, *Keywords* (Fontana, 1976).

23 Joseph Stalin, *Marxism and the National Question* (1942).
24 Herman Dooyeweerd, *A New Critique of Theoretical Thought* (Amsterdam, 1957), Part III, p. 470. Quoted in R. Tudur Jones, *The Desire of Nations* (Christopher Davies, 1974). See particularly the final chapter, 'Struggle for Community'.
25 Robert Nisbet, *The Social Philosophers* (Paladin, 1976), p. 11.
26 Saunders Lewis, *Cymru Wedi'r Rhyfel*, 2nd edn (Aberystwyth, 1942), pp. 22-3.
27 Percentage Welsh unemployment rates for December compared with those for Britain:

	Wales	Great Britain
1966	3·9	2·4
1967	4·2	2·5
1968	4·0	2·4
1969	4·1	2·5
1970	4·0	2·7
1971	5·0	3·9
1972	4·5	3·3
1973	3·1	2·1
1974*	3·9	2·7
1975	7·2	5·1
1976	7·6	5·8

(*Figures for December 1974 not available: figures for November 1974 used instead.)
28 Welsh Office, *Wales Economic Trends No. 3* (HMSO, 1976), Table 40.
29 *Regional Statistics* (HMSO, No. 12, 1976), Table 3.3.
30 *Ibid.*
31 *Ibid.*
32 *Hansard,* written answer, 7 June 1976.
33 Paul Wilding, *Poverty: The Facts in Wales* (Child Poverty Action Group, 1977).
34 Welsh Office, *Statistics of Education in Wales*, no. 1 (January 1977).
35 Welsh Education Office, *Absenteeism in the Schools of Wales*, 1975.
36 Wilding, *Poverty: The Facts in Wales.*
37 One of the most celebrated examples is the village of Rhosllannerchrug-og near Wrexham in Clwyd which, though close to the border, has a high percentage of Welsh speakers and a world-famous male voice choir. In south-eastern Wales Raymond Williams has provided an account of the Welsh community of North-Monmouthshire in his novel *Border Country* (Penguin, 1964).
38 Tom Nairn: *The Break-Up of Britain—Crisis and Neo-Nationalism* (New Left Books, 1977).

39 *Ibid.*, p. 96—Ernest Gellner: 'Nationalism', an essay in the volume *Thought and Change* (London, 1964).

40 *Ibid.*, pp. 97-8.

41 James Nicholas, *Waldo Williams* (Writers of Wales series, University of Wales Press, 1975), p. 80.

42 *Ibid.*, pp. 67-70.

43 Waldo Williams, 'War and the State' (translated by Ned Thomas in *Planet 37/38*, Gomer Press, May 1977).

44 *Ibid.*, p. 12.

45 Nicholas, *Waldo Williams*, p. 80.

PART I

Chapter 1

1 By 1976 British public expenditure had reached £45,800,000, between 50 and 60 per cent of the gross national product (Cmd 6393, *Public Expenditure to 1979-80* [1976]).

2 A. J. P. Taylor, *English History 1914—1945* (Penguin, 1970, p. 25).

3 G. C. Allen, *The Structure of Industry in Britain* (Longmans, 1961), p. 132.

4 The 1976 February *Public Expenditure* White Paper (Cmnd 6393) stated that total government spending (central and local) was some 60 per cent of the country's income. But the following October the Treasury announced to the House of Commons Expenditure Committee that it had miscalculated. It said that, hitherto, a large proportion of the interest on national debt had been counted twice over with, for example, the nationalised industries paying interest to the Treasury which itself was paying interest for the same money. The result was that the 60 per cent figure was reduced to 52 per cent (see *The Times*, 28 October 1976).

5 Examples abound, particularly at the local level. The classic case is where the activity of local government social workers can reduce feelings of responsibility that neighbours have for one another. Council tenants often refuse to carry out the simplest of repairs to the property they occupy because they can claim it is not their responsibility but the local authority's. It might even be argued that employers' efforts to refurbish factories or find new markets or products to prevent closure are reduced because they know that one way or another the state will provide a safety net, if only in the form of unemployment benefit for the redundant workforce.

6 Welsh Office Information Division, October 1976.

7 In private industry the hundred largest British enterprises produced 46 per cent of net manufacturing output in 1970 compared with only 21 per cent in 1949. The latest comprehensive data available, covering the situation at the end of 1968, measured the control of net assets in

each of the twenty-two main industrial classifications. In twenty of
them an average of just over three firms controlled half or more of the
market, sometimes exceeding 90 per cent (Monopolies Commission,
*A Survey of Mergers 1958—1968,*HMSO, 1970). By the mid-1970s
this concentration must have intensified, since the largest continuous
phase of merger activity in Britain's history took place between 1967
and 1973. For a full description of the concentration of industry and
capital in Britain see S. J. Prais, *The Evolution of Giant Firms in
Britain* (Cambridge University Press, 1976); and Leslie Hannah, *The
Rise of the Corporate Economy* (Methuen, 1976).
 8 Welsh Council Report (January 1974), *Location, size, ownership and
control tables for Welsh industry,* produced by the Department of
Economics, University College of Wales, Bangor.
 9 Ken Griffin, Deputy Chairman, British Shipbuilding Corporation,
interview with the author, October 1976.
10 Commission on the Constitution, *Written Evidence, vol. 7: Wales*
(HMSO 1972), p. 104.
11 Leopold Kohr, *Development Without Aid—The Translucent Society*
(Christopher Davies, 1973), p. 43.
12 *Digest of Welsh Statistics* (published annually by the Welsh Office).
13 *Ibid.*
14 *Ibid.*
15 *Western Mail* report, 12 May 1976, 'BSC's axe chops deepest in Wales'.
16 John Osmond, *The Centralist Enemy* (Christopher Davies, 1974),
ch. II, 'Centralisation and redundancy in steel'.
17 *Financial Times,* 22 July 1976. See also the Young Fabian pamphlet
Crisis in Steel (no. 38, June 1974) which argues cogently a similar line.
It concluded: 'The current system subsumes all the real arguments
within BSC so that the public interest as expressed by Parliament has no
real capability of getting behind the facade.' One of the key arguments
that went unanswered was that if problems of industrial relations,
supply, sales, accidents or technical hold-ups occurred at just one of the
large works in which steel-making was being centralised, there would
be large-scale disruption to the whole of Britain's steel-making capacity.
This was graphically demonstrated at the Llanwern steelworks,
Gwent, in 1975 when a year-long strike over the operation of a giant
blast furnace at the plant caused massive disruption to Britain's steel-
production, contributing to the need for steel imports, damaging to the
balance of payments.
18 See Osmond, *The Centralist Enemy,* ch. III, 'How a gas board came . . .
and went'.
19 *Hansard,* 5 August 1971.
20 See British Gas Corporation, Annual Report and Accounts 1972-3.
For instance, sales in that year were more than 27 per cent up on the
previous year. But only a very small proportion of this increase was in
the domestic sector—the industry's premium market.
21 For example, it was announced in September 1976 that an engineering
factory in Neath employing 300 workers would be closed. The firm,

Tower House Wares Ltd, had chosen to develop its Wolverhampton factory partly because gas supplies were uncertain at Neath owing to the delay in building the large gas containers (*Western Mail* report, 15 September 1976).

22 Cmnd 6388: *The Structure of the Electricity Supply Industry in England and Wales.* See also Plaid Cymru's submission to the Committee: *A National Electricity Board for Wales,* mimeographed, June 1975.

23 *Ibid.*

24 Speech to Coal Industry Society (London), 2 February 1976.

25 *Review of the Water Industry in England and Wales: A Consultative Document,* 18, 1976.

26 *Ibid.*

27 Response of the Welsh National Water Development Authority to the Government review document, para D, 28 May 1976.

28 Response of the National Water Council to the review document, para. 2.1, July 1976. See also *Western Mail* article, 2 September 1976, 'Do we need a central water authority?'

29 See Osmond, *The Centralist Enemy,* ch. IV, 'The managers take over health' for a full analysis. In September 1976 the Wales TUC launched a campaign against the 'undemocratic and inadequate' management of the health service in Wales. General Secretary, George Wright, declared the reorganised structure was a model for corporate organisation with little room for democracy and subject to Welsh Office bureaucratic control: *Western Mail* report, 9 September 1976.

30 The pre-1974 figure is made up of the 13 old Welsh counties, 4 county boroughs and 164 urban and rural districts. The post-1974 figure excludes 779 new community councils in Wales which have no statutory functions and, as a result, no effective power.

31 Speech to Wrexham constituency Labour party, 13 March 1976—one of a series on devolution he made throughout Wales in this period.

32 Figures given by Nigel Forman (Conservative MP Sutton, Carshalton) June 1975. They were compiled on the basis of replies to 64 questions put to Ministers involving 16 government departments. (*The Times* report, 28 June 1975).

33 The late Maurice Edelman (Labour MP for Coventry, North West), article in *The Times,* 14 October 1975. Figures again based on Parliamentary answers.

34 *Financial Times,* 21 August 1976.

35 *Hansard,* 12 December 1975.

36 Commission on the Constitution, *Minutes of Evidence, vol 1, Wales* (HMSO, 1970), para. 14.

37 Pembrokeshire Constituency Conference speech, 8 May 1976.

38 *Hansard,* 3 February 1975.

39 It is significant that in the United States anti-monopoly or anti-trust laws have been far more rigorously applied than in Britain. As a result the US's hundred largest firms' share of net output has remained steady

at between 30 per cent and 33 per cent since 1954, compared with the equivalent figure being doubled in Britain in the same period to around 50 per cent.

40 Labour Party, Opposition Green Paper, *The National Enterprise Board* (1972).
41 A comprehensive analysis of this development will be found in a forthcoming book by J. T. Winkler, *The Coming Corporatism,* to be published by Penguin. But the idea of corporatism in Britain has also been set out in J. T. Winkler, 'Law, state and economy: the Industry Act 1975 in context', *British Journal of Law and Society,* vol. 2, no. 2, Winter 1975. Much of the argument of this section is based on Winkler's excellent analysis. See also his article with R. E. Pahl, Professor of Sociology, University of Kent, in *New Society,* 10 October 1974, 'The coming corporatism'. A summary of their views was carried by *The Times,* 26 March 1976, 'Corporatism in Britain: why protecting industry need not mean more bureaucracy'. See also Sir Keith Joseph's response to this article, in *The Times,* 17 May 1976: 'Corporatism and liberty do not go together'; and also Paul Johnson in the *New Statesman,* 3 September 1976, 'Towards the parasite state'; and David Marquand (Labour, Ashfield) in the *Guardian,* 12 April 1976, 'State opening'.
42 Penguin, 1974.
43 Harold Macmillan, *The Middle Way* (Macmillan, 1938).
44 Anthony Wedgwood Benn, 'Heath's spadework for socialism', *Sunday Times,* 25 March 1975.
45 Peter Walker, 'The changing role of government' in M. Beesley (ed.), *Productivity and Amenity—Achieving a Social Balance* (Croom Heln, 1974).
46 Winkler, 'Law, state and economy'.
47 Winkler and Pahl, 'The coming corporatism'. In their analysis Pahl and Winkler chose the term 'nationalism' in place of 'statism' which is used here. Corporatism is a theory of state practice not community practice (in which case the term 'nationalism' would be more appropriate). Moreover, Britain, in the context of this theory of corporatism, is more of a state than a nation.
48 *Ibid.*
49 *Ibid.*
50 *Guardian,* 12 April 1976.
51 F. A. Hayek, *The Road to Serfdom* (Routledge & Kegan Paul, 1944), p. 53.
52 Ivan Illich, *Tools for Conviviality* (Calder & Boyars, 1973), p. xii.
53 Ivan Illich, *Deschooling Society* (Penguin, 1973); *Medical Nemesis* (Calder & Boyars, 1974).
54 *Tools for Conviviality,* p. xii.
55 Paul Luke, 'Illich and the devolutionists' in *Planet,* vol. 33 (Llangeitho, Tregaron, Dyfed, August 1976).
56 *Ibid.*

57 Paul Goodman, *Anarchy,* no. 96, February 1969; quoted in April Carter, *The Political Theory of Anarchism* (Routledge & Kegan Paul, 1971), pp. 9-10.

58 Dafydd Elis Thomas: 'Self-government and the community: a formula for progress' in *Y Saeth* (The Arrow), no. 1, Spring 1976, Cardiff.

59 Cmnd 6601, *Financial Aid To Political Parties* under the chairmanship of Lord Houghton, former Chairman of the Labour party, August 1976. The committee found in its opinion survey that: 'Two-thirds agreed with the view that parties opposed each other "for the sake of it",' (para. 7.12).

60 *Ibid., Minority Report* by Ian Aitken, Sir Tatton Brinton, Julian Haviland and Prof. D. N. MacCormick, para. (iv).

61 Tom Nairn, *The Left Against Europe?* (Penguin, 1973), pp. 51-2. Nairn adds that because of this 'nationalisation of class':

> Labourism constitutes, perhaps, the most important element in this astonishing homogeneity of modern Britain. In effect, the most dangerous seam of civil society, the division between the classes, runs through it rather than outside it and is constantly 'healed' politically (i.e. kept closed) by the very structure and world view of the party *(Ibid.,* p. 54).

On the Left wing inside the Labour party, Nairn comments:

> The Labour-Left almost never stands for class *against* nation, for that material reality of which Labourism is the mystical shell. Were it so, the Labour Party could not exist in its actual form, and would certainly never have survived the trials of the past 20 years without a serious split *(Ibid.,* p. 56).

62 Christopher Smallwood (lecturer in Economics, Edinburgh University), 'The economics of devolution in a European context' in *Devolution, the Left, and Europe* (Young European Left pamphlet, February 1977).

63 *Our Changing Democracy,* Cmnd 6348.

64 Leopold Kohr, *The Breakdown of Nations* (Routledge & Kegan Paul, 1957), p. 185; republished in paperback by Christopher Davies (1974).

Chapter 2

1 *Hansard,* 2 December 1975.

2 Stuart Holland, *The Socialist Challenge* (Quartet Books, 1975), p. 95.

3 Franz Fanon, 'On national culture' in *The Wretched of the Earth* (Penguin, 1967), p. 167.

4 Transmitted 10 May 1974 on BBC Wales's 'Week In, Week Out'. Transcript published in *Planet* 24/25, Gwasg Gomer, August 1974.

5 See his *Economic Theory and Underdeveloped Regions* (Duckworth, 1957).

6 Quoted in *The Times,* 23 November 1976.

7 R. A. Hart, 'The distribution of new industrial building in the 1960s', *Scottish Journal of Political Economy,* vol. XVIII, no 2, June 1971.

8 Barry Moore and John Rhodes, *Regional Policy and the Economy of Wales* (Welsh Office, 1975). See Appendix B.

9 *Hansard* (903/32 col. 580), 22 January 1976.

10 Published in *Evidence of the Labour Party in Wales to the Commission on the Constitution,* January 1970.

11 Plaid Cymru, 'The failure of regional grants: memorandum to the Secretary of State for Wales', March 1976. Written by the party's Vice-President, Dr Phil Williams.

12 *Ibid.*

13 *Ibid.*

14 *Regional Policy and the Economy of Wales,* p. 29.

15 *Ibid.,* p. 44. Moore and Rhodes define their solution as achieving a threefold objective:

   (i) equalisation of unemployment rates between Wales and the South-East and Midlands;

   (ii) equalisation of activity rates between Wales and the South-East and Midlands;

   (iii) Elimination of net-outward migration.
   Significantly, the activity-rate factor—estimated at requiring 154,000 jobs—is seen as far more significant than the migration factor, requiring only 3,000 jobs. This is the reverse of what applied in Scotland in the same period.

16 Cmnd 3334.

17 E. Nevin, A. R. Roel and J. I. Round, *The Structure of the Welsh Economy* (University of Wales Press, 1966).

18 For a fuller account of this episode see John Osmond, *The Centralist Enemy* (Christopher Davies, 1974), pp. 106-11.

19 *Regional Policy and the Economy of Wales,* p. 47.

20 Wales TUC, Second Annual Report, 1976 (Transport House, Cardiff), p. 43.

21 *Western Mail,* 'Chancellor's package a disaster for Wales', 23 July 1976.

22 Welsh Office statement, July 1975.

23 Barry Moore, John Rhodes and Peter Tyler: 'The Impact of Regional Policy in the 1970s' (Centre for Environmental Studies, *Review* No. 1, July 1977).

24 See *New Society,* 29 July 1976, for an analysis of the South-East's economic position, by Peter Hall, Professor of Geography, University of Reading.

25 Moore, Rhodes and Tyler, 'The Impact of Regional Policy in the 1970s'.

26 For example, a *Times* report (3 March 1976) recorded the pressure Leicester had exerted on the government to ease IDC policy as the city's unemployment level had risen from just under 4 per cent to 5·2 per cent in less than a year. The report, 'Leicester's hopes centre on easing IDC policy', noted,

The IDC benchmark has been raised from 10,000 square feet to 15,000 square feet for the size of establishment below which IDCs are not necessary. This gives significantly more elbow room for a campaign due to be launched later this month aimed at attracting new industry and commercial users to the city from elsewhere in Britain and abroad, particularly the Continent. The prime movers in the campaign have been the Leicester and County Chamber of Commerce and Industry, the city council and big property developers with interests in the city including MEPC and the English Property Development Corporation.

27 *Western Mail:* 'Easier rules threat to new factories' (3 April, 1976).
28 Apart from distorted priorities, Wales has done badly in terms of resources devoted to her roads. Comparable spending (pounds) per mile on roads of all classes:

Year	*England*	*Wales*
1968-69	3,130	1,630
1969-70	3,550	1,770
1970-71	4,320	2,120
1971-72	4,380	2,700
1972-73	4,820	3,110
1973-74	5,500	3,640

(Source: *Hansard*).

29 Plaid Cymru, 'The failure of regional grants'.
30 From the Welsh point of view, this is also an argument for attracting foreign investment, for instance, American and Japanese companies rather than English firms, since these are less likely to be closed.
31 Welsh Office circular, November 1975, 'South Wales structure plans— Welsh Office notes for guidance on employment/industry and population'.
32 *Western Mail,* 22 January 1976: 'Way ahead plan by Welsh Office is "out of date".'
33 Town and Country Planning Association, 'A regional strategy for South Wales', 12 July 1976.
34 John Mackintosh, review of the Commission on the Constitution's report, *Political Quarterly* (January-March 1974).
35 Routledge & Kegan Paul, 1975.
36 *Western Mail,* 3 February 1975.
37 *Guardian* report, 27 August 1976, 'Premier predicts a slump in SNP fortunes'.
38 EEC Information Division, 'Background note on the regional fund', December 1976.
39 Government statement, May 1976. See Chapter 6 for a full discussion of this development.

Chapter 3

1 Report of a special meeting of the Labour Party in Wales Executive Committee, 15 March 1975, at Transport Hall, Cardiff (Unpublished).
2 *Ibid.*
3 Michael Hechter, *Internal Colonialism: The Celtic Fringe in British National Development, 1536—1966* (Routledge & Kegan Paul, 1975).
4 Hechter is aware that the terms 'colony', 'internal colony' and 'peripheral regions' are not hard and fast. He picks on 'internal colony' for Wales, Scotland and Ireland by measuring their situation against five variables: (i) the degree of administrative integration, the extent to which laws passed for the core apply to the periphery, (ii) the extensiveness of citizenship in the periphery, (iii) the prestige of the peripheral culture, (iv) the existence of geographical contiguity, (v) the length of association between the periphery and the core.

Economic dependency is not included in these variables because it applies to all three concepts. If each of the five variables is assigned a high or low rank, then a colony is a region ranked low on all five; an internal colony is given a high rank on (i), (ii) and (iv), a medium rank on (v) and a low rank on (iii) and a peripheral region ranks highly on all variables.
5 See also S. Carmichael and C. V. Hamilton, *Black Power* (New York, 1967), pp. 4-5.
6 *Internal Colonialism*, pp. 130-3. Hechter's thesis has been rapidly absorbed into Nationalist thinking and propaganda, for example in Gwynfor Evans's *A National Future for Wales* (Plaid Cymru, 1975, pp. 26-39), and a lecture given to a November 1976 conference on 'Socialism and the National Question' at Aberystwyth by Dr Phil Williams, Vice-President of Plaid Cymru (this lecture 'The Internal Colony' was published along with the rest of the conference proceedings in *Planet 37/38*, Llangeitho, Dyfed, May 1977).

Hechter's analysis was subsequently put into a useful perspective by Tom Nairn's: *The Break-Up of Britain—Crisis and Neo-Nationalism* (New Left Books, 1977). This book is essential reading for an understanding of the significance of Scottish and Welsh nationalism in the international, and particularly, European context. The book, however, is flawed by its single-minded attempt to provide a material explanation of the forces at work through the process of uneven economic development (see Introduction). Nairn comments on Hechter's analysis as follows (p. 65):

> His account is conducted essentially in terms of over-abstract models of development: the orthodox evolutionary and diffusionist model (which foresaw the gradual elimination of peripheral nationalism) is replaced by the 'internal colonialist' one emphasizing the factors of uneven development, discrimination etc., present even in the oldest West European states. Although enlightening, the application of the theory to Britain is insufficiently historical, and

misses too many of the specifics. It omits the key question of the character of the unitary U.K. state, and has too narrow a view of the significance of imperialism for the whole British order. The differentia of this variety of 'internal colonialism' was that —like the state itself—it was a pre-modern (Absolutist or transitional) form of assimilation, which survived and acquired new vitality through successful external depredations—thus enabling real integrative tendencies to outweight those of 'uneven development' for a prolonged period. None the less, a discussion founded upon Hechter's analysis would probably be more useful than any other in the future (he himself conceded that 'the models employed here are painfully preliminary', p. 6).

7 See, for example, Ned Thomas, *The Welsh Extremist* (Gollancz, 1971 and in paperback by Y Lolfa, 1973).

8 Lord Rothschild, speech to the Letcombe Laboratory of the Agricultural Research Council, Wantage, Berkshire, 25 September 1973.

9 Lord Chalfont, 'The future of Welsh politics', BBC Radio 3, 27 September 1975.

10 See his article in the *Liverpool Daily Post*, 'Another daunting, yet rewarding watershed', 3 February 1976, and 'Why a Federal Britain?' in *New Europe* 1976/77, published by the European Movement.

11 Patricia Elton Mayo, *The Roots of Identity: Three National Movements in Contemporary European Politics* (Allen Lane, 1974), p. 2.

12 Gwynfor Evans, *A National Future for Wales* (Plaid Cymru, 1975), p. 55.

13 See David Williams, *A History of Modern Wales* (John Murray, 1950), ch. 5 and 6.

14 Eric Hobsbawm, *Industry and Empire: An Economic History of Britain since 1750* (Weidenfeld & Nicolson, 1968), pp. 252-3.

15 Bud B. Khleif, *Ethnic Boundaries, Identity and Schooling: A Socio-Cultural Study of Welsh-English relations* (Mimeographed, University of New Hampshire, 1974).

16 *Aberdare Times*, 14 November 1868. Quoted in Kenneth O. Morgan, *Wales in British Politics 1868—1922* (University of Wales Press, 1970).

17 Quoted in *Wales in British Politics 1868—1922*, pp. 107, 111.

18 Quoted in Gwynfor Evans, *Land of My Fathers* (John Penry Press, 1974), p. 412.

19 *Ibid.*

20 *Ibid.*, p. 413.

21 *Ibid.*, p. 416. Liberals had to wait until 1966 before their party was united on a Welsh basis. In that year Emlyn Hooson (first elected in Montgomery at a by-election in 1962) initiated the Welsh Liberal party in a federal relationship with the English and Scottish parties. But by this time Liberalism in Wales was a fading influence.

22 Quoted in Kenneth O. Morgan, *Lloyd George* (Weidenfeld & Nicolson, 1974), p. 26.

23 See the final section of the Conclusion: The Welsh decentralist tradition.

24 Terry Thomas, speech to the Welsh Liberal Party Council at Swansea, 6 December 1975.
25 W. L. Williams, *Cymru Fydd, Its Aims and Objects* (Cardiff, 1894).
26 *Hansard,* 1946, vol. 380, col. 1411.
27 On the Secretary for Wales Bill 1921 see *Hansard,* 1921, vol. 138, col. 441. For the other interwar efforts, see summary in the Commission on the Constitution, *Written Evidence,* vol. 1, *The Welsh Office* (1969) and also James Griffiths, *Pages from Memory* (Dent, 1969), ch. 11, which records the series of Welsh deputations that were made in favour of a Secretary of State.
28 In this period a reason advanced for why Scotland could have a Secretary of State and Wales could not was that Scotland had a separate legal system. Precisely the same argument was deployed a generation later for giving Scotland a legislative Assembly but Wales one with executive powers only.
29 See Alan Butt Philip, *The Welsh Question—Nationalism in Welsh Politics 1945—1970* (University of Wales Press, 1975), paras. 257-61, for a more detailed account. The three Welsh Liberal MPs were divided in their support for the Bill with only Clement Davies in favour.
30 Council of Wales and Monmouthshire, *Memorandum on Government Administration in Wales,* 1957 (Cmnd 53).
31 *Prime Minister's Letter to the Chairman of the Council of Wales and Monmouthshire,* 1958 (Cmnd 334).
32 Council of Wales and Monmouthshire, *Memorandum on Government Administration in Wales,* 1959 (Cmnd 631).
33 Griffiths, *Pages from Memory,* p. 162.
34 Interview with Cliff Prothero. In written communication with the author shortly before his death in 1975, Griffiths evaded the question. He merely wrote: 'This is not the first time that Nye suddenly changed his views on some crucial issue—the best known example was his change from unilateral disarmament' (March 1975). But it would be unfair to say that Bevan was entirely unaware of his Welsh roots or of the political significance of the Welsh dimension in the British context. For example, in the 1947 spring issue of the magazine *Wales* a 'Tribune' editorial by Bevan on Wales was reprinted. It included the following statement:

> Welsh National sentiment is still very strong and so far from declining, there is plenty of evidence of an upsurge of national consciousness even in those parts of Wales where Welsh is not the language of the home. In all this there is nothing to deplore. On the contrary, it is very much to the good that distinctive cultures, values and institutions should flourish, so as to counteract the appalling tendency of the times towards standardisation, regimentation and universal greyness.

In another statement Bevan said: 'Wales has a special individuality, a special culture and special claims. There may be an argument—I think there is an argument—for considerable devolution of government' *(Hansard,* 17 October 1944).

35 Richard Crossman, *Diaries of a Cabinet Minister* (Cape, 1976).
36 James Griffiths, Private Papers (deposited with the National Library of Wales at Aberystwyth—and quoted in the *Western Mail,* 8 May 1976, 'The Resignation that saved the Welsh Office').
37 Ted Rowlands, 'The politics of regional administration: the establishment of the Welsh Office', *Public Administration Journal* (Autumn 1972), pp. 333-4.
38 *Pages from Memory,* pp. 172-3.
39 Conservatives subsequently used the threat to the position of the Secretary of State as an argument against further devolution.
40 Quoted by Lord Chalfont, 'The Future of Welsh Politics', BBC Radio 3, 27 September 1975. See also account in 'The politics of regional administration', pp. 341-2.
41 *Ibid.,* p. 351.
42 Address to devolution meeting at Transport House, Cardiff, 2 April 1976: one of a series held throughout Wales by Labour during this period.
43 Commission on the Constitution, *Written Evidence, vol. 7, Wales* (HMSO, 1970), p. 104.
44 Private interview, 1973.
45 Council for Wales and Monmouthshire, *Fourth Memorandum on Government Administration in Wales,* 1959, Cmnd 631, para. 13.
46 R. A. Butler, 'How Conservatives' plan for Minister of Wales would function', *Western Mail,* 15 October 1951.
47 Welsh Grand Committee, First Sitting, 16 December 1964, 'Functions of the Secretary of State for Wales and constitutional changes in Wales', col. 10.
48 See, Alun R. Jones and Gwyn Thomas (eds), *Presenting Saunders Lewis* (University of Wales Press, 1973), particularly the essay on Lewis's 'Politics' by Dafydd Glyn Jones from which these quotations from Lewis's writings are taken.
49 See, for example, *The Times* (4 September 1976): 'The men who lit the torch that set the whole of Wales alight', by Trevor Fishlock.
50 *Western Mail,* 15 October 1936.
51 Saunders Lewis, 'Education for Citizenship', *Welsh Nationalist,* Vol. 5, 12 December 1936.
52 Translated in *Presenting Saunders Lewis.*
53 Quoted in Phillip Rawkins, *Minority Nationalism and the Advanced Industrial State: A Case-study of Contemporary Wales* (Mimeographed, University of Toronto, 1975).
54 *Western Mail,* 12 April 1976.
55 Translated in *Planet,* vol. 26/27, Winter 1974/75, Gwasg Gomer, Llandysul. The following quotation is taken from pp. 132-3.
56 Waldo Williams, *Areithiau* (Y Lolfa, 1970), p. 5.
57 November 1971, Ffransis, along with two other Society members were found guilty of entering Granada Television studios, Manchester, in July 1971 and causing damage. Ffransis subsequently served a two-year prison sentence.

58 See, for example, a pamphlet by Ioan Bowen Rees, *The Welsh political tradition* (republished by Plaid Cymru, 1975); also the final section of this book.

59 The area is the home of 'penillion'—the singing of verses to the harp.

60 Quoted in Trevor Fishlock, *Wales and the Welsh* (Cassell, 1972), p. 104.

61 Emrys Roberts, 'A note to radicals' in *Deffro* (Awake), the magazine of Cardiff North Plaid Cymru, no. 5, Autumn 1970.

62 Following its Carmarthen by-election victory in 1966, Plaid Cymru came close to winning by-elections in Rhondda (1967) and Caerphilly (1968).

63 *Western Mail,* 29 May 1955.

64 *Ibid.,* 15 November 1960.

65 *Ibid.,* 30 May 1961 and 26 May 1964.

66 *Ibid.,* 5 May 1966.

67 *Western Mail,* 6 December 1966.

68 *Ibid.,* 24 April 1968.

69 *Ibid.,* 4 June 1968.

70 'Notes of a meeting held to consider proposals to establish a Welsh Trades Union Congress, TUC', August 1968 (Unpublished).

71 *Western Mail,* 23 November 1968.

72 Private interview, October 1976.

73 Quoted in the *Morning Star,* 12 February, 1973.

74 Wales TUC, Rules and Standing Orders, Transport House, Cardiff.

75 *Western Mail,* 26 April 1976.

76 Trades Union Congress, 'TUC Regional Machinery in Wales', 2 April 1973, paras 11 and 12.

77 Much of the analysis of this section is based on a paper: 'Devolution and the Welsh Labour Party', read to a politics seminar at the University of Strathclyde in September 1976 by J. Barry Jones, of the University of Wales Institute of Science and Technology.

78 For a deeper analysis, see P. J. Madgewick, Non Griffiths and Valerie Walker, *The Politics of Rural Wales—A study of Cardiganshire* (Hutchinson, 1973).

79 At its 1975 annual conference at Llandudno the Council formally changed its designation to 'Labour Party in Wales'. There was pressure for this to be 'Welsh Labour Party' but this was resisted as being symbolic of separatist tendencies though a debate and vote was avoided. The title chosen (paralleled by the 'Conservative Party in Wales') affirmed the organisation's subordinate position within the British Labour Party. Officials have since remained ambivalent about the title, preferring, for instance, 'Labour Party, Wales'.

80 But *Radical* died a year later, swallowed up by *Labour Weekly.*

81 At this stage the referendum was seen to be purely a device to frustrate the Labour party's devolution policy.

82 Hechter, *Internal Colonialism: The Celtic Fringe in British National Development, 1536—1966.*

83 Tom Nairn, 'Scotland and Wales: notes on nationalist pre-history' in *Planet,* no. 34 (Llangeitho, Tregaron, Dyfed), November 1976, re-

produced as ch. 6 of his *The Break-Up of Britain* (New Left Books, 1977).

84 *Ibid.,* p. 5.
85 *Ibid.,* p. 4.
86 *Ibid.,* p. 5.
87 *Ibid.,* p. 8.

PART II

1 Twenty-one of the thirty-six Welsh MPs supported the guillotine. Ted Rowlands, Labour MP for Merthyr who would have supported the guillotine, was paired. George Thomas, Labour MP for Cardiff West would probably have also supported the guillotine but, as Speaker of the House of Commons, he was debarred from taking sides. The two Welsh Liberal MPs, Geraint Howells (Ceredigion) and Emlyn Hooson (Montgomery) supported the guillotine, against the line of the rest of their Parliamentary Party. The eight Welsh Conservative MPs voted solidly against, though Geraint Morgan (Denbigh) had abstained on the Second Reading vote. Of the five rebel MPs, Leo Abse (Pontypool) and Fred Evans (Caerphilly) voted against the guillotine, while Neil Kinnock (Bedwellty), Donald Anderson (Swansea East) and Ioan Evans (Aberdare) abstained.
2 Commission on the Constitution, *Minutes of Evidence, vol. 7, Wales* (HMSO, January 1970), para. 107. The Labour representative was Gwyn Morgan, then Assistant General Secretary to the British Labour party.

Chapter 4

1 These documents, which were confidential, came into the author's possession in November 1975 shortly before the publication of the Devolution White Paper.
2 Early Labour Party in Wales discussion documents referred to a Welsh Senate, viz: 'The new Welsh parliament should be established as the Senate of Wales . . .' (April 1969.) The term was revived by John Morris, then Secretary of State for Wales, during parliamentary debates in 1975. But on both occasions the term proved too provocative for more conservative party members, particularly the Welsh Labour MPs. In fact, in most of the early Labour party documents on devolution— that is, pre-1974—the term 'elected Council' is used rather than Assembly. For the purpose of clarity 'Assembly' is substituted wherever this occurs.
3 Labour Party in Wales Research Paper: 'Reform of the machinery of Government' (confidential) August 1969.
4 This last proposal was, in fact, adopted by the government in its policy for the Scottish legislative Assembly. If there was doubt about whether a Bill of the Scottish Assembly goes beyond the Assembly's legislative

competence—that is, its *vires*, the final decision would lie with the
judicial committee of the Privy Council. This Labour Party in
Wales paper was partially based on another paper written
earlier in the year (April 1969) by a sub-committee (composed of two
Cardiff lecturers, J. Barry Jones and John Reynolds, and a Cardiff
businessman, Gareth Howell) charged with examining constitutional
implications of an elected 'Council'. This sub-committee recommended
that a number of key legal areas needed further research following its
decision that the Assembly should be endowed with legislative power:
(i) what changes in the administration of justice in the courts of Wales
are envisaged as a result of the proposals for devolution ? (ii) how should
the corpus of law emerging from the Welsh Senate be best enforced?
(iii) what new legal institutions would be required? (iv) what form
should any new legal structure take? (v) what appeal procedures would
obtain?

5 *Evidence of the Labour Party in Wales to the Commission on the
  Constitution* (7 January 1970), p. 17.
6 *Western Mail,* 29 April 1974, 'Unions support Kilbrandon'.
7 Labour Party in Wales Executive Committee Statement, 29 April 1974.
8 *Ibid.*
9 Subsequently, in 1977, the Swansea Labour Association came out
  against devolution altogether (see *Western Mail* report, 18 February
  1977).
10 See *Western Mail* report, 18 May 1974.
11 HMSO, *Devolution Within the United Kingdom—Some Alternatives
   for Discussion,* 3 June 1974.
12 'A statement by the Executive Committee for consideration at a special
   delegate conference, Llandrindod Wells 22 June 1974'. It stated that the
   Welsh Assembly should have:
     (i) Power to assess the overall needs of Wales in terms of
     expenditure, to decide between the individual economic and social
     priorities having regard to the special needs of Wales and to apply
     funds within the overall financial allocation of Wales in relation to
     these needs. (ii) Power to prepare and revise comprehensive economic
     development and regional land-use plans taking into account all the
     investment, development and retrenchment plans or programmes of
     the Nationalised Industries and all large-scale commercial under-
     takings operating in and affecting Wales or any part of Wales.
     (iii) Power to prepare and review plans for investment in and develop-
     ment of health, education and other social services in Wales.
     (iv) Power to participate in policy decisions of Government-owned
     commercial and industrial undertakings in Wales.
13 The *Scotsman,* 10 July 1974.
14 The *Guardian,* 4 September 1974.
15 Issued in the name of the Labour Party Executive Committee, not the
   Labour government, 5 September 1974.
16 *Western Mail,* 30 August 1974.

17 *Ibid.*
18 Gerald Fowler, 'Address to a Chartered Institute of Public Finance and Accountancy Seminar', 15 January 1976, Cardiff.
19 See *Western Mail* report, 17 January 1974.
20 Held on 13 January 1975.
21 Plaid Cymru: 'Real power for the Assembly', statement in response to the November 1975 devolution White Paper.
22 Cmnd 6348, *Our Changing Democracy—Devolution to Scotland and Wales,* para. 189.
23 HMSO, *The New Local Authorities: Management and Structure,* 1972.
24 This is the making of decisions within the broad legislative outline of Parliament to aid the execution of policy. Many hundreds of such decisions, known as Statutory Instruments, are made by Ministers, including the Secretary of State for Wales. They are so many that Parliament physically cannot subject them to adequate scrutiny. Taken together they can have a significant impact on policy. The November 1975 devolution White Paper proposed that the Welsh Assembly should take over the role of the Secretary of State for Wales in being responsible for secondary legislation affecting Wales.
25 *Our Changing Democracy,* para. 197.
26 The document, like the other Cabinet papers referred to in this chapter, came into the author's possession in November 1975. Most have no date but it is possible to identify within a few months the period in which they were written.
27 The legislative roles of the Welsh Assembly—note by the Lord President of the Council (Cabinet paper, mid-1975, unpublished).
28 'How the Assembly should work', paper approved by Labour Party in Wales Executive Committee meeting, 10 March 1975.
29 Wales TUC, 'Recommendations on Devolution', April 1976.
30 This aspect is expanded in chapter 6.
31 *Our Changing Democracy,* paras 278-85.
32 This assumption is supported by para. 285 of the 1975 devolution White Paper: 'The Secretary of State for Wales will also retain a wide role, even in matters where it has not been necessary to create formal arrangements, in advising his colleagues in the Government on particular Welsh considerations.'
33 The Commission on the Constitution did, however, envisage the disappearance of the office, both in their legislature and executive schemes for devolution. (See paras 1148 and 1169 of the Commission's report, Cmnd 5460.)
34 *Our Changing Democracy,* paras 213, 214.
35 Wales TUC, 'Recommendations on Devolution', April 1976.
36 'The Welsh Assembly and its civil service', paper approved by Labour Party in Wales Executive Committee meeting, 10 March 1975.
37 For example, Glyn Phillips, President of NALGO, and Chairman of the Wales TUC during 1977/8, was quoted in March 1977: 'The

staff currently employed in the public services in Wales should form an
independent public service, subject, as a non-Crown body, to the
authority of the Assembly. This is the only way in which to achieve
sensible and economic use of skilled manpower resources.' (*Western
Mail*, 9 March 1977.)

38 *Our Changing Democracy,* paras 207-10.
39 *Devolution to Scotland and Wales, Supplementary Statement* (August
   1976), Cmnd 6585, para. 33.
40 Commission on the Constitution, Cmnd 5460, 1973, paras 758-61,
   'The Maintenance of Minimum Standards'.
41 *Our Changing Democracy,* para. 210.
42 See September 1974, White Paper, *Democracy and Devolution:
   Proposals for Scotland and Wales* (Cmnd 5732).
43 The Commission on the Constitution (Cmnd 5460) defined federalism
   in the following terms (para. 502):
   In a federal system sovereignty is divided between two levels of
   government. The federal government is sovereign in some matters
   and the provincial governments are sovereign in others. Each within
   its own sphere exercises its power without control from the other,
   and neither is subordinate to the other. It is this feature which
   distinguishes a federal from a unitary constitution. In the latter all
   sovereignty rests with the central government; if provincial governments exist, they are subordinate authorities, deriving their power
   from the central legislature, which may overrule them at any time by
   the ordinary legislative processes.
44 Speech to the City of London Conservative Forum, 13 November 1975.
   (The White Paper was published on November 27.)
45 Cmnd 5460, para. 539.
46 A. V. Dicey, *England's Case Against Home Rule,* 3rd edn (John
   Murray, 1887), para. 168.
47 Quoted in Enoch Powell, 'Still to Decide' (Paperfront, 1971), p. 221.
   Speech to the Association des Chefs d'Enterprises Libres, Lyons, 12
   February 1971.
48 The term 'semi-federal' was used in the text of a leading article in
   The Times, 4 June 1974.
49 Commission on the Constitution, Cmnd 5460, para. 1127.
50 *Ibid.,* para. 1126.
51 Presented at the Annual Colloquium of the United Kingdom National
   Committee on Comparative Law at Cardiff, September 1974; and
   printed, together with the other papers on devolution delivered at the
   colloquium in: *Devolution—essays edited by Professor Harry Calvert*
   (Professional Books, 1975).
52 Commission on the Constitution, Cmnd 5460, para. 1153(c).
53 Headline of a *Scotsman* leading page article by Mackintosh, 29 March
   1976, 'What Labour now offers: federalism without the faults'.
54 *Ibid.*

55 Printed as, *English Law—The New Dimension,* published under the auspices of the Hamlyn Trust (Stevens, 1974).
56 Public Lecture at University College of Wales, Cardiff, 26 April 1976.
57 *English Law—The New Dimension,* pp. 66-7.
58 Public Lecture, 26 April 1976.
59 *Ibid.*
60 *Ibid.*
61 See Peter Wallington and Jeremy McBride, 'Civil liberties and a Bill of Rights' Cobden Trust pamphlet, 1977 (obtainable from 186 Kings Cross Road, London WC1).
62 Cmnd 5460, paras 513-34.
63 Speech to the City of London Conservative Forum, 13 November 1975.
64 The case of West Germany, which changed to federalism after the Second World War, is unique. There was a desire to avoid a reconcentration of power at the centre and for this reason the occupying powers insisted on the adoption of a federal constitution. As the Commission on the Constitution commented (para. 526):

> Although federal government is evidently now in accord with the will of the West German people themselves, the federation is probably sustained as much by the continuing desire to avoid the political dangers of centralisation as by any special wish for regional diversity. It has to be remembered also that the earlier history of Germany is mainly one of political division; unity was achieved only in 1871, and it was not until 1933 that full control was exercised from the centre. The federal constitution of 1949, therefore, did not impose something entirely new and out of keeping with modern history.

65 See Commission on the Constitution, *Research Papers, vol. 2* (1973), for a full account of this development. And since the election by a large majority of the Parti Quebecois to the government of Quebec in Autumn 1976, the integrity of Canada as a unit of government has been put in severe doubt.
66 *Ibid.*
67 Welsh Office statement, 27 November 1975, the day of publication of the devolution White Paper, Cmnd 6348.
68 Cmnd 5460, para. 432.
69 See the Introductory chapter for a discussion of this point in relation to the Welsh community.
70 Saunders Lewis, *Principles of Nationalism,* August 1926. Reprinted by Plaid Cymru, 1975. For an analysis of Lewis's political philosophy see Dafydd Glyn Jones in *Presenting Saunders Lewis* (University of Wales Press, 1973).
71 *Ibid.*
72 *Ibid.*
73 *Ibid.*
74 Commission on the Constitution, Cmnd 5460, paras 426-7.
75 Plaid Cymru, *The Peaceful Road to Self-Government* (mimeographed), July 1969 (see also Commission on the Constitution, *Minutes of*

Evidence, vol. 1, Wales, pp. 29-89).
76 *Ibid.,* p. 10.

Chapter 5

1 Quoted in, *Local Government Finance—Report of the Committee of Inquiry* (Cmnd 6453, May 1976), ch. 5, para. 7.
2 *Democracy and Devolution: Proposals for Scotland and Wales* (Cmnd 5732, September 1974).
3 Cmnd 6348, *Our Changing Democracy: Devolution to Scotland and Wales,* Appendix C, 'Public Expenditure and Block Grant Consultations. An Illustrative Annual Calendar', p. 64.
4 Labour Party in Wales Research Paper, 'Reform of the machinery of government' (August 1969, confidential). The financial section was the work of a sub-committee composed of Gwynoro Jones, Labour research officer and MP for Carmarthen 1970-74; J. Barry Jones, a politics lecturer at the University of Wales Institute of Science and Technology; and Wynne Thomas, a broadcaster and Parliamentary candidate for Montgomery in 1970.
5 *Ibid.*
6 *Ibid.*
7 *Ibid.*
8 Labour Party in Wales, 'Into the Seventies', evidence to the Commission on the Constitution, 7 January 1970.
9 Commission on the Constitution, *Minutes of Evidence, vol. 1, Wales,* para. 88.
10 Labour Party in Wales, 'Devolution and Democracy', Executive Committee statement, approved by a special delegate conference, 22 June 1974.
11 *Our Changing Democracy.*
12 Cmnd 6585, *Devolution to Scotland and Wales Supplementary Statement* (August 1976), para. 34.
13 Cmnd 6453, *Local Government Finance: Report of the Committee of Inquiry,* ch. 5, para. 31.
14 *Ibid.,* para. 43.
15 Cmnd 6585, para. 34, *Devolution to Scotland and Wales Supplementary Statement.*
16 Commission on the Constitution, *Written Evidence, vol. 10, Revenue Department,* p. 162, para. 35.
17 *Our Changing Democracy,* paras 99-100.
18 Commission on the Constitution, *Written Evidence, vol. 10, Revenue Department:* H.M. Treasury—'Scope for further delegation of fiscal and economic powers' and 'Scope for regional devolution of expenditure'.
19 *Ibid.*
20 *Ibid.*

21 *Our Changing Democracy*, Cmnd 6348, November 1975, para. 95.
22 *Hansard*, col. 990 (13 December 1976).
23 Commission on the Constitution, *Research Paper, vol. 10, Financial and Economic Aspects of Regionalism and Separatism*, HMSO, 1973.
24 House of Commons Expenditure Committee (Trade and Industry sub-committee), *Minutes of Evidence*, vol. II (617—19), paras 2958-63:
    The injection of £100 million or £200 million into an economy whose gross national product is nearly £100,000 million is almost insignificant to the rate of inflation. . . . If one were thinking of an injection of demand—that is to say, expenditure on resources—of the order of £1,000 million, at that order one would admit that it had some effect on the rate of cost inflation.
25 Diane Dawson, *Revenue and equalisation in Australia, Canada, West Germany and the U.S.A.*, Commission on the Constitution, *Research Paper, Vol. 9* (HMSO, 1973).
26 Derived from figures in Central Statistical Office, *National Income and Expenditure 1964-74* (the Blue Book) (HMSO, 1975). Tables 1, 4 and 47.
27 Commission on the Constitution, *Memorandum of Dissent*, Cmnd 5460-1, p. 147, p. 27.
28 House of Commons Expenditure Committee Report, *The Financing of Public Expenditure*, para. 11.
29 *Ibid.*, para. 3.
30 *Ibid., Minutes of Evidence*, para. 99.
31 House of Commons Expenditure Committee, Report—*The Financing of Public Expenditure*, para. 19, December 1975. The most comprehensive analysis of the impact of public expenditure on regional economies has been undertaken by the Northern Region Strategy Team: 'Public Expenditure in the Northern Region and other British Regions'. See *Western Mail* report, 21 February 1977.
32 Graham Rees (Professor of Economics, University College of Wales, Aberystwyth), 'The political arithmetic of the Welsh economy' in *Population, Factor Movements and Economic Development* (University of Wales Press, 1976), p. 237.
33 Jeremy Bray, *Decision in Government* (Gollancz, 1970), pp. 172-3. Bray, now MP for Motherwell, was a Junior Minister at the Ministry of Power (1966-7) and the Ministry of Technology (1967-9).
34 *Ibid.*, p. 276.
35 *Ibid.*, p. 149.
36 *Ibid.*, pp. 277-80.
37 *Ibid.*, p. 280.
38 A. A. Tait (Walton Professor of Monetary and Financial Economics, University of Strathclyde), *The Economics of Devolution—A Knife Edge Problem* (Fraser of Allander Institute, 1975).
39 Professor A. T. Peacock, 'A Financial and Economic Scheme', Appendix B, *Memorandum of Dissent*, Cmnd 5460.
40 Layfield Committee on local government finance (Cmnd 6453, May

1976), chapter II, para. 37. Assembly control over personal income tax was advocated in the Welsh Liberal party's memorandum to the Labour government in April 1977, as part of an attempt to reach accord on devolution and continue the 'Labour—Liberal Pact in Parliament'.

41 *Ibid.,* Appendix C, para. 41.

42 This method of minimising the impact of 'spill-over' effect is based on Lord Crowther-Hunt's appendix, 'A Financial and Economic Scheme' to his *Memorandum of Dissent* to the Commission on the Constitution, Cmnd 5460, p. 160, para. 29.

43 *Western Mail,* 'Change rate-aid grant system, say councils' (24 November, 1976).

44 Commission on the Constitution, *Majority Report,* para. 662.

Chapter 6

1 Welsh Office Information Division. This figure compared with £16,218,000 spent on non-discretionary regional development grants in Wales for the financial year ending 31 March 1975 under the British Development Area programme described in Section 1 of the 1972 Industry Act. These grants are non-discretionary in the sense that they are automatic for qualifying firms. They apply equally to all the development areas and so were not considered suitable for devolution, though pressure will probably come for them to be devolved.

  Section 8 of the 1972 Industry Act gives the Secretary of State for Industry powers to encourage industrial development throughout Britain. But, unlike Section 7, these powers are not so firmly employment-oriented and are concerned mainly with large capital projects. In the financial year ended 31 March 1975 only twenty-six applications from the whole of Britain were entered under this section and only ten offers of assistance made, with none going to Wales. The Welsh Office acts as agent for the Department of Industry in operating this Section.

2 Labour Party in Wales memorandum, 'The Assembly, the Welsh Development Agency and industrial powers', 19 May 1975 (unpublished).

3 *Ibid.*

4 Labour Party in Wales memorandum, 'The Welsh Assembly and industrial powers', 25 June 1975 (unpublished).

5 *Ibid.*

6 A further discussion paper, 'How the Welsh Assembly could carry out its industrial powers' (unpublished), issued to the Executive Committee by its research department simultaneously (25 June 1975) described in detail how the Section 7 powers should be administered by the Assembly:

  Administration of the Industry Act is presently carried out by Civil Servants, and the Secretary of State bears full responsibility for their actions. These Civil Servants (formerly in the Welsh Office of the DTI) would be transferred to the Assembly, and would become its *Industrial Department*. Political control would be vested in the Assembly, and would be exercised by the Head of the Industrial Department after consultation with the Industrial Committee, in agreement with his fellow-members of the Executive Committee, and subject to the approval of the full Assembly. Clearly there would have to be a procedure by which he could take necessary urgent action without going through the full process of committee discussions.

Rules for exercising powers of selective financial assistance will be agreed between the Central Government and the Assembly, and a code of practice will be adopted to avoid undesirable competition between different parts of the UK. Enforcement of the rules could be indirect (i.e. the Assembly's actions could be challenged in the courts as being incompatible with the code) or direct (i.e. the Treasury might have to give specific financial authorisation in each proposed case of financial assistance, and would only do so if the proposal were in line with the code.) Although the second proposal might seem to restrict the freedom of the Assembly, something along these lines may be unavoidable. This is because an annual Block Grant cannot predict exactly how much expenditure will be incurred under the Industry Act 1972 during a year, and the Treasury will be continuously involved during the year with spending of this kind, as it is now with the Department of Industry.

7 *Ibid.*
8 Emrys Jones, 'The Assembly, the Welsh Development Agency, and Industrial powers: the possible choices', 8 August 1975 (unpublished).
9 *Western Mail,* 3 March 1976, 'Agency's powers a "sell-out" to business interests'.
10 *Western Mail,* 3 March 1977. Precise figures of the Agency's demands were not revealed. Negotiations between the Welsh Office and the WDA were regarded as confidential.
11 Welsh Office, *Draft guidelines for the industrial investment function of the Welsh Development Agency* (March 1976); Wales TUC, *Comments of the Wales TUC on the guidelines for the industrial investment functions of the Welsh Development Agency* (January 1976).
12 Welsh Office, *Welsh Development Agency Consultation Paper,* January 1975.
13 *Western Mail,* 'Strategic plan for Wales is Agency's number one task', 3 January 1976.
14 See, for instance, Welsh Office, *South Wales Structure Plans: Notes for guidance on employment/industry and population,* November 1975.
15 *Western Mail,* 12 November 1976.
16 See *Western Mail,* 23 November 1976, 'Strategic planning held up by politics, bureaucracy'.
17 Quoted in *The Times,* 8 November 1976, 'Quiet and practical help for Wales'.

18 Wales CBI, *Welsh Development Agency—additional comments for submission to the Welsh Office*, February 1975.
19 Wales TUC, *Comments of the Wales TUC on the guidelines for the industrial development functions of the Welsh Development Agency*, January 1976.
20 Welsh Office, *WDA Guidelines*, March 1976.
21 Wales TUC, *WDA Comments*, January 1976.
22 Welsh Office, *WDA Guidelines*, March 1976.
23 Wales TUC, *WDA Comments*, January 1976.
24 Scotland and Wales Bill (29 November 1976), part V, clause 86.
25 Labour Party in Wales, 'How the Welsh Assembly could carry out its industrial powers' (unpublished) 25 June 1975.
26 Professor Glyn Davies and Dr Ian Thomas, *Overseas Investment in Wales—The Welcome Invasion* (Christopher Davies, 1976), p. 18. Professor Davies was senior economic adviser to the Welsh Office 1967-70, since when he has been Professor of Banking and Finance at the University of Wales Institute of Science and Technology.
27 Call to the Valleys Socio-Economic Research Group, *A Socio-Economic Strategy for the Valleys* (Ty Toronto, Aberfan, November 1976).
28 *Overseas Investment in Wales*, p. 11.
29 *Transport Policy: A Consultation Document*, HMSO, 13 April 1976.
30 For a fuller critique of the 1976 Government Transport Policy Consultation document, see Plaid Cymru, *A New Transport Plan for Wales* (July 1976).
31 *Overseas Investment in Wales—The Welcome Invasion*, pp. 150-1.
32 *Ibid.*, pp. 202-3.
33 *Ibid.*, p. 18.
34 Figures in this section are taken from the Wales TUC report, *A Note on the shortage of training opportunities for young persons in Wales*, January, 1976.
35 *Ibid.*
36 *Our Changing Democracy*, para. 282. In November 1976 it was announced by the Manpower Services Commission that a central committee for Wales would be set up to monitor its work *(Towards a Comprehensive Manpower Policy*, HMSO, 1 November 1976). This would co-ordinate the work of the Employment and Training Service Agencies and the Job Creation Programme in Wales, and prepare the structure for transfer to the Secretary of State for Wales's responsibility once the Assembly was under way.
37 Taken from one of a number of confidential Cabinet documents discussing key devolution issues that came into the author's possession in November 1975, shortly before the publication of the devolution White Paper of that month.
38 *Location, Size, Ownership and Control Tables for Welsh Industry*, Welsh Council, October 1973. Research commissioned from the Economics Research Unit, University College of Wales, Bangor.
39 *Ibid.*

40 This is a possibility not only because of normal electoral changes but because the Assembly will be elected for a four-year fixed term. Thus there is a chance that the colour of the Welsh administration might change mid-term as a result of by-elections or defections.
41 *Overseas Investment—The Welcome Invasion,* pp. 18-19.

Conclusion

1 Leopold Kohr, *The Breakdown of Great Britain* (Fifty-second Conway Memorial Lecture, London, 1970). Jacques Maritain, quoted in Raymond Plant *Community and Ideology* (Routledge & Kegan Paul, 1974), p. 37,
 2 For a comparison with France, see Brian Chapman, *British Government Observed* (Allen & Unwin, 1963).
3 Gwyn Morgan, quoted in *The Times,* 22 June 1976.
4 Aristotle, *Politics* (Oxford University Press, 1942), VII, 3, 1326b.
5 Robert Nisbet, *The Social Philosophers* (Paladin, 1976), p. 392.
6 *Ibid.,* pp. 395-6.
7 *Ibid.,* p. 401.
8 Rousseau, *The Social Contract,* quoted in Nisbet, *The Social Philosophers,* p. 156.
9 *The Social Philosophers,* pp. 402-3.
10 De Montesquieu, *The Spirit of the Laws,* vol. I, book 8 (Hafner, 1962), trans. Thomas Nugent.
11 *Ibid.*
12 De Tocqueville, *Democracy in America,* vol. II (Fontana, 1968), p. 897.
13 *Democracy in America,* vol. II, pp. 898-9. The following passages are taken from these pages and from the rest of the chapter.
14 *Ibid.,* p. 868. The following passages are taken from pp. 868-74.
15 *Democracy in America,* I, p. 74.
16 Herbert Marcuse, *One-Dimensional Man* (Routledge & Kegan Paul, 1964).
17 Max Weber, *The Theory of Social and Economic Organisation,* trans. by A. M. Henderson and Talcott Parsons (Oxford University Press, 1947), p. 337.
18 See also his *The Fear of Freedom* (London, 1955).
19 M. Seeman, *On the Meaning of Alienation,* American Sociological Review, 24 December 1959.
20 See his seminal work (first translated in 1940), *Gemeinschaft und Gesellschaft*—(Community and Society)—in which he develops a distinction amongst types of society based on the character of community and social relations.
21 Robert Nisbet, *The Quest for Community* (Oxford University Press, 1953), p. 14.
22 *Ibid.,* p. 286, footnote 2. See also his *The Social Philosophers,* ch. 5 and 6 for a valuable discussion of the issues touched on in this section.
23 See Dafydd Glyn Jones's essay in *Presenting Saunders Lewis*

(University of Wales Press, 1973) for the best analysis in English of Lewis's political thought and its influence.

24 See, for example, his history of Wales, *Land of My Fathers* (John Penry Press, Swansea, 1974).

25 Lewis Mumford, *The Culture of Cities* (London, 1938), p. 358.

26 *Ibid.*, p. 367.

27 *Ibid.*, p. 358.

28 *Ibid.*, p. 368.

29 *Ibid.*, p. 367 (see also pp. 310-11).

30 *Ibid.*, pp. 351-2.

31 Robert A. Dahl and Edward R. Tufte, *Size and Democracy* (Oxford University Press, 1974), p. 135.

32 Edward Heath, *Old World, New Horizons* (Harvard, 1967).

33 Isaac Deutscher, *The Non-Jewish Jew* (Oxford University Press, 1968), pp. 113-14.

34 Proudhon, *The Solution to the Social Problem* (1848) quoted in J. C. Banks, *Federal Britain? The Case for Regionalism* (Harrap, 1971), p. 294.

35 Statement by Plaid Cymru's spokesman on European affairs, Dafydd Wigley, MP for Caernarfon, 17 February 1976.

36 For example, both county and district councils are planning authorities; districts are responsible for the collection of refuse, counties for its disposal; and districts are responsible for housing, but counties for social services—two inter-related functions.

37 Denzil Davies, speech at Glanamman, Dyfed, 13 February 1976.

38 Report by the Executive Committee of the Labour Party in Wales to its annual conference at Llandudno, May 1977.

39 See T. P. Ellis, *Welsh Tribunal Law and Custom in the Middle Ages* (Oxford University Press, 1926), 'The vitality of the cymwd, as a territorial unit, is, in fact, one of the striking features of early Wales' (vol. I, p. 25).

40 Cmnd 6453, May 1976.

41 See Ioan Bowen Rees's key work, *Government by Community* and particularly chapters 6 and 7, which discuss the Swiss experience (Charles Knight, 1971).

42 See Ghita Ionescu's introductory essay in his *The Political Thought of Saint-Simon* (Oxford University Press, 1976).

43 Proudhon, Letters, 1864. Quoted in *Selected Writings of Pierre-Joseph Proudhon*, ed. Stewart Edwards (Macmillan, 1969).

44 Nisbet, *The Social Philosophers*, p. 433.

45 Robert Owen, *Report to the County of Lanark* (1820). See A. L. Morton, *The Life and Ideas of Robert Owen* (Lawrence & Wishart, 1962).

46 Roughly translatable as: law, society, co-protection, help, and assemblies. The Welsh prefix 'cyf' or 'cym' means 'together'.

47 Tom Ellis, *Addresses and Speeches*, p. 22.

48 Dafydd Jenkins, *Law and Government in Wales before the Act of Union*

(Welsh Studies in Public Law, University of Wales Board of Celtic Studies, University of Wales Press, 1970), p. 7.

49 Ioan Bowen Rees, *Government by Community,* pp. 212-13. On this point Rees added:

Of all the religious denominations, the most unauthoritarian and, indeed, anarchic of all—the Congregationalist—probably has not only the best educated ministry but the ministry most receptive to new ideas. Each Congregational congregation is completely autonomous and directly democratic, while the Welsh Congregational Union itself is a voluntary organisation which anyone can join as a voting member, and which only has persuasive powers over the affiliated churches. Autonomy does not mean isolation, however, and one wonders whether social workers and teachers would not be happier and more efficient as independent contractors (individually or in partnership) than under the direct supervision of Directors.

50 *The Miners' Next Step*—Being a Suggested Scheme for the Reorganisation of the Federation: Issued by the Unofficial Reform Committee, 1912 (re-published with an introduction by R. Merfyn Jones, Pluto Press, 1973).

51 *Ibid.*

52 *Ibid.*

53 When he died in 1970, J. R. Jones had been Professor of Philosophy at University College, Swansea, for eighteen years. But his influence only began to emerge in the late 1960s. Most of his writings are in Welsh.

54 Waldo Williams, 'Pa Beth Yw Dyn?' (What is Man?) in *Dail Pren* ('Leaves of a Tree') (Gwasg Gomer, 1956), p. 67. The quotation is in response to the question raised in the poem: Beth yw gwladgarwch? (What is a patriotism?). The poem is essentially about man's search for identity. 'Adnabod' (recognition) is only attained between man and man when the common root is discovered:

Beth yw adnabod? Cael un gwraidd
Dan y canghennau.

(What is recognition? To find one root
Beneath the branches.)

Index

A

Abercynon, 72
Aberdare, 4, 73
Aberdare (constituency), 129
Aberfan, 87
Aberporth, 110
Aberystwyth, 221
Ablett, Noah, 249
Abse, Leo, 127, 137, 147
Act of Union, Wales with England, 91, 248
Adfer, 132
Afan (district), 127
Africa, 49
Agriculture (Welsh administration of), 39, 100
Aitken, Ian, 50n
alienation, 238-9
Ailen, G. C., 24n
Althusius, Johannes, 232, 233-4
anarchism, 19-20, 48, 246-7
Anderson, Donald, 127, 137, 147
Anglesey, 11
Anglesey (constituency), 123, 124
Aristotle, 231-2, 233, 245
Association of District Councils, 256

B

Bains Committee, 150
Bakunin, Michael, 48
Bala, 96, 113
Bangor, 221
Barcelona, 131
Basque County, see Euzkadi
Bavaria, 167
BBC, 36, 108
BBC Wales, 59
Bedwellty (constituency), 129
Beeching, Lord, 34
Beesley, M., 43n
Belfast, 131
Belgium, 79
Benn, Tony, 23, 33, 43
Betts, Clive, 267
Bevan, Aneurin, 23, 102, 236
Bidault, George, 141
Bilbao, 131
Bill of Rights, 8, 165, 167-9

Bird, Ald. Roberts, 97
Birmingham, 15, 17
Blackpool, 9
Bluestreak, 43
Bodin, Jean, 233
Bonald, Louis de, 239
Bonn, 197
Bradford, 70
Bray, Jeremy, 195-7
Brecon, 100
Brecon and Radnor (constituency), 123, 124
Brecon, Lord, 34
Bratton, Sir Tatton, 50n
Bristol, 15
British Airways, 34
British Columbia, 167
British Gas Corporation, 30, 31, 32
British Railways, 30
British Steel Corporation, 29, 30, 31, 35, 40
Brittany, 131
Brooks, Jack, 120
Brown, Lord George, 66, 104
Brynmawr, 73
Burke, Edmund, 232, 239
Burning of the Bombing School, 109-10
Butler, R. A., 100, 107n
Butt-Philip, Alan, 101n

C

Cabinet Office Constitution Unit, 141, 223
Caerleon, 88
Caernarfon, 88, 116, 221
Caernarfon (constituency), 123
Caerphilly (constituency), 122, 129
Cairncross, Alec, 193
Callaghan, James, 1, 9, 77, 79, 123, 190
Calvert, Prof. Harry, 166n
Cambrian Airways, 34
Canada, 164, 171n, 192
cantons (Swiss), 149, 244
Capel Celyn, 113
Cardiff, 29, 68, 71, 99
Cardiff (district), 127
Carmarthen, 88
Carmarthen (constituency), 122, 123, 124, 125
Carmichael, S., 83n

Carter, April, 48n
Catalonia, 131
Central Electricity Generating Board, 30
centralisation, financial, 27; in industry, 28-9, 225; in research and development, 29-30; in coal industry, 30-1; in steel industry, 31; in gas industry, 31-2; in electricity industry, 32-3; in water industry, 33-4; in railways, 34; in telephone service, 34; in local government, 34-5.
Central Policy Review Staff, 84
Ceredigion (constituency), 123
Chalfont, Lord, 85, 105n
Chester, 34
Civil Service, increase in, 24, see Welsh Office
class conflict, 23, 40, 247
Clerical and Administrative Workers' Union, 118
Clwyd (county council), 127, 220
Clwyd, Ann, 146
coalmining, 55
Cole, G. D. H., 236
Commission of Inquiry (1846—The Blue Books), 99-100
Commission on the Constitution, 28, 38, 64, 73, 77-8, 82, 100n, 106, 125, 126, 138, 142, 143, 144, 158n, 159, 161, 164n, 165-6, 170, 171n, 172, 175, 176, 180, 182, 183, 189, 191-2, 200, 203, 207, 232
Common Market, see European Economic Community
communications (Wales), 71-3, 218-21
Communist Party (Wales), 8
Community Councils, 244, 265
community, ideas of, 10-12, 230; and capitalism, 18; and the state, 18-20, 25-6, 84; and sovereignty, 172-7; and Welsh history, 98
community socialism, 112
Concorde, 43
confederalism, 173-7
Confederation of British Industry (Wales), 69n, 213, 215
Conservative party, 45
Conservative Party in Wales, development, 92-3; electoral performance, 127-9; and devolution, 7-8; and Welsh Office, 105.
Conwy (constituency), 123, 124

corporation, 24-5, 41-6, 51, 229
Corsica, 131
Council for the Principality, 254-5, 258, 262
Council for Wales and Monmouthshire, see Welsh Council
Craig, F. W. S., 89
Crossman, R. H. S., 23, 77, 103
Crowther, Lord, 138, 183
Crowther-Hunt, Lord, 34, 82
Cwmbran, 221
cymdeithasiaeth, 112
Cymdeithas yr Iaith Gymraeg, 48, 96, 110-14
Cymru Fydd, 95-7, 99, 132, 248
Cynffig, 221

D

Dahl, Robert A., 241
Daniel, Sir Goronwy, 38, 66, 106
Davies, Clement, 101n
Davies, Denzil, 243
Davies, D. Ivor, 119
Davis, Sir Dai, 214
Davies, Prof. Glyn, 218, 221, 222, 226-7
Davies, S. O., 101, 123, 124
Dawson, Diane, 192n
Deeside, 221
Deffro (magazine), 115n
demand management, 186, 191-4, 196-8, 206-7
Denmark, 79, 176
Department of the Environment, 33
Department of Trade and Industry, 157
Derfel, R. J., 112
Deutscher, Isaac, 241
development area policy, 61-6, 70-1, 73, 75
Development Corporation for Wales, 226
devolution, problems of definition, 1-4, 24-6, 35, 49; economic pressure for, 53-7; as a British policy, 81-2; as a tactic to allay protest, 77-8; and Welsh economy, 217-18; and EEC, 242-3; and local government, 6-7, 243-5; and Bill of Rights, 168; and nominated bodies, 6; government approach to Wales and Scotland on, 141-2, 146-7; and Scottish politics, 145-6; and finance, 138; Scotland

and Wales Bill, 137, 162; separate Bills policy, 138, 150, 162. See also, Welsh Assembly, patronage, corporatism, class conflict.
Dicey, A. V., 3, 165
Donelly, Desmond, 126
Dooyeweerd, Herman, 11
Durkheim, Emile, 239
Dusseldorf, 198
Dyfed, 127, 128, 220, 256

E

Eastern Europe, 49
East Moors (Cardiff), 31, 55
Ebbw Vale, 31, 73, 77, 123
economic activity, 13, 53, 57
Eden, Sir John, 32
education, 14, 99-100
Edward I, 91
Edwards, Ness, 102, 103
Edwards, Nicholas, 8, 39
Edwards, O. M., 11
Edwards, Wil, 124
Eire, 51, 75, 79
Electrical trades union, 116, 118
Elizabeth I, 93
Ellis, Tom (MP for Meirionydd), 95-7, 248
Ellis, Tom (MP for Wrexham), 85-6
Employment Act (1972), 38
Employment Service Agency, 157, 223
Emrys ap Iwan, 96, 98
Engineering Workers' Union, 120
European Convention on Human Rights, 169
European Economic Community, 9, 12, 46, 50, 69-70, 75, 79, 85, 106, 108, 167-8, 212, 230-1, 242-3
Euzkadi, 17, 131
Evans, Fred, 137n, 147
Evans, Gwynfor, 84n, 92, 96, 111, 113, 114, 239-40
Evans, Ioan, 137n

F

Falange, 45
Fanon, Franz, 59
farming, 55, also see agriculture

federalism, 8-9, 163-70, 171, 246
Ffransis, Ffred, 111-13
Financial Times, 31
Finland, 176
Fishguard, 19
Fishlock, Trevor, 109n, 113n
Foot Michael, 1, 150, 162, 187, 188, 230
Foundry Workers' Union, 116
Fowler, Gerald, 147
Francis, Dai, 120
Friesland, 131
Fromm, Erich, 238

G

Gaitskell, Hugh, 102
Galicia, 131
Gellner, Ernest, 17
general elections (Wales), 89
Gladstone, Ewart, 8, 10
Goodman, Paul, 48
Gower, Sir Raymond, 8
Gray, Ian, 214, 215
Gray, Stephen, 31
Greece, 75
Greenland, 79
Griffin, Ken, 28n, 118
Griffiths, James, 100n, 102-4, 107, 123, 124
Griffiths, Non, 123n
Grimond, Jo, 2
Gruffydd, W. J., 11n
Gwent, 11, 76, 128, 219, 256
Gwilym, Eurfyl ap, 114
Gwynedd, 69, 73, 127, 128, 220

H

Hailsham, Lord, 8
Hall, Prof. Peter, 69n
Hamburg, 75, 198
Hamilton, C. V., 83n
Hannah, Leslie, 27n
Hardie, Keir, 4, 95, 236
Hart, R. A., 62n
Haviland, Julian, 50n
Hay, Will, 249
Hayek, F. A., 47
Healey, Denis, 69n

health authorities, 37, 265
health service, 34, 160
Heath, Edward, 42, 43, 84, 241
Hechter, Michael, 78, 82, 83, 84n, 130-1
Henderson, Arthur, 4-5
Highlands of Scotland, 131
Hirwaun, 32
Hobsbawm, Eric, 94
Holland, Stuart, 55
Home Rule, 96; see also devolution
Hooson, Emlyn, 9, 97n, 137n
Houghton Committee, 50
housing, 13, 72
Howell, Gareth, 143n
Howells, Geraint, 9, 137n
Hughes, Cledwyn, 123, 147, 258
Hywel Dda, 91

I

Iceland, 176
Illich, Ivan, 47
Industrial Relations Act (1971), 42, 168
Industrial Development Certificates, 62-3, 69, 70-1
Industrial Reorganisation Corporation, 42
industrial re-training, 222-4
Industry Act (1972), 38, 42, 62, 157, 209, 212
Industry Act (1975), 43-4
industry, Welsh structure of, 74, 224-5
Intermediate Education Act (1889), 99
internal colonialism, 78, 83, 130
International Monetary Fund, 69
Ionescu, Hgita, 246n
Ireland, see Eire and Northern Ireland
Islwyn (district), 127
Italy, 72, 75, 79

J

Jenkins, Dafydd, 248n
Johnson, Paul, 41n, 85
Jones, Alec, 147
Jones, Alun, 253
Jones, Alun R., 107n
Jones, Dafydd Glyn, 107n, 173, 239n
Jones, Emrys, 81, 125, 126, 143, 182, 212

Jones, Glyn, 267
Jones, Gwynoro, 124, 126, 180n
Jones, J. Barry, 122n, 143n, 180n
Jones, J. E., 114
Jones, Prof. J. R., 250-1
Jones, Mervyn, 28
Jones, Michael D., 96, 98
Jones, R. Mervyn, 249
Jones, R. Tudur, 12n
Jones, Tom, 117, 118
Jones, T. W., 123
Jones, Sir William, 101
Joseph, Keith, 41n

K

Kane, Vincent, 59-60
Kay, Dr John, 31
Kelsall, Ian, 69n
Khlief, Bud, 94
Kilbrandon Commission, see Commission on the Constitution
King, Dr David, 191
Kinnock, Neil, 40, 46, 50, 124, 127, 137n, 147
Kohr, Leopold, 28, 47, 51-2, 229, 245
Korea, 19
Kroptokin, Peter, 48

L

Labour party, 41, 50-1, 78, 102
Labour Party in Wales, growth in influence, 125-7; annual conference, 126-7; designation, 125n; electoral performance, 5-6, 122-4, 127-9; attitude to devolution, 4-7, 81-2; debate over Assembly constitution, 142-9, 156; debate over Assembly's finance, 180-3; debate over Assembly's economic powers, 210-12; attitude to Secretary of State for Wales, 125, 211-12; attitude to Welsh Civil Service, 160; and Welsh Development Agency, 217; and regional policy, 64; and local government, 243-4, 254, 256, 258, 262, 264-5; relationship with Wales TUC, 120; response to community, 98
Labour Party in Scotland, 6

Labour Weekly, 126n
Land Authority for Wales, 37
Länder, 149, 197-8
Latin America, 49
Lawrence, Geoffrey, 113
Layfield Committee, 179, 186-7, 202, 244
Leicester, 70, 71n
Lewis, Saunders, 9-10, 96, 108-9, 173-5, 232, 239-40
Liberal party, 8-9, 42, 50, 82; see also Welsh Liberal Party
libertarianism, 246
Liverpool, 15, 113
Llandudno, 6, 9, 53
Llanelli (constituency), 128
Llantrisant, 73, 221
Llantrisant New Town, 76
Llanuwchllyn, 11
Lloyd George, 95-7
Lloyd George, Megan, 123
Lloyd, Tal, 120
local government reorganisation, 34-5
London, 23, 70, 75, 132
Lovering, J., 74
Lower Saxony, 198
Luke, Paul, 48
Luther, 173
Luxembourg, 79

M

M4, 76-7
Macchiavelli, 173
MacCormick, Prof. D. N., 50n
Mackintosh, John, 77, 166-7
Macmillan, Harold, 42
Madgewick, Peter, 123n, 267
Madrid, 131
Mainwaring, Will, 249
Malatesta, 48
Manchester, 70
Manpower Services Commission, 157, 223
Marcuse, Herbert, 237
Maritain, Jacques, 229
Marquand, David, 41n, 46
Marsh, Richard, 105
Marx and Marxism, 236, 238, 246-7, 250
Mayo, Patricia Elton, 86

McBride, Jeremy, 169n
Meirionnydd, 11, 116
Meirionnydd (constituency), 123
Merthyr Tydfil, 4, 72, 95, 221
Merthyr (constituency), 129
Merthyr (district), 127
Mid Glamorgan, 76, 127, 128, 256
Milford Haven, 221
Miners' Union, 117, 119, 120, 144
The Miners' Next Step, 249-50
Minister for Welsh Affairs, 101, 107
Mold, 111
Monmouth (constituency), 123
Monopolies Commission, 27n
Montesquieu, 234
Moore, Barry, 62, 65-9, 71
morbidity (in Wales), 13
Morgan, Elystan, 124
Morgan, George Osborne, 94
Morgan, Geraint, 137n
Morgan, Gwyn, 138n, 143, 182-3, 231
Morgan, Kenneth O., 95n, 98n
Morgan, Rhodri, 78
Morris, John, 37, 68-9, 81, 121, 142n, 148, 253, 254
Morton, A. L., 248n
Multi-Role Combat Aircraft, 43
Mumford, Lewis, 240
Munich, 198
Mutualism, 246
Myrdal, Gunnar, 60-1, 75

N

Nairn, Tom, 16, 50-1, 84n, 130-2
Nalgo, 160
National Coal Board, 30
National Economic Development Organisation, 42
National Enterprise Board, 41, 43, 46, 78, 225
National Front, 45
nationalism, meaning of, 11-12; nation and state, 2; English, 165, 170; Welsh, 173-5; and foundation of Plaid Cymru, 108-10
National Library of Wales, 99
National Museum of Wales, 99
National Scientific Society (Wales), 29, 30
Nazis, 45

Neath, 32n
Neath (constituency), 128
Netherlands, 79
Nevin, Prof. Edward, 66-7
Newport, 97
Newport (district), 127
New Society, 41n, 69,
New York, 23
Nicholas, James, 19
Nisbet, Robert, 12, 231, 233-4, 239, 247
Nordic Union, 176
Northern Ireland, 8, 10, 55, 60, 62, 88,
    131, 166, 237
North-South Wales, division of, 15, 118,
    121-2
Norway, 176

O

Occitania, 131
Owain Glyndwr, 91, 94
Owen, Margaret, 97
Owen, Robert, 247-8

P

Pahl, R. E., 41n, 44, 45
Pandy, 11
Paris, 75
Parliament for Wales Campaign, 101
Parti Quebecois, 171n
patronage, 36-9
Pay and Price Board, 37
Pembroke (constituency), 123, 126
Pembrokeshire, 20
Peacock, Prof. A. T., 200, 205n
Phillips, Glyn, 160n
Plato, 231-2, 245
Plaid Cymru, founding of, 95-6;
    philosophy, 12, 173-7, 239-40;
    development, 107-15, 116; electoral
    performance, 77, 124-5, 127-9; atti-
    tude to devolution, 9-10, 149; economic
    policies, 64-5, 73, 219n, 220-1,
    240; and local government, 244;
    also, 32n, 46, 50, 76, 85, 87, 98, 102.
Planet, 48n, 60n, 110n
Plant, Raymond, 229n
Plowden Committee, 32-3
pluralism, 232-45

Pontarddulais, 116, 221
Pontypool, 221
Pontypridd (constituency), 129
Port Talbot, 31
Portugal, 45, 75
Powell, Enoch, 1, 7, 46, 59-60, 164-6,
    170
Powys, 127, 220
Prais, S. J., 27n
Prestatyn, 7
Proudhon, 242, 246-7
Prices and Incomes Board, 37
primary products (value to Wales),
    15-16
Prothero, Cliff, 102, 125
public spending, in Wales, 14-15; as
    proportion of GNP, 24; growth of,
    24, 25

Q

Quebec, 171n
Queensland, 167

R

Rawkins, Phillip, 110n
Rees, Prof. Graham, 195
Rees, Ioan Bowen, 3, 111n, 245n, 248-9
Rees, Les, 144
Rees, Noah, 249
referendum (on devolution), 124, 127,
    147-8
regional policy, the problem, 53-5;
    centralist versus decentralist analysis,
    57-9; impact on Wales, 61-6; why
    it cannot succeed, 67-74
Regional Employment Premium, 62, 67,
    68-9, 195
Reynolds, John, 143n
Rhodes, John, 62, 65-9, 71
Rhodri Fawr, 91
Rhondda, 72, 249
Rhondda (constituency), 122, 129
Rhoose, 34
Rhosllannerchrugog, 15n
Rhymney (district), 127
Richard, Henry, 94-5
roads (in Wales), 71-2
Roberts, Emrys, 114

Roberts, Goronwy, 101, 123, 124
Roel, A. R., 66n
Rolls Royce, 43
Rosebery, Lord, 96
Ross, William, 77
Rothschild, Lord, 84
Round, J. I., 66n
Rousseau, 233
Rowlands, Ted, 81, 104, 105-6, 253

S

Saint-Simon, 239. 246
Salazar, Dr Antonio de Oliveira, 45
Sartre, 238
Saunders, Graham, 118
Scarman, Leslie, 167-9
Schumacher, E. F., 47
Scotland, 8, 17, 32, 51, 53, 60, 62, 70, 79, 88, 130-2, 195, 196, 199, 221, 237
Scottish Assembly, 141, 143n, 145, 149, 150, 152, 166-7, 168
Scottish Council, 221
Scottish Development Agency, 59, 78
Scottish Labour Party, 16
Scottish National party, 6, 46, 50, 77, 145
Secretary of State for Scotland, 101
Secretary of State for Wales, creation of, 101-6, 123; relationship with Assembly, 156-9, 211-12; economic role, 157, 209-10, 216, 224
Seeman, M., 238
Sharp, Baroness, 103
Short, Ted, 146, 153-5
Shotton, 31, 55
Shrewsbury, 34
Smallwood, Christopher, 51
Smethwick, 70
South-East (of England), 69-70, 194, 219-20
South Glamorgan, 76, 78, 127, 256
sovereignty, location of, 137-8, 139, 164, 172-7; and community, 18; and pluralism, 232-3; and Parliament, 3, 8, 170; and EEC, 86
Spain, 45, 75, see Euzkadi, Catalonia
Stalin, 11
state, and nation, 2; and community, 25-6; growth of, 24-5
steel industry, 55, 68, see British Steel Corporation

Stuttgart, 198
Swansea, 29, 71
Swansea (district), 127
Swansea Labour Association, 144
Sweden, 176
Switzerland, see Canton
syndicalism, 98, 246, 249-50

T

Tait, Prof. A. A., 198-9
Taylor, A. J. P., 24
Teeside, 196-7
Thomas, Dafydd Elis, 48-9, 114
Thomas, George, 61, 85, 105, 106, 126, 137n, 143
Thomas, Gwyn, 107n
Thomas, Dr Ian, 218, 221, 222, 226-7
Thomas, Ned, 84n, 267
Thomas, Roy, 203
Thomas, R. S., 81
Thomas, Terry, 98
Thomas, Wynne, 180n
The Times, 14, 41n, 166n
Tocqueville, 234-7
Tomkins, C., 74
Tonnies, Ferdinand, 238-9
Tonypandy, 249
Town and Country Planning Association 77
Trade Councils, 117, 119, 120-1
Training Services Agency, 157, 223
Transport and General Workers' Union, 117, 118, 119
Treasury, 158, 180, 182, 185, 186, 188, 189-94, 199, 200, 203, 206
Tryweryn, 11, 109, 113-14
Tudors, 91-2, 173-4, 248
Tufte, Edward R., 241
Turkey, 75

U

Ulster, see Northern Ireland
unemployment, 13, 54-5, 57, 66-8, 108, 222
United States of America, 41n, 190, 192
University Grants Committee, 36
University of Wales, 99, 160

V

Vile, Prof. M. J. C., 171

W

Wales Radical Cymru (newspaper), 126
'Wales: the Way Ahead' (1967 White
Paper), 66, 76, 214
Wales TUC, creation of, 87, 116-19;
constitution, 120-1; General Council,
120; influence, 121-2; and Labour
Party in Wales, 120, 125; and Welsh
Assembly, 144-5, 156, 160; and dev-
olution referendum, 148; and Welsh
Development Agency, 213-17; and
regional policy, 68; and industrial
re-training, 222-3; and health service,
34n
Walker, Peter, 43
Walker, Valerie, 123n
Wallington, Peter, 169n
Walters, Donald, 93
Wass, Sir Douglas, 191-2
Watkins, Tudor, 123
Webbs, 236
Weber, Max, 232, 238
Welsh Assembly, executive powers, 150,
152-5; primary legislation, 152-4; secondary legislation, 152n, 154-5;
committee structure, 150-1, 155-6;
block grant, 157-8, 179-80, 184-9,
190, 202, 204, 206-7; budget, 201,
203; tax powers, 182, 187-8, 190-1,
202-3; economic powers, 209-12; and
Welsh Development Agency, 79, 217;
economic aspirations of, 157-8, 223-4;
UK reserve powers, 160-62; and
nationalised industries, 35, 81-2, 145,
160; and civil service, 143, 159-60;
membership, 145, 150; fixed term,
150-1, 158; and Welsh Office, 143;
and Secretary of State for Wales,
156-9; and local government, 230,
243-5, 253-66; see also devolution,
and Labour Party in Wales   .
Welsh Board of Education, 99
Welsh Board of Health, 100
Welsh Council, creation of, 100-2;
campaign for Secretary of State for
Wales, 101-2, 107; and economic

planning, 66-7; and industry research,
74, 224-5
Welsh Council of Labour, see Labour
Party in Wales
Welsh Counties Committee, 254, 258-9
Welsh Development Agency, 37, 59, 69,
78-9, 145, 157, 210-17, 224-5
Welsh Economic Council, see Welsh
Council
Welsh economy, 218-28
Welsh Grand Committee, 9, 38, 107n
Welsh Hospital Board, 34, 38
Welsh Language, 13, 88, 91, 93, 96,
132, 267-8
Welsh Language Society, see Cym-
deithas yr Iaith Gymraeg
Welsh Liberal Party, rise in nineteenth
Century, 92, 95, 97; attitude to devol-
ution, 9, 101n, 202n; philosophy, 98;
and local government, 244
Welsh nationalism, see Plaid Cymru
Welsh National Water Development
Authority, 34, 37, 160, 260
Welsh Office, campaign for, 101-3; and
national identity, 107, 132; develop-
ment of, 103-4; impact of, 105-6, 117,
119, 112; as a governing elite, 37-9;
and economic planning, 66-7, 76-7,
214, 221; and regional policy, 62-4,
68-9; and Welsh Development
Agency, 213-17; and health service,
34; and water industry, 33; devol-
ution unit, 152
Welsh radical tradition, 49
Western Mail, 70, 77, 109, 117, 121, 147
West Germany, 79, 164, 171n, 190,
197-8
West Glamorgan, 76, 127, 256
Whitelaw, William, 46
Wigley, Dafydd, 114, 243n
Wilding, Paul, 13n, 15, 53
Williams, Dafydd, 114
Williams, David, 93
Williams, D. G. T., 166
Williams, Phil, 64n, 84n, 114
Williams, Raymond, 11, 15n
Williams, Waldo, 18-20, 111, 251
Williams, W. L., 99n
Wilson, Harold, 1, 37, 103, 253
Winkler, J. T., 41n, 44, 45
Wolverhampton, 32n, 70
Woodcock, George, 118